Study Guide
with Worked Examples

Study Guide with Worked Examples

for use with

International Economics

Robert C. Feenstra Alan M. Taylor

Stephen Ross Yeaple
University of Colorado at Boulder

WORTH PUBLISHERS

Study Guide with Worked Examples
by Stephen Ross Yeaple
for use with ***Feenstra/Taylor: International Economics***

ISBN 13: 978-1-4292-0592-4
ISBN 10: 1-4292-0592-X

First Printing

Printed in the United States of America

Worth Publishers
41 Madison Avenue
New York, NY 10010
www.worthpublishers.com

CONTENTS

Part Eight
Applications and Policy Issues

Answers to Study Guide Problems A-1

PREFACE

Robert Feenstra and Alan Taylor have written an excellent textbook that identifies the important issues in international economics and presents and explains a wide range of microeconomic and macroeconomic models that can be used to analyze these issues. This ***Study Guide with Worked Examples*** complements the textbook by providing students additional opportunities to develop their knowledge of international economics through active learning. Active learning strategies are useful not only in academics but also in sports, music, or the arts. A good coach or teacher (1) *identifies* an important skill for a player or student to develop, (2) *demonstrates* that skill to the player or student, (3) *confirms* that the player or student is executing the technique properly, and finally (4) *drills* the player or student until the skill becomes second nature. In most higher education settings, materials are made available to you that can take you through these steps, but it is up to you to take those steps.

The strategy employed in the ***Study Guide with Worked Examples*** has two components. First, for each section of each chapter in the textbook, the essential concepts are reviewed and key terms are presented to make students aware of what material they need to know. In places, fundamental economic principles from introductory microeconomic and macroeconomic courses are reviewed. Students are also invited to provide the definition of the key terms that form the basic vocabulary of international economics.

The second component involves problem solving. For each section of each chapter questions are asked that (1) test students' knowledge of essential concepts and (2) help reinforce the logical structure of economic analysis. The problems vary considerably in difficulty, occasionally asking students to extend the uses of economic principles beyond the applications discussed in the textbook. Although space is provided for answers directly after each question, students are encouraged to use additional space to provide careful explanations because most of the value created from answering stimulating questions is in the practice of writing detailed answers. To identify common mistakes and to demonstrate common features of different types of economic problems, tips are provided immediately following questions that delve into particularly important or difficult topics. Finally, detailed answers for every question are provided at the end of the book.

The more time and effort that you put into your studies, the more rewarding your experience will be and the more you will appreciate the quality of the textbook that Robert Feenstra and Alan Taylor have written.

ACKNOWLEDGMENTS

I would like to thank Rob Feenstra, Alan Taylor, and Sarah Dorger, Acquisitions Editor at Worth Publishers, for encouraging me to write this study guide. I thank all of the people at Worth Publishers who gave me direction and helped in putting this book together, especially Marie McHale, Development Editor, and Stacey Alexander, Production Manager. I am deeply grateful to my wife, Katherine, for proofreading much of the book. Thanks also to the students in my International Trade class at Princeton University for commenting on the earliest drafts of the manuscript. Finally, I thank my children for their enthusiasm.

Stephen Ross Yeaple
University of Colorado at Boulder

Study Guide
with Worked Examples

1

Trade in the Global Economy

Overview

The term "globalization" means many things: the flow of goods and services across borders; the movement of people and firms; the spread of culture and ideas between countries; and the tight integration of financial markets around the world. In this book we analyze the flows of goods and services, people, and capital between countries and the policies that governments use to influence these flows. The volume of these flows is huge and is growing very rapidly. In addition to attempting to understand the forces that drive these flows, we will also delve deeply into the impact of these flows on welfare. How does trade affect a nation's material well-being? Does international trade increase the gap between the rich and the poor? What is the impact of immigration on workers?

This chapter presents a broad view of the flows in goods and services, people, and capital across borders. We will see that these flows are complex and difficult to summarize, but there are patterns in these flows that can be explained.

1 International Trade

ESSENTIAL CONCEPTS

International trade occurs when the residents of one country sell *merchandise goods* or *services* to residents of another country. The volume of international trade between countries is huge. In 2000 the total value of exports of goods was $10.2 trillion and the total volume of exports of services was $2.4 trillion. This chapter presents a large amount of information on the size and direction of international trade flows that may be hard to digest. We attempt to boil down some patterns in the international trade data.

- Countries with large *gross domestic product* (GDP) account for most international trade.
- Small countries engage in proportionately more trade relative to their GDP than do large countries.
- The volume of trade between two countries falls off rapidly in the distance between the two countries.

- Trade occurs between very similar countries and between very different countries.
- Two-way trade between countries is common; for example, the largest market for U.S. exports is Canada, and Canada is the largest source country for U.S. imports.
- Trade volumes have increased more rapidly than gross domestic product since the 1950s.
- Tariffs have fallen steadily since the 1950s.
- Technological progress in shipping has dramatically reduced international trade costs.

Why do countries engage in international trade? What affect does international trade have on the wealth of nations? What impact do these trade volumes have on the distribution of income? These are the big questions within the field of international trade, and various answers to these questions are given in Chapters 2 to 7. Chapters 2 to 4 and Chapter 7 present models that explain the motive for trade between countries with different characteristics, such as access to technology and natural resource abundances. Chapter 6 presents a model that explains why very similar countries, perhaps even identical countries, can gain from engaging in international trade and why most international trade between countries occurs between large developed countries that are in close proximity to each other.

Government policies toward trade have a big impact on the volume of trade. During periods when trade barriers, such as tariffs and quotas, have been low, international trade has flourished, whereas during periods of high trade barriers, such as the years between World War I and World War II, trade volumes have contracted. The effect of trade policies on the volume of international trade and on welfare are the subject of Chapters 8 to 11. Throughout this section of the book, we discuss the role of an important international institution, the World Trade Organization (WTO), in coordinating trade policies among its member countries and facilitating the growth of international trade.

KEY TERMS

Use the space provided to record your notes on the following key terms.

Exports __________

Imports __________

Merchandise goods __________

Service exports __________

Trade balance __________

Trade surplus ______________________________

____

____

Trade deficit ______________________________

____

____

Bilateral trade balance ______________________________

____

____

Gross domestic product ______________________________

____

____

Trade barriers ______________________________

____

____

Import tariffs ______________________________

____

____

Import quota ______________________________

____

____

REVIEW QUESTIONS

Problem 1: Why is a bilateral trade balance often a misleading measure? Explain.

____

____

____

Problem 2: Table 1-2 in the textbook shows the share of trade in gross domestic product. What characteristics appear to be important in explaining how reliant a country is on international trade?

____

____

____

Problem 3: According to Table 1-2 in the textbook, the international trade volumes of Hong Kong and Malaysia exceed their GDP. How is this possible?

____

____

____

Problem 4: Consider the following assertion: "Globalization is an irresistible force drawing countries together." Does the historical record support this assertion?

____

____

____

TIPS

The statistics presented in the chapter are "aggregate" volumes, lacking any detail about the types of goods and services traded. The actual motives for trade are obscured. In later chapters we will see that there are patterns in the composition of trade between countries.

Problem 4 is meant to point out that trade barriers between countries affect the volume of international trade. Historically, tariffs and quotas have occasionally increased rather than decreased. This is one reason for the fact that the two "golden eras" of globalization are separated by many years.

2 Migration and Foreign Direct Investment

ESSENTIAL CONCEPTS

International *migration* is a contentious topic in many countries. Many concerns raised by immigration are economic in nature. How does immigration affect wages? Do immigrants take jobs away from native-born residents? Given these fears, it is not surprising that all countries have restrictions on inward migration, and it is a safe bet that in the absence of these restrictions there would be substantially more international migration of labor. Chapter 5 presents an economic analysis of the effects of migration and shows that from the perspective of theory, immigration's effect on wages is primarily a short-run phenomenon. In the long run, the economy can absorb an increase in labor force without major changes in wages. The trade models presented in Chapter 4 also demonstrate that international trade acts as a substitute for immigration: A worker may not be able to enter the U.S. labor market, but the goods produced by the worker can.

Foreign direct investment occurs when a firm in one country owns a company in another country. Flows of foreign direct investment (FDI) between countries are substantial. A common perception is that multinational companies primarily invest in low-wage countries in order to reduce their costs of production. Although this type of foreign direct investment does occur, most foreign direct investment is between developed countries. A key example is the vast network of assembly plants in the United States owned by the Japanese firm Toyota. This type of foreign direct investment is often called *horizontal FDI* because it involves replicating the same production activity in many locations. The motive for this type of FDI is typically explained by the desire of firms to produce near their customers. *Vertical FDI* occurs when a multinational opens a plant in a low-wage country. Much of the vertical FDI of U.S. multinationals is in Mexico. Although the numbers for vertical FDI are considerably smaller than the numbers for horizontal FDI, vertical FDI is more controversial.

KEY TERMS

Use the space provided to record your notes on the following key terms.

Migration

Foreign direct investment

Horizontal FDI

Vertical FDI

Reverse-vertical FDI

Exchange rate

REVIEW QUESTIONS

Problem 5: Worker migration between countries is almost entirely from the lowest-wage countries to the highest-wage countries. True or false? Explain.

Problem 6: Why might a multinational produce the same good in many different countries? Explain.

Problem 7: Foreign direct investment can affect the volume of trade. Would you expect that vertical and horizontal FDI have a different or similar impact on trade volumes? Explain.

TIPS

The book measures migration by the number of foreign-born people in a country, and it measures foreign direct investment by the change in the level of foreign ownership of companies in a given time period. The first is a "stock"; the second is a "flow." The actual sales of the foreign companies owned by multinationals are much larger than the flow of new investments.

Problem 7 points out that the flows of trade and foreign direct investment are interrelated.

2

Trade and Technology: The Ricardian Model

Overview

Trade patterns between countries display regularities that can be explained using economic theory. Different facts suggest different economic mechanisms. This chapter introduces a model developed by the nineteenth-century economist David Ricardo that relates a particular country characteristic, its technology, to its trade pattern. Ricardo showed that a country could be technologically "backward" in every industry and still gain from trading with more productive countries. The analysis of Ricardo's model illustrates the principle of *comparative advantage,* one of the most fundamental concepts in economics. Many of the economic mechanisms found in Ricardo's model are also to be found in the more complicated models discussed later in the book. For this reason, it will pay to be especially vigilant in your study of this chapter!

The next four chapters explore various other models that offer explanations for particular regularities in the pattern of trade across countries. In addition to providing some explanation for these trade patterns, the models can also be used to understand the impact of international trade on welfare.

1 Reasons for Trade

ESSENTIAL CONCEPTS

The pattern of trade between countries, both in the aggregate statistics presented in Chapter 1 and in the example of U.S. imports of snowboards presented at the beginning of this chapter, suggests that there are a range of explanations for why countries trade with each other. Many of these explanations involve differences across countries in terms of the characteristics of their economies. For instance, countries may differ in their access to *technology* or in their supply of productive *resources.* Differences in technology will lead some countries to have *absolute advantages* in the production of some goods. That is, in the production of some goods they may be the world's productivity leaders. The actual explanation for trading patterns lies not in a country's absolute advantage, however, but rather in its *comparative advantage.* A country has a comparative advantage in the good that it is relatively better able to produce. Comparative advantage can be due to differences in technology, but it can also stem from a country's endowment of *resources,* be those resources natural (such as arable land or coal) or artificially created (such as capital).

Finally, geography matters for the structure of trade in many ways. Aside from geography's impact on a country's endowments of natural resources, geography also determines the distances between countries. A key regularity in the data is that the amount of trade between two countries falls in the distance between them. Trading relationships that are fostered by *proximity* are often strengthened by government policy. Canada, Mexico, and the United States have traditionally traded a great deal with each other because of the ease of transport and communication. A *free trade area* agreed to by these countries has also deepened their trading ties.

KEY TERMS

Use the space provided to record your notes on the following key terms.

Exports ______________________________

Imports ______________________________

Proximity ______________________________

Resources ______________________________

Natural resources ______________________________

Labor resources ______________________________

Capital ______________________________

Factors of production ______________________________

Absolute advantage ____

____

____

Comparative advantage ____

____

____

Technology ____

____

____

Free trade area ____

____

____

Foreign direct investment ____

____

____

Outsourcing ____

____

____

2 The Ricardian Model

ESSENTIAL CONCEPTS

This chapter uses a simple general equilibrium model developed by David Ricardo to illustrate the principle of *comparative advantage.* In a general equilibrium model, an economy has a supply of *factors,* or resources used to produce goods. *Technology* determines how factors are turned into goods. Demand for these goods is determined by consumers' income, which depends on the economy's output; by consumers' preferences, which are represented by *indifference curves;* and by *relative prices.* Finally, a general equilibrium model specifies how people and firms compete. In this chapter, *perfect competition* prevails in every market.

The economy's *production possibility frontier* (PPF) summarizes what the economy can produce given its technology and factor endowment. In Ricardo's model, the marginal product of labor (MPL) in each industry is constant so that an industry's output is just its marginal product of labor multiplied by the number of workers employed in the industry. By moving labor between industries, we can trace out a country's PPF. The slope of this PPF tells us the *opportunity cost* of expanding the output of the good on the X axis in terms of the good on the Y axis. A country has a comparative advantage in a good if its opportunity cost of production of that good is lower than the opportunity cost of that good in other countries.

The level of consumer demand for goods depends on (1) consumers' budget constraints, (2) consumers' tastes, and (3) relative prices. Because these concepts are used in many of the book's chapters, it is worth reviewing them. Suppose a consumer has income I to spend on apples and shirts. The number of apples she demands is D_A and the number of shirts she demands is D_S. The price of apples is P_A and the price of shirts is P_S. If she spends all her income, then

$$I = P_A \cdot D_A + P_S \cdot D_S \Rightarrow D_S = \frac{I}{P_S} - \frac{P_A}{P_S} \cdot D_A.$$

Note that P_A / P_S is called the *relative price* of apples. The relative price tells us the *opportunity cost* of an apple to a consumer given the prices of the two goods, or how many shirts need to be given up to buy an additional apple. For simplicity, the country is treated as one consumer that has its own budget constraint. Where on the budget constraint a consumer chooses to purchase depends on her preferences, which are represented by *indifference curves* as shown in Figure 2-1.

There are two assumptions behind the way that indifference curves are drawn: (1) consumers want *more* of all goods, and (2) *ceteris paribus* consumers get diminishing returns out of consuming more of the same good. From these assumptions it follows that indifference curves are convex (as shown) and higher indifference curves imply greater utility. Changes in income and relative prices change a consumer's budget constraint but have no impact on the consumer's tastes. That is, the map of indifference curves never changes, just which curve we can reach. The tastes of the entire country are represented using a single set of indifference curves that tell us which bundle on their budget constraint consumers choose and how well off they are.

Finally, we assume that there is perfect competition. Because firms take prices and wages as given in making their hiring decision, the relative prices that they charge exactly reflect the opportunity cost of production facing the economy. Because firms make

FIGURE 2-1

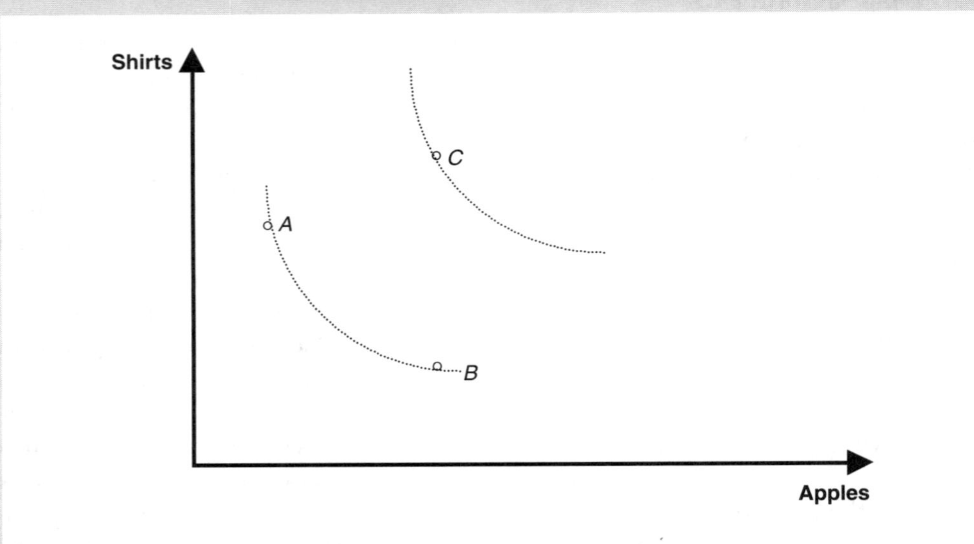

Indifference Curves

zero profits, their earnings are passed on to workers so that workers can consume what is produced.

An equilibrium occurs when firms supply goods and hire workers to maximize their profits, consumers demand goods to maximize their utility, and supply equals demand. In a "no-trade equilibrium" there is only domestic demand, so the level of domestic production must equal the level of domestic demand. When international trade is allowed, foreign demand and supply must be taken into account.

KEY TERMS

Use the space provided to record your notes on the following key terms.

Factors ____________________

Marginal product of labor ____________________

Production possibilities frontier ____________________

Opportunity cost ____________________

Perfect competition ____________________

Relative price ____________________

Indifference curves ____________________

Utility ____________________

REVIEW QUESTIONS

Problem 1: Home is endowed with 100 workers who can produce two goods: shirts and apples. Worker's *marginal product* of labor in shirts (MPL_S) is 2. (One worker can produce 2 shirts.) The marginal product of labor in apples is 5.

1a. Graph Home's PPF with output of shirts (Q_S) on the Y axis and apples (Q_A) on the X axis; label the intercepts and the slope.

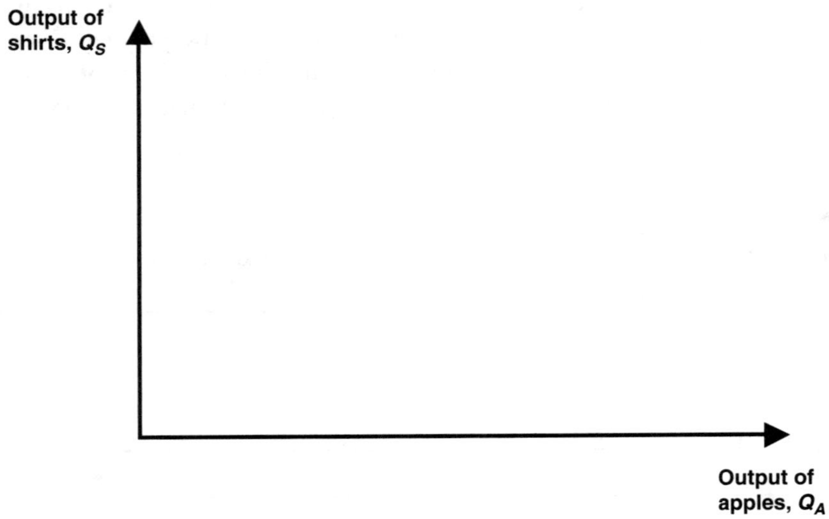

1b. Explain why the PPF is a straight line.

1c. What is the opportunity cost of apples in terms of shirts?

1d. What is the opportunity cost of shirts in terms of apples?

1e. How would you change the graph that was the answer to 1a if the number of workers in the country fell to 50? Show in the axes provided below.

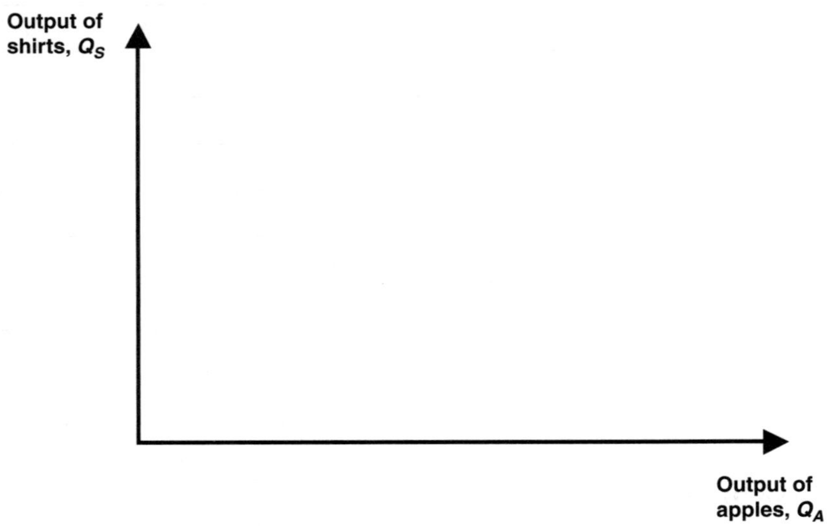

1f. Does this change the opportunity costs of the goods?

1g. Suppose that the workers wake up feeling sick one day and their marginal product in both goods is half as much as it was before ($MPL_S = 1$ and $MPL_A = 5/2$). How would this change the PPF relative to your answer in 1a? Show in the axes provided below.

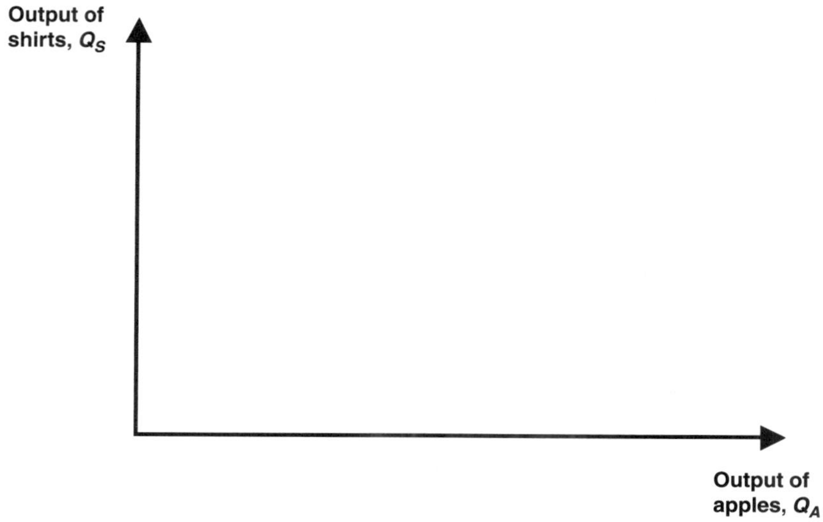

1h. Now suppose that the bumblebees in Home become depressed and so are less able to pollinate the apple trees. As a result, the MPL_A falls from 5 to 2. How does this change affect Home's PPF? Show the "before" and "after" cases in the axes provided below.

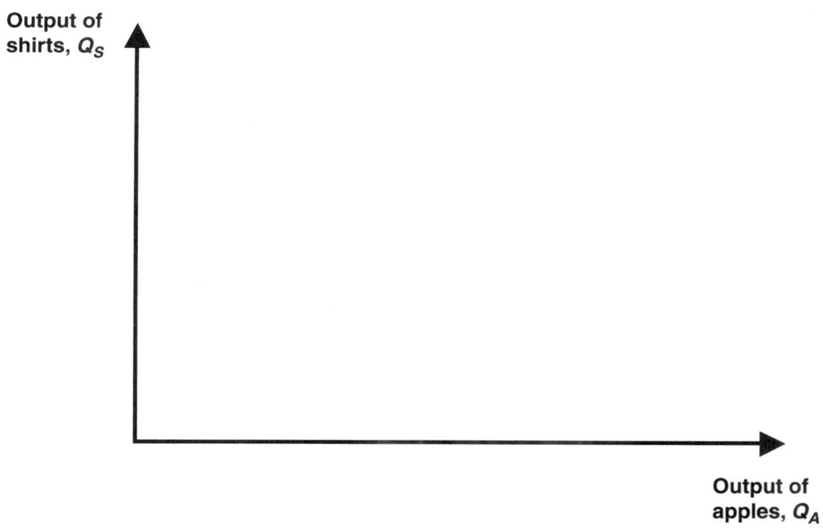

1i. How does "the great bee depression" affect the opportunity cost of apples in terms of shirts? ____

____

____

TIPS

In the Ricardian model the PPF is always straight, never curved. This is because there is only one factor and its marginal product in each industry is assumed to be constant. Later we will see models with "curved" PPFs.

The opportunity cost of good *A* in terms of good *B* is only equal to the slope of the PPF if good *A* is on the X axis.

The problems above can be used as a "cookbook" for other problems. Experiment with different numbers for stock of factors and for technology to get more practice.

Problem 2: Home is endowed with 100 workers. The marginal product of labor in shirts (MPL_S) is 2. The marginal product of labor in apples is 5. Suppose the price of a shirt is $5 and the price of an apple is $2.

2a. Given the information provided in problem 2, where on the PPF will the economy produce?

____

____

2b. Suppose the price of an apple rises to $4. What will firms produce?

____

____

TIPS

There is perfect competition. Given prices, firms adjust output to maximize their profits and in the process generate demand for factors. Prices of factors then adjust to guarantee that firms make zero profits.

Because marginal products are constant in Ricardo's model, firms are willing to supply *any* level of output along the PPF as long as relative prices are equal to the slope of the PPF.

For any other relative price, the economy *must* specialize in one good.

Problem 3: An apple costs 20¢ (P_A = \$1 / 5), a shirt costs 50¢ (P_S = \$1 / 2), and the consumer's income is \$100.

3a. What is the equation for the budget constraint? Graph this budget constraint, being careful to label all the relevant information.

3b. How would your graph change if income is \$200, the price of apples is 40¢, and the price of a shirt is \$1?

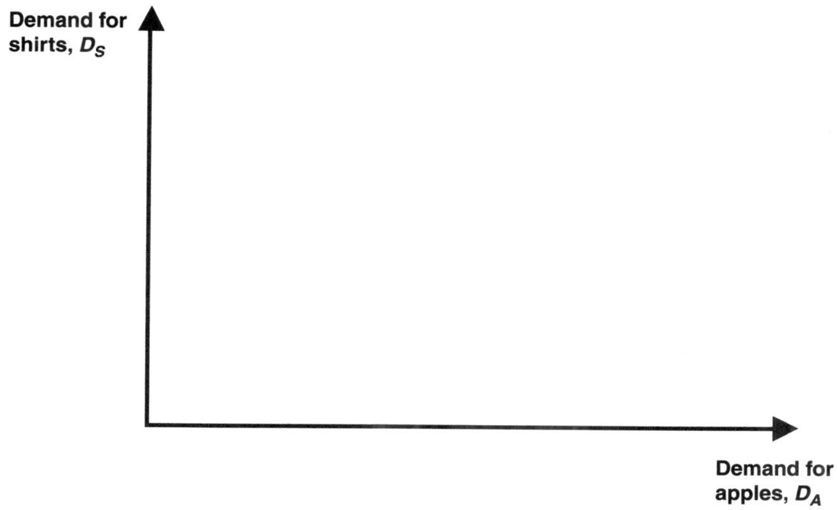

3c. Starting from the case in which income is \$200, the price of apples is 40¢, and the price of shirts is \$1, show how the graph changes when the price of shirts falls to 50¢ and everything else stays the same. How has the opportunity cost of apples been affected by the change in the dollar price of shirts? ______________________________

____

____

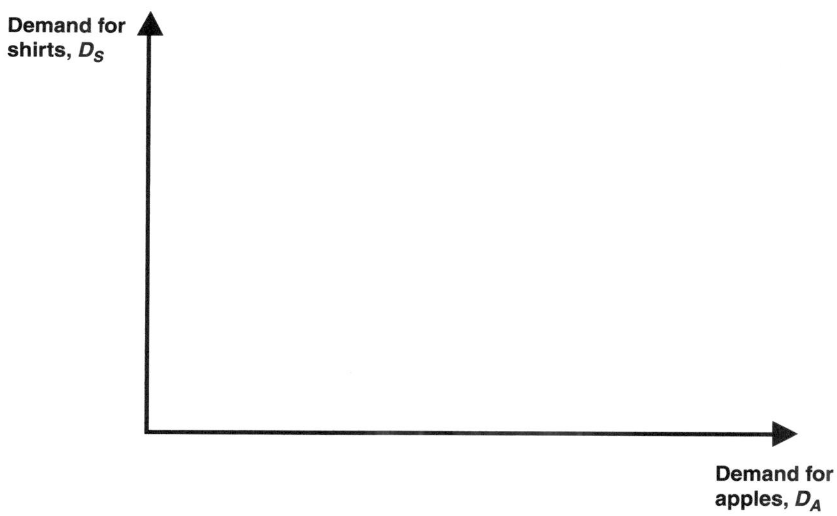

3d. Show how the graph changes when the price of shirts is \$1 and the price of apples falls to 20¢. How has the opportunity cost of shirts been affected by the change in the price of apples? ______________________________

____

____

TIPS

It is important to remember that the slope of the budget constraint is the price of the good on the *X* axis divided by the price of the good on the *Y* axis.

Relative prices do *not* involve dollar signs! They are "real" in the sense that they tell us the tradeoff facing consumers in actual goods.

In the Ricardian model, international trade will be like a change in relative prices as shown in problems 3c and 3d. Consumers can afford more of both goods as long as the consumer spends his income on both goods.

Problem 4: Consider the information in Figure 2-1. The dotted lines are indifference curves, and *A, B,* and *C* are three different bundles of goods.

4a. Given the choice of *A, B,* or *C,* which bundle would the consumer select? ______

______

______

4b. Given the choice of *A* or *B,* which bundle would the consumer select? ______

______

______

4c. A consumer's income is \$200, the price of apples is 40¢, and the price of a shirt is \$1. Graph the consumer's budget constraint. Draw an indifference curve that determines the consumer's demand. Label this demand.

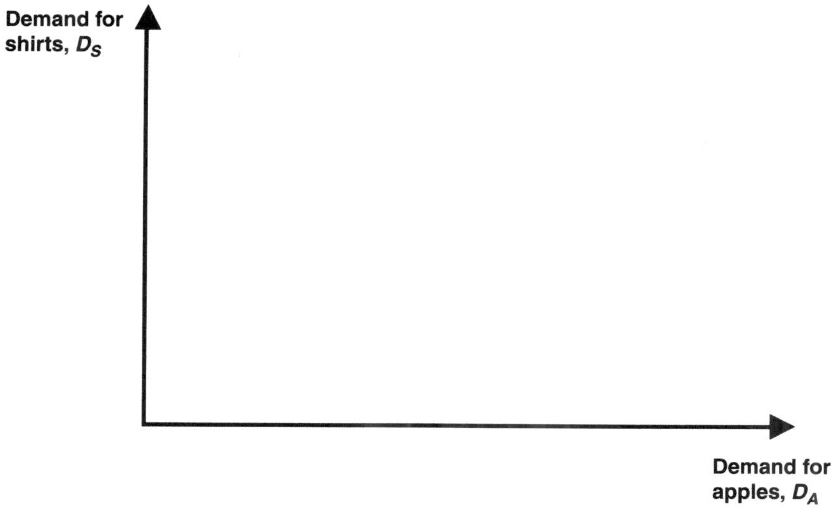

4d. Show how the graph changes when the price of shirts falls to 50¢ and everything else stays the same. Show the new indifference curve and demand levels.

TIPS

It is imperative not to draw indifference curves so that they appear to cross. Indifference curves *cannot* cross because otherwise they could not involve different levels of "utility."

We often draw two indifference curves, one representing utility before a change and one representing utility after a change. In principle, there are an infinite number of indifference curves corresponding to all other possible levels of utility, but we don't draw them to avoid cluttering up the picture.

Problem 5: Home's stock of factors is 100 workers. Two goods are produced: shirts and apples. Workers' marginal product of labor in shirts is 2, and the marginal product of labor in apples is 5.

5a. Graph a no-trade equilibrium for this economy that shows the country's PPF (with axes labeled) and an indifference curve that shows demand levels. Indicate the relative prices.

5b. Suppose that a technology improvement leads to an increase in the marginal product of labor in apples to 10. Show how the equilibrium changes.

5c. Going back to the initial information, suppose the economy is given the opportunity to trade as much as it wants with the outside world at the *fixed* international relative price of apples of 1. On the next page, draw a figure showing how producers and consumers respond to this opportunity.

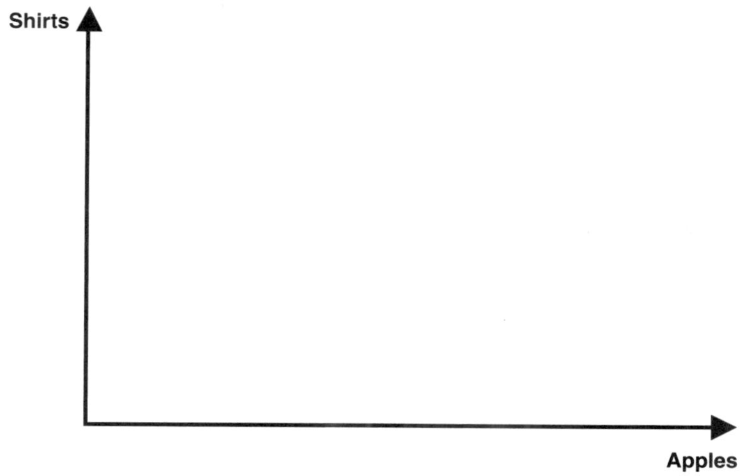

TIPS

Problem 5c demonstrates a general feature of the Ricardian model. Being allowed to trade with the outside world at *any* relative price that is different than the no-trade equilibrium price must make the country better off.

You should notice a similarity in the answers to problems 5b and 5c. Technical progress and the ability to trade at fixed world prices have the same effect: They shift out the consumption possibilities frontier.

3 Determining the Pattern of International Trade

ESSENTIAL CONCEPTS

To analyze how different technologies across countries affect the trading pattern, the model includes two countries. One of these countries will have an *absolute advantage* in both goods. That is, it will have a better technology for producing both goods. A country has an *absolute advantage* in a good if its marginal product of producing that good is higher than in another country. A country has a *comparative advantage* in a good when it has a lower opportunity cost of producing it than does another country. Because the relative price of a good in a no-trade equilibrium reflects the opportunity cost of producing that good, the country with a lower relative price for a good in a no-trade equilibrium has a comparative advantage in that good.

Consider the following example. Suppose that Home worker's *marginal product* of labor in shirts (MPL_S) is 2, and the marginal product of labor in apples is 5. Foreign worker's marginal product of labor in shirts is 8, and the marginal product of labor in apples is 8. Hence, Foreign has an absolute advantage in the production of both goods. The opportunity cost of apples in Home is 2 / 5 shirts, whereas the opportunity cost of apples in Foreign is 1 shirt. By definition, then, Home has a comparative advantage in apples and Foreign has a comparative advantage in shirts.

By reorganizing production toward their comparative advantage, countries increase the quantity of world output. To see this, suppose that the two countries are producing both goods. If Home expands production of apples by 1 unit, it has to cut shirt production by 2 / 5 units. If Foreign cuts apple production by 1 unit, it will free enough labor to produce another shirt. Apple output is unchanged, while shirt output has *risen* by 1 − 2 / 5 = 3 / 5 units. Reorganizing production toward countries' comparative advantage and allowing international trade give rise to *gains from trade* due to the more efficient use of the world's resources. The distribution of these gains between countries depends on the *terms of trade* on world markets.

KEY TERMS

Use the space provided to record your notes on the following key terms.

Absolute advantage

Comparative advantage

International trade equilibrium

Gains from trade

World price line

REVIEW QUESTIONS

Problem 6: Suppose that Home has a marginal product of labor of 4 making apples and a marginal product of labor of 4 making shirts.

6a. Foreign has a marginal product of labor of 6 making apples. Choose a number for the marginal product of labor in Foreign for shirts that gives Foreign a comparative advantage in apples.

6b. Choose numbers for the marginal product of labor in apples and in shirts in Foreign so that the wage rate is twice as high in Foreign, but there are no gains from trade.

Problem 7: Explain why a country will export the good in which it has a comparative advantage and import the other good if trade is balanced.

Problem 8: Suppose that Home has 100 workers, a marginal product of labor of 4 making apples, and a marginal product of labor of 4 making shirts. Foreign has 100 workers, a marginal product of labor of 8 making apples, and a marginal product of labor of 6 in shirts.

8a. What range of relative prices could be observed in a trading equilibrium? Explain.

8b. Draw the production possibilities frontier, world price line, and indifference curves for each country for a trading equilibrium when the relative price on world markets is halfway between their autarky relative prices. Label the intercepts of the world price line and PPF.

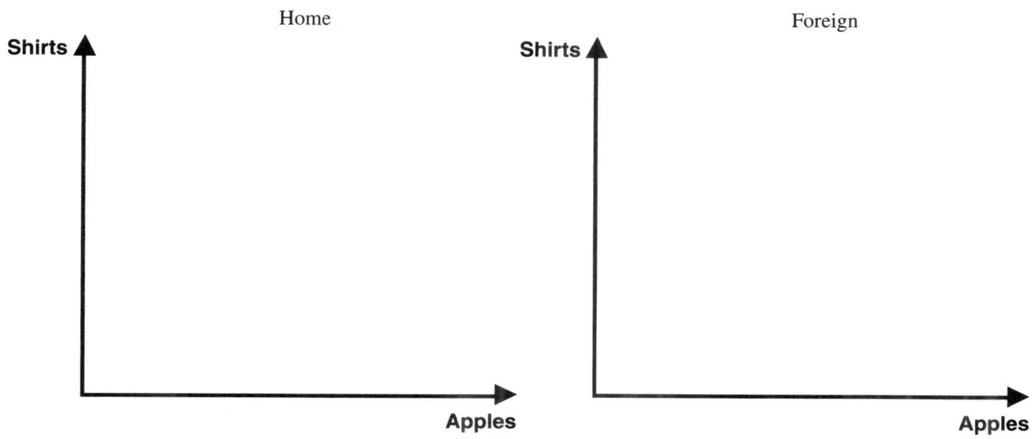

TIPS

Gains from trade have nothing to do with wage differences between countries. Wage differences are due to absolute advantage, but it is comparative advantage that creates gains from trade.

From your work with production and budget constraint you should notice that the greater the difference between world relative prices and relative prices in a no-trade equilibrium, the more the country gains from trade.

4 Solving for International Prices

ESSENTIAL CONCEPTS

International prices are determined by international supply and demand for goods. The model includes two goods, but it is sufficient to think about just one good for determining the *one* relative price. If trade is balanced, then the value of Home's exports is equal to the value of its imports of the other good *and* to the value of Foreign's imports. Exports are domestic production minus domestic consumption. By varying the relative price of the good, we observe how a country's production and consumption change and so predict how the country's desire to trade is affected. The relative price that makes one country's export supply equal the other country's import demand is the equilibrium international price, or the *terms of trade.*

KEY TERMS

Use the space provided to record your notes on the following key terms.

Export supply curve ______________________________

Import demand curve ______________________________

Terms of trade ______________________________

REVIEW QUESTIONS

Problem 9: Suppose that Home has 100 units of labor with a marginal product of 4 making apples and a marginal product of 4 making shirts. In the no-trade equilibrium, suppose that consumers in Home demand 175 apples. Foreign has 100 units of labor with a marginal product of 8 making apples and a marginal product of 6 in shirts. In a no-trade equilibrium Foreign consumes 400 apples. It may help you to consult your answers to problem 8 for the following problems.

9a. Draw Home's export supply curve.

Home's Export Supply

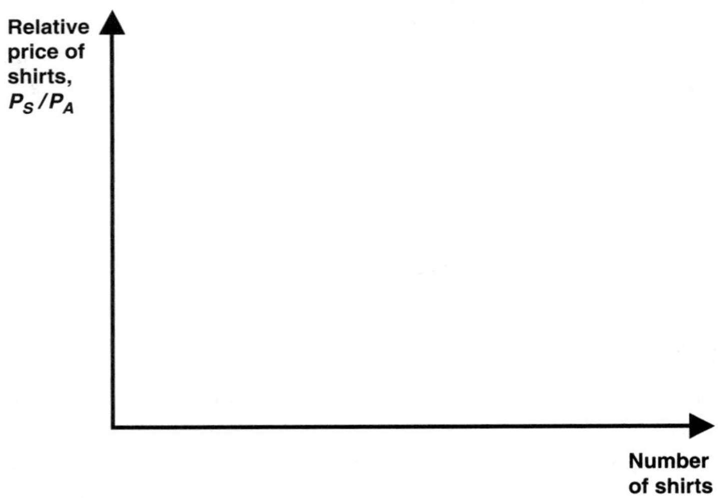

9b. Add Foreign's import demand curve to the diagram so that the world relative price of shirts is between the two countries' no-trade relative prices.

9c. Suppose the number of workers in Home were to double. How would this change shift Home's export supply curve? Show in your original diagram.

TIPS

If instead the problem had asked about Foreign's export supply and Home's import demand, the graph would have looked different but the information would be the same!

The answer to 9c displays a general result in trade models: Larger countries are less likely to gain from trade. Relative prices in the international trade equilibrium are not much different for the large country than in a no-trade equilibrium. This is because Foreign demand is small relative to Home supply. As we saw in earlier problems, countries gain more the bigger the difference is between no-trade and trade relative prices.

3

Who Gains and Who Loses from Trade?

Overview

Chapter 2 demonstrated that there are gains from trade in the sense that countries that engage in international trade can consume more than countries that do not. This chapter analyzes the way that international trade affects the actual spending power, or real income, of individuals rather than countries. As the title of the chapter suggests, it is possible for a country to gain from trade while some (but not all!) individuals living in that country are made poorer by international trade.

International trade affects the welfare of individuals through its effects on the real earnings of the factors that they own. Some people get most of their income by working, whereas others get income from their ownership of land or of capital. International trade increases the earnings of some factors and lowers the real earnings of other factors. As a result, some individuals will gain from international trade and others will lose. To get at these issues, it is critical to use a model that has more than one type of factor.

The *specific-factors model* that is introduced in this chapter features three factors. This model shows that there are clear winners and clear losers from international trade. The idea that a country gains from trade has a very specific meaning: The gains to those that benefit from international trade exceed the losses of those that are harmed by international trade.

1 Specific-Factors Model

ESSENTIAL CONCEPTS

The model assumes that one industry (agriculture) uses labor and land and the other industry (manufacturing) uses labor and capital. This model is called the specific-factors model because land is *specific* to the agriculture sector and capital is *specific* to the manufacturing sector; labor is used in both sectors, so it is not specific to either one. Labor is sometimes referred to as the *mobile factor* because it can move freely between the two industries.

Adding a specific factor to production in each industry gives rise to the key feature of the specific-factors model: *diminishing returns.* To produce agricultural products, a firm needs land and labor. Land is in fixed supply, so output can only be expanded by adding labor (i.e., moving it out of manufacturing). As more workers are put to work using the same amount of land, the marginal product of labor in agriculture decreases. In the manufacturing industry the same assumption applies. Because the amount of capital is fixed, the marginal product of labor in manufacturing is decreasing in the level of manufacturing employment because as the number of workers in manufacturing rises there are fewer machines for each worker to use.

One important implication of diminishing returns is that it causes a country's PPF to be bowed out (or concave). This means that when the country goes to trade with the outside world, it will increase the output of the good whose relative price has risen and decrease the output of the other good, but it will not completely specialize in the production of either good. This is because moving labor from one industry to another causes the marginal product of labor to fall in the expanding industry and rise in the contracting industry. For example, if the relative price of manufacturing goods rises because of international trade, the opportunity cost of manufacturing goods will also rise as the country expands the production of manufacturing goods (falling MPL_M) and contracts the production of agricultural goods (rising MPL_A).

When countries are not engaged in international trade, the opportunity costs of production differ across countries. Trade allows the countries to expand the production of the goods in which they have a lower opportunity cost in the no-trade equilibrium and contract production of the goods in which they have a higher opportunity cost. Hence, there are gains from trade.

KEY TERMS

Use the space provided to record your notes on the following key terms.

Specific-factor model ______________________________

Diminishing returns ______________________________

Embargo ______________________________

Autarky ______________________________

REVIEW QUESTIONS

Problem 1: Suppose that the technology for creating manufacturing goods is $Q_M = \sqrt{\overline{K} \cdot L_M}$, where Q_M is manufacturing output; $\overline{K}$ is the country's endowment of capital, the factor specific to manufacturing; and L_M is the amount of the mobile factor, labor, used in manufacturing.

1a. How much does Q_M rise if both inputs ($\overline{K}$, L_M) are doubled? ____________________

1b. Now suppose that $\overline{K}$ is fixed at 100. How much does Q_M rise if L_M is doubled? ________

____

1c. Is the cost of lost manufacturing output associated with reducing manufacturing employment by one employee larger or smaller when the initial level of employment is 100 or 10? ____

____

____

Problem 2: Suppose that there are two goods: Agriculture (A) and Manufacturing (M). Agriculture is produced with Land and Labor and Manufacturing is produced with Capital and Labor. Labor is mobile between industries. The next two questions refer to Figure 3-1.

FIGURE 3-1

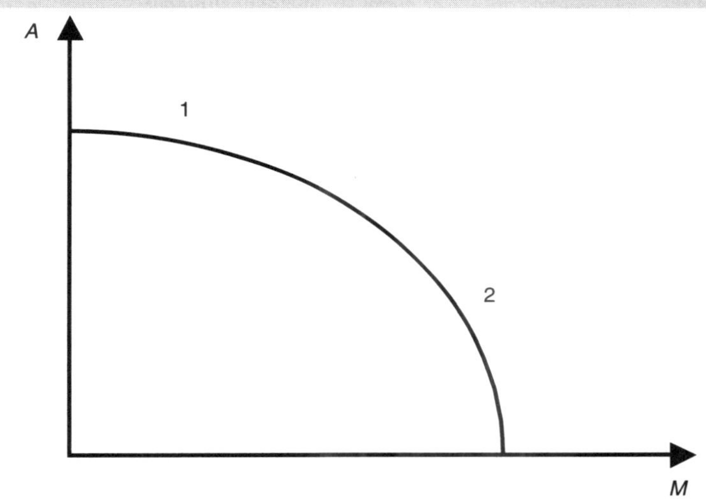

PPF

2a. Is the opportunity cost of M in terms of A higher at point 1 or point 2 in Figure 3-1?

____

2b. Provide an intuitive explanation for why the PPF is "bowed out" in Figure 3-1.

____

____

2c. If the price of a manufactured good is P_M = \$10/unit and the marginal product of labor in manufacturing is 2 units per worker, what must the wage paid to a unit of labor be?

____

____

2d. If $P_M > P_A$, in which industry is the marginal product of labor higher? ______________

____

____

2e. Suppose you own a manufacturing firm. If $P_M = \$10$/unit, the wage is \$25, and the marginal product of labor is 4 units per worker, are you hiring too many, too few, or the right amount of labor? ______________

____

____

2f. Suppose the price of manufactured goods in terms of agricultural products falls. What would we expect to happen to the marginal product of labor in agriculture?

____

____

TIPS

Problem 1 explores the fundamental concept of diminishing marginal product. Do not go into an exam until you are completely comfortable with this concept!

An important implication of the diminishing marginal product of labor in the specific-factors model is that the PPF displays increasing opportunity costs. That is, the more of a good that is produced, the higher the opportunity cost of producing more.

Problem 3: An economy called Home makes autos from capital and labor and bananas from land and labor. Labor is mobile between the two industries. Home is in a no-trade equilibrium, but it is considering opening to international trade with the rest of the world. The relative price of autos in terms of bananas is higher in Home than the fixed price on world markets.

3a. Create a diagram with a PPF, indifference curves, and an international price line showing how production and consumption in Home changes from its no-trade levels to its post-trade levels. Indicate the trade pattern on the diagram.

3b. Explain how your diagram shows how the country as a whole is better or worse off with trade than without trade. ____

3c. Now suppose that there are two countries in the world, Home and Foreign. The countries are not initially engaged in international trade and the relative price of autos is higher in Foreign than in Home. If the countries engaged in international trade, which country would export bananas? ____

3d. Once the two countries are engaged in trade, in which country is the opportunity cost of producing autos higher in terms of bananas? ____

TIPS

Make sure that you can correctly identify production and consumption on a PPF-indifference curve diagram. This is fundamental!

Study carefully how the indifference curves are drawn in the answer to problem 3a. Trade allows the country to get to a higher indifference curve. It is *not* shifting indifference curves.

Care must be taken in drawing the diagram to avoid the suggestion that the indifference curves would ever cross.

The answers to problems 3c and 3d illustrate an important point. Without trade, the opportunity cost of production is different in the two countries, whereas with trade it is the same. When the opportunity cost of production is the same in both locations, world resources are being used efficiently: No country is "low cost" or "high cost."

2 Earnings of Labor

ESSENTIAL CONCEPTS

How does trade affect the livelihoods of people who get their income from their labor? To answer this question, one needs to understand how trade affects the buying power of a worker's wage (W). This is known as the *real wage*. There are two ways to measure the buying power of the wage. If the two goods being produced are agricultural products and manufacturing products, we can measure the buying power of the wage in terms of agricultural products (W/P_A) or in terms of the buying power of the wage in terms of manufacturing products (W/P_M).

To see this, consider a worker's budget constraint. The worker earns nominal income (in dollars) W and pays P_A for autos and P_B for bananas. Her budget constraint is then

$$W = P_A D_A + P_B D_B,$$

which is plotted in panel (a) of Figure 3-2. If both W/P_A and W/P_B were to increase, then the worker's budget constraint shifts out and the worker can afford more of both

FIGURE 3-2

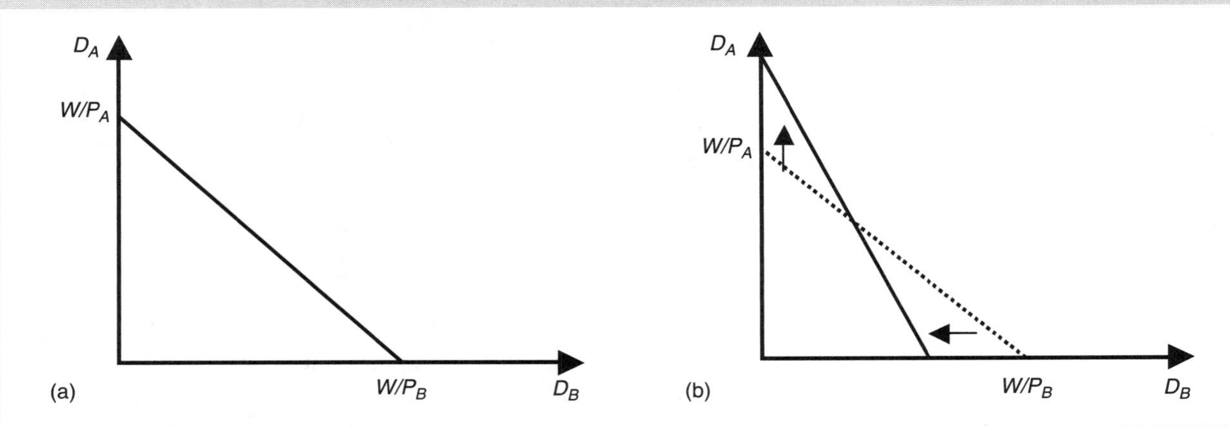

The Effect of Trade on Worker's Budget Constraint

goods. The opposite is true if W/P_A and W/P_B were to decrease. The case where these two measures of welfare do not move in the same direction creates complications. This case is shown in panel (b) of Figure 3-2, where W/P_A increases but W/P_B decreases.

The dotted line is the budget constraint before the price change, and the solid line is the budget constraint after the change. If the worker spends all her income on autos, she is better off. If the worker spends all her income on bananas, she is worse off. The actual impact depends on how much the consumer values autos relative to bananas.

The effect of international trade on the real income of a worker can be determined by the profit-maximizing equation for firms and the knowledge of how labor moves from one industry to another. For instance, the hiring equation for agriculture is $P_A \cdot MPL_A = W$, which can be rewritten $W/P_A = MPL_A$. If employment in agriculture went up, then MPL_A went down and so too did the earnings of a worker relative to the price of agricultural goods. If employment in agriculture went down, then the opposite conclusion is reached. The real wage in terms of manufacturing goods can be analyzed in the same way.

KEY TERMS

Use the space provided to record your notes on the following key terms.

Real wage ______________________________

____

____

Trade adjustment assistance ______________________________

____

____

Services ______________________________

____

____

REVIEW QUESTIONS

Problem 4: A country called Home makes autos from capital and labor and bananas from land and labor. Labor is mobile between the two industries. The country is in a no-trade equilibrium, but it is considering opening to international trade with the rest of the world. The relative price of autos in terms of bananas is higher in Home than the (fixed) price on world markets.

4a. The diagram below shows the real wage in terms of bananas (how many bananas a unit of labor can buy) and the allocation of labor across industries in the no-trade equilibrium. Use this diagram to show these variables in a trading equilibrium.

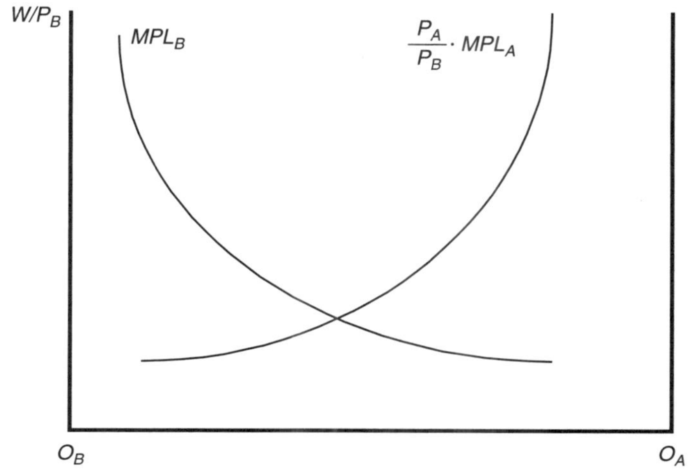

4b. If workers spend all their income on autos, does trade make workers better off or worse off? ______________________________

____

4c. If workers spend all their income on bananas, does trade make workers better off or worse off? ______________________________

____

4d. If workers spend their income on both goods, what can you say about the effect of trade on workers' well-being? ______________________________

____

TIPS

The effect of trade on the real income of the mobile factor (labor) must always be ambiguous in the specific-factors model because the movement of labor between industries raises the marginal product in the contracting industry and lowers it in the expanding industry.

Notice that the marginal products diagram in problem 4 has been reformulated by dividing all the nominal variables (wage, value of marginal products, etc.) by P_B. A change in the relative price has exactly the same effect on real variables as a change in the nominal price of one, holding fixed the other price. In other words, an increase in P_A holding P_B fixed has the same consequences as a decrease in P_B holding P_A fixed. The key difference is in how the diagram works when drawn this way. Either type of price change affects only the curve that is "attached" to the relative price P_A/P_B. A good exercise would be to redo problem 4 with all prices in terms of autos.

Problem 5: Consider the following questions concerning worker mobility.

5a. Suppose that wages in a country were $15 per hour in one industry and $12 per hour in another. Is labor perfectly mobile in this country? Explain. ______

______

______

5b. Provide an explanation for why it is often the case that displaced workers earn less in their new jobs than they did in their previous job. ______

______

______

Problem 6: Suppose a country makes computers with capital and labor and tulips with land and labor. When the country goes from a no-trade equilibrium to a trade equilibrium, the price of computers rises while the price of tulips stays the same. Suppose that labor is not allowed to move between industries.

6a. What is the effect of trade on the real income of computer workers? ______

______

______

6b. What is the effect of trade on the real income of tulip workers? ______

______

______

TIPS

Both problems 5 and 6 illustrate the role that labor mobility plays in the specific-factors model. It is important to understand that there is only one wage because workers can move freely between industries. If there were some reason labor couldn't move, such as a trade union or government-imposed barrier to entry, then there would be two wages.

3 Earnings of Capital and Land

ESSENTIAL CONCEPTS

Although the specific-factor model makes "wishy-washy" predictions about the effect of international trade on the real income of the mobile factor, it makes strong predictions about the effect of international trade on the real income of specific factors. International trade increases the real income of the factor specific to the export industry and decreases the real income of the factor specific to the import industry. This has a very intuitive explanation. Trade induces the export sector to expand and the import sector to contract. Because the amount of the specific factor is fixed in the export sector, the only way to expand production is to increase the amount of labor in that sector. As more labor enters the export sector and there are more workers using the fixed quantity of the specific factor, the specific factor becomes more valuable. As labor leaves the import sector, the specific factor has fewer workers using it and that factor becomes less valuable. In terms of the marginal product of a specific factor, an increase in the amount of labor using that fixed factor increases the marginal product of that factor. The higher the marginal product of the factor, the greater the real income of that factor when measured in terms of the output of that sector.

KEY TERMS

Use the space provided to record your notes on the following key terms.

Rental on capital ______________________________

Rental on land ______________________________

Nominal protection coefficient ______________________________

REVIEW QUESTIONS

Problem 7: Two countries, Home and Foreign, produce autos from capital and labor and bananas from land and labor. Labor is mobile between the two industries. The no-trade equilibrium in the two countries is illustrated in the diagram below.

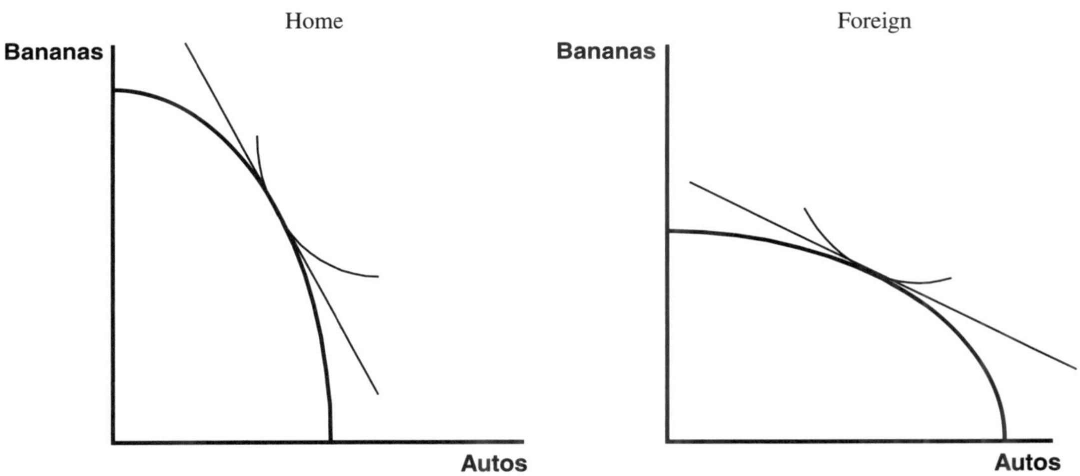

7a. In the diagram above, show a candidate equilibrium if the two countries are trading with each other. Indicate how production and consumption have changed in the two countries.

7b. How has the real rental to capital changed in Home? Explain. ______________________________

7c. How has the real rental to capital changed in Foreign? ______________________________

7d. What happens to the demand for land in Home? ______________________

____

____

7e. If the winners could without cost compensate the losers, would the countries engage in free trade?

____

____

TIPS

When the ratio of factors used in production changes, it means (1) that the marginal products of each factor has changed and (2) that the change of the marginal product of one factor moves in exactly the opposite direction as the marginal product of the other factor. If capital and labor are used in production and the capital/labor ratio increases, then the marginal product of labor goes up (more machines per worker) and the marginal product of capital goes down (fewer workers per machines).

Because the marginal products of different factors used in production move in opposite directions in response to changes in the price of goods, the incomes of factors move in opposite directions. Trade is always controversial in the specific-factors world.

A specific factor is just an input into production that is used only in that industry. In the textbook, Land is specific to agriculture and Capital is specific to Manufacturing. In reality, there are many inputs into production that are specific to an industry. Machines are designed for uses that are specific to an industry. Worker skills can also be industry specific (pastry cooks have skills that do not translate well into law enforcement).

4

Trade and Resources: The Heckscher-Ohlin Model

Overview

This chapter outlines the structure of a "long-run" model of international trade that relates a country's factor endowment to its trade pattern. This model is called the Heckscher-Ohlin model after the economists Eli Heckscher and Bertil Ohlin, who sought to understand the rapid increase in international trade in the late nineteenth century. The model predicts a country's trade pattern on the basis of its endowments, and it predicts how international trade affects the real income of the owners of a country's capital and labor. As in the specific-factor model, a country gains from trade in the sense that it can consume more goods, but some (perhaps many!) individuals within the country will find that their real income has fallen. The chapter concludes with an assessment of the model's ability to explain world trading patterns and a discussion of how the model can be extended to improve its predictive ability.

1 Heckscher-Ohlin Model

ESSENTIAL CONCEPTS

The classic *Heckscher-Ohlin model* is a world in which there are two countries, two goods, and two factors. For convenience we call the factors capital and labor and the countries Home and Foreign. Both goods use capital and labor in their production and both factors are free to move from one industry to another. This is the sense in which this is a "long-run" model. (In the short run it is easy to imagine that factors are stuck in their industry.) The key way that the two goods are different from each other (aside from how consumers use them) is in their *factor intensity.*

Factor intensity is a key concept that merits some review. Suppose that computers and shoes both use capital (K) and labor (L) in their production. The going market rate for a unit of capital is R and the going rate for a unit of labor is W. The relative demands for labor in the computer and shoe industry are shown in Figure 4-1.

FIGURE 4-1

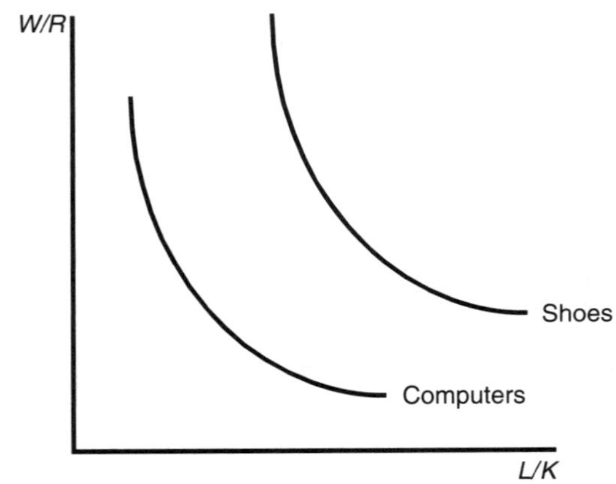

Factor Intensity

The technology used to produce these goods allows producers some degree of substitutability between these factors. Hence, as W rises relative to R, firms in both industries use a mix of inputs that features relatively less L and relatively more K, as Figure 4-1 shows. We say that shoes are *labor intensive* compared with computers because whatever level of W / R prevails in factor markets, the firms that produce shoes use a higher ratio of labor to capital than the firms that produce computers. Alternatively, we could say that computers are *capital intensive* relative to shoes.

The assumption that goods differ in their factor intensity is important because it tells us something about the shape of a country's PPF. First, because goods differ in their factor intensity, the PPF is concave (or bowed out), as shown in Figure 4-2.

FIGURE 4-2

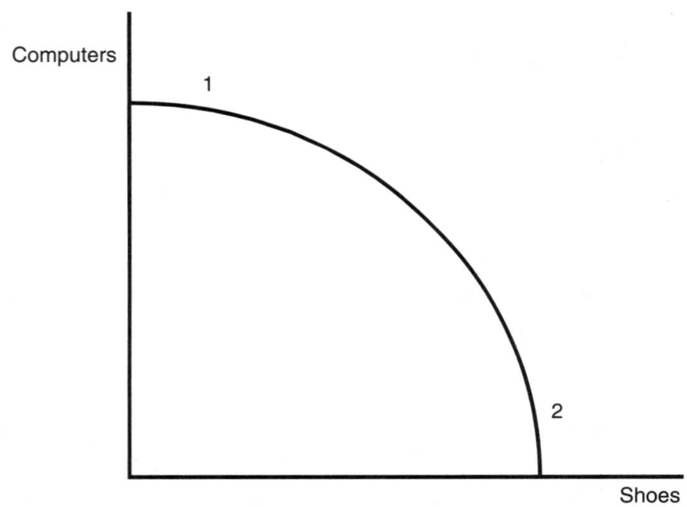

The PPF

To see why the PPF is concave, consider the effect of reallocating capital and labor across industries. At a point such as 1 in Figure 4-2, nearly all the country's factors are being used to make the capital-intensive good, computers. The opportunity cost of shoe production is very low at point 1 because a lot of labor and a little capital can be pulled out of computer production to produce a substantial quantity of shoes with only a little reduction in computer production. As we move from point 1 to point 2, most of the labor has been extracted from the production of computers so that the expansion of shoe production can only be accomplished by extracting a lot of capital and a little labor from computer industry. This results in a small increase in the output of the labor-intensive shoe industry and a large drop in the output of the capital-intensive computer industry.

The second important implication of goods that differ in their factor intensity is the effect on the shape of the PPF of changing a country's endowment. Suppose that we were to add capital to a country's endowment. Because the country has a larger stock of factors and because both goods use both factors, the PPF shifts outward: More of both goods can be produced. However, because computers are capital intensive and shoes are labor intensive, the PPF shifts out in favor of computers, as shown in Figure 4-3.

The two countries are identical in every dimension except in terms of their endowments. They have identical tastes and technologies, but they have different *factor abundances.* Factor abundance is measured as the ratio of capital to labor (or its inverse). The *capital-abundant* country has a higher ratio of capital to labor in its endowment than the *labor-abundant* country, which has a higher ratio of labor to capital. From our discussion in the previous paragraph, this means that the two countries have systematically different PPFs: The capital-abundant country has a PPF skewed out toward the capital-intensive good, whereas the labor-abundant country has its PPF skewed out toward the labor-intensive good. Faced with the same relative price of computers, the capital-abundant country will supply relatively more computers and fewer shoes than the labor-abundant country, which will supply relatively more shoes than computers. Because the two countries have the same tastes, they will consume the two goods in the same ratio. This means that in a trading equilibrium, the capital-abundant country will export the capital-

FIGURE 4-3

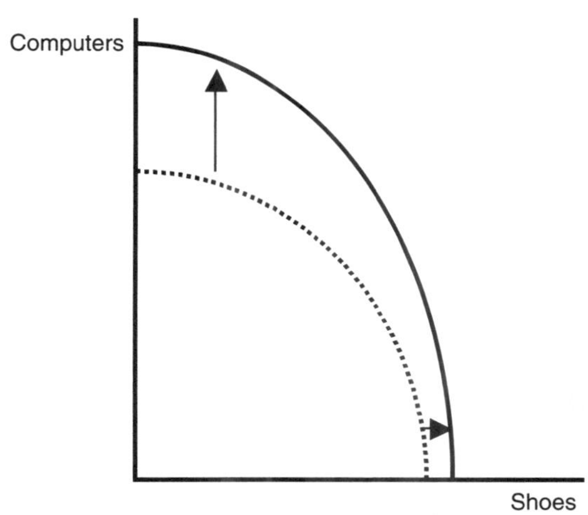

The Effect on the PPF of an Increase in the Capital Stock

intensive good and the labor-abundant country will export the labor-intensive good. This is the *Heckscher-Ohlin theorem*.

As intuitively sensible as the prediction of the Heckscher-Ohlin model sounds, it actually has some difficulty explaining trade patterns. A number of empirical studies have shown that the two-country, two-good, two-factor model does a poor job predicting trade patterns. The most famous of these studies is the *Leontief paradox*. Keep in mind that the model is designed to isolate one possible reason for international trade: unequal distribution of the world's factors. When the model fails to capture pieces of the trading pattern between countries, it suggests that the model ignores important features of the actual world in which we live.

KEY TERMS

Use the space provided to record your notes on the following key terms.

Heckscher-Ohlin model ______________________

____

____

Free-trade equilibrium ______________________

____

____

Reversal of factor intensity ______________________

____

____

Abundance in that factor ______________________

____

____

Scarce in that factor ______________________

____

____

Heckscher-Ohlin theorem ______________________

____

____

Leontief paradox ______________________

____

____

REVIEW QUESTIONS

Problem 1: The two countries are Home and Foreign, the two factors are capital and labor, and the two goods are shoes and computers.

1a. Shoes and computers are produced using capital and labor. Using the following diagram, draw a *factor intensity reversal* between shoes and computers.

1b. Home is endowed with 200 units of capital and 100 units of labor. Foreign is endowed with 100 units of capital and 40 units of labor. Which country is capital-abundant? ________

____

____

TIPS

It is very easy to accidentally say (or write on an exam) *factor intensity* when *factor abundance* is meant or vice versa. This slip up will likely result in a lower grade, so don't do it!

Problem 2: There is a world with two countries called Home and Foreign. Home and Foreign produce computers and shoes using capital and labor. Computers are capital intensive relative to shoes. It is unknown what the factor endowments of each country are, but it is known that the relative price of computers is higher in Home than Foreign in a no-trade equilibrium.

2a. Which country is capital-abundant? ______________________________

____

____

2b. Which country is producing a higher ratio of computers to shoes in a no-trade equilibrium? ____

____

____

Problem 3: There is a world with two countries called Home and Foreign. Home and Foreign produce airplanes and shirts using capital and labor. Airplanes are capital intensive relative to shirts and Foreign is capital-abundant relative to Home. All the Heckscher-Ohlin assumptions hold.

3a. Which country is exporting shirts? ______________________________

____

____

3b. The consumers in Home are buying twice as many shirts as airplanes. What is the ratio of shirt to airplane consumption in Foreign? ______________________________

____

____

3c. Suppose that Foreign's endowment of capital is increased. What happens to the relative price of airplanes in terms of shirts on world markets? Use the diagrams below in answering your question. ______________________________

____

____

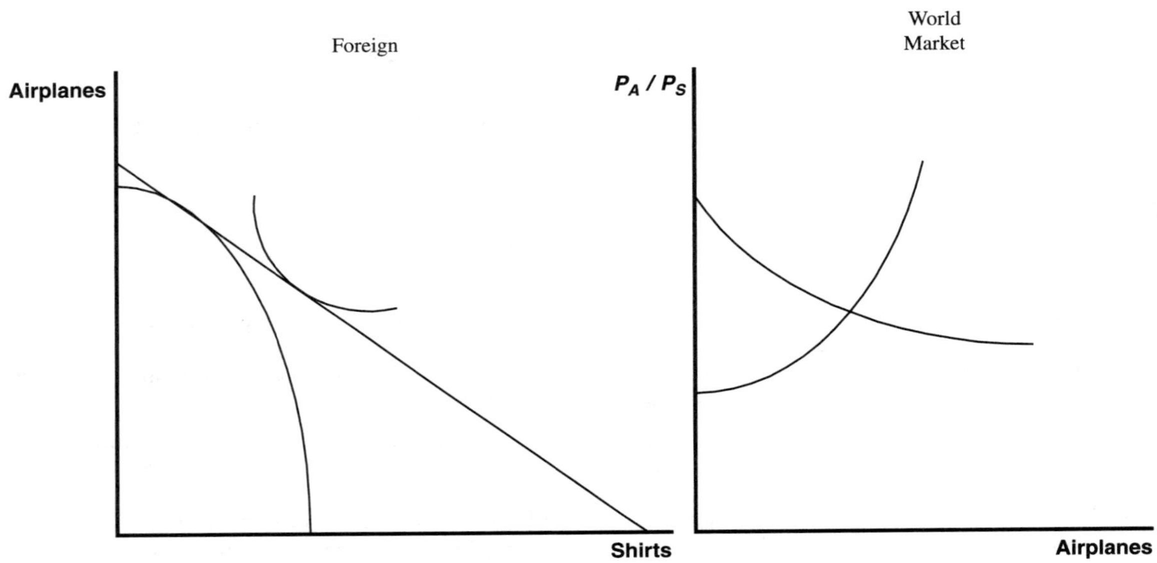

3d. Suppose that Foreign's endowment of capital is increased. What happens to the level of national welfare in Home (can it reach a higher indifference curve)? ______________________________

____

____

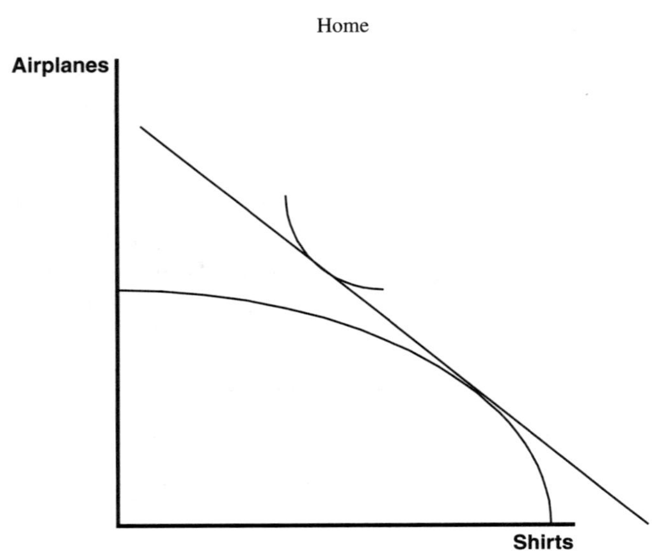

Problem 4: An important assumption in the Heckscher-Ohlin model is that the tastes are the same in both countries. Suppose that tastes are different in the Home and Foreign. Is it possible for a capital-abundant country (Foreign) to export the labor-intensive good (shirts) if tastes are different? If so, draw a PPF-indifference curve diagram for Home and a PPF-indifference curve diagram for Foreign that illustrates this case in the following space.

Problem 5: Consider the assumptions of the Heckscher-Ohlin model. What three failures of these assumptions could explain the Leontief paradox? ____________________

____

____

Problems 4 and 5 illustrate the importance of assumptions in a model. Change an assumption and you change the model's predictions.

TIPS

2 Effects of Trade on Factor Prices

ESSENTIAL CONCEPTS

We now consider the effect of changes in goods prices induced by international trade on the prices of factors in the long-run Heckscher-Ohlin model. As in the specific-factors model, international trade causes the real incomes of factor owners to change, with some factors seeing their real incomes rise and others seeing their real incomes fall. The types of predictions are very different in the long-run Heckscher-Ohlin model than in the specific-factors model. In the specific-factors model, we see that there is a divide across industries in the effect of international trade on real income: The factor specific to the export industry sees its real income rise with trade, whereas the factor specific to the import industry sees its real income fall. In the Heckscher-Ohlin model there is no specific factor. Instead, the *Stolper-Samuelson theorem* has the key implication that the owners of the factor in which the country is abundant gain from international trade, whereas the owners of the factor in which the country is scarce are hurt by international trade. It becomes possible then that an individual could see her real income fall in the short run (factor specific to import industry) and rise in the long run (abundant factor).

To think about the economics of the Stolper-Samuelson theorem, consider Figure 4-2. An increase in the relative price of shoes shifts production away from point 1 and toward point 2. An increase in shoe production requires a decrease in computer production. But because shoe producers demand a lot of labor and a little capital and computer producers demand a lot of capital and a little labor, shutting down computer output releases "too much" capital and "too little" labor. This is why W / R has to rise to get firms to use less labor and more capital. Because firms in both industries increase the ratio of capital to labor that they use in production, the marginal product of labor rises and the marginal product of capital falls in *both* industries. A decrease in the relative price of shoes has exactly the opposite effect.

KEY TERMS

Use the space provided to record your notes on the following key term.

Stopler-Samuelson theorem ______________________________

____

____

REVIEW QUESTIONS

Problem 6: Consider the relative demand curve for a country shown in Figure 4-4. *RD* stands for relative demand and *RS* stands for relative supply. The two industries are computers and shoes.

FIGURE 4-4

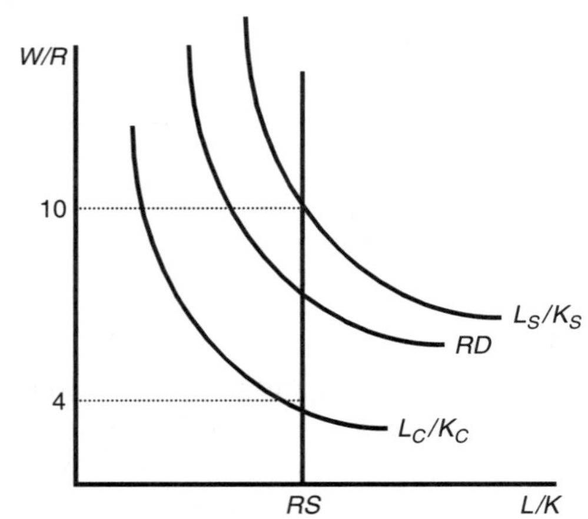

Relative Demand

6a. What is the highest relative wage that we could observe in this economy? ______________

____

____

6b. What causes the relative demand curve for labor in a country to shift up? ______________

6c. Suppose there is an upward shift in the relative demand curve for labor. What happens to the ratio of labor to capital used in production in each industry? ______________

Problem 7: Consider the real-sounding but fictional country of Ubetcha. Ubetcha produces two goods, autos and hats, using capital and labor. Autos are capital intensive relative to hats. The country has long enjoyed its isolation from the world but is now considering free trade. The top Ubetchan economist traveled abroad and noticed that the relative price of autos is lower on world markets than it is in Ubetcha. All Heckscher-Ohlin assumptions hold.

7a. Suppose the country were to institute free trade with the rest of the world. How would the capital/labor ratio used by Ubetchan's producers of autos and hats change? ______________

7b. If Ubetcha engages in free trade with the rest of the world, how will the marginal product of capital change in the auto and hat industries? ______________

7c. Suppose there is an organization in Ubetcha, the Union of Ubetchan Capitalists, or UUC for short, which represents the interests of capital owners in the country. Would that organization support or lobby against the free-trade idea? Explain. ______________

Problem 8: The National Election Study (NES) survey in the United States in 1992 found that workers with higher levels of education were more likely to support free trade than less educated workers.

8a. Assuming that the United States is a relatively skill-abundant country, is this result consistent with the Heckscher-Ohlin model? Explain. ______________

8b. Suppose that the same questionnaire were asked in a skill-scarce country. What would the Heckscher-Ohlin model predict about the responses of workers? ______________

Problem 9: Suppose that the world was one large, happy country that produced doughnuts and sofas using capital and labor. Sofas are capital intensive relative to doughnuts. International trade is *not* allowed. The following questions build on one another.

9a. Suppose that the world is divided into two identical countries (Home and Foreign); that is, they receive the same amount of labor and capital. Would there be any motive for immigration (i.e., would laborers want to move) between the two countries? Explain. ______

______

______

______

9b. Now suppose that some of the capital is moved from Foreign to Home so that Home is capital-abundant relative to Foreign. Trade is still not allowed. What happens to the real income of labor in each of the two countries? ______

______

______

9c. If laborers are free to move internationally, which way do they move?

______

______

9d. What does the migration do to real incomes of laborers in Home and Foreign?

______

______

9e. If you were a capitalist in Home, would you be in favor of immigration? Explain.

______

______

______

TIPS

Note that in problem 9, international trade is not allowed but immigration is. The problem shows that trade and immigration have similar effects on income distribution.

Problem 10: Your well-meaning but excessively enthusiastic relative, Bob, wants you to sign a petition to ban trade with a developing country. He claims that trade will encourage the expansion of labor-intensive "sweatshop" industries in the developing country and so will reduce the welfare of workers (the abundant factor) in that developing country. Does the Heckscher-Ohlin model necessarily imply that developing country workers will be hurt by trade? ______

______

______

______

Problem 11: What kind of result could Leontief have found that would have not been called a paradox? ______

______

______

3 Extending the Heckscher-Ohlin Model

ESSENTIAL CONCEPTS

A world where there are two goods, two factors, and two countries is relatively easy to analyze. Unfortunately, the world is not so simple, and we need to be careful taking what we can learn from the Heckscher-Ohlin setting considered earlier to the real world. Fortunately, it is not that hard to extend the Heckscher-Ohlin model to many goods, many factors, and many countries. To do so, we need a new concept of factor abundance. A country's relative abundance in a factor can be measured as its share of the world's endowment of that factor relative to its share of the world's income. If every country has the same tastes, then every country consumes goods in the same ratio. A factor's *services* can be thought of as *embodied* in the goods that we consume in the sense that a certain number of worker and machine hours "went in" to the finished product. Hence, consumers can be thought of as consuming factor services indirectly through their consumption of goods, and because goods can be traded, so too can factor services.

For example, if the United States has 26.6% of the world's GDP, it should consume 26.6% of the world's goods, and 26.6% of all the services of capital (i.e., the time the capital was used to make the goods), and 26.6% of all the services of land, and so on. If the U.S. has 50.7% of the world's research and development (R&D) scientists, then the goods that the United States exports to the rest of the world should have more R&D services embodied in them than the goods that the United States imports from the rest of the world.

One can measure the factor content of trade by measuring the inputs into the production of all goods and then use trade data to infer how much of each factor service is embodied in each. This is the idea of the *extended Heckscher-Ohlin theorem,* and it is this concept that is most appropriate for thinking about actual world trading patterns.

Another problem with the Heckscher-Ohlin model that we have discussed is its assumption that technologies are the same everywhere. It is clearly not true that factor prices are the same everywhere or that technologies are the same everywhere, and these two discrepancies are probably linked. If workers from country A can produce twice as much as workers from country B, then we need to be careful in how we measure a country's endowment of labor. This is the idea of measuring a country's *effective labor force,* and the idea occurred to Leontief many years ago. More generally, the productivity of all factors may vary across countries in such a way as to confound the predictions of the extended Heckscher-Ohlin model. By controlling for a factor's productivity in a given country, the model can be made to fit the data better.

KEY TERMS

Use the space provided to record your notes on the following key terms.

Extended Heckscher-Ohlin theorem ________________________________

____

____

Factor content of exports ________________________________

____

____

Factor content of imports ______________________________

____

____

Effective labor force ______________________________

____

____

Effective factor endowment ______________________________

____

____

Abundant in that effective factor ______________________________

____

____

Scarce in that effective factor ______________________________

____

____

Sign test ______________________________

____

____

REVIEW QUESTIONS

Problem 12: Suppose Home has 15% of the world's capital, 7% of the world's labor, 5% of the world's arable land, and 10% of the world's GDP.

12a. What does the extended Heckscher-Ohlin model predict about the labor content of Home's net exports? ______________________________

____

____

12b. Suppose that Home's workers are much better paid than workers in the rest of the world. Why might you expect the sign test to fail when measuring the labor content of Home's net exports? ______________________________

____

____

12c. Is it possible for a country to appear scarce in all factors? ______________________________

____

____

TIPS

A model that fails to predict reality is not necessarily a "failure." Even if a model doesn't predict reality well, it can be very useful if one can identify the assumptions that are the culprit for the model's poor performance! Empirical studies of the extended Heckscher-Ohlin model suggest that the assumption that technologies are the same across countries is inappropriate.

5

Movement of Labor and Capital between Countries

Overview

This chapter analyzes the effects that movements in factors between countries have on (1) factor rewards (wages, rental, etc.), (2) the pattern of production across countries, and (3) the size of global output. Two kinds of factor flows are considered: immigration (the movement of labor) and foreign direct investment (movement of capital). To analyze the short-run effects of immigration and foreign direct investment we use the specific-factors model introduced in Chapter 3. To analyze the long-run effect of factor movements we use the Heckscher-Ohlin model introduced in Chapter 4. To keep the analysis simple, we assume that in both the short run and the long run the international prices of goods are fixed.

A key point made in this chapter is that the short-run and long-run effects of factor movements on factor rewards are very different. Immigration and FDI alter the distribution of income across factors in the short run but have no effect on real income in the long run. The effects of factor flows on the pattern of production are also very different in the short run than in the long run. The chapter concludes by considering the gains from factor flows. Both immigration and foreign direct investment lead to a more efficient use of the world's resources and therefore to greater output given the same world resources.

1 Movement of Labor between Countries

ESSENTIAL CONCEPTS

Immigration causes the supply of labor to fall in one location and to rise in another. Hence, the effects of immigration on the real incomes of different factors and the output of each industry are treated as changes in countries' endowments of labor. How does the economy absorb the new workers, and what effect does it have on the people living in that country? The answer to this question depends on whether one considers the short run, when factors are limited in their ability to move across industries, or the long run, when factors are perfectly mobile across industries.

Because the specific-factors model is built upon the assumption of limited factor mobility across industries, it is appropriate for analyzing the short-run effects of immigration. To be consistent with Chapter 3, the specific factors are called land and capital and the mobile factor is called labor. (Of course, the specific factors could be different types of capital or labor.) To keep things as simple as possible, we assume that the country is trading freely with the rest of the world at fixed prices.

In the specific-factors model, new workers must be absorbed into both industries. When a worker is hired in an industry, the marginal product of labor in that industry must fall because there is now less of the specific factor per worker. Because prices are fixed, the decline in the marginal product of labor must be accompanied by a decline in the real wage in that industry. If workers were to enter only one industry, then the wage in that industry would fall below the wage level in the other industry. Hence, labor must be absorbed in both industries. Changes in the remaining economic variables are driven by the increase in labor employed in both industries. First, output of both industries must increase because there are more factors being used in production. Second, because there is more labor and the same amount of specific factor, the marginal products of both specific factors must rise. Hence, immigration increases the real income of the specific factors.

How does a country absorb an increase in its labor endowment in the long run? There are two possible channels that we will discuss in the context of a specific example. Suppose there are two industries, A and B. Industry A is labor intensive relative to industry B. The country is endowed with $\overline{K}$ units of capital and $\overline{L}$ units of labor. Because all factors are used, we have $\overline{K} = K_A + K_B$ and $\overline{L} = L_A + L_B$. In Chapter 4, we learned that the condition that the relative supply of labor $\overline{L}/\overline{K}$ must be equal to the relative demand for labor (a weighted average of relative demand in each industry) can be written

$$\frac{\overline{L}}{\overline{K}} = \left(\frac{K_A}{\overline{K}}\right)\left(\frac{L_A}{K_A}\right) + \left(\frac{K_B}{\overline{K}}\right)\left(\frac{L_B}{K_B}\right).$$

From this expression, we see that an increase in the endowment of labor $\overline{L}$ due to immigration can be absorbed either (1) by increasing the labor-to-capital ratio in each industry (L_A / K_A and L_B / K_B) or (2) by increasing the weight of the labor-intensive industry A (with its higher labor/capital ratio) in relative demand (increasing $K_A / \overline{K}$ and decreasing $K_B / \overline{K}$).

It turns out that the first channel plays *no* role in absorbing new workers in the long run. The labor/capital ratios used in each industry cannot change as long as the prices of goods are held fixed. This is hard to show formally, but we provide some intuition. The key insight follows from the fact that for a fixed set of goods prices, there is only *one capital-to-labor ratio* for each industry that makes (1) the value of the marginal product of labor the same in both industries, and (2) the value of the marginal product of capital is the same in both industries. In the short run, the rental on capital can be different across industries (think specific-factors model) so that employment can increase in both industries. This is not so in the long run. In the long run labor is absorbed into the economy exclusively through an increase in the output of the labor-intensive good and a decrease in the output of capital-intensive good.

To see how changing the mix of output can absorb the increase in labor, consider the following numerical example as an alternative to the *box diagram*. Suppose that the production of good A requires 1 unit of labor and 1 unit of capital, whereas the production of good B requires 1 unit of labor and 5 units of capital. If Q_A is the output of good A and Q_B is the output of good B, then if all factors are being used we have

$$\overline{K} = 5 \cdot Q_B + 1 \cdot Q_A$$

and

$$\overline{L} = 1 \cdot Q_B + 1 \cdot Q_A.$$

Doing a little algebra, we find that

$$Q_A = \frac{5\overline{L} - \overline{K}}{4} \text{ and } Q_B = \frac{\overline{K} - \overline{L}}{4}.$$

From these two expressions, it is clear that an increase in the labor endowment, $\overline{L}$, increases the output of the labor-intensive good A and decreases the output of the capital-intensive good B. This example illustrates the *Rybczynski theorem* and the *Factor price insensitivity result*. A change in endowments for whatever reason leads to a change in the mix of the country's outputs rather than a change in the country's factor prices when the prices of goods are held fixed.

KEY TERMS

Use the space provided to record your notes on the following key terms.

Specific-factors model ________________________________

Rybczynski theorem ________________________________

Factor price insensitivity ________________________________

REVIEW QUESTIONS

Problem 1: Consider a country called Home that produces manufactured goods (M) and agricultural products (A). M is produced using capital and labor. A is produced using land and labor. (Hence, this is a short-run problem.) Labor is perfectly mobile between industries. Suppose that the country is trading with the rest of the world at fixed prices (P_M and P_A). Initially, the country has the same wages as the rest of the world.

1a. Suppose that the country's endowment of land expands. What impact does this expansion of land have on the wage (W)? Use the diagram provided below to support your answer.

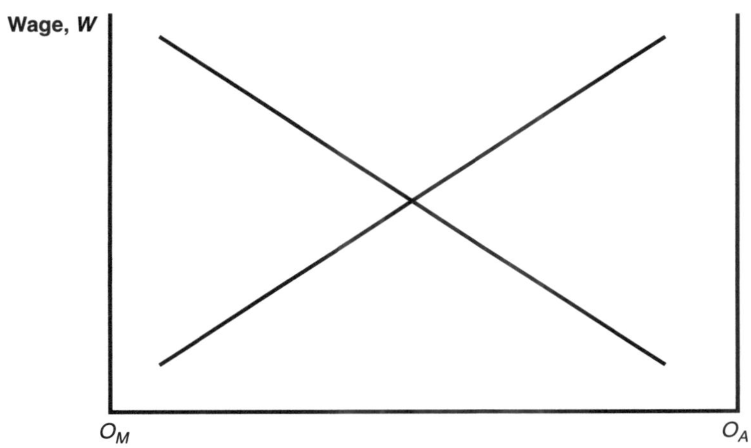

1b. Suppose that the wage is higher in Home than in the rest of the world so that Foreign labor will move to Home. What is the impact of the increase in labor for the wage in Home? Use the diagram provided below to support your answer. ______________________

____

____

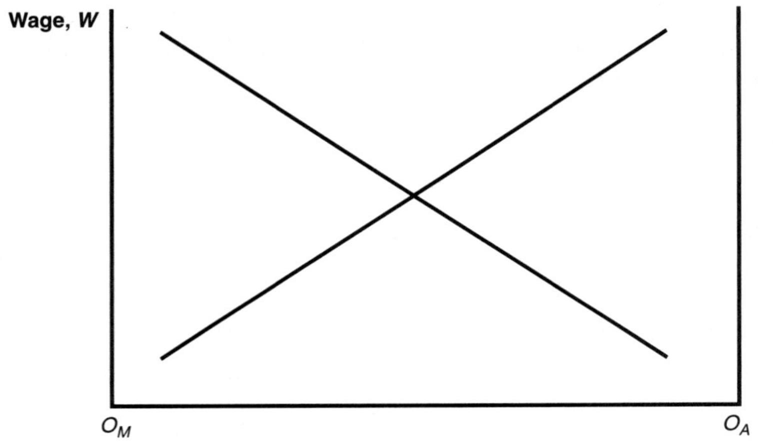

1c. What is the impact of the immigration to Home on the real earnings of a unit of capital in Home and on the real earnings of a unit of land in Home? ______________________

____

____

1d. Using the axes below, show how the output of both goods is affected by the immigration into the country. Explain your diagram. ______________________

____

____

TIPS

It is important to understand why adding more of a specific factor shifts up the marginal product of labor in the industry using that factor.

When the stock of the endowment of the mobile factor changes, it is always the case that in the short run the output of both goods and the real return to both specific factors must change in the same direction. It is not possible without additional information, however, to say which industry is affected the most.

It does not matter whether one shifts the axes O_M or O_A when increasing the size of the labor force.

To convince yourself that you know the material well, run all the questions in problem 1 in reverse (consider an outflow of labor). All the answers should be reversed.

Problem 2: Consider a country that produces two goods: airplanes and shirts. The country is trading with the rest of the world at fixed goods prices. Airplane producers are using 5 units of capital and 3 units of labor to produce one unit of airplanes and shirt producers are using 2 units of capital and 2 units of labor to produce one shirt. Both factors are mobile between industries.

2a. Which good is capital intensive? ______________________________

____

____

2b. Suppose there is a sudden emigration (outflow of labor). What happens to the level of employment in the airplane industry in the long run? Show using the box diagram below.

____

____

____

2c. Can you derive an equation that relates the country's output to its endowments? ________

____

____

2d. Use the axes below to show how the emigration of labor alters the shape of the production possibilities frontier in the long run. Indicate the level of production of both goods before and after the outflow of labor.

TIPS The Rybczynski theorem can be used to explain why a country's PPF is skewed toward the good that is intensive in the country's relatively abundant factor. It would be helpful to convince yourself that this is so.

Problem 3: Consider a country that produces two goods, computers and shirts, using capital and labor. In the short run, labor is specific to its sector because workers need particular skills to be productive in the industry. In the long run, labor is perfectly mobile between industries. Capital is perfectly mobile in both the short and long run. The country is engaged in free trade at fixed world prices.

3a. Suppose there is an inward flow of computer workers into the country. What is the short-run impact of the immigration on the real incomes of both computer and shirt workers already in the country? Explain using the axes below. ______________________________

____

____

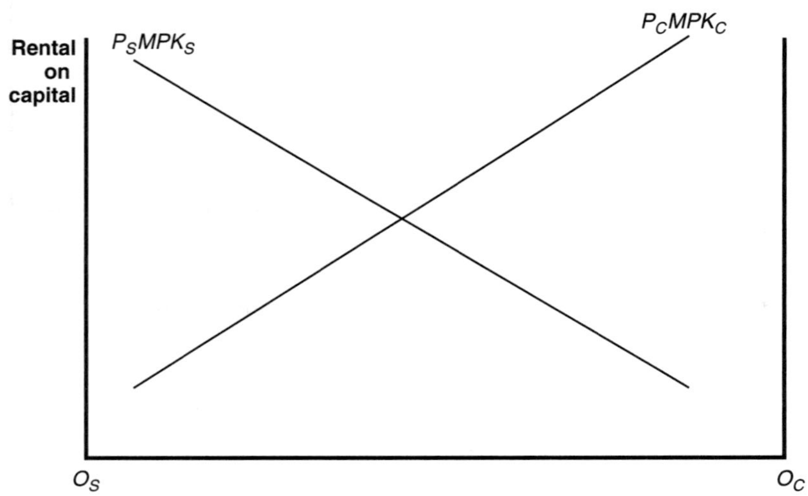

3b. What is the impact of the influx of computer workers on real wage in the long run (i.e., when workers are free to move between industries)? ______

3c. What is the effect of the immigration in the short and long run on the real income of capital? ______

TIPS

The assumptions that economists make regarding the nature of technology have important implications for how they perceive the effects of immigration. To answer any problem correctly, you must identify what factors are assumed to be mobile.

The contrast between the short-run and the long-run implications of immigration on factor prices is important. Any calculation of the impact of immigration on factor prices depends on the assumptions that were made to generate those estimates!

In the example considered here, workers have skills that are specific to particular industries. This is probably closer to truth than assuming that workers are perfectly mobile between sectors. By giving factors different names, we can use the same framework to think about other real-world cases.

Problem 4: Answer the following questions "true," "false," or "uncertain," and **explain** your answer.

4a. Most immigrants into the United States enter the country legally. ______

4b. Almost all immigrants (both legal and illegal) into the United States are very low skilled.

4c. The response of Miami's output to the Mariel boat lift is consistent with the Rybczynski theorem. ______

2 Foreign Direct Investment

ESSENTIAL CONCEPTS

Foreign direct investment (FDI) occurs when a company from one country obtains a production plant in a foreign country. If the plant is built from scratch, it is a greenfield investment. If instead the plant already existed under a different firm's ownership, the investment is called acquisition FDI. The chapter focuses mostly on greenfield investment because this type of FDI better fits the way FDI is modeled. In the short run, FDI is modeled as an increase in a country's endowment of one of the specific factors, capital. The key result is that an increase in the endowment of one of the specific factors drives up the demand for labor and its real wage. The real rental to both specific factors must fall. With respect to the outputs of goods, in the short run an increase in the stock of one specific factor increases the output of that specific factor and reduces the output of the other industry. The reduction in the output of the other industry occurs because the growth in the industry receiving FDI attracts workers out of agriculture.

In the long run, we assume that all factors are perfectly mobile between industries and that industries are characterized by their factor intensity; therefore, the effect of an inflow of capital is symmetrical to the case of an inflow of labor. Both the Rybczynski theorem and the factor price insensitivity result are still valid. FDI changes the country's output but has no impact on its factor prices in the long run.

KEY TERMS

Use the space provided to record your notes on the following key term.

Foreign direct investment ____

____

____

REVIEW QUESTIONS

Problem 5: Agricultural products (A) are produced with land and labor, and manufacturing products (M) are produced using capital and labor. Labor is perfectly mobile between industries but cannot move internationally.

5a. Suppose there are two countries, Home and Foreign, that are identical except that Home has a larger endowment of labor than Foreign. The two countries are engaged in free trade. Given this scenario, is there any motive for capital to move internationally? If so, which direction would it move? ____

____

____

5b. Assume that the international prices of A and M do not change and that capital moves from Foreign to Home. What will FDI do to Home's level of production of M and of A? Show using the following diagram. ____

____

____

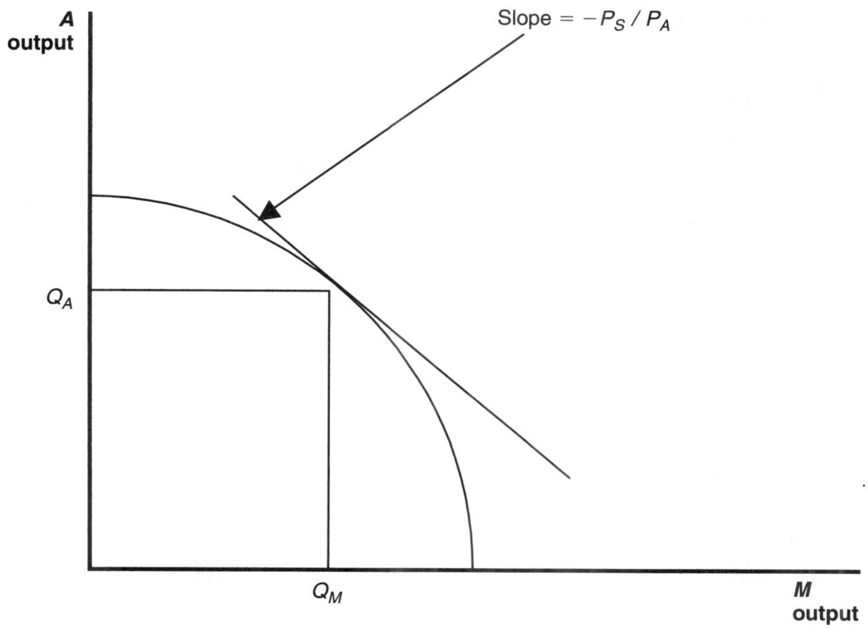

5c. What is the impact of this inward FDI on the real wage of labor, the real rental of capital, and the real rental of land in Home?

5d. How does the outward investment affect the real earnings of labor in Foreign?

TIPS

Note the difference in the answers to problems 5c and 5d. The factors that are helped in Home are the factors that are hurt in Foreign and vice versa.

Problem 6: Consider a country that produces airplanes and shirts using capital and labor. Shirts are labor intensive relative to airplanes. Labor and capital are perfectly mobile between industries. The country is engaged in free trade at fixed world prices. Suppose that some of the capital used to make shirts is transferred abroad via outward foreign direct investment.

6a. What is the impact of the transfer of capital abroad on the production of shirts in the long run?

6b. What is the long-run impact of the outward foreign direct investment on the real wage?

3 Gains from Labor and Capital Flows

ESSENTIALS CONCEPTS

Thus far, the analysis has highlighted how changes in endowments due to labor and capital flows alter real incomes of various factors and the output of different goods. How do these flows affect the national welfare of the country that is the source of these flows and the national welfare of the country that is the destination for these flows? To answer this question, keep in mind that labor moves from the low-wage country to the high-wage country and capital moves from the low- to the high-rental country. Because factor prices reflect the value of the marginal product, factors move from countries with low marginal products to countries with high marginal products. This means that factor flows increase world output: There are gains from factor movement. In general, both source and destination countries share in the gains, but the disruptive effect of the change in income distribution can be very large relative to the total welfare gain.

KEY TERMS

Use the space provided to record your notes on the following key term.

Real value added ______________________________

____

____

REVIEW QUESTIONS

Problem 7: There are two countries, Home and Foreign. The two countries are identical except that Home has a labor force of 100 and Foreign has a labor force of 200. Given this allocation of labor across Home and Foreign, the value of the marginal product of labor in Home is 30 and the value of the marginal product of labor in Foreign is 20. If labor were to be free to move, the wage in both countries would be 25. Figure 5-1 summarizes this situation.

FIGURE 5-1

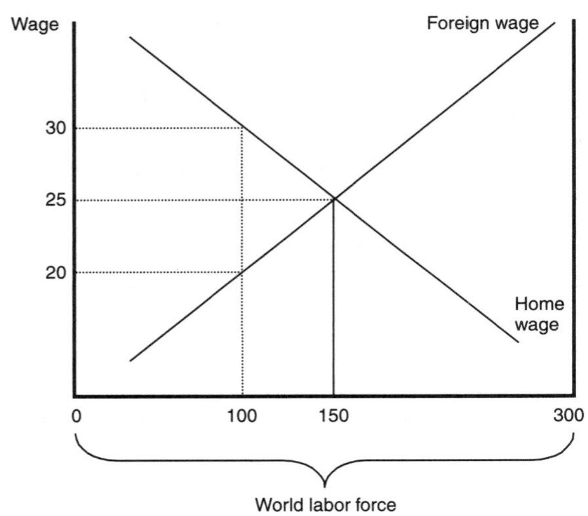

Marginal Product of Labor in Foreign and Home

7a. If immigration were free between countries, how much would the value of output change in Home? ______________________________

____

____

7b. What is Home's national gain in allowing immigration? ______________________________

____

____

7c. Who benefits from this immigration in Home and how much? ______________________________

____

____

TIPS

The analysis of the gains from FDI is conceptually identical to that of immigration. The marginal product of capital and the rental are considered instead of the marginal product of labor and the wage. One could repeat problem 7 for FDI renaming all the variables appropriately.

Problem 8: Why are younger people more likely to immigrate than older people?

____

____

____

6

Increasing Returns to Scale and Imperfect Competition

Overview

This chapter begins with an example of actual trading patterns, U.S. imports and exports of golf clubs. Two aspects of this trading pattern cannot be explained by the models of comparative advantage presented in earlier chapters. First, the United States simultaneously imports golf clubs from a wide range of countries at very different prices. Second, the United States exports golf clubs to many of the same countries from which it is also importing golf clubs! This kind of *intra-industry trade,* or "two-way" trade in the same good between countries, is pervasive, occurring between many trading partners in many goods.

This chapter shows that models built on the assumption of *imperfect competition* improve our understanding of trade patterns and provide additional insight into the gains from trade. The centerpiece of the chapter is the model of trade under *monopolistic competition.* Firms in a monopolistically competitive industry have a monopoly over their own particular brand or "variety" of a *differentiated* good. There is an element of competition, however, in the sense that the demand for a firm's variety depends on the actions of other firms. Firms produce their variety using an *increasing returns to scale* technology. Firms face fixed product development cost and constant marginal costs of production, so their average cost falls as they produce larger volumes of output.

The monopolistic competition model makes predictions that are distinct from those of a comparative-advantage–based model. With respect to trade patterns, the model predicts intra-industry trade between similar countries and gives rise to the *gravity equation,* which is an accurate predictor of the volume of trade between countries. With respect to the gains from trade, the model identifies two channels through which trade affects welfare. International trade expands the range of variety available to consumers and allows firms to better exploit economies of scale by expanding the size of their operations.

The chapter concludes with an alternative model built on imperfect competition. Rather than assume that products are differentiated, the model assumes that goods are homogeneous. It shows that imperfect competition can explain a common phenomenon known as *dumping,* in which a firm charges a lower price in the foreign market than in its home market. Finally, it shows that imperfect competition alone can give rise to intra-industry trade even in the absence of product differentiation and economies of scale.

1 Basics of Imperfect Competition

ESSENTIAL CONCEPTS

The first section is designed (1) to review the theory of monopoly and (2) to introduce the concept of *product differentiation* in the context of a *duopoly.* A monopolist faces a downward-sloping demand curves and chooses its output (and hence the price of its product) to maximize its *economic profits.* A firm's profit is equal to the difference between its sales revenue and its total costs of production. By choosing to sell one more unit, the firm increases its revenue by the value of its *marginal revenue* and increases its total cost by its marginal cost. Suppose a firm is selling Q units at a price of P. The additional revenue raised by this firm if it sells one more unit is

$$P - \Delta P \cdot Q.$$

The firm earns P from selling one more unit but because the firm has to cut its price by ΔP on all the units it had been selling, it loses $\Delta P \cdot Q$. If the marginal revenue exceeds marginal cost, then the firm can increase its revenue by more than its cost by selling one more unit. If the marginal revenue is less than marginal cost, a firm can raise its profits by selling one less unit of its good because cutting production by one unit lowers revenue by less than it lowers total cost. Hence, a profit-maximizing firm chooses output so that marginal revenue is equal to marginal cost.

In the case of duopoly with differentiated products, there is a single demand curve for an industry's output, D, but each firm faces a demand curve that is specific to its variety of that industry's good. When the two firms charge the same price, industry demand is divided equally among varieties so that each firm sells $D / 2$. Because products are differentiated, a firm cannot grab the entire market by lowering its price below that of its competitor. Instead, a firm that reduces its price attracts new customers to its product, some of whom would have chosen to purchase the product of the firm's competitor. The demand curve for the firm, d, is flatter than the demand curve $D / 2$, because the firm can steal some of its competitor's customers by lowering its price.

KEY TERMS

Use the space provided to record your notes on the following key terms.

Imperfect competition ______________________________

____

____

Duopoly ______________________________

____

____

Marginal revenue ______________________________

____

____

Marginal cost ____

Differentiated goods ____

Economic profits ____

Monopoly profits ____

REVIEW QUESTIONS

Problem 1: After extensive market research a firm discovers that it faces the demand curve recorded in the following table.

Quantity Sold	Price, $	Revenue, $	Marginal Revenue, $
1	7		
2	6		
3	5		
4	4		
5	3		
6	2		
7	1		

1a. Calculate the revenue and the marginal revenue associated with each output level and fill in the columns in the table.

1b. If the marginal cost is $2.5 per unit, what level of production should the firm choose to maximize its profits? Explain. ____________________

1c. Calculate the profits associated with this level of output. ____________________

Problem 2: A firm faces the demand curve, marginal revenue curve, and marginal cost curve shown in the following diagram. Add to this diagram the optimal level of output and show geometrically on this diagram the level of a firm's profits.

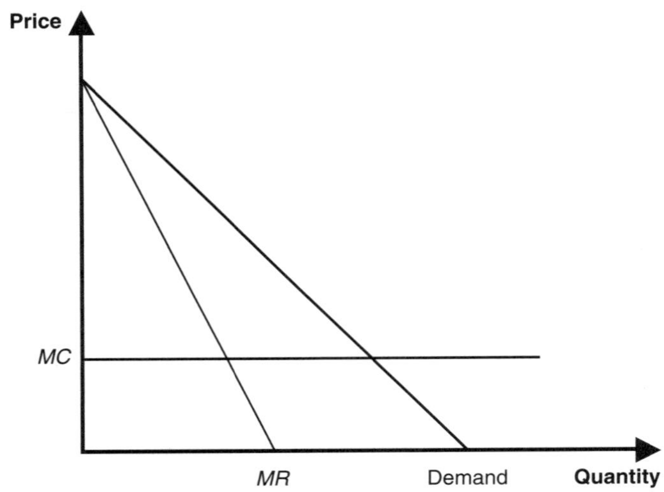

Problem 3: Consider a duopoly. In the diagram below, D / 2 is industry demand divided by the two differentiated varieties in the market when each variety has the same price and d is the demand curve specific to each firm.

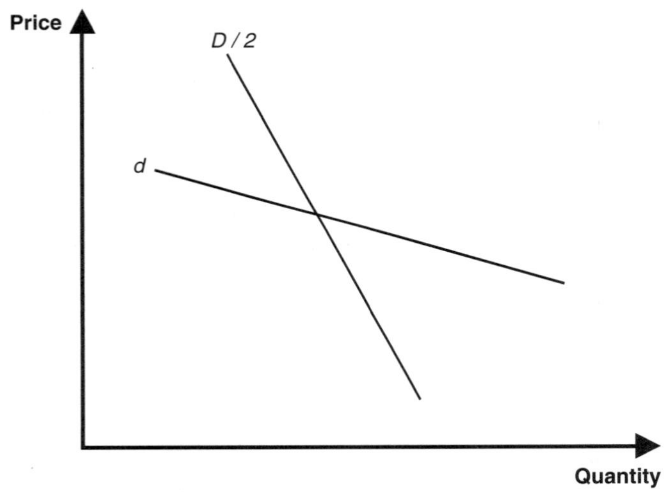

Why is the d curve flatter than the D / 2 curve? ____

____

____

2 Trade under Monopolistic Competition

ESSENTIAL CONCEPTS

The model of monopolistic competition is based on four assumptions. First, each firm produces a good that is similar to but differentiated from the goods that other firms in the industry produce. Because each firm's product is somewhat different from the goods of the other firms, a firm can raise its price without losing all its customers to other firms; that is, each firm faces a downward-sloping demand curve for its product. Second, there are many firms in the industry. Third, firms produce using a technology with increasing returns to scale: average costs of production fall as the quantity produced increases. Fourth, firms can enter and exit the industry freely, so that monopoly profits are zero in the long run. In monopolistic competition, firms have some monopoly power, and yet in a long-run equilibrium each firm's profits are zero.

The model neatly captures two gains from trade that are very different than those due to comparative advantage: International trade results in (1) a wider variety of goods available and (2) lower prices due to the better exploitation of economies of scale. Opening to trade induces a rationalization effect: Some firms close when exposed to the increased competition in a larger global market, but the ones that remain produce at a larger scale. Increasing returns to scale mean that as a firm expands its output, its average costs are falling. The drop in average cost is passed on to consumers in the form of lower prices.

The model also allows us to better understand trade patterns between countries. Each variety is produced in one location but is demanded in all trading countries. Hence, there is one-way trade in each variety. Because each country produces distinct varieties, there is two-way or *intra-industry trade* within goods.

KEY TERMS

Use the space provided to record your notes on the following key terms.

Increasing returns to scale ________________________________

Economies of scale ________________________________

Monopolistic competition ________________________________

Intra-industry trade ________________________________

REVIEW QUESTIONS

Problem 4: A firm faces a fixed cost of $100 and a marginal cost of $2 per unit of output. If the firm is planning to sell 10 units, what is the lowest price that the firm can charge that will allow it to break even?

Problem 5: In the following diagram, D / N is industry demand divided by the number of differentiated goods when each good has the same price and d is the demand curve facing each individual producer of a differentiated good.

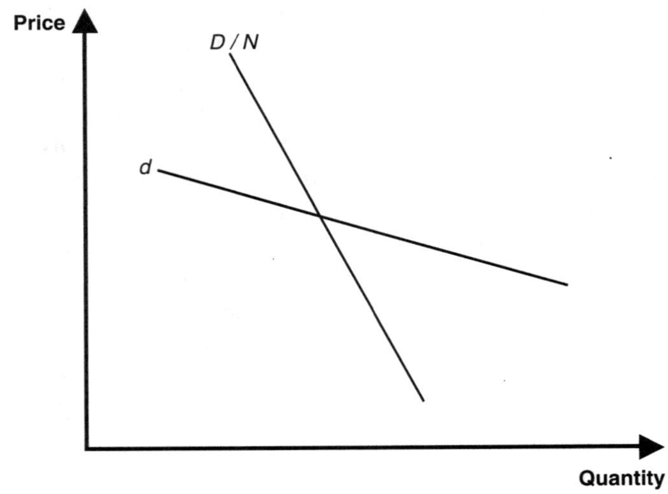

5a. Draw in the diagram the effect on d and D / N of an increase in N, the number of competing varieties.

5b. Explain why you drew the demand curves as you did. ________________________

____

____

TIPS Understanding the response of demand curves D / N and d is critical to understanding many of the key implications of the monopolistic competition model.

Problem 6: The marginal and average cost curves facing a firm are drawn in the following diagram.

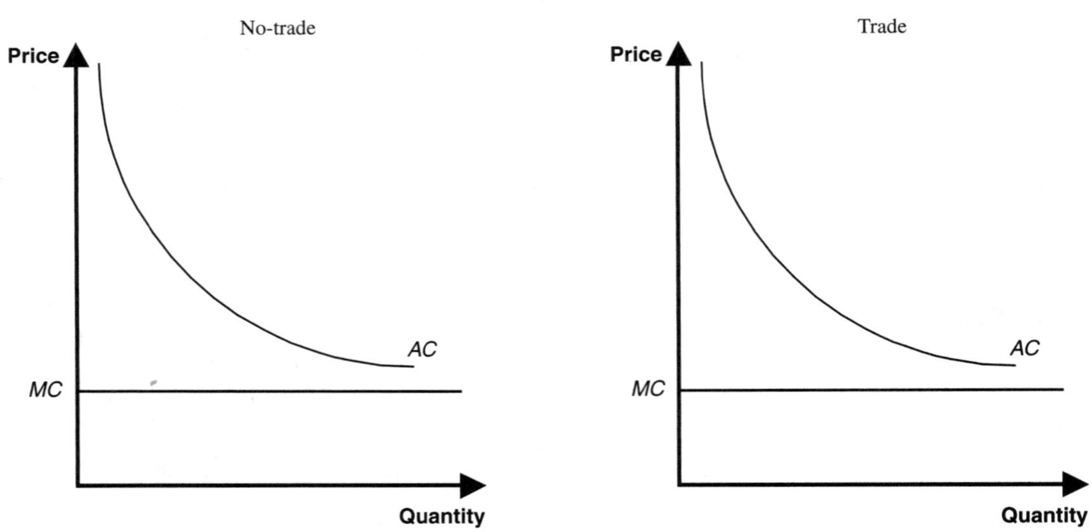

6a. In the left-hand panel, draw demand curves D / N and d, a marginal revenue curve, and the level of the optimal price and quantity for a firm in a long-run no-trade equilibrium.

6b. In the right-hand panel, draw demand curves D / N and d, a marginal revenue curve, and the level of the price and quantity for a firm in a long-run trading equilibrium for the case of two identical countries.

6c. Explain *how* the two panels are drawn differently. ______________________

____

____

6d. Explain *why* the two panels are different. ______________________________

____

____

6e. What are the gains from trade, and how can they appear in the difference in the way the two panels were drawn? ____

____

____

6f. What are the adjustment costs associated with international trade, and how do they appear in the way the two panels were drawn in the previous diagram? ______________

____

____

Problem 7: Consider a world with two countries. One of the countries is large and the other is small. There is one monopolistically competitive industry that uses labor as the only input.

7a. In autarky, in which country has the highest real wage? Explain. ______________

____

____

7b. Which country gains the most from international trade? Explain. ______________

____

____

Problem 8: Essentially only two producers in the world make wide-bodied aircraft. Would monopolistic competition be an appropriate model for this industry? Why or why not?

____

____

TIPS

The monopolistic competition model is popular among economists because it is neat and tidy. Because the number of firms is large, we abstract from messy "strategic behavior" across firms. When the number of firms is small, however, we can no longer avoid thinking about strategic behavior.

A key observation is that the gains from trade are essentially gains to market size. Large markets allow for more variety at lower prices. The gains from trade come from consolidating two small markets into one large global market.

3 Empirical Applications of Monopolistic Competition and Trade

ESSENTIAL CONCEPTS

This section shows that the monopolistic competition model is helpful in understanding key parts of international trading patterns. First, the model helps to explain the gains from trade between similar countries, such as the United States and Canada. Evidence produced from the North American Free Trade Agreement (NAFTA) suggests that there are high short-term adjustment costs that are balanced by growth in the productivity and the employment of the surviving firms. Second, the monopolistic competition model predicts that intra-industry trade should be highest in industries in which there is a high degree of product differentiation. The *index of intra-industry trade* measures the extent to which trade is two-way between countries. As predicted by the monopolistic competition model, the index is high for goods that exhibit a high degree of product differentiation. Third, the monopolistic competition model predicts that international trade patterns should be well predicted by a *gravity equation,* which is given by

$$TRADE = \frac{GDP_1 \cdot GDP_2}{DIST^{\eta}}.$$

The gravity equation predicts that the volume of trade between two countries (here countries 1 and 2) is increasing in the gross domestic product of either country and is decreasing in their distance from each other. This relationship comes from the fact that each country produces a distinct set of varieties that are demanded in each country. The share of a country's GDP (the value of the output of its varieties) that is sold to a given foreign country is increasing in the foreign country's income or GDP and decreasing in distance between the two countries because transport costs rise with distance. The gravity equation is an accurate predictor of the volume of trade between countries.

KEY TERMS

Use the space provided to record your notes on the following key terms.

Free-trade agreements __________

Regional trade agreements __________

Trade adjustment assistance __________

Index of intra-industry trade __________

Gravity equation __________

Border effects

Tariffs

Quotas

REVIEW QUESTIONS

Problem 9: Different soil conditions generate variation in the character of grapes and the wine that is made from them. Is it possible that intra-industry trade can be high in certain industries even in the absence of imperfect competition?

Problem 10: Consider a country that opens to trade with a neighboring country. The immediate effect of this opening is an increase in unemployment. Workers eventually find jobs, but most workers find themselves employed in a different industry. Is the main motive for trade between these two countries most likely to be monopolistic competition or comparative advantage? Explain.

Problem 11: Would you expect the gravity equation to explain trade patterns best between a set of countries that are similar in terms of their endowments or a set of countries that are different in their endowments? Explain.

Problem 12: How could you use data on international trade flows to assess which industries display a high degree of product differentiation and which ones do not?

TIPS

As indicated in the answer to problem 9, product differentiation alone can give rise to high levels of intra-industry trade.

Problems 10 to 12 demonstrate that there are many things at work in trading patterns between countries. Because different models have different implications, it is important to know which model is appropriate for which phenomenon.

Problem 13: Explain how the gravity equation can be used to measure the "border effect."

Problem 14: How has NAFTA affected the range of product variety available in the United States?

4 Imperfect Competition with Homogeneous Products: The Case of Dumping

ESSENTIAL CONCEPTS

This section shows that imperfect competition can explain the common phenomenon of *dumping.* Dumping occurs when a firm sells a product abroad at a price that is either less than the price it charges in its local market or less than its average cost of production. As we will learn later in the book, government policies toward dumping are the source of substantial friction between countries.

Two examples of dumping are considered. In the first example, a monopolist is choosing how much of its good to sell in its home market and in foreign markets. If it is difficult for consumers to arbitrage price differences across countries, then the firm can engage in *price discrimination* across countries. The firm chooses output so that the marginal revenue in each market is equal to the marginal cost of production. Firms will often find that selling its product at a lower price abroad than at home is a profit-maximizing strategy.

The second example involves two firms located in two different countries. The firms produce identical profits under the same conditions, and it is costly to transport the good between countries. Under these circumstances *reciprocal dumping* will arise: Each firm invades the other firm's domestic market, driving down the price in that market. Dumping arises in the model in the sense that the price charged in the foreign market is less than the price in the firm's home market plus the additional cost of transporting the good abroad. The two key points are (1) dumping is a natural phenomenon in many monopolistic and oligopolistic markets, and (2) intra-industry trade can result from imperfect competition even when there is no product differentiation.

KEY TERMS

Use the space provided to record your notes on the following key terms.

Price discrimination

Discriminating monopoly

Dumping ______________________________

____

____

Antidumping duty ______________________________

____

____

Oligopoly ______________________________

____

____

Reciprocal dumping ______________________________

____

____

REVIEW QUESTIONS

Problem 15: Suppose a monopolist located in Home has a constant marginal cost of $2 and can sell its good in two countries, Home and Foreign. Consumers are assumed to be unable to arbitrage any price difference across countries. Demand at Home is given by $P = 10 - Q$ and demand in Foreign is $P = 6 - Q$.

15a. What is the equation for the marginal revenue curve facing the monopolist in the Home and Foreign markets? ______________________________

____

15b. At what price is the firm selling its product in the two markets? ______________________________

____

15c. In the following diagrams, draw demand and marginal revenue curves in Home (its domestic market) and Foreign (its export market) so that the firm chooses to "dump" its product abroad.

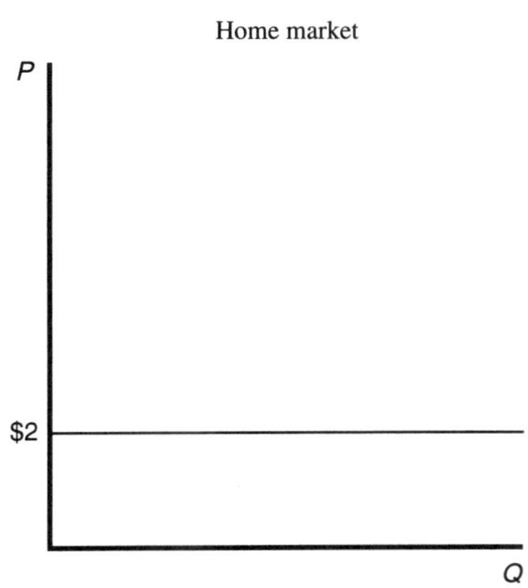

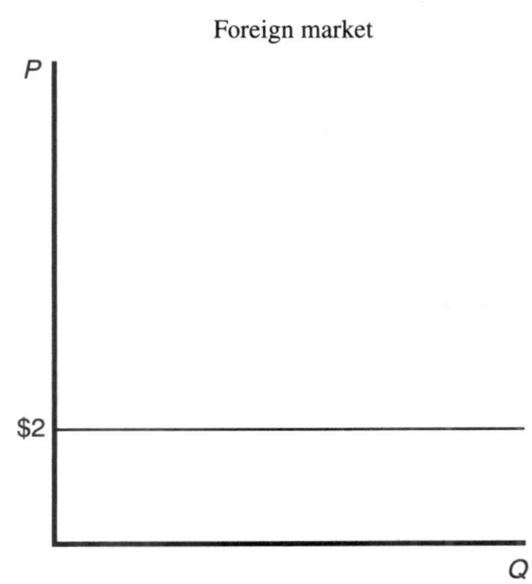

TIPS It is important to know how to derive the marginal revenue equation from a linear demand curve. If you get stuck at this step, then you cannot answer fully any subsequent question! For a linear demand curve, the marginal revenue curve always has the same Y intercept and a slope that is twice as large (in absolute value) as the demand curve.

Problem 16: Suppose that a firm charges \$10 for a good in its home market and \$10 in its export market. Could this firm be accused of dumping? Explain.

Problem 17: A firm located in country H produces the sleep medication Beddybuy. The firm faces a downward-sloping (linear) demand curve in its home market. In the neighboring country F, the government imposes prices controls so that there is a ceiling on the price that the firm can charge for Beddybuy.

17a. Use the following axes to show the case where the firm is willing to sell Beddybuy in country F and charges a higher price for Beddybuy in H.

17b. Suppose some sleep-deprived consumers in country H learn that they can get Beddybuy in country F for the lower price from Internet pharmacies. Is it possible that this would cause the firm to stop selling its product in F? Explain.

Problem 18: A politician argues against free trade area in a particular industry that produces a homogenous good. She argues that because there is no difference in the cost of production in the two countries in the free trade area there are no gains from trade. Assess this argument.

Problem 19: Suppose that there are two countries. There is one producer of wheat in each country. Each producer has a marginal cost of \$10. Demand in each country is given by $P = 95 - Q$, where P is the price and Q is the total amount sold in that country.

19a. Suppose the two countries are in autarky. Provide the equation for the marginal revenue curve facing each producer in its home market. ______

______

19b. What is the profit-maximizing price charged by firms in autarky? ______

______

19c. What is the economic profit earned by each firm? ______

______

Now suppose that the two firms can sell their product in each other's market but there are transport costs between countries so that each good costs $5 to ship.

19d. Provide an equation for the marginal revenue facing a firm in its home market and an equation for the marginal revenue facing a firm in its export market.

______

______

19e. Solve for the quantity sold by a firm in its home market and in the export market. ______

______

______

19f. In what sense, if any, are the firms engaged in dumping in the foreign market? ______

______

______

19g. What is the effect of the opening of international trade on firms' profits? ______

______

______

7

Foreign Outsourcing of Goods and Services

Overview

Outsourcing occurs when the production process for a *final good* is broken down into individual activities that are then relocated to different countries. As outsourcing becomes more pervasive, increasingly countries are specializing in parts of production processes, such as product development, *intermediate input* production, and assembly, rather than in final goods, such as computers and shirts. This phenomenon appears in trading patterns as an increase in the share of trade that is in intermediate inputs and business services and as a decrease in the share of trade accounted for by final goods.

The first goal of this chapter is to develop a model to analyze the role of outsourcing in the growing gap in the wages between skilled and unskilled workers. Firms in the model choose where to locate production activities given wage differences across countries. Changes in transport costs induce firms to outsource a larger set of production activities to low-wage countries. Because the additional activities that are being outsourced are low-skill intensive from the perspective of the high-wage country and high-skill intensive from the perspective of the low-wage country, outsourcing expands the relative demand for skilled labor in both countries.

The second goal of the chapter is to discuss the gains from trade associated with outsourcing. As in other models, outsourcing leads to a more efficient use of the world's resources and so makes it possible to produce more output with the same stock of factors. These gains from trade show up in the data as an increase in productivity. The model highlights the importance of a country's terms of trade across production activities in determining the size of the gains from trade.

The final goal of this chapter is to examine the newest form of outsourcing, the outsourcing of *business services* such as accounting, computer programming, and order processing. This form of outsourcing has led to growing consternation among professional workers in developed countries as jobs that had previously been insulated from international trade become vulnerable to outsourcing.

1 A Model of Outsourcing

ESSENTIAL CONCEPTS

The model of outsourcing is built upon the key concept of the *value chain*. The production process for making a final good involves many different activities (or steps) that can be done in different locations. Each activity requires some skilled and unskilled labor plus some additional factors (such as capital and infrastructure), but activities have different skill intensities. For instance, the production of a good may involve some high-technology parts that are very skilled-labor intensive and some low-technology parts that are very unskilled-labor intensive. The value chain is an ordering of these activities according to their relative skill intensity.

In the model, factor prices differ across countries. For instance, assume that Home has high wages for skilled and unskilled workers and low capital rentals relative to Foreign. Assume further that the relative wage for skilled workers is higher in Foreign than in Home. The difference in factor prices across countries and the difference in the skill intensity across activities (the ratio of skilled to unskilled workers used in the activity) mean that some activities will be cheaper to do in Home and other activities will be cheaper to do in Foreign.

An example is shown in Figure 7-1. The vertical axis in this diagram is the cost of an activity, and the horizontal axis is the value chain. Each activity in the value chain is a point on the horizontal axis. As we move right on the horizontal axis, the skill intensity of the activity is increasing so that assembly would be found near the bottom of the value chain and research and development (R&D) would be found near the top. In drawing the diagram, capital costs (and any transport costs) have been assumed to be uniform across activities.

FIGURE 7-1

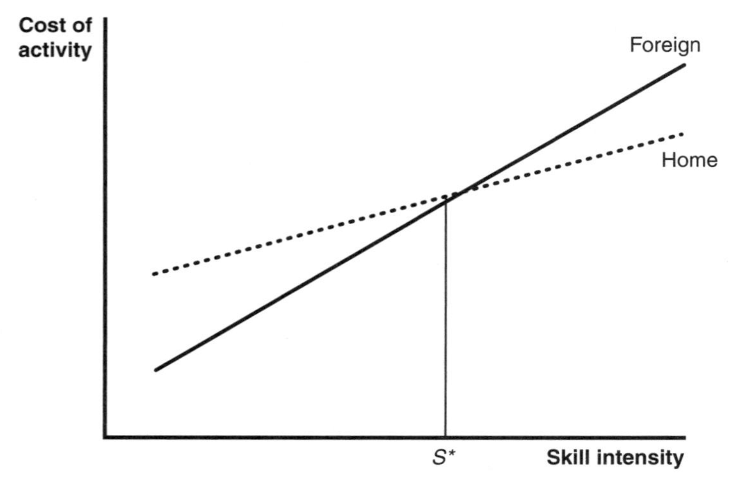

Slicing the Value Chain

The solid line shows Foreign's cost per activity, and the dotted line shows Home's cost per activity. Because the relative wage of skilled workers is higher in Foreign than in Home, Foreign's cost line is steeper than Home's cost line. Given the factor prices in each country, a Home firm would *slice the value chain* by producing all activities with a skill intensity less than S^* in Foreign and by producing all activities with a skill intensity greater than S^* in Home. In summary, the least skill-intensive activities are outsourced.

A reduction in transport or capital costs in Foreign induces additional outsourcing into Foreign. The downward shift in Foreign's cost line induces a rightward shift in S^* so that some activities that had previously been done in Home would be outsourced to the Foreign. The shift in S^* to the right raises the average skill intensity of activities done in both Home and Foreign. This implies that the relative demand for skilled labor and the relative wage of skilled labor rise in both countries.

The economic effects of an increase in outsourcing are very difficult to tell apart from the effects of *skill-biased technical change.* In both cases the relative demand for skilled labor rises in all countries, pushing up the relative wage of skilled workers. Recent empirical studies show that both outsourcing and technical change explain part of the growing wage gap between skilled and unskilled labor, but the exact contribution of each is hard to identify.

KEY TERMS

Use the space provided to record your notes on the following key terms.

Value chain ______________________________

____

____

Foreign outsourcing ______________________________

____

____

Offshoring ______________________________

____

____

Skill-biased technical change ______________________________

____

____

REVIEW QUESTIONS

Problem 1: A good is produced using three production activities (a, b, and c) that each use skilled and unskilled labor. The following table shows the number of skilled and unskilled workers needed to produce one unit in each production stage.

	a	b	c
Skilled labor	1	2	3
Unskilled labor	4	3	2

There are two countries: Home (H) and Foreign (F). The skilled worker wage is $4 in H and $5 in F. The unskilled worker wage is $2 in H and $1 in F. Transport costs of $2 per unit must be added to cost of a production stage if that production stage is outsourced to F.

1a. Given this information, which production activities are done in which country? ______

______

1b. If the transport cost falls to zero, what happens to the location of production of each stage (assume that the wages don't change)? ______

______

______

1c. How has the reduction in transport cost in Foreign affected the relative demand for skilled labor in each country? ______

______

______

1d. If instead of activities, we renamed a, b, and c final goods, would there be any difference in the effect of a reduction in transport costs on relative wages? ______

______

______

TIPS

Problem 1d asks the question, "How different is outsourcing from traditional trade in goods?" The model presented in the chapter is designed to determine the impact of outsourcing, but it could equally have been applied to determining specialization in final goods production when the costs of production differ across countries. The effect on relative demand for labor would be the same, but the way it might appear to individuals in society would be very different.

Note that the analysis ignores the changes in the wages caused by the shift in activities across countries. The changes in wages caused by outsourcing would tend to shift the costs of doing activities in each country.

Problem 2: Suppose a low-wage country banned inward foreign direct investment. In the outsourcing model, how would such restrictions affect the range of production activities performed in the country? ______

______

______

Problem 3: The Heckscher-Ohlin model is built on the concept that goods can be ranked in terms of their factor intensity. What complications arise when activities can be outsourced?

______

______

Problem 4: It is a well-documented fact that the ratio of white collar jobs to blue collar jobs has risen in U.S. manufacturing over the last two decades.

4a. How could outsourcing explain this fact? ______

______

______

4b. Why does the Heckscher-Ohlin model have difficulty explaining this fact? ______

______

______

4c. Can there be explanations for this fact that do not involve international trade? ______

______

______

2 The Gains from Outsourcing

ESSENTIAL CONCEPTS

As in the more standard models of international trade discussed in the earlier chapters of the book, the ability of firms to relocate some production activities abroad leads to gains from trade through a more efficient allocation of world's resources. To make this point, we reinterpret the Heckscher-Ohlin model, which was developed in Chapter 4, in order to analyze the gains from outsourcing.

This reinterpretation occurs in three steps. First, label the axes of the production possibilities frontier as inputs into the production of the final good rather than the final goods. Examples of such inputs are research and development and components. Second, replace indifference curves with *isoquants*. The inputs in the PPF are used to produce a final good rather than utility. Third, imagine that a country's resources are divided over a number of identical firms so that each firm has an equal share of the country's resources and a PPF. Given this reinterpretation, countries have comparative advantages at stages of production rather than in final goods. The gains from trade in inputs are very similar to the gains from trade in final goods, only they show up as increases in productivity: Firms can produce more final good output with the same amount of inputs.

Although there are gains from outsourcing, changes in global market conditions can cause changes in the terms of trade. If developing countries become more adept at activities in which the developed world has a comparative advantage, then the developed world can experience a terms-of-trade loss. Any terms-of-trade loss is bad for a country because it means that the country's budget constraint has shifted inward. This is the point made by Professor Samuelson. The possibility that changes in the terms of trade on global markets could reduce the welfare of developed country workers does not mean that outsourcing is bad for a country. It just means that developed countries may someday gain less from trade than they are currently.

KEY TERMS

Use the space provided to record your notes on the following key terms.

Isoquant ______

______

______

Business services ______

______

______

REVIEW QUESTIONS

Problem 5: The country of Home has many identical firms that produce a single final good using R&D and components. R&D and components are in turn produced using skilled and unskilled labor. R&D is relatively skill intensive compared with components production. The country is initially in autarky.

5a. Suppose that Home is now able to trade with Foreign, which is relatively skilled-labor scarce. Show, using the following diagram, the impact of trade on the output of a typical firm in Home.

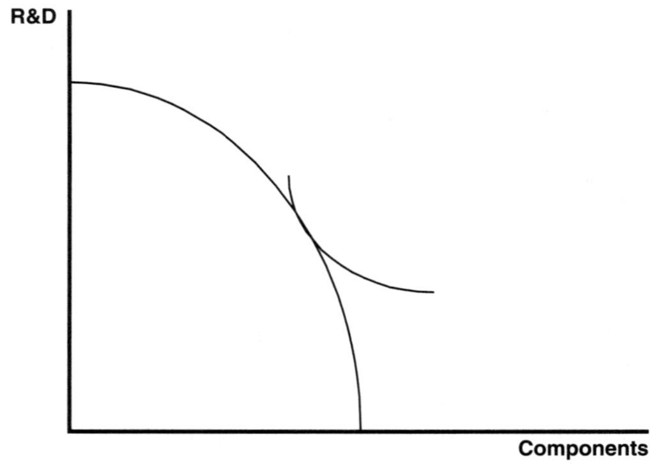

5b. Describe the pattern of trade between Home and Foreign. ______________________

____

____

5c. Describe the gains from trade for Home. ______________________

____

____

5d. What is the effect of trade on the relative demand for skilled labor in Home? ________

____

____

5e. Now suppose that Home's terms of trade improve. Show the effect of the terms of trade improvement in the following diagram.

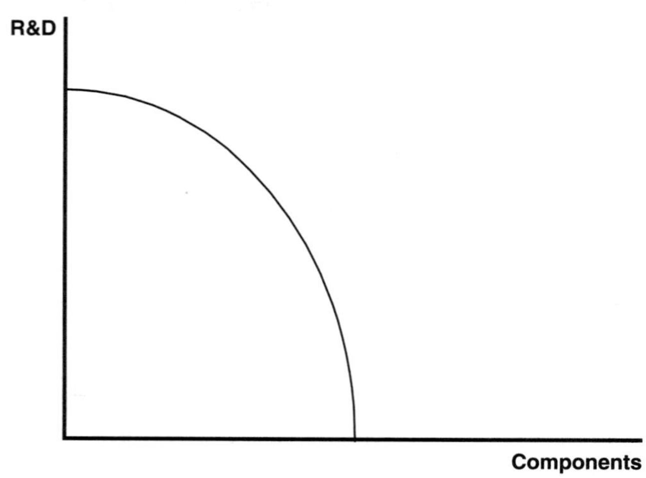

5f. What is the effect of a terms-of-trade improvement on the observed productivity of the typical firm in Home? Explain. ______

______

______

Problem 6: Output is produced from business services and components. Home has an absolute advantage in both business services and components and a comparative advantage in business services relative to Foreign.

6a. If Home could increase Foreign's productivity in components by giving some of its technology to Foreign, would this make Home better or worse off? Explain. ______

______

______

6b. If Home could increase Foreign's productivity in business services by giving some of its technology to Foreign, would this make Home better or worse off? Explain. ______

______

______

TIPS

A deterioration in a country's terms of trade has negative implications for that country whether they involve the prices of intermediate inputs or the prices of final goods. The same analysis could have been applied in any of the models of comparative advantage.

It should be clear that this simplified model of outsourcing is just a reinterpretation of the Heckscher-Ohlin model.

Problem 7: According to the study of Amiti and Wei cited in the textbook, what portion of U.S. productivity growth can be attributed to outsourcing? ______

______

______

3 Outsourcing in Services

ESSENTIAL CONCEPTS

Most workers in developed countries are employed in services industries. For years, these workers were not directly exposed to international trade because services were largely impossible to trade. Advances in information technology have meant, however, that many services workers have found that their jobs could be outsourced. As a result, there has been a general increase in the anxiety of service workers in developed countries regarding international trade.

In recent years skilled workers in developed countries have found that many skill-intensive activities are being outsourced to developing countries such as India. The value chain model introduced in this chapter can be used to think about this phenomenon with two slight adjustments. First, skilled workers in India are currently paid considerably less than their developed country counterparts (although skilled labor wages are rising rapidly in India). Second, the assumption is dropped that transport costs are uniform across activities. Instead, it is assumed that transport costs are very high in low-skill-intensive activities and very low in high-skill-intensive activities. This assumption is motivated by conditions in India, the largest destination for service outsourcing. In India, physical infrastructure such as roads is rudimentary, whereas information technology infrastructure is relatively advanced.

KEY TERMS

Use the space provided to record your notes on the following key term.

Business services ____

REVIEW QUESTIONS

Problem 8: The following diagram shows the cost per activity in Home and Foreign if transport costs were the same in both countries. By assumption the cost of activities in Foreign are lower for all activities (represented by the Foreign curve) than in Home (represented by the Home curve).

8a. Now suppose that there are transport costs in Foreign that are not uniform across activities: They are "high" for a set of the most unskilled labor activities and "low" for a set of the most skilled labor activities. Draw in the Foreign cost, inclusive of transport costs, so that the most highly skilled activities are outsourced from Home to Foreign.

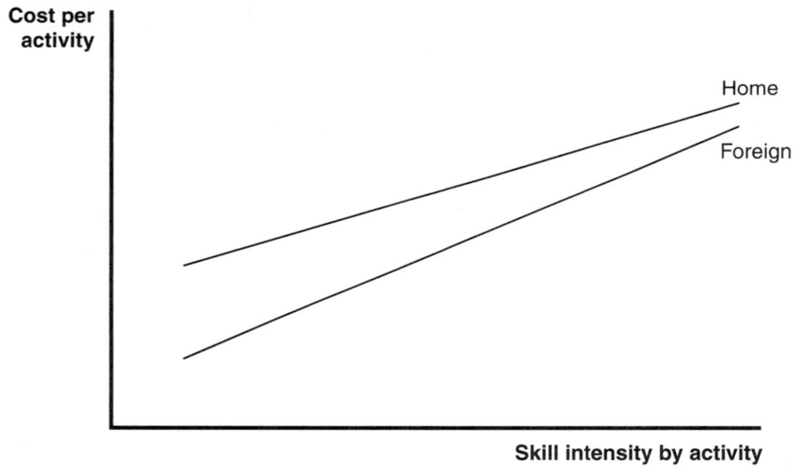

8b. Is it possible to construct an example in which both very high and very low skill-intensive activities are outsourced while the moderately skill-intensive activities are not? __________

Problem 9: Why might India's growing success in business services be potentially "bad news" for the United States? ______________________________

Problem 10: Until recently, many services could not be traded internationally. Could the increased tradability of services result in a further decline in manufacturing employment in the United States? ______________________________

____

____

TIPS

As problem 8 demonstrates, it is possible to generate all kinds of different outcomes with respect to outsourcing if one is free to choose any pattern of transportation costs one wants.

"Bad news" in trade models generally comes from a deterioration in a country's terms of trade.

8

Import Tariffs and Quotas under Perfect Competition

Overview

As trade creates gains between countries and winners and losers within countries, a country's *trade policy* affects the welfare of other nations and redistributes income within its borders. Because one country's policies can negatively affect other countries, the *World Trade Organization* acts as a forum for countries to come to a collective agreement on trade policies and resolves disputes between countries when they arise. The structure and history of the WTO affect all relevant aspects of trade policy.

The chapter introduces a perfectly competitive, partial equilibrium model to analyze the welfare impact of two types of trade policies: the import *tariff* and the import *quota*. The tariff, which is a tax on imports, is the most common way that countries reduce the volume of their imports. The analysis suggests that import tariffs lower the welfare of *small* importing countries but can actually improve the welfare of *large* importing countries. Large countries' gain is at the expense of their trading partners, however, explaining some of the conflicts that arise between countries. The import quota is a direct restriction on the number of imports allowed into a country. In the perfectly competitive model, the welfare effects associated with import *quotas* are much like those of the import tariff. Like tariffs, quotas raise domestic prices above world price and so aid producers and harm consumers. Governments typically enforce quotas in a way that ensures that they lower national welfare.

1 A Brief History of the World Trade Organization

ESSENTIAL CONCEPTS

Prior to World War II the world was in a major economic slump commonly referred to as the Great Depression. During this period, countries used trade policies to aid domestic producers, but the collective effect of a simultaneous rise in tariffs across all major countries was to reduce the volume of trade for all countries. The loss of the gains from trade is generally thought to have contributed to the seriousness of the Depression.

In 1947, the General Agreement on Tariffs and Trade (GATT) was established, with the goal of reducing trade barriers. In addition to providing a forum for negotiating the reduction of trade barriers, the GATT contained 24 articles that regulated countries' use of trade policies. Under the GATT, countries met periodically for negotiations, called *rounds,* with the purpose of lowering trade barriers and introducing rules for the conduct of trade policy.

In 1994 the GATT was replaced by the World Trade Organization. The articles of the GATT were written into the WTO agreement. Unlike the GATT, the WTO is a formal institution that has a mechanism, or procedure, for settling disputes that arise when countries are accused of violating the rules. This subsection introduces some of the key rules of the WTO and the GATT before it.

KEY TERMS

Use the space provided to record your notes on the following key terms.

Trade policy ______________________________

Import tariff ______________________________

Dumping ______________________________

Import quota ______________________________

Export subsidies ______________________________

Regional trade agreements ______________________________

Free-trade areas ______________________________

Customs unions ______________________________

Safeguard provision ____

____

____

Escape clause ____

____

____

REVIEW QUESTIONS

Problem 1: The following questions test your knowledge of the WTO's rules.

1a. How would you know if a foreign firm was dumping its product in your domestic market? ____

____

____

1b. Suppose that several countries decided to reduce tariffs exclusively on each others' products but maintain their tariffs on other countries' products. Would this agreement violate the WTO's "most favored nation" principle? Why or why not? ______________________

____

____

1c. Why is "most favored nation status" called "normal trade relations" in the United States?

____

____

TIPS

Memorize the appropriate article in GATT for each of the relevant key terms.

Be patient. Each of the articles highlighted in this section will be featured at some point in the next several chapters.

2 The Gains from Trade

ESSENTIAL CONCEPTS

A simple partial equilibrium framework is introduced to analyze the effect of Home's trade policy on its welfare. There are two types of actors in Home, consumers and producers. In Figure 8-1, Home's consumers are represented by a demand curve (*D*) and Home's producers are represented by a supply curve (*S*). When Home is in autarky, the price (P^A) and quantity (Q_0) in this market is determined by the intersection of supply and demand. Now suppose that the country could trade with the outside world at fixed world prices. If the price on the world market is below the price in Home in autarky, then Home's consumers will expand their demand and its producers will contract their supply. When Home's demand exceeds its domestic supply, the country must import the difference. Home's import demand curve is shown on the right-hand panel of Figure 8-1. Given a world price P^W, a country imports M_1, which is equal to $D_1 - S_1$.

FIGURE 8-1

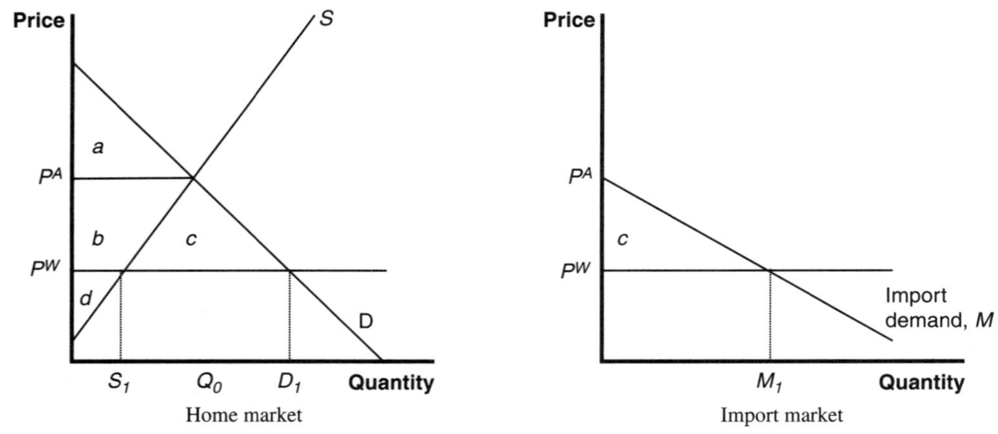

International Trade in Partial Equilibrium

To measure welfare in this framework, we rely on the concepts of *consumer surplus* and *producer surplus.* The surplus that accrues to a consumer who buys D_1 units of a good when the price is P^W is equal to the area under the demand curve up to D_1 (the total utility of consuming that much of the good), less the amount that the consumer had to pay, or price P^W multiplied by D_1 (the foregone utility of consuming other goods). In Figure 8-1, given a price of P^W, the consumer surplus is equal to the sum of the areas *a, b,* and *c.* Because international trade lowers the price of the import good, trade improves the well-being of consumers by the area $b + c$, as shown in the left-hand panel of Figure 8-1.

The producer surplus associated with selling S_1 units at a price P^W is the revenue earned ($P^W \cdot S_1$) less the total payments to variable factors (the area under the supply curve up to S_1). In Figure 8-1, the producer surplus given a price of P^W is the area *d.* International trade lowers the price in an import industry relative to autarky and so harms producers whose revenues fall by more than their variable costs. In Figure 8-1, the loss imposed on producers by international trade is the area *b.*

International trade creates winners and losers in this model, but the gains to the winners exceed the losses to losers. In Figure 8-1, the gains from trade are measured by the area *c.* Notice that this welfare effect is measured by the area of a triangle. The area of a triangle is easy to calculate: It is one half of the product of the base and height of the triangle. Finally, notice that the gains from trade can also be measured by triangles in either diagram.

KEY TERMS

Use the space provided to record your notes on the following key terms.

Consumer surplus ____

____

____

Producer surplus ____

____

____

Import demand curve ____

____

____

Small country ____

____

____

REVIEW QUESTIONS

Problem 2: Anne is willing to buy one tomato if the price of tomatoes is \$3 and two tomatoes if the price of tomatoes is \$2. If the price of tomatoes is \$2, what is Anne's consumer surplus?

____

____

Problem 3: Suppose tomatoes are grown using land (a specific factor) and labor (a mobile factor). If the revenue of tomato growers is \$100 and the wage bill (amount paid to the mobile factor) is \$60, what is the producer surplus in the tomato industry? ______________

____

Problem 4: Figure 8-2 shows the trading equilibrium for a small country with import demand M facing a fixed world price for a good.

FIGURE 8-2

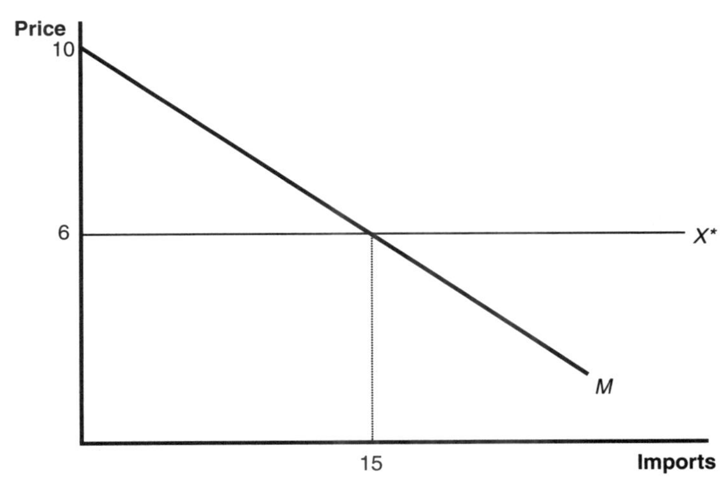

The Import Market

4a. What is the autarky price in this small country? ______________________

4b. What are the national welfare gains from trade for this economy compared with national welfare in autarky? ______________________

____

____

4c. The following Home Market diagram shows Home's domestic supply and demand for the good. Fill in the information from Figure 8-2 (prices and imports) and your answer to problem 4b (gains from trade) in this diagram.

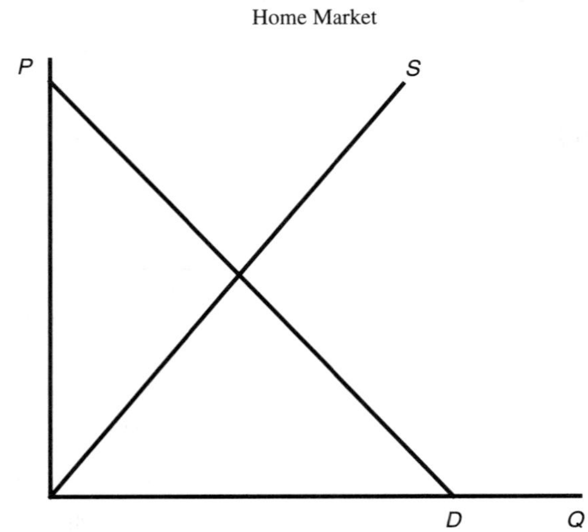

TIPS

When a country goes from autarky to free trade, the price on the world market becomes the price in the importing country. Home's producers would not be able to sell any goods for a price higher than the world level.

The diagrams used in the book have linear supply and demand curves. This means that the measurement of deadweight losses always involves calculating the area of triangles. The area of a triangle is one half of the product of the triangle's base and its height.

3 Import Tariffs for a Small Country

ESSENTIAL CONCEPTS

A *small country* faces a horizontal export supply curve. It cannot affect the world price of its imports by changing its behavior. When Home puts a tariff of size t into place, the price facing home consumers and producers is equal to the fixed world price P^W plus the tariff t. As shown in Figure 8-3, consumers reduce their demand and producers increase their supply and imports fall.

The increase in the price in the home market lowers consumer surplus by the area $a + b + c + d$. At the same time, the increase in price in Home increases its producer surplus by the area a. Because the country is an importer, the loss of consumer surplus is always greater than the gain in producer surplus. The tariff also raises revenue for the government, however, and this revenue has value equal to $t\ M_1$, where t is the tariff rate and

FIGURE 8-3

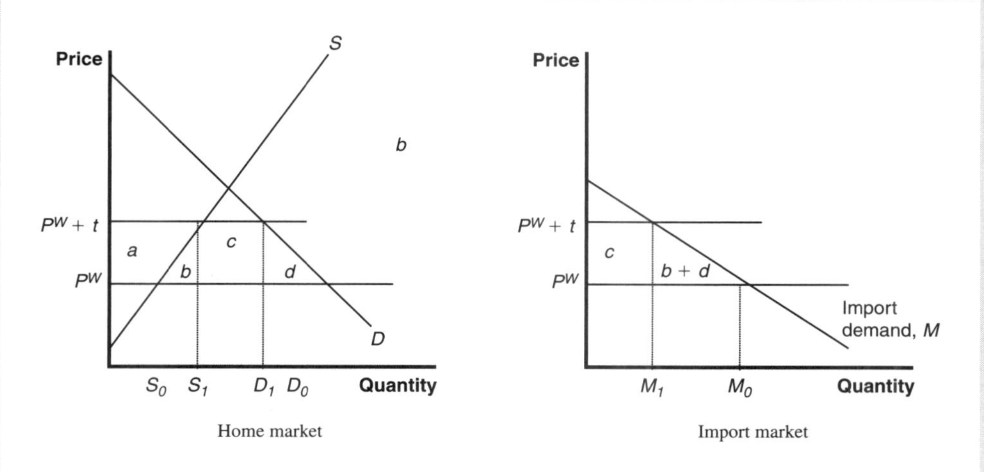

Effect of a Tariff, Small Country

M_1 is the amount of the good imported. In Figure 8-3 (both panels) this is the area *c*. On net, a tariff imposed by a small country must reduce the welfare of that country by the area $b + d$. These welfare losses are called the *deadweight loss* of the tariff and are equal to the sum of the *production loss* (area *b*) and *consumption loss* (area *d*). The deadweight loss appears in both the Home Market and Import Market diagrams and can be easily calculated using the formula for the area of a triangle.

KEY TERMS

Use the space provided to record your notes on the following key terms.

Deadweight loss ______________________________

____

____

Production loss ______________________________

____

____

Consumption loss ______________________________

____

____

Dispute settlement system ______________________________

____

____

Tariff war ______________________________

____

____

REVIEW QUESTIONS

Problem 5: Consider the information in Figure 8-2. Now suppose that this country puts in a tariff of $2 per unit imported. Suppose that the country's imports fall from 15 units to 7.5 units.

5a. What is the effect of the tariff on the domestic price? ______________________

5b. What is the value of tariff revenue raised by this tariff? ______________________

5c. What is the effect of the tariff on national welfare (provide a number)? ______________

____

Now suppose that the tariff causes the revenue of domestic firms to rise by $9 and the payments to variable factors of production to rise by $4.

5d. What is the effect of the tariff on producer surplus? ______________________

5e. Given your answers to questions 5b through 5d, what is the effect of the tariff on consumer surplus? ____

____

5f. Fill in as much of the information as possible in the following domestic supply and demand diagram.

Home Market

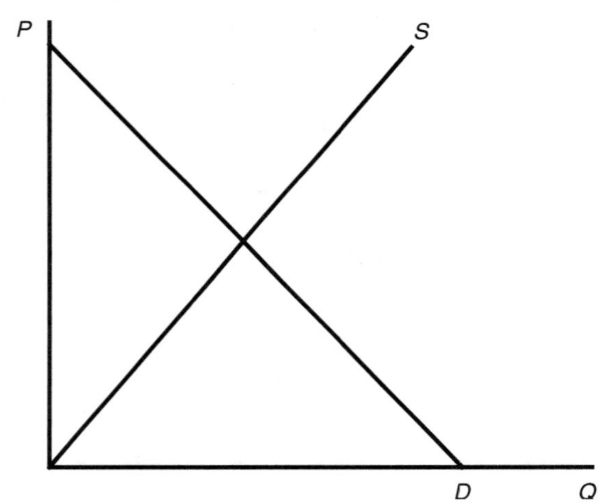

TIPS You should be comfortable understanding the relationships between the information in the Home Market diagram and the Import Market diagram.

Problem 6: Home has a tariff of $2 on the import of a pair of shoes. Home is small, and the price of shoes on the world market is $15. Home had been producing 100 pairs of shoes and consuming 300 pairs of shoes. Now suppose that Home gets rid of its tariff entirely. As a result, consumption of shoes rises by 25 pairs and production of shoes falls by 25 pairs. Assume that Home's supply and demand curves are linear.

6a. What is the impact of the tariff removal on producer surplus? (Provide a number.)

____

6b. What is the impact of the tariff removal on consumer surplus? (Provide a number.)

____

6c. What is the impact of the tariff removal on government revenue? (Provide a number.)

____

6d. Is the country better or worse off after the tariff is removed and by how much? ______

____

6e. Use the following diagram to illustrate the information provided in the questions and answers to the other parts of the problem.

Home Market

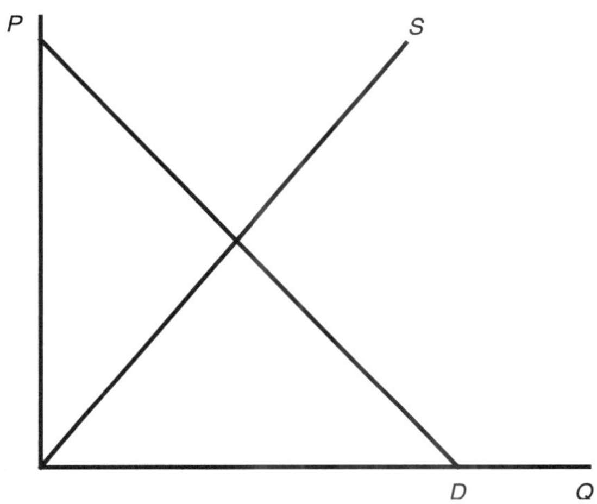

4 Import Tariff for a Large Country

ESSENTIAL CONCEPTS

If Home is a *large country,* it can alter world prices by changing its demand on the world market. To model a large country, we assume that the country faces an export supply curve that has a positive slope, as shown in the right-hand panel of Figure 8-4. By imposing a tariff, the government raises the price in Home, inducing producers to supply more and consumers to demand less so that imports contract for any given world price. This reduction in demand pushes down the world price in Import Market, shown in Figure 8-4 as the decrease in the world price P_0^W to P_1^W. Meanwhile, the domestic price rises from P_0^W to $P_1^W + t$.

The reduction in the world price is called the *terms-of-trade gain* for Home, and it represents an increase in Home's welfare. The gain occurs because Home has pushed some of the incidence of the tariff onto foreign producers. Total tariff revenue accruing to the government is shown in both panels of Figure 8-4 as the area $c + e$, of which the area e is paid by foreign producers. The remainder of the welfare analysis for Home is similar to the case of the small country. Because the price rises in Home (P_0^W to $P_1^W + t$), consumer surplus falls by the area $a + b + c + d$ and producer surplus rises by the area a. The total impact of the tariff on national welfare is then $e - (b + d)$. The key result is that if the government chooses its tariff carefully, then the terms-of-trade gain exceeds the dead-

FIGURE 8-4

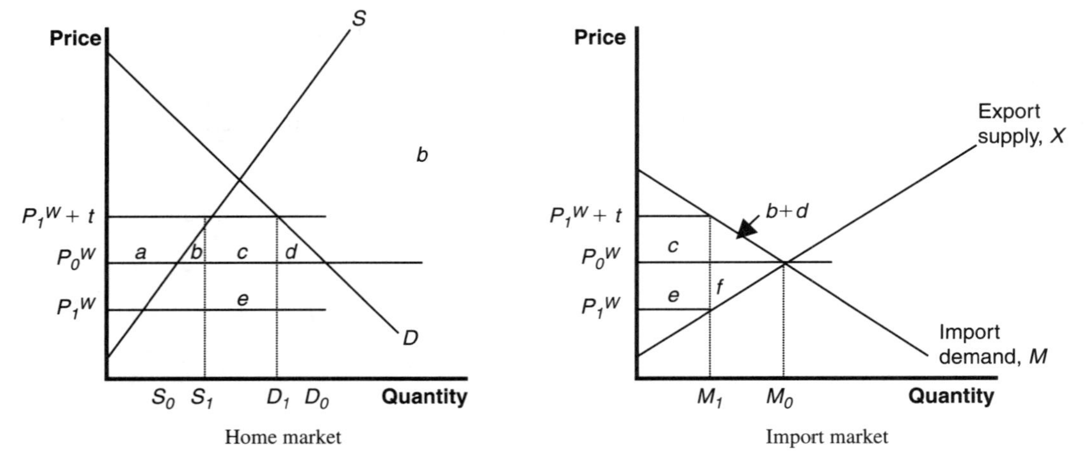

Effect of a Tariff, Large Country

weight loss and Home is better off with a tariff than it is with free trade. The tariff rate that maximizes the welfare gain for Home is called the *optimal tariff.*

Home's welfare gain comes at the expense of its trading partner, where producer surplus falls by more than consumer surplus rises in response to the lower world price. Total losses to the exporting country are shown as the area $e + f$ in the Import Market in Figure 8-4. By imposing a tariff, Home might precipitate a *trade war* by inducing its trading partner to impose *retaliatory* tariffs on Home products as punishment. Finally, because free trade maximizes global efficiency, a tariff necessarily leads to welfare losses through production and consumption losses, which are equal to $-(b + d + f)$.

KEY TERMS

Use the space provided to record your notes on the following key terms.

Large country

Terms of trade

Terms-of-trade gain

Optimal tariff

REVIEW QUESTIONS

Problem 7: Suppose Home is importing 100 units of a good at a world price of $10/unit. Home then puts in a tariff of $2 per unit. As a result of the tariff, the price paid in Home rises to $11 per unit and imports fall to 50 units.

7a. What impact has the tariff had on the world price? ____________________

____

7b. What tariff revenue is raised by this tariff? ____________________

7c. Assuming that the country's import demand curve is linear, what is the deadweight loss in Home caused by this tariff? ____________________

7d. By how much did this tariff raise or lower Home's welfare?

____

7e. By how much did this tariff raise of lower Foreign welfare?

____

7f. What is the effect of the tariff on world welfare? ____________________

7g. Use the following domestic supply and demand diagram for the exporting country to illustrate the welfare impact of Home's tariff on consumer surplus, producer surplus, and national welfare. Where possible, provide numbers.

The exporter's domestic market

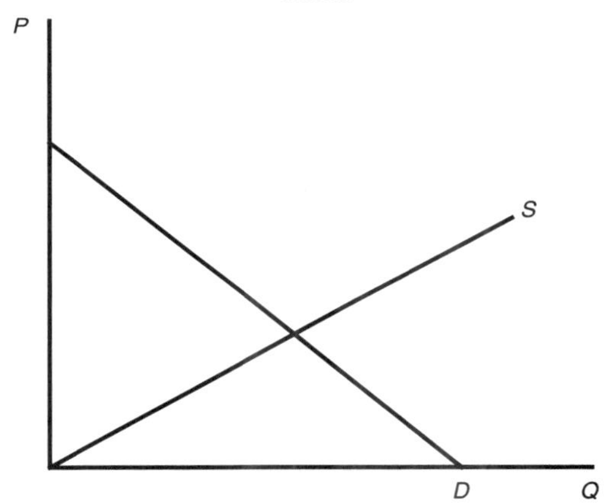

When Home imposes a tariff, its consumers and producers react to a price that exceeds the world price by the size of the tariff. When the tariff is imposed, the price in Home increases by *t*, causing consumers to demand less and producers to supply more. The demand for imports then falls, pushing down the price on the world market. The new equilibrium occurs when at the new world price plus the tariff, Home consumers and producers want to import the same quantity that Foreign producers and consumers want to sell at the new world price.

TIPS

Problem 8: The optimal tariff formula states that the tariff that raises national welfare the most is inversely related to the elasticity of the export supply curve. Provide an intuitive explanation for why this is so. ____________________

____

____

TIPS A tariff is just a tax on imports. As we know from introductory economics, the incidence of a tax falls on both suppliers and consumers. If we think of the importing country as the consumer and the exporting country as the supplier, then it makes sense that the steeper the supply curve, the more the effect of a tax is borne by the exporting country.

5 Import Quotas

ESSENTIAL CONCEPTS

A quota is a limit on the number of imports allowed into a country. If Home imposes a quota, its government requires anyone importing the good to have a *quota license.* In the presence of a quota, the price in Home rises above the world price in order to make Home's excess demand (equal to domestic demand minus domestic supply) equal the amount of the quota. As in the case of the tariff, a higher domestic price reduces consumer surplus by more than it increases producer surplus. The fact that the price in Home exceeds the world price means that quota licenses have value as they give their owner the right to buy low at the world price and sell high at the domestic price. The total value of quota licenses is called the *quota rent.*

Who gets the quota rents? There are several possibilities. First, if the government auctions the quota licenses in a perfectly competitive market, then the quota rents accrue to the government. In this case, the welfare effect of a quota is *equivalent* to a tariff that restricts imports by the same amount. The diagrams for a quota would be drawn in exactly the same way that they would be for a tariff. Second, the quota rents could be given away. One potential problem with giving the quota licenses away is that people engage in *rent-seeking* behavior: They use real resources to lobby the government in order to obtain quota licenses. In fact, quota rents are often given to the governments of the exporting countries to distribute as they please. When quota rents are given to foreigners, the effect of the quota on national welfare is unambiguously negative in both the small- and large-country cases.

KEY TERMS

Use the space provided to record your notes on the following key terms.

Quota licenses ______________________________

____

____

Quota rents ______________________________

____

____

Equivalent import tariff ______________________________

____

____

Rent seeking ______

Voluntary export restraint (VER) ______

Voluntary restraint agreement (VRA) ______

Multifiber arrangement (MFA) ______

REVIEW QUESTIONS

Problem 9: Consider two scenarios for a small country. In one case, the government imposes a tariff on the import of a good. In the second case, the government imposes a quota that restricts imports by the same amount as the tariff and distributes the quota licenses by selling them on a perfectly competitive market.

9a. Compare and contrast the welfare effects of these two policies given the fixed world price. ______

9b. Now suppose that the protected good's price falls on world markets after the tariff and quota are in place. If you were a producer in the protected market, would you rather be protected by the tariff or by the quota? Explain. ______

Problem 10: Consider a large country that is importing 100 units of a good at $10 a piece. The government of the importing country puts in a quota of 50 units, which is enforced by having the government of the exporting country distribute these licenses. As a result of this quota the Home price rises to $13 and the price on the world market drops to $8.

10a. What is the value of the quota rent? ______

10b. What is the effect on the export country's total welfare (provide a number)? ______

10c. What is the effect on the import country's total welfare (provide a number)? ______

10d. Illustrate the welfare effects on the importer and exporter countries in the following export-import diagram.

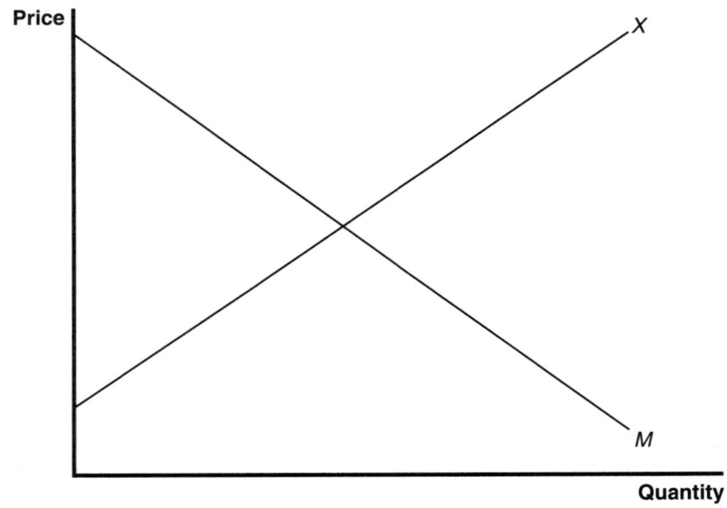

10e. If instead the importing country allowed the exporting country to sell the import licenses, what would be the welfare effect of the quota on the two countries? ______

______

______

______

Problem 11: Why would a country give the quota rents to the exporting country? ______

______

______

TIPS The effect of a quota on national welfare depends on how the quota rents are distributed. Read problems on quotas carefully.

9

Import Tariffs and Quotas under Imperfect Competition

Overview

Perfect competition is a useful abstraction that economists use as a starting point in their analyses. No market is perfectly competitive, however, so it is important to consider the affects of trade policies when markets are imperfectly competitive. This chapter considers two broad types of imperfect competition. The first type occurs when firms, either domestic or foreign, have *market power.* Firms with market power have some control over the prices that they receive for their output. The second type occurs when there are *market failures,* such as *imperfect capital markets* or the existence of *externalities.* Market failures often justify government intervention.

Trade policy can have very different welfare effects when firms have market power. One benefit of international trade is that imports limit the ability of domestic firms to exploit their market power. These pro-competitive effects of international trade remain even when the government implements a tariff, but they are largely eliminated when the government implements an import quota. The differential effect of the two policies arises because a tariff continues to allow imports to respond to price changes in the home market, whereas a quota does not.

When a country is served by a single foreign monopolist, a country's tariff policy interacts with the price-setting behavior of the foreign firm. Home is always large in the sense that its tariff policy alters the price received by the foreign firm, but terms-of-trade gains only arise when the demand curve has a particular shape. Finally, the nature of a government's tariff policy also matters in the welfare implications. An *antidumping* policy threatens foreign firms with tariffs if they set a price in the home market that is below some measure of "fair value." When foreign firms raise their price in the home market to avoid these tariffs, the home market's consumer surplus falls and no tariff revenue is collected.

Market failures that are distinct from the existence of the market power of firms also have important implications for trade policy. When capital markets are imperfect and it takes time for firms to learn how to produce efficiently, potentially prosperous industries may never come into being because firms have no way to cover short-term losses. When there are positive externalities across firms, such as *knowledge spillovers,* industries may only be viable if they reach a certain size. Market failures of these sorts justify *infant industry protection:* Temporary trade barriers give new industries time to become internationally competitive.

1 Tariffs and Quotas with Home Monopoly

ESSENTIAL CONCEPTS

To analyze the effect of trade policies when the Home industry is imperfectly competitive, we adjust the partial equilibrium model by assuming that Home has only one firm with an upward-sloping marginal cost curve. In autarky, the Home firm is a monopolist and so faces a downward-sloping marginal revenue curve. The firm maximizes its profits by choosing the quantity that sets marginal revenue equal to marginal cost. As a result, the price facing Home consumers is greater than the firm's marginal cost. We assume that Home is small in the sense that there is a fixed world price for the good. With free trade, the Home price becomes the fixed world price and so the monopolist becomes a price taker. Because the Home firm has no incentive to restrict output, competition from imports can lead to an increase in the amount that the Home firm is willing to sell!

Tariffs and import quotas have different effects on welfare because they affect the market power of the Home firm differently. With a tariff, the Home firm would lose all its sales if it raised its price above the world price plus the tariff. Hence, the Home firm continues to be a price taker. As long as the Home firm is a price taker, the welfare effect of a tariff is the same as in the case of many Home firms. With a quota, imports cannot respond to price increases by the Home firm. The quota reduces the demand facing the domestic firm, but the firm still faces a downward-sloping demand curve for its output and so has an incentive to restrict output to raise the price. Hence, the quota leads to a higher price and less consumption than does a tariff.

KEY TERMS

Use the space provided to record your notes on the following key terms.

Market power ____

Marginal revenue ____

REVIEW QUESTIONS

Problem 1: Consider an industry in which Home (a small country) has a single firm with an upward sloping marginal cost curve. The price on world markets is P^W.

1a. In the following diagram, show the quantity sold and price charged by the monopolist if international trade is not allowed.

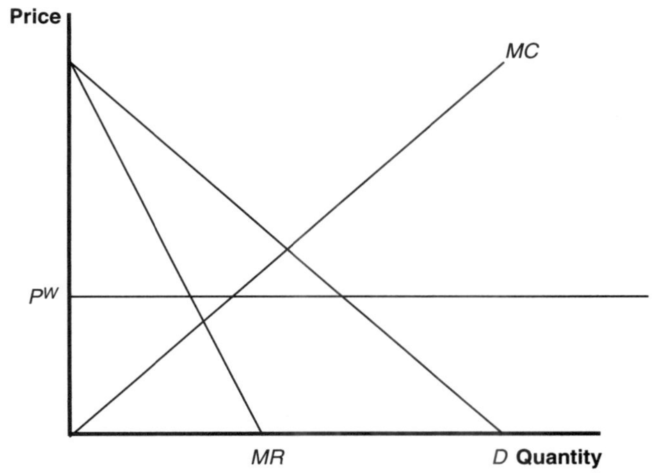

1b. What price is charged by Home's single firm if international trade is allowed? ________

1c. How does international trade affect the quantity sold by Home's single firm? Illustrate your answer in the previous diagram. ________

1d. How does going from autarky to free trade affect the welfare of the monopolist? ________

1e. How does going from free trade to autarky affect consumers' welfare? ________

1f. How does going from autarky to free trade affect national welfare? ________

1g. Suppose the world price were very low (below the intersection of *MR* and *MC*). In this case, how would the monopolist's output react to being exposed to free trade? ________

TIPS

Although producer surplus and profit are different concepts, the producer surplus here continues to be the excess of revenue (price times quantity sold) over the payments to variable factors of production (the area under the marginal cost curve). The difference here is that we are no longer measuring producer surplus with a triangle but with a trapezoid.

Problem 2: Could free trade increase consumer surplus relative to autarky even if it did not lead to any imports? Explain. ________

Problem 3: Consider an industry in which Home (a small country) has a single firm with an upward sloping marginal cost curve. The price on world markets is P^W. The country is originally engaged in free trade and it imposes a (nonprohibitive) tariff of size *t*.

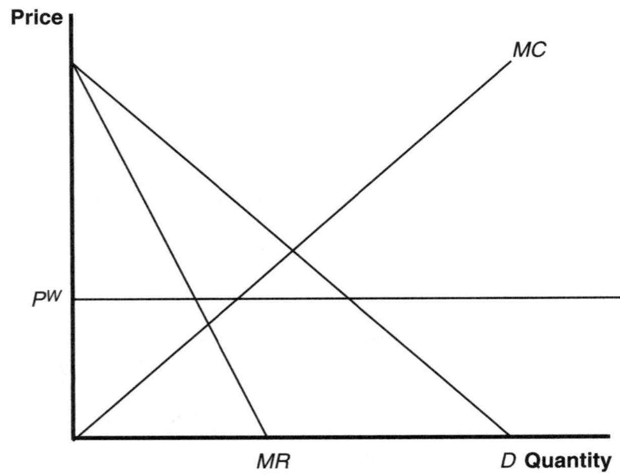

3a. Use the previous diagram to show the effects of this tariff on producer surplus, consumer surplus, and government revenue.

Now suppose instead that the government imposed a quota that yielded the same level of imports as the tariff *t*.

3b. Which policy (the quota or the tariff) has a larger effect on consumer surplus? Explain.

____

____

3c. Would the quota rent created by this quota be bigger than, smaller than, or exactly the same as the revenue generated by the tariff? Explain. ____________________

____

TIPS

With a tariff the Home firm continues to be a price taker, whereas with a quota the firm has market power. The difference is that with a quota imports cannot respond to a higher price charged by the Home firm.

2 Infant Industry Protection

ESSENTIAL CONCEPTS

This section addresses different kinds of *market failure* that are sometime used to justify policies that restrict imports. A key assumption of the model considered in this section is that there is some form of increasing returns to scale over time. Domestic firms have high costs in the short run, but they could have low costs in the long run if they expand their output. Market failures can keep these kinds of increasing returns from being exploited. Two types of market failures, (1) imperfect lending markets and (2) positive *externalities,* are considered. To analyze the effect of imperfect capital markets, we suppose that there is a single firm that has high costs because it has little experience. This firm would make negative profits in the short run because of its high costs, but over time its costs would fall if it were to gain sufficient experience. The firm might be viable in the long run but still fail if it cannot get loans to cover its losses in the short run. A tariff would reduce the firm's losses in the short run (at the expense of lower consumer surplus) but would no longer be needed in the long run once the firm's costs fell to internationally competitive levels. To understand the role of externalities, consider the example of *knowledge spillovers.* Suppose that (1) firms learn from experience so that the knowledge created by one firm is increasing in its output; (2) knowledge from one firm is learned by another (i.e., it spills over); and (3) knowledge lowers a firm's costs. In this setting, firms do not produce enough knowledge and so industry-wide costs are high.

A tariff that expands industry output lowers industry cost, and so firms in the industry can then become competitive on world markets. A tariff that is intended to give firms "time to grow" is called *infant industry protection.* Under the right circumstances, the tariff will help the industry lower its costs so that it will no longer need to be supported by tariffs in the future. A government contemplating this type of policy needs to weigh the short-run cost to consumer surplus induced by a tariff against the long-run benefit of increased producer surplus. This type of argument can also be used to justify protecting existing firms that have fallen behind their international competitors. If a firm has good prospects but is currently struggling and cannot obtain loans from banks, then the government can protect the industry temporarily. An example of such an experience is discussed in the Harley-Davidson case study in the textbook.

KEY TERMS

Use the space provided to record your notes on the following key terms.

Infant industry ______________________________

____

____

Externality ______________________________

____

____

Market failure ______________________________

____

____

Knowledge spillover ______________________________

____

____

Problem 4: Suppose you are a government official in charge of tariff policy. A businessperson approaches your office and argues that she could establish a world-class cucumber operation if only a tariff were applied to cucumber imports for next 5 years.

4a. What costs would the proposed policy have on the country? ______________________________

____

4b. If the world price of cucumbers were P, what would have to be true about the cost of production in cucumbers now and in 5 years to make this a reasonable policy? ______________

____

____

4c. If capital markets in the country were perfect, would that change your opinion about the validity of this proposal? ______

4d. What other policies could you suggest that would also serve to support an infant industry?

______

Problem 5: A foreign multinational opens an affiliate in Home. The multinational is the only firm in the industry, and it lobbies the government for infant industry protection.

5a. If the multinational's argument for protection were that capital markets were imperfect, would it be in Home's best interest to follow a policy of infant industry protection in this industry? Explain. ______

5b. If the argument were that there are knowledge spillovers in this industry, would it be in Home's best interest to follow a policy of infant industry protection? Explain. ______

Problem 6: What kind of market failure would justify the protection of Harley-Davidson?

______

TIPS

For infant industry protection to make sense, a government must be able to identify a real market failure. How would the government know that the industry will eventually become competitive?

3 Tariff with Foreign Monopoly

ESSENTIAL CONCEPTS

When a foreign monopolist supplies the Home market, Home can influence the price charged for its imports. A monopolist chooses to supply the level of output that sets its marginal revenue equal to its marginal cost, and in turn this level of output determines the price in the market. A tariff on a foreign monopolist increases the marginal cost of serving the market and so influences both the level of output supplied by that monopolist and the implied price.

Home can increase its welfare by applying a tariff if the marginal revenue curve facing the monopolist is steeper than the demand curve (as is the case with linear demand). The reason for this is that the monopolist optimally chooses not to pass on all of the tariff increase to consumers, creating a terms-of-trade–like gain for the country. That is, the monopolist bears some of the cost of the tariff. If this gain outweighs the consumer surplus loss (remember there are no producers in Home!), then the country will be better off. The example of the tariff on Japanese trucks illustrates this effect. When the tariff on Japanese trucks was raised from 4% to 25%, the price of a truck to U.S. consumers rose by 12%.

REVIEW QUESTIONS

Problem 7: The demand in Home for a good produced by a foreign monopolist is given by the equation $P = 100 - Q$, where P is the price and Q is the quantity sold. The marginal revenue curve facing the foreign monopolist is then $MR = 100 - 2Q$. Suppose that the foreign monopolist has a constant marginal cost of \$10 per unit.

7a. What price does the foreign monopolist charge if there is no tariff? __________

7b. Now suppose that Home puts a \$10 per unit tariff on imports of the good. What price does the foreign monopolist charge? __________

7c. What is the impact of the tariff on Home's welfare? __________

Problem 8: Consider the demand and marginal revenue curves in Figure 9-1. These curves are drawn so that the marginal revenue curve is "flatter" than the demand curve ("constant elasticity," for those who care).

8a. Use the following diagram to confirm that a tariff will raise domestic prices by more than the amount of the tariff.

FIGURE 9-1

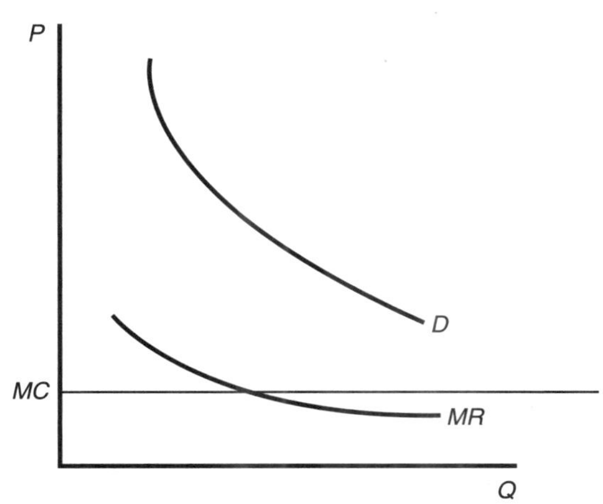

Demand Curve Steeper than the Marginal Revenue Curve

8b. In this case, can a tariff on the foreign monopolist raise national welfare? Explain. ______

______

______

TIPS

Home can always affect the price charged by the foreign firm, but whether there is a terms-of-trade gain from the tariff depends on the shape of the demand curve.

The equation for marginal revenue for a linear demand curve was derived in Chapter 6. Review that discussion.

4 Policy Response to Dumping

ESSENTIAL CONCEPTS

As discussed in detail in Chapter 6, the phenomenon of "dumping" naturally arises in models of imperfect competition. An imported product is being dumped (a) if its price is below the price that the exporter charges in its own local market or (b) if the exporter's local price is not available; then dumping is determined by comparing the import price with (1) a price charged for the product in a third market or (2) the exporter's average costs of production. Under the rules of the WTO, an importing country is entitled to apply an antidumping tariff when a foreign firm is dumping its product and this dumping has caused "material injury" to domestic firms.

Unlike other trade policies, such as the *safeguard tariff,* a foreign firm can influence the level of a tariff that it faces in a market by changing the price that it charges for its good. The antidumping duty (the tariff) that is actually applied will be equal to the difference between the price charged by the firm and its "fair value." By raising its price to the "fair value," the foreign firm can avoid a tariff on its product altogether. It is for this reason that antidumping policy creates a situation in which the home country loses from the mere existence of the policy. Prices are high because of the threat of the antidumping duty, but the antidumping duty is never applied so there is no tariff revenue.

The application that is presented in the chapter is crucial reading because it illustrates the excessive usage of antidumping policy. Evidence that antidumping policy often leads to a change in the behavior of foreign firms is the high percentage of antidumping cases that are withdrawn and settled. U.S. antidumping law actually permits U.S. firms to withdraw their case and agree with foreign firms on the level of prices and market shares. That is, the law encourages collusion between domestic and foreign firms in the U.S. market.

KEY TERMS

Use the space provided to record your notes on the following key terms.

Dumping ______

______

______

Antidumping duty ______

______

______

Countervailing duty ______________________________

____

____

Material injury ______________________________

____

____

Discriminating monopoly ______________________________

____

____

Safeguard tariff ______________________________

____

____

REVIEW QUESTIONS

Problem 9: Consider the following (fictional) claim of a government official. "Since we implemented our antidumping policy, we have not applied antidumping duties to any foreign products. Therefore, the policy could not have had any effect on foreign producers." Discuss.

____

____

____

Problem 10: Why do firms make claims of dumping so often? ______________________________

____

____

Problem 11: Under the antidumping procedure in the United States, can antidumping duties be applied if there is no domestic competitor? ______________________________

____

____

TIPS

There was a time when antidumping was justified by the fear of "predatory pricing." Modern treatments of dumping rarely mention this possibility because the way that antidumping laws are applied tends to reduce rather than increase competition.

10

Export Subsidies in Agriculture and High-Technology Industries

Overview

Export and production subsidies provided by developed-country governments to local farmers are perhaps the single most contentious issue in the current WTO negotiations. The effects of these subsidies are analyzed using the perfectly competitive, partial equilibrium model first introduced in Chapter 7. The assumption of perfect competition in agriculture is reasonable given the relatively large number of farms. Both export and production subsidies aid the producers that receive them, but both types of subsidies inevitably reduce the national welfare of the country offering them. Of the two types of subsidies, the production subsidy raises producer surplus with the least amount of harm to national welfare because it does not lower consumer surplus. This result is an example of the *targeting principle:* Policies that have a direct impact on a government objective are more efficient than policies that have an indirect impact.

Export and production subsidies tend to lower the terms of trade of a large exporting country. The change in the terms of trade has an impact on foreign countries. Importing countries are made better off as the lower price increases their consumer surplus by more than it reduces their producer surplus. Other countries that export agricultural products are hurt, however, as their terms of trade deteriorate as well. In general, producers not receiving the subsidies are made worse off, and this helps explain why subsidies are a hot button issue in the current WTO negotiations.

Subsidies are also relatively common in high-technology industries where imperfect competition is the normal state of affairs. Because strategic behavior is common in imperfect competition, *game theory* is used to understand the *strategic* impact of government subsidies. Unlike the case of perfect competition, subsidies in imperfectly competitive industries are shown to have the potential to increase the welfare of the country that offers them. These welfare gains arise if the subsidy can cause profits that would otherwise be enjoyed by foreign producers to be *shifted* to domestic producers. The benefits of subsidies in these industries are not guaranteed, however, and depend on the details of the international competition in that industry. The well-publicized case of Boeing and Airbus' competition in the global market for large, wide-bodied aircraft is used to illustrate the issues involved.

1 WTO Goals on Agricultural Export Subsidies

ESSENTIAL CONCEPTS

Agriculture is one of the important issues at the current Doha negotiations of the WTO. Progress has been made in the negotiations to eliminate agricultural export subsidies, but production subsidies and tariffs on agricultural products continue to be sticking points. The agricultural subsidies and tariffs imposed by developed countries have a serious impact on the terms of trade of many developing countries, such as Brazil, because these countries have a comparative advantage in agriculture. On the flip side, developed countries want developing countries to open their markets in service industries where developed countries have a comparative advantage. One goal of the current negotiations is to improve the access of developing countries to developed countries' markets in manufacturing industries. Currently, the target is to allow developing countries to have tariff-free access to developed countries' markets in 97% of imported products. The key issues to absorb from this section are largely factual. Table 9.1 in the textbook summarizes the negotiating agenda.

KEY TERMS

Use the space provided to record your notes on the following key terms.

Common agricultural policy (CAP) ______________________________

____

____

Indirect subsidies ______________________________

____

____

Domestic farm supports ______________________________

____

____

REVIEW QUESTIONS

Problem 1: Why would developed-country food aid to developing countries be an area of discussion in trade talks? ______________________________

____

____

Problem 2: Could a tax credit on the purchase of fertilizer be an issue at the WTO? Explain.

____

____

TIPS

The focus of the GATT at its inception in 1947 was to lower trade barriers in manufacturing. Agriculture and services were largely ignored at the time. This is one reason for the importance of these areas in recent rounds of negotiations.

2 Agricultural Export Subsidies in a Small Home Country

ESSENTIAL CONCEPTS

The perfect competition, partial equilibrium model introduced in Chapter 7 is used to analyze the impact of an export subsidy. In the case of a small Home country, the world price is fixed at P^W. An export subsidy of size s raises the amount that producers earn by selling their product on world markets to $P^W + s$. Because producers would be unwilling to sell their product in Home for any less than what they can receive by exporting their output, the domestic price rises to $P^W + s$. The higher domestic price induces Home producers to expand their supply and Home consumers to contract their demand, leading to an increase in the volume of the country's exports. Because at any given world price, Home is willing to export more, the export supply curve is shifted to the right in the world market diagram.

Because Home is an exporter of the subsidized good, the higher price in Home expands producer surplus by more than it reduces consumer surplus. Home's national welfare falls, however, because the cost of the subsidy to the government is greater than the gain in producer surplus. Hence, the export subsidy creates deadweight loss equal to the sum of the production and consumption losses (producers are making too much and consumers are demanding too little). In the case of linear supply and demand, the deadweight loss can be calculated as the area of a triangle. The triangle has height equal to the size of the subsidy, and the base is the increase in exports.

KEY TERMS

Use the space provided to record your notes on the following key terms.

Consumption loss ________________

____

____

Production loss ________________

____

____

REVIEW QUESTIONS

Problem 3: Explain why a country that imposes an export subsidy often enacts an import tariff on the same product simultaneously. ________________

____

Problem 4: Figure 10-1 illustrates Home's export supply curve. Home is small and faces a world price of $10, at which it is willing to sell 100 units. Suppose that Home's government offers an export subsidy of $1 per unit export and exports rise to 120 units.

4a. What is the cost of the subsidy to the government? ________________

____

____

FIGURE 10-1

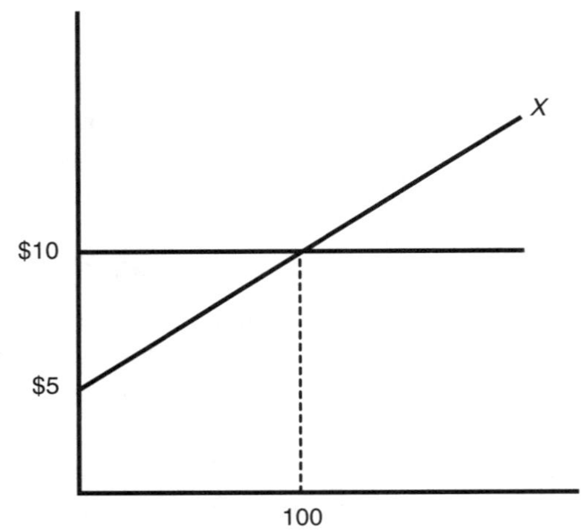

The Export Supply of a Small Country

4b. What is the effect of the subsidy on national welfare? ______________________________

____

____

4c. Show the deadweight loss and cost of the subsidy in Figure 10-1.

Problem 5: A small home country imposes an export subsidy of size *s*. The effects of the subsidy are shown in Figure 10-2.

FIGURE 10-2

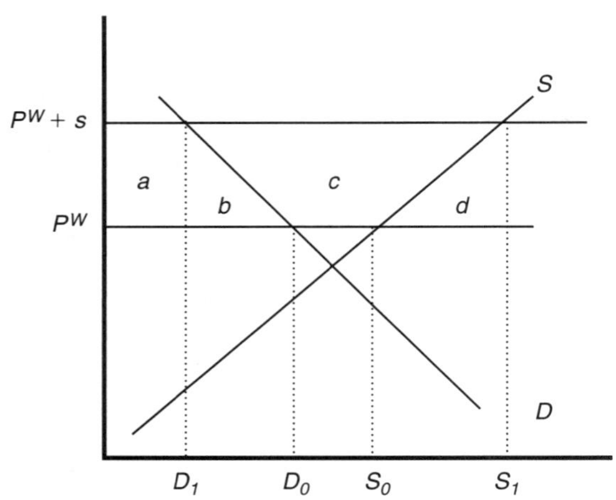

The Effect of an Export Subsidy in the Home Market

5a. What is the cost of the subsidy to the government? ______________________

5b. What is the effect of the subsidy on producer surplus? ______________________

5c. Using the information on prices and quantities, provide a formula for the size of the consumption loss. ______________________

Problem 6: Suppose Home is an importer of chocolate. The country is small and so the price of chocolate on world markets is fixed. Could the country use an export subsidy to turn the country into an exporter of chocolate? Explain. ______________________

____

____

TIPS

There are gains from trade between countries, but this does not mean that exports should be subsidized. This is not obvious to many who have not taken a class in international trade.

3 Agricultural Export Subsidies in a Large Home Country

ESSENTIAL CONCEPTS

In the perfect competition, partial equilibrium model, an export subsidy hurts a large exporter even more than it hurts a small exporter. An export subsidy induces Home to increase its supply on world markets. Because Home is large, it faces a downward-sloping import demand curve and the increased supply of the good on world market drives down the world price. Thus, an export subsidy gives rise to a *terms-of-trade loss* for the exporting country. This loss represents a transfer of welfare from the Home country's government to foreign consumers. Home's welfare falls by the sum of the deadweight loss and the terms-of-trade loss of the subsidy.

KEY TERMS

Use the space provided to record your notes on the following key term.

Terms of trade ______________________

____

____

REVIEW QUESTIONS

Problem 7: Home is a large exporter of bikes on international markets. The country exports 100 bikes for $100 apiece. The government imposes an export subsidy of $10 per bike. As a result, exports rise by 50 units and the world price of bikes falls to $95 per bike.

7a. What is the cost of the export subsidy to the government? ______________________

____

7b. What is the effect of the subsidy on Home's welfare? (Provide a number.) ______________________

____

____

7c. What is the effect of the subsidy on Foreign's welfare? (Provide a number.)

____

____

7d. Show the effect of the export subsidy on the welfare of consumers and producers in the importing country Foreign on the following diagram.

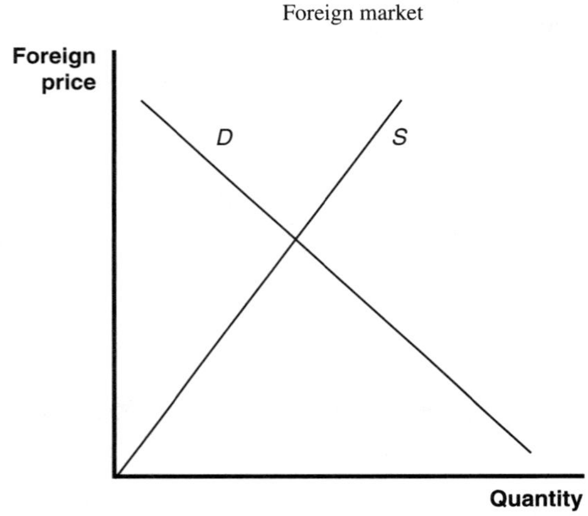

7e. Use the following world market diagram to illustrate the terms-of-trade effects and deadweight losses to each country.

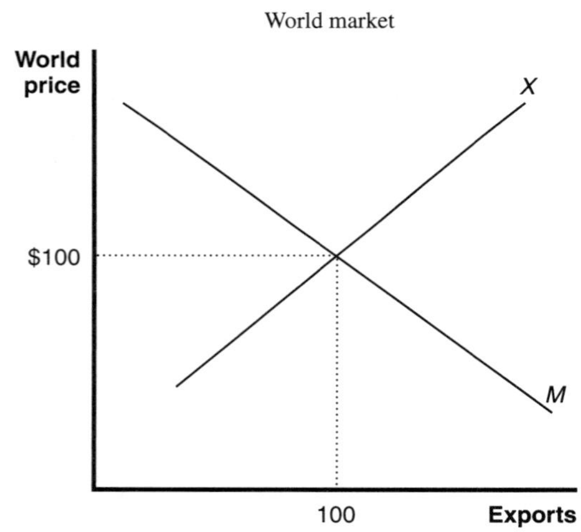

7f. Could Foreign accuse Home firms of "dumping" their product in their market?

____

7g. What other WTO-sanctioned trade policy could be implemented by Foreign in this situation? ____

____

TIPS

It is important to notice that Home's terms-of-trade loss exceeds Foreign's national welfare gain. This motivates the argument that if increasing Foreign's welfare is the main objective of a policy, a direct cash payment to Foreign is more efficient.

Export subsidies create price gaps between exporting and importing countries that could result in the importing country charging the exporting country with dumping.

Problem 8: Suppose that Home imposes an export *tax* so that to export one unit of a good, an exporter would have to pay *T*. Home is large on world markets.

8a. Using the following diagram, illustrate the effect of the export tax on the volume of exports, the price on world markets, and the price in the home market.

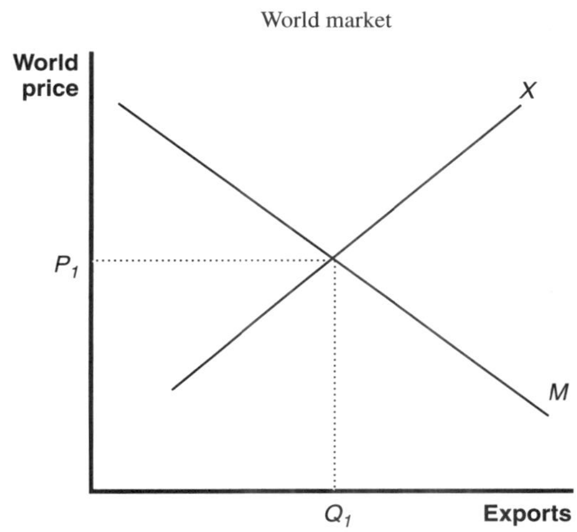

8b. What is the effect of the export tax on Home's producer surplus, consumer surplus, and government revenue? ______________________________

____

____

8c. Compare and contrast the effect of an export tax on national welfare with that of an export subsidy. ______________________________

____

____

TIPS

An export tax is just a negative export subsidy. As such, its welfare effects are exactly opposite those of an export subsidy. Whereas an export subsidy inevitably causes a loss of national welfare, an export tax (like an import tariff) can raise domestic welfare.

4 Agricultural Production Subsidies

ESSENTIAL CONCEPTS

Export subsidies lower a country's welfare but raise the surplus enjoyed by its producers. If the primary goal of the policy is to increase producer surplus, then a *production subsidy* will accomplish this goal at a lower cost than an export subsidy. To see this, consider a small home country. A production subsidy raises the price paid to producers to the world price plus the subsidy, but it has no impact on the price paid by consumers. Because the price paid by consumers does not change, there is no loss in consumer surplus when a production subsidy is paid. Hence, a production subsidy raises producer surplus in a manner similar to that of an export subsidy, but there is no consumption distortion associated with the production subsidy. Because a production subsidy achieves the same objective as an export subsidy while causing less damage, it is the preferred policy. The *targeting prin-*

ciple holds that it is best to use the policy instrument that achieves the objective most directly.

Both types of subsidies will result in terms-of-trade effects if the exporter is a large country. For this reason, a production subsidy also falls under Article XVI of the GATT. However, because domestic consumption does not fall in the case of the production subsidy, the effect of the subsidy on exports is smaller than it would be if an export subsidy were used to raise producer surplus by the same amount. Hence, the terms-of-trade loss caused by a production subsidy is smaller than the loss caused by an export subsidy.

KEY TERMS

Use the space provided to record your notes on the following key terms.

Production subsidy ______________________________

Targeting principle ______________________________

REVIEW QUESTIONS

Problem 9: Consider the information in Figure 10-3. A subsidy of size s = \$5 has altered the production of a small home country.

FIGURE 10-3

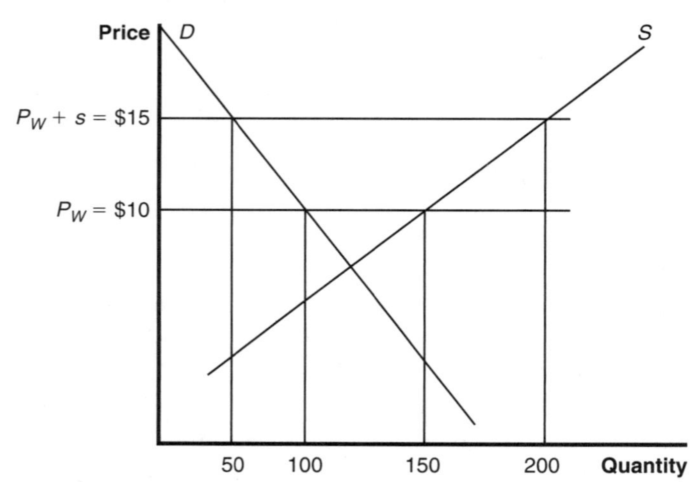

Production versus Export Subsidy

9a. Is the budgetary cost to the government to induce producers to make 200 units higher for a production or export subsidy? ______________________

____

9b. What is the size of the production loss (provide a number) of either a production subsidy or an export subsidy? ______________________

____

9c. What is the size of the consumption loss for the two types of subsidies? ____________

____

9d. How large is the additional national welfare loss if an export subsidy is chosen rather than a production subsidy? ______________________

____

9e. If Home were a large country, which type of subsidy would have the biggest impact on Foreign's producers? ______________________

____

____

9f. If Home were a large country, what would be the effect of a production subsidy on consumer surplus in Home? Explain. ______________________

____

____

TIPS

Any policy that has an impact on world prices has an effect on foreign welfare.

Problem 10: Suppose Home, a small country, is importing a good and the government wishes to raise the producer surplus by offering a production subsidy. Could the subsidy induce the country to become an exporter of the good? ______________________

____

____

TIPS

Problem 10 illustrates just how distortionary subsidies can be. An import tariff could never induce a country to become an exporter in this framework.

5 High-Technology Export Subsidies

ESSENTIAL CONCEPTS

Our analysis of the model with perfect competition led to the very strong implication that subsidies, whether they are subsidies to exports or to production, lowered the subsidizing country's welfare. Yet, such subsides are common. There are two possible explanations. First, these subsidies may worsen national welfare but are implemented by governments that favor producers over consumers, perhaps for political reasons. Second, there is something important missing in the model and these subsidies are actually in the national interest. It is this second possibility that is explored in the final section of this chapter.

One possible motive for subsidies is to increase the volume of an activity that provides positive *externalities* to others. Such externalities are thought to be important in high-technology industries. Because this argument is familiar to the earlier discussion on infant industry protection in Chapter 9, this possibility is not discussed in any detail here.

Another possible motive for subsidies occurs when there is *imperfect competition* in an industry. When an industry is imperfectly competitive, two issues arise. On one hand, firms in these industries behave strategically and their actions are best understood using *game theory.* On the other hand, firms in imperfectly competitive industries may earn profits. Under these conditions, it is possible that government subsides can change the nature of competition between firms in such a way that profits earned by foreign firms are shifted to domestic firms. Such a shift of profits can improve the national welfare of the country offering the subsidy.

The classic critique of this argument is that for such "strategic trade policy" to be desirable the conditions in an industry have to meet a number of criteria, and these conditions are not easily assessed by the government. When these criteria are not met, the subsidy could reduce national welfare in much the same way that it would reduce welfare in the perfectly competitive model. Whatever the effect of the subsidy on the welfare of the country imposing the subsidy, the subsidy always has an impact on the welfare of the other country.

Because game theory will be used more than once in this book and because not all introductory economics classes deal with game theory, it is worth some review. In the games considered in this book, there will always be two players who have to decide which of two actions they will take. Each action taken by one player yields a payoff to the player, but the size of this payoff depends on the action taken by the other player. It is this fact that gives rise to the need for a player to have a "strategy:" If the other player chooses action A, I will choose action B. A Nash equilibrium to a game occurs when each player is choosing the action that gives the highest payoff to that player given the action chosen by the other player.

Consider the following example. The two players are Hank and Mick, who have been arrested by the police for two crimes. The police have hard evidence that each is guilty of a minor crime and believe that they have committed a more serious crime. They are being separately questioned by the police, and each can take two actions: They may (1) *confess* to the serious crime or (2) keep *quiet.* If both Hank and Mick choose to keep quiet, they will both be convicted of the minor crime and will serve 2 years in jail. If both Hank and Mick confess, they will each serve 4 years. If only one of the two confesses, then the one that confesses will serve only 1 year in jail and the other will serve 6 years in jail. Hank and Mick want to serve as little jail time as possible.

This game is known as the "prisoner's dilemma," and it is used as an example at several junctures in the book. The key point made by this example is that two players (in this book, generally governments conducting policy) would be better off if they could cooperate, but each player has an incentive to deviate from cooperative behavior. As a result, the strategic behavior of the players results in their being made worse off. To see this, let us analyze the game. The first step is to organize the information so that the relationship between the payoffs to each player and the actions of each player is clear. This is done in the following payoff matrix.

		Mick	
		Confess	Quiet
Hank	Confess	−4 (Mick) / −4 (Hank)	−6 (Mick) / −1 (Hank)
	Quiet	−1 (Mick) / −6 (Hank)	−2 (Mick) / −2 (Hank)

In this payoff matrix, each row corresponds to the action taken by Hank and each column corresponds to an action taken by Mick. In each box, the number in the lower left-hand corner corresponds to the payoff to Hank and the upper right-hand corner corresponds to the payoff to Mick given the permutation of actions chosen by the two players. For instance, if Mick confesses and Hank does not, Hank will get a payoff of −6 and Mick will get a payoff of −1. (Jail time is bad, so the numbers are negatives!)

The *Nash equilibrium* to the game occurs when each player is choosing the action that yields the highest payoff to that player *given the action chosen by the other player.* Suppose Mick was to confess; then the best action for Hank to take would be to confess as well, because −4 is greater than −6. If Mick were to stay quiet, Hank's best action would be to confess, because a payoff of −1 is better than a payoff of −2. Given the symmetry of Mick's payoffs to Hank's payoffs, the Nash equilibrium of this game is that both Hank and Mick confess because only then will each player be choosing the best action given the action of the other.

Although the prisoner's dilemma example has a single equilibrium, other games with different payoffs can have more than one. This is the case in the Boeing-Airbus game presented in the textbook. To see how sensitive the equilibrium is to the payoffs, suppose that in the Mick and Hank example both players can avoid any jail time if neither confesses while all the other payoffs remain the same. In this case, the game has two equilibria: one in which both confess and one in which both stay quiet. Without any additional information, we cannot predict which equilibrium will be observed.

KEY TERMS

Use the space provided to record your notes on the following key terms.

Duopoly ______________________________

____

____

Game theory ______________________________

____

____

Nash equilibrium ______________________________

____

____

First mover advantage ______________________________

____

____

Externality ____

____

____

Payoff matrix ____

____

____

REVIEW QUESTIONS

Problem 11: Consider the Airbus-Boeing model outlined in the textbook.

11a. Is there any welfare loss analogous to the deadweight loss in this model? __________

____

____

11b. What would happen to welfare in the two countries if the United States were to retaliate against European Union subsidies by offering a subsidy of its own? ______________

____

____

11c. Given your answer to 11b, explain the motivation for the United States and the European Union to sign their 1992 trade agreement on large aircraft. ______________

____

____

TIPS

The argument made in this section fits the details of the Airbus-Boeing relationship quite well, but few other industries fit the description this well.

As well as conditions in the large-body aircraft fit the model, the subsequent distress that Airbus has experienced suggests that one should be careful using the model to interpret the situation in the industry.

11

International Agreements: Trade, Labor, and the Environment

Overview

International agreements impose restrictions on the policies of their signatories. Countries allow their own policy options to be restricted by an agreement because the agreement also restricts the policies of the other participating countries. For instance, countries that belong to the WTO are expected to adhere to a set of obligations, such as the most favored nation principle. This chapter discusses international agreements that influence polices in areas that are relevant to international trade, including trade policy, labor standards, and environmental regulation.

The World Trade Organization is the result of a *multilateral trade agreement* that is designed to overcome a particular *prisoner's dilemma* between countries. Countries have an incentive to protect domestic industries, but tariffs and quotas have a negative impact on their trading partners. If everyone has an incentive to protect, then the outcome can result in collectively small gains from trade. Each party would be better off with free trade but, given the protection offered by other countries, sees it in its best interest to offer protection as well.

A *regional trade agreement* (RTA) requires its adherents to allow free trade to its signatories while maintaining tariffs on countries outside the agreement. These agreements can create trade between participating countries, but they can also divert trade from countries outside the agreement. Regional trade agreements often include *side agreements* on *labor standards.* These standards involve regulations on labor issues such as occupational safety and child labor. Developing countries accept these labor standards in order to be allowed into regional trade agreements with developed countries. Policymakers in developing countries and many trade economists worry that these agreements might be *disguised protectionism,* inspired at least in part by a desire to increase the cost of production in low-wage countries.

The final type of international agreement discussed in the chapter is *multilateral environmental agreements,* which deal specifically with environmental policy. Many issues arise within the context of the WTO, which allows countries to maintain their own environmental regulations as long as these regulations are equally applied to foreign and domestic firms. A larger, perhaps more contentious, issue is whether international trade tends to harm the environment. This concern has theoretical justification, particularly in the case of *common property.* International trade can exacerbate the *tragedy of the commons,* leading to more rapid depletion of natural resources, and can give rise to a different form of the prisoner's dilemma. Once again, the existence of a prisoner's dilemma suggests the need for more extensive international agreements.

1 International Trade Agreements

ESSENTIAL CONCEPTS

Multilateral trade agreements and regional trade agreements are designed to reduce trade barriers between countries. Multilateral agreements involve a wide range of countries, whereas RTAs are often limited in scope to as few as two countries. With more than 140 member countries, the WTO is the crowning example of a multilateral trade agreement. The WTO owes its existence to the desire among its members to overcome a prisoner's dilemma. To illustrate the nature of the prisoner's dilemma, consider a world with two countries, Home and Foreign. Home exports good A and imports good B, and Foreign imports good A and exports good B. By imposing the optimal tariff on good B, Home can increase its welfare at Foreign's expense because its terms-of-trade gain exceeds its deadweight loss. Foreign's welfare falls by the sum of its terms-of-trade loss and its deadweight loss. Foreign can increase its welfare at Home's expense by applying a tariff on good A. When both countries apply a tariff, the terms-of-trade gains in their import goods are exactly canceled out by the terms-of-trade losses in the export goods, so all that is left is deadweight loss in both industries. The outcome is the Nash equilibrium to the prisoner's dilemma game. The WTO is designed to overcome the prisoner's dilemma by (1) imposing rules on the application of trade policies, (2) providing a forum for countries to negotiate lower tariffs on each other's goods, and (3) providing a dispute settlement mechanism.

An alternative to multilateral trade agreements is *regional trade agreements.* RTAs occur when several countries eliminate trade barriers between signatories to the agreement but maintain tariffs against countries outside the agreement. These agreements are inherently discriminatory because countries outside the agreement do not get the same treatment. This exception to the MFN principle is allowed in Article XIV of the GATT. Because these agreements are inherently discriminatory, their detractors often refer to them as *preferential trade agreements.*

RTAs come in two forms: *free-trade areas* and *customs unions.* Although both types of agreements involve free trade between members, customs unions require member countries to share a single tariff code on countries outside the agreement, whereas free-trade areas allow countries to have different tariff codes. Countries impose *rules of origin* to avoid the importation of goods into the lower-tariff country in a free-trade area followed by trans-shipment to the higher-tariff country.

Although RTAs lower trade barriers between countries, they may or may not increase welfare. RTAs have two types of effects on trading patterns. *Trade creation* occurs when a member country imports a product from another member country that it formerly produced for itself. *Trade diversion* occurs when a country switches its import supplier from a country outside the agreement to a country inside the agreement. Trade diversion can lead to a welfare loss for the importing country because it no longer collects tariff revenues. From a global point of view, trade diversion causes a less efficient use of the world's resources as production is reallocated away from a low-cost producer to a high-cost producer.

KEY TERMS

Use the space provided to record your notes on the following key terms.

Multilateral agreement ______________________________

Terms-of-trade gain ______________________________

Prisoner's dilemma ______________________________

Regional trade agreements ______________________________

Preferential trade agreements ______________________________

Free-trade area ______________________________

Customs union ______________________________

Rules of origin ______________________________

Trade creation ______________________________

Trade diversion ______________________________

REVIEW QUESTIONS

Problem 1: The prisoner's dilemma set out in the textbook featured a world with two large countries. Would this logic hold if there were only one large country and many small countries? Explain. ____________________

Problem 2: Suppose that many small countries were to form a customs union. What impact might the customs union have on the prisoner's dilemma? ____________________

TIPS The assumption that the two countries are identical in the formulation of the prisoner's dilemma is important. If one country gains more from following its optimal tariff than the other, it becomes less clear that country would benefit from international trade agreements.

Problem 3: Suppose that Home joins a free-trade area. Is it possible that Home simultaneously imports a homogeneous good from outside the free-trade area and exports the same good to a member of the free-trade area? Explain.

Problem 4: Use the diagram for Home's market to show an example of trade creation in a RTA.

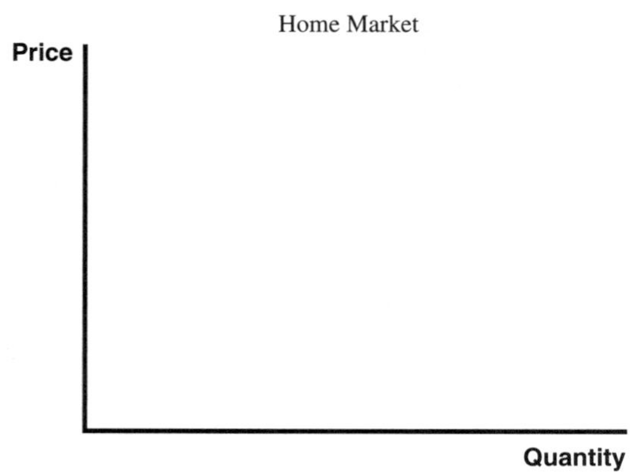

Problem 5: Home's market could be served by its own producers, who have constant marginal cost of C_H; by country B, whose producers have marginal cost C_B; or by country A, whose producers have marginal cost C_A. Home has the largest marginal cost and country A has the smallest marginal cost. Home initially applies the most favored nation tariff t to both A and B.

5a. If Home forms a regional trade agreement with country A, could this agreement lead to trade diversion? If so, under what circumstances? ____________________

5b. If Home forms a regional trade agreement with country B, could this agreement lead to trade creation? If so, under what circumstances? ______

______

______

Now suppose that Home does not produce the good at all. The marginal costs for countries A and B and Home's demand are shown in Figure 11-1.

5c. Illustrate the case of trade diversion in Figure 11-1 by drawing the effect of the tariff on the cost of the country outside the regional free-trade arrangement.

FIGURE 11-1

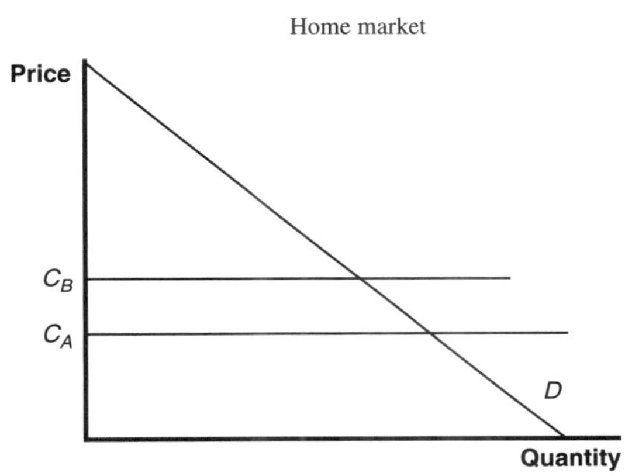

Trade Creation or Diversion

5d. In your diagram answer to question 5c, is there any welfare benefit from the RTA? Explain. ______

______

______

TIPS

It is possible that even in a particular industry a regional trade diversion could improve a country's welfare if it leads to a substantial increase in imports. Experiment with different drawings of Figure 11-1 so that an RTA results in different magnitudes of changes in consumer surplus relative to loss tariff revenue.

2 International Agreements on Labor Issues

ESSENTIAL CONCEPTS

RTAs are often accompanied by *side agreements* that are not directly related to trade policies. When the levels of economic development differ substantially across countries within the RTA, these side agreements are often over *labor standards,* which cover areas such as occupational health and safety, child labor, and minimum wages. Consumers and policymakers favor labor standards out of concern for working conditions abroad. Labor unions often push for labor standards as part of trade agreements out of concern that poor labor standards abroad create more competition for U.S. workers.

Economists and policy makers in developing countries are skeptical about the motive for and benefits of attaching labor standards to trade agreements. Many see the emphasis on labor standards as a form of *disguised protectionism* because the regulations may result in much higher costs of production in the affected countries. Of particular concern is pressure to require developing country firms to pay a *living wage.* Although a living wage is not well defined, it can be construed to mean a wage that is higher than the norm in developing countries. Economic theory suggests that wages that are well above the market wage would either increase unemployment in developing countries or would force people into the unregulated informal sectors.

Finally, some evidence is presented that nongovernmental organizations (NGOs) have been effective at reducing some of the most egregious forms of abuse in developing countries by pressuring firms to improve their working conditions. Their successes suggest that bad publicity can be an effective tool for changing firms' behavior.

KEY TERMS

Use the space provided to record your notes on the following key terms.

Labor standards ____________________

Living wage ____________________

REVIEW QUESTIONS

Problem 6: According to a survey by the National Bureau of Economic Research, consumers were willing to pay a premium for items made under good working conditions. How could a NGO use this sentiment to improve working conditions in developing countries?

Problem 7: Explain why economists are wary of trade agreements with developing countries that include labor standards? ____________________

Problem 8: Suppose there are two sectors in an economy: the formal sector, which is subject to government regulations, and the informal sector, which is not subject to government regulations. Each sector has a specific factor associated with it, and labor is mobile between the two sectors. Prices of the goods produced by the two sectors are fixed on world markets. Suppose the government imposed a "living wage" on the formal sector that was above the market wage.

8a. What would happen to employment in the formal sector? Explain. ____________________

8b. What would happen to the wage paid in the informal sector? Explain. ______________

____

____

____

3 International Agreements on the Environment

ESSENTIAL CONCEPTS

Many environmentalists are suspicious of international trade in general and the WTO in particular. Policies toward the environment can run afoul of WTO rules when they have consequences for international trade. For instance, the U.S. Marine Mammal Protection Act requires that tuna fishers use nets that do not inadvertently catch dolphins. When imports of tuna from Mexico were banned by the United States in 1991, the GATT (the WTO did not yet exist) ruled that the ban violated GATT rules on nondiscrimination. In looking at WTO rules, however, it is not obvious that they are stacked against the environment. *Article XX* of the GATT allows countries to adopt any environmental laws they please, provided that these laws are applied uniformly to domestic and foreign producers. The problem arises when a country regulates the *production process method* rather than the product itself. Past WTO rulings have not allowed countries to ban imports on the basis of their production process method, ruling that such a ban is essentially an effort to force one country's regulations onto another. The WTO has had no problem, however, with products being labeled in such a way to report the production process method so that concerned consumers can avoid products made in an environmentally unfriendly way.

Does international trade by its very nature accelerate the degradation of the environment? This is an open question, and plenty of examples can be found to support either side of the argument. For instance, in the United States the most fuel-efficient cars tend to be built by foreign manufacturers, so limiting these imports would worsen fuel efficiency in the United States. Those who are concerned that international trade has a negative impact on the environment can find plenty of theoretical support for their argument. This is particularly true in areas in which natural resources are *common property.* Common property tends to be overused, a phenomenon commonly referred to as the *tragedy of the commons.* International trade can exacerbate the tragedy of the commons by directing global demand toward the resource of a particular country or region, so that there is even more overuse of natural resources under free trade. Examples abound. For instance, the overharvesting of tropical wood is certainly encouraged by a large global market. Global pollutants, such as carbon dioxide emissions, present a problem similar to the tragedy of the commons: Weak regulation can give a country a production advantage while all countries suffer the consequences of the pollution. As another example of a prisoner's dilemma, this situation calls for multilateral agreements.

KEY TERMS

Use the space provided to record your notes on the following key terms.

Multilateral environmental agreements ______________________

____

____

Tragedy of the commons ______________________________

Common property ______________________________

Kyoto protocol ______________________________

REVIEW QUESTIONS

Problem 9: Home requires the use of at least 40% recycled paper in cardboard boxes and bans imports of Foreign boxes because they use no recycled paper.

9a. If Foreign complains to the WTO, how is the WTO likely to rule? ______________________________

9b. If Home were to require cardboard boxes manufacturers to label the recycled paper content of their boxes, would this violate WTO rules? ______________________________

Problem 10: Suppose that rich countries have stronger feelings toward the environment than poor countries, goods differ in the amount of pollution they create, and pollution regulations impose higher costs on "dirtier" industries. How might a reduction in tariffs brought about by the WTO affect pollution? ______________________________

Problem 11: The "sneed" industry produces a product that everyone needs as well as a great deal of pollution. Suppose that many identical countries have sneed firms. The pollution can be controlled using alternative production techniques, but this raises the marginal cost of production.

11a. If the pollution created by the sneed industry is primarily local, is an international agreement necessary? ______________________________

Now suppose that the pollution created by the sneed industry is global.

11b. If all countries require the sneed industry to use the low pollution production technique, what happens to the price of sneeds on world markets? ______________________________

11c. Suppose that your country is the only one not to sign on to an international agreement requiring the use of low pollution production techniques. What happens to producer surplus in your sneed industry once the agreement is put into place? ______________________

____

____

____

11d. Given your answer to 11c, explain why might it be hard to get all countries to sign on to an international agreement on sneed production techniques? ______________________

____

____

TIPS

Problem 10 gets at the "pollution haven hypothesis." The hypothesis is that tariff reduction is likely to lead to a migration of the production of dirty industries to poor countries with poor environmental regulations.

Problem 11 makes the point that when there are many countries there is an incentive for individual countries to free ride on the beneficial actions of others.

12

The Global Macroeconomy

Overview

This chapter provides a brief overview of the topics covered in the remainder of the book. These topics are organized into three categories. Because the exchange rate is the most important price in the economy, affecting the well-being of all of a country's citizens, the structure of the foreign exchange market and the theory of the exchange rate come first. The causes and implications of financial globalization are next on the agenda. The ability to borrow and lend on international financial markets is shown to improve a country's well-being, but there are limits to a country's activities on international markets and dramatic consequences when countries cannot fulfill their international obligations. Finally, in virtually every chapter there is some analysis of the policy decisions facing governments. These policies span the mundane, such as fiscal policy, through very intricate decisions, such as whether a country would be well served by joining the Eurozone.

1 Foreign Exchange: Of Currencies and Crises

ESSENTIAL CONCEPTS

The exchange rate is the price of one country's currency in terms of another. It is the single most important price in an open economy because its level determines how expensive foreign goods and services are relative to domestic goods and services and because changes in the exchange rate affect the relative return on foreign assets. The foreign exchange market, where currencies are traded, is the largest market in the world. The structure and operation of the market are laid out in Chapter 13 and a theory of the monetary forces that determine the exchange rate is laid out in Chapters 14 and 15.

Movements in the exchange rate can have a big impact on an economy's performance because the exchange rate affects demand for a country's goods and services and can directly alter a country's wealth. A sudden sharp drop in the exchange rate, known as an *exchange rate crisis,* can have serious economic implications, including a large drop in economic output, a rise in poverty, and widespread bank failures. The economic dislocation caused by such crises occasionally spills over into the political arena in the form of riots and government failures. The *International Monetary Fund* is the international institution charged with helping countries in crisis. The tools to understand the links between countries are developed in Chapter 16, whereas the effect of exchange rate movements on the economy is the subject of Chapter 18. Chapter 20 explores the causes and consequences of exchange rate crises.

To avoid the effects of a changing exchange rate, some governments choose to have a *fixed* exchange rate. To do so, they must be prepared to buy and sell their currency for foreign currency. Other countries prefer to let their exchange rate *float,* allowing market forces to determine the exchange rate. Some countries group together and adopt a common currency. The relative merits of different exchange rate regimes is the focus of Chapter 19, whereas the euro, the common currency of many European countries, is discussed in detail in Chapter 21.

KEY TERMS

Use the space provided to record your notes on the following key terms.

Fixed exchange rate ______________________________

____

____

Floating exchange rate ______________________________

____

____

Exchange rate crisis ______________________________

____

____

Default ______________________________

____

____

International Monetary Fund (IMF) ______________________________

____

____

World Bank ______________________________

____

REVIEW QUESTIONS

Problem 1: Why do economists call the exchange rate "the single most important price in the economy"? ______________________________

____

____

Problem 2: How can a movement in the exchange rate affect a country's exporters?

____

____

2 Globalization of Finance: Of Debts and Deficits

ESSENTIAL CONCEPTS

When a household spends more than it earns, it must either drawdown its savings or sell assets (borrow). Countries find themselves in the same situation. A country whose *expenditure* exceeds its *income* is running a current account *deficit* and must sell assets to another country that is running a current account *surplus.* Countries that persistently spend less than their income build up their external *wealth,* whereas countries that run current account deficits run down their wealth. As is the case with households, *capital gains* and losses also affect a country's wealth. The *balance of payments* is an elaborate accounting system designed to follow international transactions and the evolution of its external wealth. The balance of payments accounts are closely integrated with a country's national accounts, which follow the flow of spending within a country. The national accounts and balance of payments are explained in Chapter 16.

Financial globalization allows countries to separate their savings from their investment, thereby helping countries that are experiencing bad times or that have high investment needs. The downside is that countries occasionally find themselves unwilling to repay their debts to international creditors. Countries considered likely to default on their foreign debts pay higher interest rates due to their *country risk.* The benefits of financial globalization are the subject of Chapter 17, risk premiums are discussed in Chapter 20, and the problem of sovereign default is covered in Chapter 22.

KEY TERMS

Use the space below to record your notes on the following key terms.

Income ______________________________

____

____

Expenditure ______________________________

____

____

Surplus ______________________________

____

____

Deficit ______________________________

____

____

Wealth ______________________________

____

____

Capital gains ______________________________

____

____

Country risk ______________________________

____

____

Balance of payments ______________________________

____

____

REVIEW QUESTIONS

Problem 3: Suppose that it costs Brazil 10% interest to borrow and in the United States only 4%. What is the level of Brazilian country risk? ______________________________

____

____

Problem 4: Suppose that Home runs a current account deficit.

4a. What should happen to Home's external wealth, *ceteris paribus?* ______________________________

____

____

4b. What phenomenon could make Home's external wealth move in an unexpected direction?

____

____

____

3 Governments and Institutions: Of Policies and Performance

ESSENTIAL CONCEPTS

The implications of various *policies* are discussed throughout the half of the book devoted to international macroeconomics. Some of these policies are more fundamental than others. *Regimes* are sets of rules that define the parameters within which policy is implemented. Even more fundamentally, *institutions* cover the most basic legal, political, and social structures that influence economic behavior.

The process of globalization is driven in large part by governments reducing their restrictions on the economic integration of their country with other nations. Countries have reduced their barriers to trade in goods and services and have increasingly removed restrictions on capital flows in and out of the country. A definite pattern arises across countries in terms of the extent of liberalization, with the *advanced countries* liberalizing the most, *emerging markets* liberalizing some, and *developing countries* still largely outside the global economy. The benefits of financial integration are discussed in Chapter 17, and the barriers to financial integration are touched on in Chapter 22.

One of the most important policies facing a country is its choice of exchange rate regime. A country that fixes its exchange rate avoids the uncertainties created by exchange rate fluctuation but limits its ability to carry out an independent monetary policy. Moreover, it may become more susceptible to exchange rate crises. Some countries have starkly integrated their economy with those of others by adopting a *common currency* or by engaging in *dollarization*. The monetary implications of a fixed exchange rate are addressed in Chapter 15, and the criteria for preferring a fixed exchange rate over a flexible system are elaborated in Chapter 19. The role of fixed exchange rates in causing currency crises are discussed in Chapter 20. Finally, the reasons for and consequences of a common currency system are the focus of Chapter 21.

KEY TERMS

Use the space below to record your notes on the following key terms.

Policies ______________________________

Regimes ______________________________

Institutions ______________________________

Advanced countries ______________________________

Emerging markets ______________________________

Common currency ______________________________

Dollarization ______________________________

The Great Divergence ______________________________

Income per person ______________________________

Income volatility ______________________________

Developing countries ____________________

____

____

REVIEW QUESTIONS

Problem 5: What forces propel globalization?

____

____

TIPS

If this chapter has been a bit of blur, do not worry too much. You will get the opportunity to work through it all carefully in the next 10 chapters.

13

Introduction to Exchange Rates and the Foreign Exchange Market

Overview

The exchange rate is the price of one country's currency in terms of another country's currency. The exchange rate is one of the most important prices in the entire economy because movements in the exchange rate alter the competitiveness of a country's goods and change the rate of return on domestic assets relative to foreign assets. This chapter begins with a short description of the global market for foreign exchange covering (1) the types of foreign exchange contracts traded on this market, (2) the chief players in the market, and (3) the manner in which the market functions.

The chapter also introduces the important concept of arbitrage. By buying low and selling high, arbitrageurs alter supply and demand conditions so as to guarantee that all exchange rates are consistent across countries. In addition, it follows from the principle of arbitrage that if investors are not concerned about risk then the expected returns on all assets must be the same regardless of the currency in which they are denominated. This insight is used to derive the uncovered interest parity equation, which can be used to calculate the level of the exchange rate that equilibrates foreign exchange markets.

1 Exchange Rate Essentials

ESSENTIAL CONCEPTS

This section introduces some simple terms and conventions concerning the *exchange rate* that will be used throughout the remainder of the book. The exchange rate is the relative price of two currencies. A relative price and its reciprocal convey exactly the same information, but it is critical that the two are not confused because an increase in a relative price is associated with a decrease in its inverse. The important convention to remember is that the home country's exchange rate is the number of units of its own home currency that must be given up to buy one unit of the foreign country's currency. An increase in a country's exchange rate is called a *depreciation* because it takes more units of the domestic currency to buy foreign currency. A decrease in the exchange rate is called an *appreciation*. There are over a hundred currencies in the world, and it is possible that a country's exchange rate may be depreciating against one currency and appreciating against another. *Effective exchange rates* are used to measure the average change in the value of a country's currency. Changes in a country's effective exchange rate are equal to the weighted average of changes in its exchange rate across all of that country's trading partners. The weight Country A's currency receives in Country B's effective exchange rate is equal to Country A's share of Country B's total trade.

A key point made in this chapter is that if the prices of goods are fixed in a country's own currency then their foreign currency price moves proportionately with changes in the country's exchange rate. Hence, if the dollar appreciates against the yen, the dollar price of Japanese products becomes more attractive relative to American products. If the dollar depreciates against the yen, the dollar price of Japanese products becomes less attractive relative to American products.

KEY TERMS

Use the space below to record your notes on the following key terms.

Exchange rate ______________________________

____

____

Appreciation ______________________________

____

____

Depreciation ______________________________

____

____

Effective exchange rate ______________________________

____

____

REVIEW QUESTIONS

Problem 1: On day one the U.S. dollar bought one euro or 100 Japanese yen. On day two one euro cost 1.2 U.S. dollars, whereas one U.S. dollar bought 120 Japanese yen.

1a. Write the day two exchange rate between the dollar and the euro first in American terms and then in European terms. ______________________________

____

____

1b. Between day one and day two, did the U.S. dollar appreciate or depreciate against the euro? By how much in percentage terms? ______________________________

____

____

1c. Between day one and day two, did the euro appreciate or depreciate against the dollar? By how much in percentage terms? __________

1d. Write the day two exchange rate between the dollar and the yen first in American terms and then in Japanese terms. __________

1e. Between day one and day two did the dollar appreciate or depreciate against the yen? By how much in percentage terms? __________

1f. Suppose that the U.S. trade with Europe is worth $200 billion and its trade with Japan is worth $400 billion. Between day one and day two, did the effective exchange rate of the dollar appreciate or depreciate? (The basket of currency includes only the euro and the yen.) By how much? __________

TIPS

It is easy to mix up an appreciation with a depreciation and vice versa. Using the common convention, a country's currency is appreciating (often said to be rising or getting stronger in the media) when its exchange rate is going down. Think of an appreciation as allowing you to get more foreign currency for your dollar.

The big discrepancy between the amount that the dollar depreciated against the euro in problem 1b and the amount that the euro appreciated against the dollar in problem 1c is due to the very large size of the exchange rate movement. The bigger the movement in the exchange rate, the larger the discrepancy.

Notice that although the dollar depreciated against the euro by more than it appreciated against the yen, the effective exchange rate appreciated because (in this example anyway) the U.S. trades more with Japan than it does with Europe.

Problem 2: Volker, a disheveled businessman, travels frequently between Boston and his home town of Munich, Germany. The price of a glass of his favorite ale is $2 in Boston and €3 in Munich.

2a. At what U.S. exchange rate is the price of the ale the same in both countries when measured in a common currency? __________

2b. In which city is the ale cheaper if one dollar currently buys one euro? __________

TIPS When the prices of goods are sticky in their own currency, a depreciation of home's currency makes all of its goods become more attractively priced relative to foreign goods.

2 Exchange Rates in Practice

ESSENTIAL CONCEPTS

An *exchange rate regime* describes the amount of effort that a government exerts to control the exchange rate. At one extreme, the government may not make any effort whatsoever to control the exchange rate, leaving the exchange rate to be freely determined on foreign exchange markets. This type of regime is known as a *floating (or flexible) exchange rate regime.* At the other extreme, the government may exert as much effort as is necessary to keep the exchange rate constant. This is what is known as a *fixed (or pegged) exchange rate regime.* When looking at exchange rate data, it is easy to distinguish a fixed exchange rate regime from a floating exchange rate regime because the fixed exchange rate is constant, whereas the floating varies (sometimes substantially) from day to day.

Most governments follow a policy toward their exchange rate that lies between the two extremes. For instance, a country might allow its exchange rate to float within a *band,* or range around some rate, but will take action if the exchange rate moves outside this band. Another problem that arises in classifying exchange rate regimes is a country might follow a fixed exchange rate system only to abandon it when the cost of maintaining that regime is high. In this case, the variability of the exchange rate can be very low at some times only to become very high at other times (exchange rate crises).

Countries that wish to maintain very stable exchange rates occasionally adopt a *currency board* system, under which governments tie their hands so as to make it harder to drop the fixed exchange rate. Still other countries dump their currency altogether in favor of adopting a relatively stable currency. Ecuador's adoption of the U.S. dollar as its currency in 2000 is an example of *dollarization.* Finally, some countries collectively share a single currency in a *currency union* so that there is no exchange rate variability across countries within the union. For instance, the euro is shared by an increasing number of European countries.

KEY TERMS

Use the space below to record your notes on the following key terms.

Exchange rate regime ______________________________

____

____

Fixed (or pegged) exchange rate regime ______________________________

____

____

Floating (or flexible) exchange rate regime ______________________________

____

____

Band ______________________________

Dollarization ______________________________

Currency board ______________________________

Currency union ______________________________

Free float exchange rate regime ______________________________

Managed float ______________________________

Exchange rate crises ______________________________

Crawl ______________________________

REVIEW QUESTIONS

Problem 3: Suppose that a country called Home has many trading partners and each trading partner has its own currency.

3a. If each trading partner allows its currency to float, is it possible for Home to fix its exchange rate against all of its trading partners? Explain. ______________________________

3b. If Home wishes to reduce the variability of its effective exchange rate, what kind of exchange rate regime might it choose? Explain. ______________________________

TIPS At this stage of the book, the study of exchange rate regimes is mostly memorization. The distinction between regimes becomes critical when we delve into a government's economic objectives and the policies that it can take to achieve these objectives.

3 The Market for Foreign Exchange

ESSENTIAL CONCEPTS

Exchange rates, or the price of one currency in terms of another, are determined in the *foreign exchange market*. This market, which is a collection of electronically linked corporations and institutions spread out over the globe, is the largest in the world, with over $1.9 trillion worth of transactions per day. Foreign exchange transactions can take many forms, but most of these transactions (90%) are simple *spot contracts* for the immediate delivery of a foreign exchange. The rate at which currencies exchange is known as the *spot exchange rate*.

Newspapers typically report single exchange rates, but in fact different individuals pay different rates. Traders of foreign exchange advertise rates at which they sell a given currency and rates at which they buy the same currency. The difference between these rates is called a *spread*. These spreads, which reflect *market frictions* or *transactions costs,* differ between different clients and are lowest between the main players in the foreign exchange market, the commercial banks. Most foreign exchange transactions involve a transfer of deposits between commercial banks, known as *interbank trading*. In addition to other private players in the foreign exchange market, such as *non-bank financial institutions,* governments often intervene to affect exchange rates. Governments occasionally attempt to suppress foreign exchange trading by imposing *capital controls* or by *intervening* in the market by buying and selling foreign exchange rates.

Finally, there are many types of contracts in the foreign exchange market, including *forwards, swaps, futures,* and *options*. These contracts are termed *derivatives* because their prices are derived at least in part from the spot exchange rate. Because these contracts involve future trades in foreign exchange, they allow investors to hedge against risk or to take risk through speculation.

KEY TERMS

Use the space below to record your notes on the following key terms.

Foreign exchange (forex) market ______________________________

____

____

Spot contract ______________________________

____

____

Spot exchange rate ______________________________

____

____

Spread ____

Market friction ____

Transaction cost ____

Derivatives ____

Forwards ____

Swaps ____

Futures ____

Options ____

Commercial banks ____

Corporations ____

Interbank trading ____

Nonbank financial institutions ____

Capital control ______________________________

Official market ______________________________

Black market ______________________________

Intervention ______________________________

REVIEW QUESTIONS

Problem 4: Why are the spreads facing individuals in their foreign exchange dealing larger than the spreads in transactions between large market players such as commercial banks?

Problem 5: Suppose the dollar–euro spot rate is 1.20 and the current 30-day forward rate is 1.25.

5a. You have an obligation to pay a French supplier of wine 10 million euros in 30 days and have contracted with a U.S. distributor to sell the wine for $13 million. How many dollars can you make if you hedge your risk using the forward market? ______________

5b. Is it possible that you could lose money if you do not hedge your risk? ______________

5c. Suppose that you could get a call option that would allow you to buy euros in 30 days at 1.27. Describe the merits of buying this option relative to using the forward market as in problem 5a.

5d. Now suppose you are a speculator facing the same spot and forward rates as above and you have $1 million. Suppose you bought euros forward. In 30 days, the spot rate for the dollar turns out to be 1.3. How many dollars did you make or lose from this transaction?

5e. Now suppose instead that the spot rate stayed the same over the next 30 days. If you bought euros forward, how many dollars did you make or lose from this transaction?

As in your high school science classes, it is important to keep track of the units. If you are dividing where you should be multiplying or vice versa, then the units won't be correct, and you will spot your mistake.

TIPS

4 Arbitrage and Spot Exchange Rates

ESSENTIAL CONCEPTS

Although foreign exchange traders are spread out across the globe, fiber optic cables, computers, and the principle of *arbitrage* ensure that there is a single, unified foreign exchange market. For instance, suppose that a dollar will buy more euros in New York than in Paris. A quick investor will buy euros in New York, transfer them to Paris, and then sell them at the higher rate prevailing there. By buying low and selling high, the investor makes a profit, and her actions tend to raise the price of euros in New York and lower it in Paris until the prices are the same.

Arbitrage also ensures that all *cross rates* are the same in every market. Suppose a dollar investor wants to buy British pounds. The investor could buy pounds directly, or the investor could buy euros with the dollars and then use the euros to buy pounds. If the foreign exchange market is in equilibrium (and if transactions costs were very low), it should not matter which way the dollar investor obtains the pounds because the cross rates should be identical. That is, $E_{\$/£} = E_{\$/€}E_{€/£}$. If instead, $E_{\$/£} > E_{\$/€}E_{€/£}$, then the dollar investor could get more pounds by buying euros and then selling them for pounds than by buying them directly. Further, the investor could sell the pounds for dollars and actually make dollars in the transaction.

Whenever arbitrage opportunities arise, the market quickly adjusts to eliminate them. The foreign exchange market is in *equilibrium* when there are no opportunities for arbitrage (the so-called *no-arbitrage condition*). Finally, although there are over 160 different currencies in the world, almost all trading activity is limited to a handful of developed country currencies such as the U.S. dollar. This is because such *vehicle currencies* are sufficiently traded so that all traders are willing to buy or sell them, whereas the same cannot be said for rarely traded currencies.

KEY TERMS

Use the space below to record your notes on the following key terms.

Arbitrage

Equilibrium ______________________________

____

____

No-arbitrage condition ______________________________

____

____

Cross rate ______________________________

____

____

Vehicle currency ______________________________

____

____

REVIEW QUESTIONS

Problem 6: Suppose $E_{\$/€} = 3/2$ and $E_{\$/£} = 2$. What cross rate between the euro and the pound must prevail if there are no arbitrage opportunities?

a. $E_{€/£} = 3/4$

b. $E_{€/£} = 3$

c. $E_{£/€} = 3/4$

d. $E_{£/€} = 1/3$

Problem 7: Suppose that $E_{¥/\$} = 100$, $E_{\$/€} = 2$, so

a. $E_{€/¥} = 0.005$

b. $E_{\$/¥} = 0.01$

c. $E_{¥/€} = 200$

d. All of the above

e. None of the above

Problem 8: Suppose that you have \$1 million. While staring at the computer screen, you notice that $E_{\$/£}=2$, $E_{¥/\$}=100$, and $E_{¥/£}=220$. If you have time for three quick trades, what dollar profit could you realize? Explain. ______________________________

____

____

Problem 9: Could capital controls cause an exchange rate to be different in two cities? Explain.

____

____

TIPS

Problem 8 demonstrates how arbitrage opportunities can arise when the cross rates are inconsistent. Don't expect to make money this way, however, unless you have a supercomputer and lightning-speed communications!

5 Arbitrage and Interest Rates

ESSENTIAL CONCEPTS

When arbitrage is possible, then two equivalent items must have the same price. In financial markets this means that two assets, even if they have different names, must have the same price as long as the characteristics for which investors care are the same. In general, there are three characteristics of an asset that are important to investors: (1) its *rate of return,* (2) its *liquidity,* and (3) its *risk*. If two assets are identical in terms of their liquidity and risk, then they should have the same rate of return if investors are free to choose assets. For the bulk of this book, it is assumed that assets are identical in terms of their risk and liquidity so that we may apply simple, no-arbitrage conditions.

In comparing the rates of return for assets whose price, and whose return, is valued in different currencies, we must distinguish between the asset's local currency return and its return in foreign currencies. For instance, the dollar return on a foreign deposit is equal to the interest rate on the foreign deposit (local return) plus the percent change in the dollar exchange rate between the time when the foreign deposit was purchased and the time when the deposit was sold (rate of depreciation). A dollar-based investor must decide how to convert foreign currency earnings back into dollars. On the one hand, they might use the forward market to "lock in" the percent change in the exchange rate. On the other hand, they may calculate the expected return on the foreign asset (rather than its "for sure" return), using the expected rate of dollar depreciation over the period that they own the foreign deposit. The first method avoids risk, but if investors care only about expected returns, then the two methods should be equivalent in the eyes of an investor choosing between them.

The *uncovered interest parity (UIP)* condition holds when arbitrage equalizes the expected common currency return on domestic and foreign deposits. For instance, if the interest rate on U.S. deposits is $i_\$$ and the interest rate on British deposits is i, then the (approximated) uncovered interest parity condition is

$$i_\$ = i_£ + \Delta E^e_{\$/£} / E_{\$/£},$$

where the right-hand side of this equation is the expected dollar rate of return on British deposits (the local currency return i and the *expected rate of depreciation* of the dollar $\Delta E^e_{\$/£} / E_{\$/£}$) and the left-hand side of this equation is the dollar return on U.S. deposits. It is very important to understand that the home country return on assets denominated in a foreign currency has two components, whereas the return on home assets only has one. This means that if the interest rate in the U.S. exceeds the interest rate in the U.K. then the dollar must be expected to depreciate relative to the pound. If in addition one knew the expected future spot rate, then one could compute the spot rate that must prevail on foreign exchange markets.

KEY TERMS

Use the space below to record your notes on the following key terms.

Forward exchange rate ______________________________

____

____

Covered interest parity ____

____

____

Expected exchange rate ____

____

____

Uncovered interest parity ____

____

____

Rate of return ____

____

____

Risk ____

____

____

Liquidity ____

____

____

Expected rate of return ____

____

____

Expected rate of depreciation ____

____

____

Forward premium ____

____

____

REVIEW QUESTIONS

Problem 10: Suppose that the U.S. nominal interest rate is 5% and the European nominal interest rate is 3%. The dollar is expected to

a. appreciate by 8%
b. depreciate by 8%
c. appreciate by 2%
d. depreciate by 2%
e. depreciate by 15%

Problem 11: Suppose the interest rate in U.S. deposits is 5% per year and the interest rate in Germany is 3% a year. The spot rate for the dollar is $E_{\$/€} = 1.25$. You are an investor with $1 million.

11a. Suppose you used all of your dollars to buy euro deposits. What would the value of these deposits (in euros be)? __________

11b. At the end of one year, how many euros would you have? __________

11c. If instead you used your $1 million to buy U.S. deposits, how many dollars will you have at the end of the year? __________

11d. What would the one-year forward exchange rate have to be for you to be indifferent between these two investments? Assume that international transactions are costless. Explain.

____

____

11e. Why would the forward rate that is your answer to 11d be a coherent predictor of the spot rate one year in the future? __________

____

____

11f. Given your answer to 11e, what is the expected rate of depreciation of the dollar?

____

____

11g. If dollar deposits were perceived to be more liquid and less risky than German deposits, then how might you adjust your answer to 11e? __________

____

____

Problem 12: Assume that uncovered interest parity holds. In the following questions, assume that all other exogenous variables (everything but the exchange rate) stay the same.

12a. What would happen to the spot rate $E_{\$/£}$ if British interest rates rose? __________

____

____

12b. If U.S. interest rates rise, what must happen to the expected dollar return on British deposits? __________

____

____

12c. What could explain a sudden depreciation in the dollar if U.S. and British rates do not change? Explain. __________

____

____

TIPS

The uncovered interest parity condition is perhaps the most important equation in the international macroeconomics portion of the book. The sooner you understand its implications, the better off you will be.

The uncovered interest parity condition is used to predict the spot rate *given* the expected future spot rate. That is, the current price in the market must reflect what people expect the spot rate to be in the future. This is the source of frequent confusion.

Expectations about the future can change instantaneously and without warning, and when they do, they affect the economy immediately. The study of how expectations are formed is central to macroeconomics.

Note that the approximation used in the book is fine for small interest rates. As interest rates get higher, the approximation can become quite poor.

14

Exchange Rates I: The Monetary Approach in the Long Run

Overview

In the long run, countries experiencing rapid money supply growth also tend to experience high inflation and a depreciating currency. This chapter presents a model that relates the price level and exchange rate in the long run to monetary conditions and so is called the *monetary approach to the exchange rate*. The monetary approach is built on three assumptions: (1) Goods are freely traded, (2) assets are freely traded, and (3) prices are perfectly flexible. This last assumption in particular gives the model a distinctly long-run flavor.

Because goods can be freely traded in international markets, goods' prices must be the same in all countries when measured in the same currency, a situation known as purchasing power parity (PPP). Given price levels in each country, the long-run exchange rate, therefore, must adjust to ensure PPP. Because assets are freely traded, uncovered interest parity holds. When uncovered interest parity and PPP hold simultaneously, a country's interest rate must be equal to the world *real interest rate* plus the expected rate of inflation in that country. Standard monetary theory and the assumption of perfectly flexible prices complete the model. Prices and the rate of inflation depend on the level and rate of change of nominal money supply and of real money demand.

Because the model relies on perfectly flexible prices, it is not an appropriate model of the exchange rate in the short run. However, because short-run models of the exchange rate rely on expectations of the long-run level of the exchange rate, the long-run model is a crucial input into short-run models of the exchange rate.

1 Exchange Rates and Prices in the Long Run: Purchasing Power Parity and Goods Market Equilibrium

ESSENTIAL CONCEPTS

Suppose that we lived in a world in which goods and services cross borders without cost and prices are perfectly flexible. In such a world, the prices of all goods and services would have to be the same in every country when measured in the same currency, for if they were not, arbitrageurs would buy goods in low cost locations and sell them in high cost locations. The *law of one price (LOOP)* states exactly this. Further, the prices of any given basket of goods when measured in a common currency would have to be the same in every country. This is the idea of *absolute purchasing power parity (APPP).*

It is useful to define the relative price of a basket of goods and services in two different countries as

$$q_{Japan/US} = (E_{\$/¥} \times P_{Japan}) \; / \; P_{US}$$

where P_{US} is the price in dollars of the basket in the U.S., P_{Japan} is the price in dollars of the basket in Japan, and $E_{\$/¥}$ is the dollar–yen exchange rate. This relative price is called the real exchange rate because it describes the rate at which real (rather than nominal) things are traded. When $q_{Japan/US}$ is less than one, the U.S. dollar is said to be *overvalued* because it takes less than one American basket to buy the exact same basket in Japan. The dollar is said to be *undervalued* when the real exchange rate is above one. APPP holds only when the real exchange rate is equal to one.

A similar concept that can hold even when the real exchange rate is not equal to one is *relative purchasing power parity (RPPP),* which relates rates of change in exchange rates to the difference of rates of change in inflation rates across countries. When the real exchange rate is constant, changes in prices in Japan or in the U.S. must be offset by changes in the nominal exchange rate to keep the relative price of Japanese and U.S. goods constant. Hence, if inflation is higher in Japan than in the U.S., $P_{Japan} \; / \; P_{US}$ is increasing, so $E_{\$/¥}$ must be falling at the same rate.

Concepts of PPP are important because they provide a method of predicting the exchange rate. Suppose that APPP were to hold. Then, given price levels P_{Japan} and P_{US}, the exchange rate that makes PPP hold is

$$E_{\$/¥} = P_{US} \; / \; P_{Japan}.$$

In such a world, all we would need to do to forecast exchange rates would be to forecast price levels. In the real world, APPP is a reasonable approximation over a horizon of many years or decades, but it has little to say about short-run movements in exchange rates. This is because the real world involves many frictions in the international exchange of goods, including (1) transaction costs (such as trade barriers such as tariffs and quotas and shipping costs), (2) the existence of non-traded goods, (3) imperfect competition that gives firms pricing power in different markets, and (4) stickiness in domestic price levels. Despite its drawbacks as a predictor of exchange rates in the short run, APPP is useful because it provides a guide to the exchange rate in the long run, where long run is defined as the time necessary for prices to be flexible and for firms to overcome trade barriers.

KEY TERMS

Use the space below to record your notes on the following key terms.

Monetary approach to exchange rates ____________________________

Law of one price (LOOP) ____________________________

Purchasing power parity (PPP) ______________________________

Real exchange rate ______________________________

Real appreciation ______________________________

Real depreciation ______________________________

Overvalued ______________________________

Undervalued ______________________________

Absolute PPP ______________________________

Inflation ______________________________

Relative PPP ______________________________

REVIEW QUESTIONS

Problem 1: The price of an apple in the U.S. is \$1, and the exchange rate is $E_{\$/€} = 1.25$. If international trade in apples is frictionless, then what must the price of an apple be in Germany?

Problem 2: Suppose that in the United States, the price of guns is \$200 and the price of doctor's visits is \$150. Suppose that in France, the price of guns is €300 and the price of doctor's visits is €50. Guns and doctor's visits receive an equal weight in a basket of goods.

2a. Is there any exchange rate that would make the law of one price hold for both goods?

2b. What is the dollar price of a U.S. basket?

2c. What is the euro price of a French basket?

2d. If $E_{\$/€} = 1$, does APPP hold?

2e. Suppose that $E_{\$/€}$ were to increase. Would this result in a real appreciation or a real depreciation of the dollar?

2f. Provide any value of $E_{\$/€}$ such that the dollar is overvalued. Explain.

2g. If, instead, guns received a weight of 3/5 in an American basket and only 2/5 in a French basket, would APPP hold when $E_{\$/€} = 1$?

TIPS

Problem 2 provides an example in which the law of one price may not hold for any good but APPP holds. Problem 2g gets at a practical problem in comparing price levels across countries: if different countries use different baskets, then different exchange rates are implied for PPP than if all countries used the same baskets.

Problem 3: Home's currency (the dollar) is depreciating relative to Foreign's currency (the blot) at a rate of 5%. Home's inflation rate is 8%. Foreign's inflation rate is 2%. Is Home's real exchange rate appreciating or depreciating and by how much?

Problem 4: (Multiple Choice) Suppose that money growth in Home is 6%, and money growth is 1% in Foreign. Then,

a. Home's real exchange rate is appreciating.

b. RPPP would predict that Home's currency will buy fewer of Foreign's currency next year.

c. Real interest rates are higher in Home than in Foreign.

d. none of the above

Problem 5: (True or False. Please explain your answers.) Assess the following statement, "relative PPP is a better approximation of reality when one of the two countries is suffering hyperinflation and the other is not."

____

____

Problem 6: (Multiple Choice) If the law of one price holds for all goods and services, then

a. The real exchange rate must equal one.

b. APPP holds.

c. RPPP holds.

d. all of the above

e. none of the above

Problem 7: (Multiple Choice) Which of the following might explain why PPP doesn't hold in the short run?

a. Prices are sticky.

b. Governments impose tariffs on goods.

c. Firms face imperfect competition.

d. all of the above

e. none of the above

2 Money, Prices, and Exchange Rates in the Long Run: Money Market Equilibrium in a Simple Model

ESSENTIAL CONCEPTS

Given information on future price levels in the long run, PPP can be used to make predictions on future exchange rates. Developing a model of future price levels is therefore the focus of this section. In the long run, price levels are determined by equilibrium in the market for *money.* To keep the analysis simple, we assume that the *central bank* directly determines the *money supply, M. Money demand, M^d,* is generated by its three key uses: as a store of value, as a unit of account, and as a medium of exchange. Specifically, we rely on the *quantity theory of money* to provide a demand equation: the demand for money is equal to the price level (P) multiplied by real output (Y) multiplied by a constant ($\overline{L}$) or

$$M^d = P \times Y \times \overline{L}$$

The idea is that people require a certain amount of money to carry out their transactions, and the volume of transactions is equal to the size of the economy, $P \times Y$. In equilibrium, the price must adjust so that the demand for money is equal to the supply of money made available by the central bank. Hence, for the United States, the price level should be

$$P_{US} = \frac{M_{US}}{\overline{L}Y_{US}}$$

A similar equation would have to hold for each other country.

By combining the APPP equation with one price equation for each country, we have the *fundamental equation of the monetary approach to exchange rates:*

$$E_{\$/¥} = \left(M_{US} \big/ M_{Japan}\right)\left(\frac{\overline{L}_{Japan} Y_{Japan}}{\overline{L}_{US} Y_{US}}\right)$$

This equation tells us what matters for the exchange rate in the long run. For instance, holding everything else equal, an increase in real output in the United States will tend to raise money demand and so will lower prices in the United States. Lower prices in the United States will make the dollar appreciate. Other variables that matter are the relative supplies of monies in the two countries and the proportion of real income that people want to hold in real balances. The fundamental equation can also be expressed in terms of changes over time. For instance, holding fixed all other variables, if the U.S. money supply grows faster than real output, then it must be that the dollar depreciates at the rate at which M_{US} / Y_{US} is increasing.

KEY TERMS

Use the space below to record your notes on the following key terms.

Money ____________________

Central bank ____________________

Money supply ____________________

Money demand ____________________

Quantity theory of money ____________________

Fundamental equation of the monetary model of the price level ____________________

Fundamental equation of the monetary model to exchange rates ____________________

REVIEW QUESTIONS

Problem 8: Home's money supply grows at 3% and Foreign's grows at 5%. Home's currency should

a. appreciate at a rate of 2%

b. appreciate at a rate 3/5%

c. depreciate at a rate of 5/3%

d. depreciate at a rate of 2%

e. none of the above

Problem 9: In the United States, the level of real output is 100 units, and money demand is equal to half of nominal output. In Japan, the level of real output is 80 units, and money demand is equal to three quarters of nominal output. The money supply in the United States is $25. Assume that the monetary approach to the exchange rate holds.

9a. What is the price level in the United States? ______________________

9b. If $E_{\$/¥}$ is 0.1, then what is the price level in Japan? ______________________

9c. Given your answer to 9b, what is the supply of money in Japan? ______________________

Problem 10: Suppose that U.S. money growth is 5% per year and U.S. economic growth is 3% a year. Suppose that money growth in Canada is 7% a year and the economy is shrinking at 2% a year.

10a. What is the inflation rate in the U.S.? ______________________

10b. What is the inflation rate in Canada? ______________________

10c. What does the monetary approach to the exchange rate predict about the movement of the Canadian dollar? ______________________

TIPS

The monetary approach to the exchange rate is really pretty simple. In the long run, PPP (one equation) and the quantity theory of money (two equations) hold. End of story.

3 The Monetary Approach: Implications and Evidence

ESSENTIAL CONCEPTS

This short section presents evidence on the link between money growth rates and exchange rates movements. As predicted by the monetary approach, there is a tight positive relationship between monetary growth rates and inflation rates over the long run. In addition, the evidence presented in this section suggests an improvement that can be made over the approach presented in the previous section. In the previous section, we assumed that money demand was a fixed proportion of nominal output. The evidence suggests that real money demand (M / P) falls dramatically as inflation rates become very high. The empirical evidence motivates a need to generalize our model of money demand, which is done in the next section.

KEY TERMS

Use the space below to record your notes on the following key term.

Hyperinflation ____

____

____

REVIEW QUESTIONS

Problem 11: Provide an intuitive explanation for why demand for real money balances collapses during periods of very rapid money growth (hyperinflations).

____

____

Problem 12: There are two countries, Home and Foreign. Assume that the monetary approach to the exchange rate accurately predicts the exchange rate. What is the effect on Home's exchange rate if Home's demand for liquidity constant, $\bar{L}$, were to decrease?

____

____

4 Money, Interest, and Prices in the Long Run: A General Model

ESSENTIAL CONCEPTS

In this section the monetary approach to the exchange rate is improved by using a more standard, and realistic, model of money demand. Rather than assume that money demand is a fixed, constant proportion of nominal output, it is assumed that the liquidity ratio is a decreasing function of the interest rate i. In this case the demand for real balances can be written

$$\frac{M^d}{P} = L(i) \times Y,$$

where $L(i)$ is the liquidity ratio (decreasing in i) and Y is real output. The assumption that demand for real balances falls with the interest rate is motivated by the following logic: Because money does not pay interest, an increase in the interest rate on deposits increases the opportunity cost of holding money and so reduces demand for money. Put another way, individuals are more willing to put up with the inconvenience of having their money tied up in less liquid assets if the return to those assets is higher.

Now that we have the interest rate in the money demand equation, we need to have a model of what determines interest rates when prices are perfectly flexible. The first step is to notice that the uncovered interest parity condition links interest rate differentials to expected changes in the exchange rate which relative PPP links in turn to differences in inflation rates across countries. For two countries, Home and Foreign, this means

$$i_H - i_F = \pi_H^e - \pi_F^e$$

If the interest rate is higher in Home than in Foreign in the long run, then it must be because Home's expected rate of inflation (π_H^e) is higher than the expected rate of inflation in Foreign (π_F^e). This is known as the *Fisher effect*.

Up until now, we have spoken exclusively about nominal interest rates, which tell us the return of a deposit in terms of money. The *real interest rate* is the return of an investment in terms of how much goods and services we can buy, or the nominal interest rate minus the rate at which money is expected to lose value relative to goods and services: $r = i - \pi^e$. By rearranging the Fisher effect equation, we find that as long as uncovered interest parity and RPPP hold, then real interest rates must be the same in both countries and equal to the *world real interest rate*. Arbitrage in financial and goods markets causes *real interest parity*. For a country taking real interest rates as given (determined on world markets), the nominal rate of interest must be equal to the sum of the fixed world interest rate r and the expected local rate of inflation π^e. In the long run the rate of inflation is equal to the rate of money growth less the rate of output growth. This observation completes the model. Monetary policy simultaneously determines (1) price levels and inflation rate, (2) interest rates, and (3) exchange rates and depreciation rates.

Relative to the monetary approach described earlier in the chapter, the more general approach differs in two important respects: (1) Changes in monetary policy alter the nominal interest rate, and (2) changes in this interest rate have direct effects on price levels and exchange rates. Hence, a sudden change in money growth rates leads to a leap in prices and exchange rates that work through changes in money demand that in turn are induced by changes in interest rates.

KEY TERMS

Use the space below to record your notes on the following key terms.

Real money demand function ______________________________

____

____

Fisher effect ______________________________

____

____

Real interest rate ______________________________

____

____

Real interest parity

World real interest rate

REVIEW QUESTIONS

Problem 13: In a long-run equilibrium, Country A has an interest rate of 10%, whereas Country B has an interest rate of 7%. Real output in each country is growing at 2% per year. The money growth rate in Country B is 6%.

13a. Which country has a higher inflation rate?

13b. Which country has a higher real interest rate?

13c. What is the inflation rate in Country B?

13d. What is the money growth rate in Country A?

Suppose that the central bank of Country B announces at time *T* that the country will henceforth have a money growth rate that will be 2% per year.

13e. What is the effect of the decrease in money growth on nominal interest rates in Country B at time *T*?

13f. What is the effect of the decrease in money growth rate on the liquidity ratio $L(i)$?

13g. What is the effect of the decrease in the money growth rate on the price level in Country B?

13h. What is the effect of the decrease in the money growth rate on Country B's exchange rate at time *T*?

13i. How does Country B's exchange rate change after time *T*?

Problem 14: (Multiple Choice) Which of the following could explain a sudden depreciation in a country's exchange rate?

a. a decrease in the expected rate of inflation
b. an increase in the real level of output
c. a decrease in the money supply
d. all of the above
e. none of the above

Problem 15: (Multiple Choice) Suppose that prices are perfectly flexible. Home is growing at a faster rate than Foreign. Money supplies in each country are fixed. Which of the following is predicted by the monetary approach?

a. Home's currency is depreciating relative to Foreign's currency.
b. The exchange rate is constant between the two countries.
c. Interest rates are lower in Home than in Foreign.
d. none of the above

Problem 16: Imagine a world with two countries, Home and Foreign. Home's currency is the dollar and Foreign's currency is known as the blot. Trade in goods and in assets is completely free. In a long-run equilibrium Home's money supply grows at 10%, and Foreign's money supply grows at 5%. Assume that *prices are perfectly flexible.*

16a. At what rate does Home's currency appreciate or depreciate? ____________________

____

____

16b. Is Home's interest rate higher or lower than Foreign's interest rate and by how much?

____

____

Suppose that at time *t*, Home's central bank announces that henceforth the money growth rate will be 5% instead of 10%.

16c. What happens to Home's interest rate at time *t?* ____________________

____

____

16d. What happens to Home's exchange rate at time *t?* ____________________

____

____

16e. After time *t*, what happens to the value of the dollar relative to the blot?

____

____

TIPS

In the long-run model presented in this section, a country with higher inflation also has a higher interest rate. This positive relationship between interest rates and inflation rates may seem backwards to students raised in low inflation countries. The important thing to remember is that this is a *long-run model.*

The more complicated money demand equation affects only some of the model's predictions. An increase in money growth rate will alter the rates of changes of prices and exchange rates in the same way, but the "jump" at time *T* happens only because of the adjustment in the interest rate.

5 Monetary Regimes and Exchange Rate Regimes

ESSENTIAL CONCEPTS

High and/or volatile inflation rates tend to destabilize an economy and retard its long-run growth. For this reason, countries frequently set an *inflation target* and structure their monetary policies to achieve this target. To meet long-run targets, governments often choose a *monetary regime* featuring a *nominal anchor.* The government chooses a nominal variable to target the rate of inflation in prices, another nominal variable.

Three potential nominal anchors are considered. The first nominal anchor is motivated by RPPP. Rearranging the basic RPPP equation yields

$$\pi_H = \frac{\Delta E_{H/F}}{E_{H/F}} + \pi_F$$

While Home's government has no control over Foreign's inflation rate, it can target the rate at which its currency appreciates or depreciates relative to Foreign's currency. In this case, the government imposes an *exchange rate target*. For instance, a government could fix its exchange rate vis-à-vis a low-inflation country so that Home's inflation becomes equal to Foreign's inflation rate. The second nominal anchor is the growth rate of the nominal money supply. The fundamental equation for the price level implies that the rate of inflation is

$$\pi_H = \mu_H - g_H,$$

where g_H is the rate of growth of real output and μ_H is the nominal anchor, the growth rate of the money supply. In this case the government announces a *money supply target*. Finally, the Fisher effect implies another nominal anchor, the nominal interest rate. Because the nominal interest rate is equal to the real interest rate plus inflation, and because the real interest rate is fixed from the perspective of the government, a government that controls nominal interest rates *(inflation plus interest rate target)* also controls inflation rates.

The key problem facing a government pursuing a monetary regime with a nominal anchor is that the government must be committed to its target. This means that a country with a nominal anchor sacrifices monetary policy autonomy in the long run. To be able to pursue such a policy (which often has negative, short-run political consequences), it is often necessary for *central bank independence* so that government officials cannot order the bank to change its policies.

KEY TERMS

Use the space below to record your notes on the following key terms.

Inflation target ______________________________

____

____

Nominal anchors ______________________________

____

____

Monetary regime ______________________________

____

____

Exchange rate target ____

Money supply target ____

Inflation target plus interest rate policy ____

Central bank independence ____

REVIEW QUESTIONS

Problem 17: Suppose the economy of Home grows at a rate of 3% and inflation in Foreign runs at a rate of 5%. Home's inflation target is 2%.

17a. What exchange rate target would allow Home to meet its inflation target?

17b. What money supply target would allow Home to meet is inflation target?

17c. If foreign interest rates are 8%, what interest rate should the government target to meet its inflation target? ____

17d. If the growth rate of real output were to fall to 1%, how would the government have to adjust its nominal anchor policies? Consider all three nominal anchors. ______________

15

Exchange Rates II: The Asset Approach in the Short Run

Overview

The theory of exchange rates is built on two arbitrage arguments. First, if assets can be traded internationally, then the expected return of deposits in each country should be the same when measured in the same currency. Second, if goods and services can be procured from different countries, then the exchange rate should adjust so that a given basket of goods and services has the same price in each country when measured in the same currency. The first arbitrage condition, uncovered interest parity (UIP), applies at all times. Given interest rates on deposits in different countries, UIP tells us how much a currency is expected to change in value over a given time horizon, but it does not tell us the expected level of the exchange rate. The second arbitrage condition, purchasing power parity (PPP), is assumed to apply only after some time has passed. Given expected levels of prices in the long run, PPP tells us the level of the exchange rate to expect in the long run. Only by using the two arbitrage conditions together can we predict the effect of various economic shocks on the level of spot exchange rate.

In order to make use of either arbitrage condition, we need to be able to predict monetary phenomenon. To use PPP to forecast expected exchange rates, we need to be able to forecast expected price levels. To use the UIP condition (in conjunction with PPP) to forecast spot rates, we need to be able to predict interest rates in the short run. By assuming that price levels are sticky in the short run but perfectly flexible in the long run, we are able to use the same equation for equilibrium in the money market to predict the effect of economic changes on both the short-run interest rate and the long-run price level.

Once formulated, our complete theory of exchange rate determination shows that permanent monetary and economic shocks have much larger impacts on the exchange rate than do temporary monetary and economic shocks. That is, permanent shocks result in exaggerated exchange rate movements in the foreign exchange (FX) market that cause the exchange rate to overshoot its new long-run level. Finally, our theory can be used to demonstrate some fundamental results in international economics: Countries that allow free trade in financial assets cannot independently target both the exchange rate and the money supply simultaneously.

1 Exchange Rates and Interest Rates in the Short Run: UIP and FX Market Equilibrium

ESSENTIAL CONCEPTS

The asset approach to exchange rates is built upon the idea of arbitrage in the international market for financial assets. According to UIP, free international trade in financial assets causes the common currency return on deposits denominated in different currencies to be equal. For the case of the United States and Europe, the UIP condition is

$$i_{\$} = i_{€} + (E^{e}_{\$/€} - E_{\$/€}) \ / \ E_{\$/€}$$

which states that the expected return on European deposits measured in dollars (the right-hand side) is the same as the return on deposits in the United States (the left-hand side). This equation can be rewritten

$$E_{\$/€} = E^{e}_{\$/€} \ / \ (1 + i_{\$} - i_{€}).$$

The UIP equation is the *fundamental equation of the asset approach to exchange rates* because it predicts the current spot rate $E_{\$/€}$ as a function of three different monetary variables: (1) interest rates in a "home" country, $i_{\$}$; (2) interest rates in a "foreign" country, $i_{€}$; and (3) expected future spot exchange rates, $E^{e}_{\$/€}$, between home and foreign currencies. If an investor can predict these three monetary variables, then the investor can predict the exchange rates. The *FX market diagram* expresses this information in graph form: Given interest rates and expected future exchange rates, there is only one exchange rate that equalizes home and foreign returns.

KEY TERMS

Use the space below to record your notes on the following key terms.

Asset approach to exchange rates ____

Fundamental equation of the asset approach to exchange rates ____________________

FX market diagram ____

REVIEW QUESTIONS

Problem 1: Suppose that the U.S. nominal interest rate is 5% and the European nominal interest rate is 3%. The dollar is expected to

a. appreciate by 8%

b. depreciate by 8%

c. appreciate by 2%

d. depreciate by 2%

e. none of the above

Problem 2: Suppose that the interest rate on one-year deposits is 4% in the United States and 2% in the European Union. UIP is assumed to hold.

2a. How much is the U.S. dollar expected to depreciate against the euro over the next year?

2b. If the current U.S. dollar–euro exchange rate were one, then what does the foreign exchange market expect the spot rate to be next year?

2c. Suppose that the American interest rates increased to 5% at time *T.* Has the expected rate of dollar depreciation over the next year increased or decreased? Explain.

2d. If the future expected spot rate remained unchanged after the increase in interest rates at time *T,* what happens to the spot rate at time *T?*

2e. In the diagram below, draw the expected dollar return on American and European assets as a function of the American exchange rate before and after the change in American interest rates.

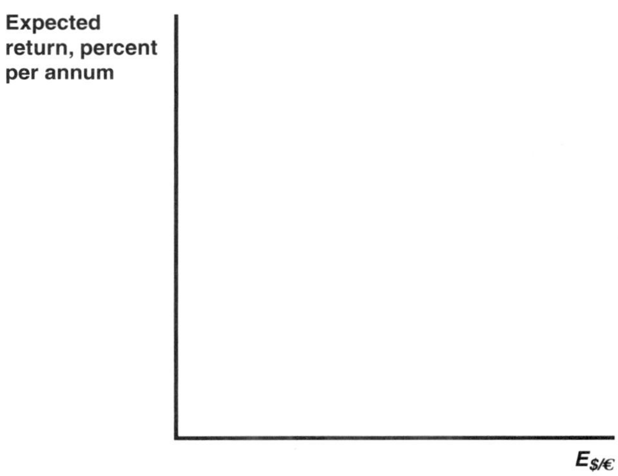

Suppose that U.S. interest rates are 4% per year and E.U. interest rates are initially at 2% per year. At time *T,* E.U. interest rates rise to 3% per year.

2f. At time *T,* does the rate of expected depreciation of the dollar increase or decrease? Explain.

2g. If at time *T* the expected future spot rate were to remain unchanged, what would happen to the current spot rate? Explain.

2h. In the diagram below, draw the expected dollar return on U.S. and European assets as a function of the U.S. exchange rate before and after the change in European interest rates.

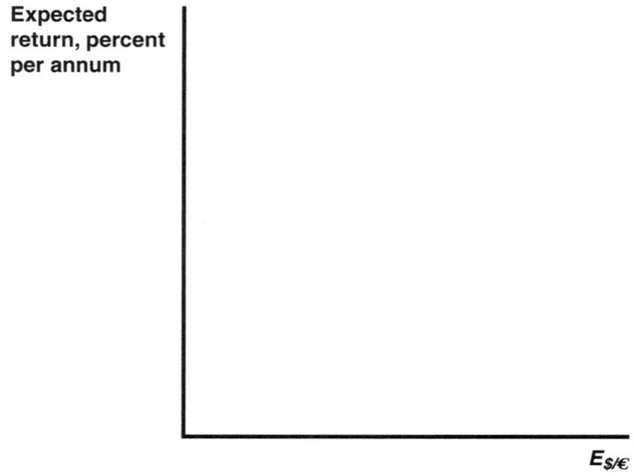

TIPS

Problem 2 highlights an important feature of equilibrium in the foreign exchange market. The increase in the U.S. interest rate caused the dollar to appreciate when it occurred, but it also led to a greater rate of expected depreciation of the dollar over the next year.

The diagrams above may look like supply and demand diagrams, but they are not. If the return on one kind of asset is greater than the return of an equivalent asset, then *everybody* prefers the asset with the higher return, and markets must adjust.

Notice that the textbook takes the trouble to review the concept of UIP in great detail. This demonstrates the importance of this material!

2 Interest Rates in the Short Run: Money Market Equilibrium

ESSENTIAL CONCEPTS

Economists have long observed that an increase in the money supply will eventually lead to an increase in prices if everything else is held equal. They have also observed that the process of price adjustment can be quite slow and that prices may reasonably be treated as fixed in the short run. In this section, we explore the implications of this short-run *nominal rigidity* for our model of exchange rates.

Equilibrium in the money market requires (in both the short and long run) that the supply of real balances be equal to the demand for real balances:

$$\frac{M}{P} = L(i)Y$$

If the price level P and real output Y are fixed in the short run, then equilibrium in the money market requires that interest rate (i) adjust so that people are willing to hold the quantity of money supplied by the central bank (M). A temporary increase in M has no long-run effect on the price level P, but it must lower the interest rate. A permanent increase in the money supply must also reduce the interest rate in the short run because prices are fixed in the short run, even if it will increase prices (i.e., cause inflation) in the long run. Note that temporary or permanent changes in Y have the opposite effects of temporary or permanent changes in M.

KEY TERMS

Use the space below to record your notes on the following key term.

Nominal rigidity ______________________________

____

____

REVIEW QUESTIONS

Problem 3: Consider a country that has seen its money supply (*M*) and real gross domestic product (GDP) (*Y*) fixed for a long time. At time *T*, *M* unexpectedly increases by 10% and stays constant at that level forever. Assume that prices are sticky in the short run.

3a. What is the effect of the increase in *M* on prices at time *T*? ______________________________

____

____

3b. What is the effect of the increase in *M* on the interest rate at time *T*? Use the following diagram to answer the question. ______________________________

____

____

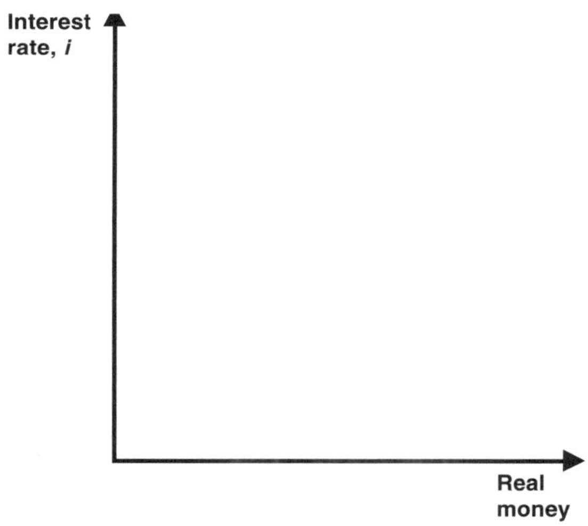

3c. What is the long-run effect of the increase in *M* on the price level?

____

____

3d. What is the long-run effect of the increase in *M* on the interest rate?

____

____

Problem 4: Consider a country that has seen its money supply (*M*) and real GDP (*Y*) fixed for a long time. At time *T*, *Y* unexpectedly increases by 10% and stays constant at that level forever. Assume that prices are sticky in the short run.

4a. What is the effect of the increase in *Y* on prices at time *T*?

____

____

4b. What is the effect of the increase in *Y* on the interest rate at time *T*? Use the following diagram to answer the question.

____

____

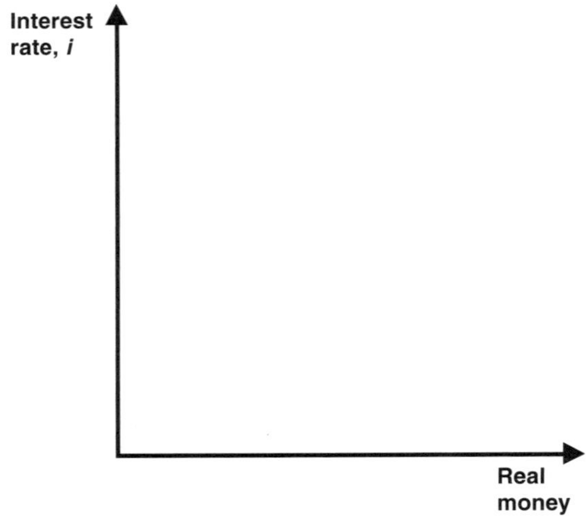

4c. What is the long-run effect of the increase in *Y* on the price level?

____

____

4d. What is the long-run effect of the increase in *Y* on the interest rate?

____

____

TIPS

How long is the short run? How short is the long run? These are quite reasonable questions that students frequently ask. There is no easy answer to this question because the degree to which prices are sticky is not well understood.

Problems 3 and 4 emphasize the difference between the long run and the short run. Note that there is no long-run effect on the interest rate because in the long run, money supply growth is expected to be zero, so there is NO long-run inflation.

Note that in problems 3 and 4, real and nominal interest rates move in the same direction in the short run because the Fisher effect only applies to the long run.

3 The Asset Approach: Applications and Evidence

ESSENTIAL CONCEPTS

In this section, the UIP condition (or fundamental equation to the asset approach to exchange rates) is combined with the money market equilibrium condition in order to consider the effect of temporary changes in the money supply on the exchange rate. Because the changes in money supply are temporary, they have no effect in the long run and so do not have an effect on the expected future spot rate. However, because price levels are fixed in the short run, changes in the money supply or in real output in either of the two countries cause interest rate differentials to change and so affect the current spot rate through the UIP condition.

REVIEW QUESTIONS

Problem 5: Use the diagrams below to show the effect of a temporary increase in Home's money supply on its interest rate and on its exchange rate. (All nominal variables are in terms of Home dollars.) Explain your diagram.

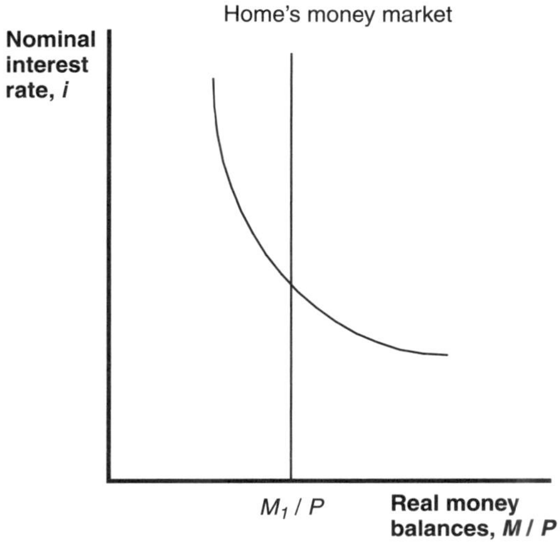

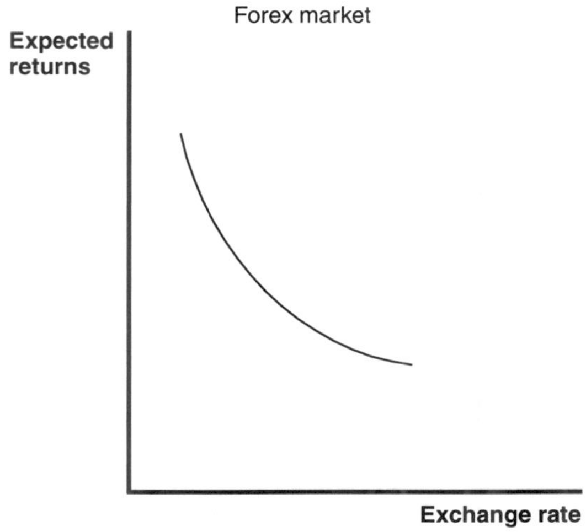

Problem 6: Use the diagrams below to show the effect of a temporary increase in Home's GDP (Y) on its interest rate and on its exchange rate. Explain your diagram.

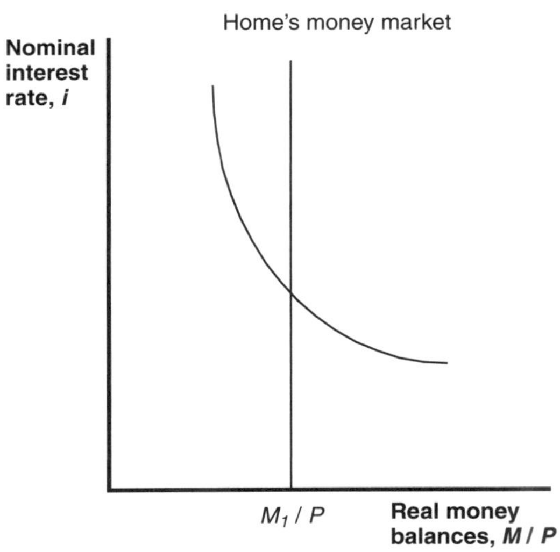

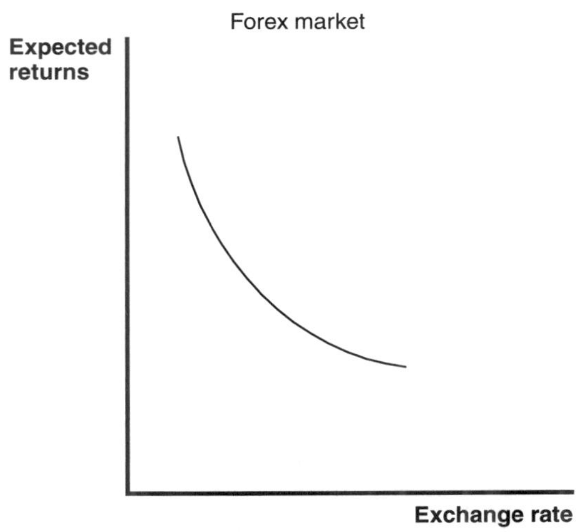

Problem 7: Use the diagrams below to show the effect of a temporary increase in Foreign's GDP (Y) on its interest rate and on the exchange rate (Home dollars in terms of Foreign). Explain your diagram. ____

____

____

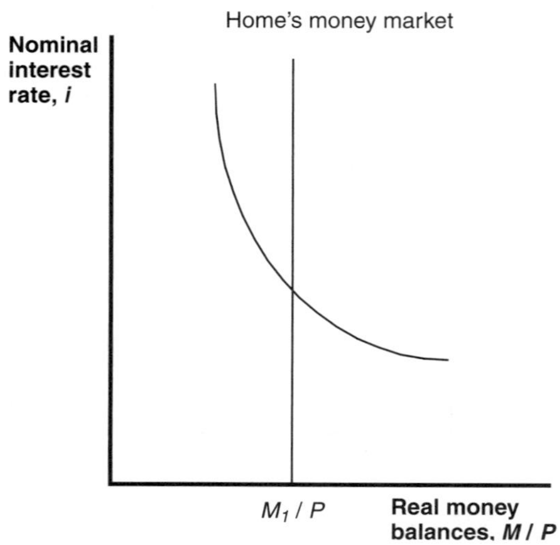

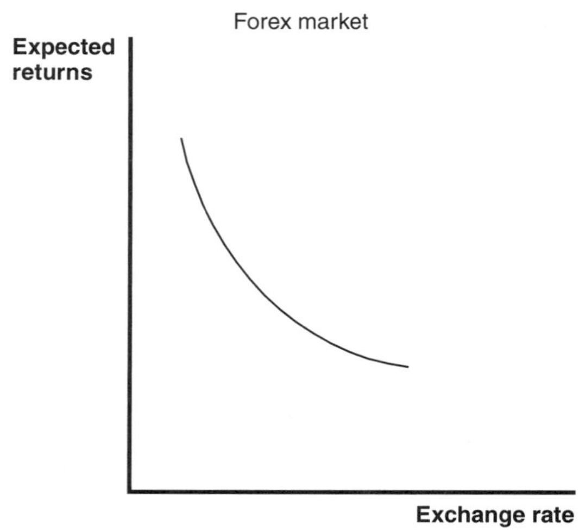

TIPS

Because capital controls prevent arbitrage in expected returns, they break the link between interest rates and exchange rates.

It is crucial that the word "temporary" appeared in each question. Permanent changes would alter future expectation and would have an additional impact on the exchange rate as we will learn in the next section.

The problems also highlight the fact that temporary shocks to the supply of real balances (M / P) can have similar effects to temporary shocks to the demand for real balances caused by changes in Y.

Sometimes it is asserted in the media that "strong economies have strong currencies." The problems above rationalize this type of statement. An increase in real output raises money demand and so leads to an appreciation of the currency.

4 A Complete Theory: Unifying the Monetary and Asset Approaches

ESSENTIAL CONCEPTS

The complete theory uses the equilibrium in the home and foreign money markets to solve for all three variables in the fundamental equation of the asset approach to the exchange rate. In the short run, monetary equilibrium plus sticky prices determines the interest rate in each country. In the long run, monetary equilibrium plus the Fisher effect determines expected price levels in each country, and PPP translates expected price levels into an expected future spot rate.

The benefit of the complete model is that it allows us to analyze the effect of *permanent* shocks to the money supply or to real output. Permanent shocks have the same short-run effects on interest rates as temporary shocks. For instance, a permanent increase in Home's money supply lowers the interest rate on Home's deposits in the short run. A permanent increase in the money supply (or decrease in real output) must also increase the long-run price level and so must lead to higher (depreciated) exchange rate in the long run. Foreign exchange arbitrageurs immediately anticipate the long-run change in the exchange rate: The expected future spot rate shifts up at the **same** time that interest rates fall. Thus, the short-run and long-run effects reinforce one another in immediate response of the exchange rate to the permanent increase in the money supply, leading to a sharp jump in the exchange rate. The sharp depreciation is followed by a slow appreciation of the exchange rate toward its new long-run level as the short-run effect dissipates. Thus, the complete model predicts that permanent shocks to the money supply cause the exchange rate to *overshoot* its new long-run level. An immediate implication of the model is that countries that do not have compelling nominal anchors are likely to experience very high levels of exchange rate volatility.

KEY TERMS

Use the space below to record your notes on the following key term.

Overshooting ______________________________

REVIEW QUESTIONS

Problem 8: True, False, or Uncertain. Please explain your answer.

8a. If prices were perfectly flexible, then exchange rates would never overshoot. __________

8b. Suppose the dollar were to depreciate sharply. Does this necessarily imply an increase in the expected rate of inflation in the United States? __________

8c. Does an increase in interest rates predict an exchange rate appreciation? __________

Problem 9: Consider the exchange rate of the dollar for the euro. Suppose that the liquidity function $L(i)$ is the same in both the United States and in Europe. The United States and Europe are initially in long-run equilibrium. The money supply in the United States is \$1,000, and its real GDP is 10,000 units. The price level in the United States in this long-run equilibrium is \$1 per unit of output. The money supply in Europe is €500, and its real GDP is 5,000 units. At time T, the United States permanently (and unexpectedly) increases its money supply to \$1,500. At time T, interest rates in the United States fall from 5% to 2%.

9a. What is the exchange rate prior to time T? __________

9b. What is the expected future spot rate at time T (after permanent increase in the money supply)? __________

9c. What are interest rates in Europe before and after time *T*? ______

9d. What is the expected rate of depreciation/appreciation of the dollar immediately following time *T*? ______

9e. What is the exchange rate immediately after the permanent increase in the money supply in the United States at time *T*? ______

Problem 10: Suppose the spot exchange rate between the U.S. dollar and the euro is well described by the "overshooting" model. The countries are in a long-term equilibrium when U.S. GDP increases permanently. No other exogenous variables change.

10a. What is the immediate impact of this "shock" on the U.S. interest rate and on the current spot exchange rate? Use the following diagrams to answer the following questions.

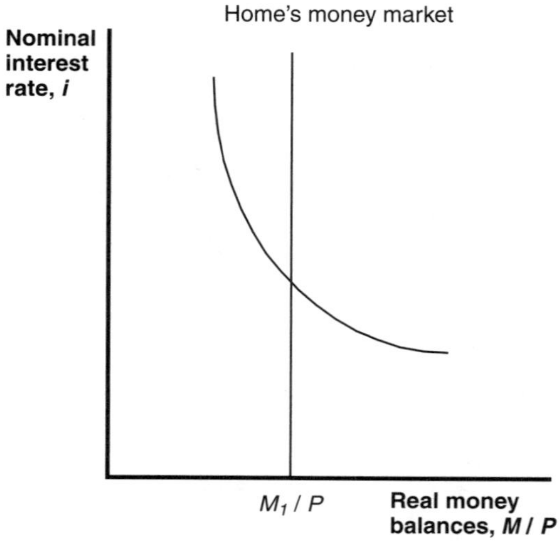

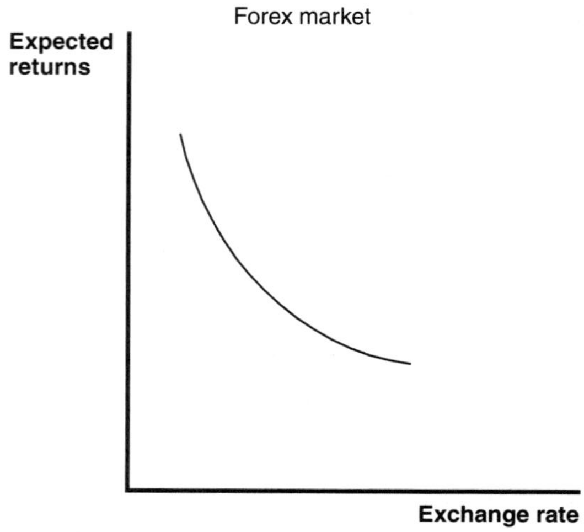

______

10b. What is the impact of this "shock" on the U.S. interest rate, the U.S. price level, and the spot exchange rate in the long run?

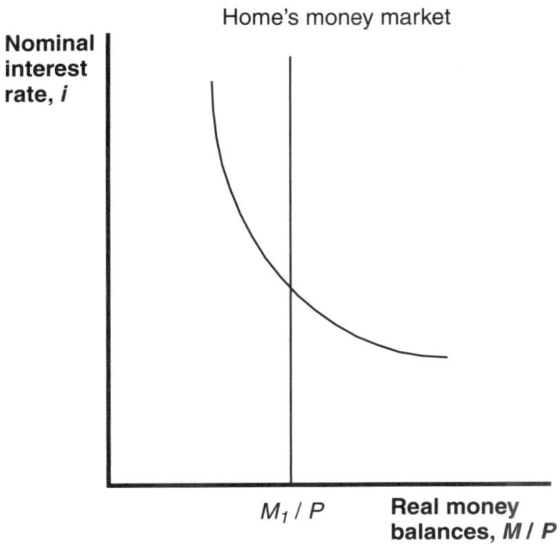

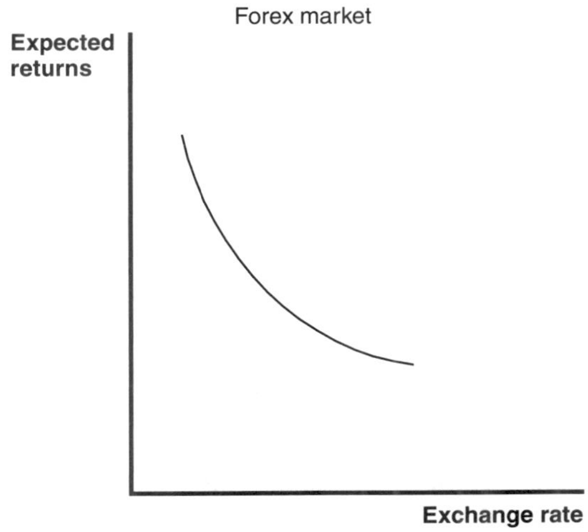

____

____

____

TIPS

Note that the problems in this chapter do not consider cases of long-run inflation as in Chapter 14. This simplifies matters considerably because the long-run interest rate is unchanged.

Problem 9 illustrates using numbers to "overshoot" of the exchange rate.

Problems 9 and 10 are quite involved, but they do make use of most of the concepts discussed in this chapter. If you can understand each step, you are in good shape.

5 Fixed Exchange Rates and the Trilemma

ESSENTIAL CONCEPTS

As noted in Chapter 13, countries often choose to fix their exchange rate. What does the complete theory tell us about fixed exchange rate systems? A key result in all of international economics is that a country that fixes its exchange rate and does not impose capital controls loses its control over its monetary policy. To see this, note that under a fixed exchange rate system, the expected depreciation of the exchange rate becomes zero. This means that the interest rate in the country fixing its exchange rate must be exactly equal to the interest rate abroad. The textbook shows that this happens in practice: When Denmark fixes its currency relative to the euro, Danish interest rates converge to Eurozone levels. Using the money demand equation, it is then clear that a country with a fixed exchange rate does not have control over its money supply in the short run because there is only one level of the money supply that keeps interest rates equal to foreign levels. In summary, a country that maintains free mobility of capital faces a dilemma: it can either choose its exchange rate or its money supply, but it cannot do both.

When a country imposes capital controls, it becomes much harder for investors to arbitrage differences in interest rates across countries, and the UIP condition no longer holds. Hence, a country that imposes capital controls regains control over both its exchange rate and its money supply at least in the short run. Why don't countries impose capital controls? Countries benefit from being able to engage in international borrowing and lending with the rest of the world. (This is a topic that is covered in detail in Chapter 17.) Therefore there exists a *trilemma*. It is impossible to choose both the exchange rate and the money supply and to allow for capital mobility simultaneously.

KEY TERMS

Use the space below to record your notes on the following key term.

Trilemma ________________________________

REVIEW QUESTIONS

Problem 11: Suppose PPP holds in the long run. In the *long run,* does a country imposing capital controls have control over both the exchange rate and the money supply? Explain.

Problem 12: Suppose that Home has pegged its currency to Foreign's currency. Home and Foreign allow free movement of capital.

12a. If Foreign's interest rate increases, what happens to the interest rate in Home?

12b. Suppose that Home's national output (Y) increases. What must happen to the money supply in Home?

TIPS

Problem 11 makes the point that control over the money supply and exchange rate separately is only relevant in the short run. In the long run, PPP ties down the exchange rate as a function of the money supply via the price level.

16

National and International Accounts: Income, Wealth, and the Balance of Payments

Overview

Sound economic policy relies on careful measurement of economic phenomenon. The national income and product accounts and the balance of payments are the two intricate accounting systems used to keep track of the circular flow of payments within and between economies. This chapter explains these important accounting concepts and uses them to analyze features of the international economic system. The chapter begins by deriving a series of "identities" that relate national income to national expenditure and to transactions with foreigners. The national income identity will play a crucial role in our macroeconomic analysis later in the book.

The balance of payments accounts summarize a nation's transactions with the rest of the world. The balance of payments accounts balance because every transaction involves an exchange of two items of equal value so that each credit is offset by a debit. The balance of payments can be used to analyze how a nation finances the gap between the value of its expenditures and its output. The financial flows that are documented in the balance of payments are one component of the evolution of countries' external wealth. A country that consistently spends less than it produces will tend to see its wealth increase. A country that persistently spends more than it produces will tend to see its wealth decline. Finally, the importance of capital gains and losses on countries' external wealth are analyzed.

The chapter is very vocabulary-intensive and requires a substantial amount of memorization. The subject matter is important to master because economic analysis of real-world phenomenon requires sensible measurement, as the chapter illustrates through a series of case studies.

1 Measuring Macroeconomic Activity: An Overview

ESSENTIAL CONCEPTS

This section presents an overview of the accounting systems used by macroeconomists to trace economic activity. To introduce the accounting concepts, the chapter begins with the simple case of the closed economy (i.e., an economy that is not linked to the outside world). In a closed economy, one can easily perceive a "circular flow of payments." In the national product and income accounts of a closed economy, the amount that the consumers of final goods and service spend, or *gross national expenditure (GNE),* is equal to the value of goods and services created, or *gross domestic product (GDP).* GDP, which only counts *value added* at each stage of production by the economy's productive resources (factors), generates income, or *gross national income (GNI),* which is paid out to domestic citizens. Completing the circle of payments, GNE is financed out of GNI.

In an open economy, the links with the rest of the world in an open economy occur at each stage along the circular flow of payments. Not all expenditures on goods and services are spent on domestically produced goods and services. For instance, some expenditure falls on *imports,* whereas some of the value of final output is sent abroad as *exports.* The difference between GNE and GDP is equal to the difference between exports and imports, which is called the *trade balance.* GDP and GNI tend to differ in an open economy because some of the value of domestic output accrues to foreign factors, such as the domestic affiliates of multinational firms or foreign workers working in the country (an example of *factor service imports*), and some of the national income is generated by the country's factors working abroad, such as interest payments on outstanding loans to foreigners (an example of *factor service exports*). Hence, GNI is equal to GDP plus *net factor income from abroad (NFIA).* Finally, the amount of disposable income has to be adjusted because some of the income may either be given away to residents of foreign countries or residents of foreign countries may transfer income to domestic residents *(net unilateral transfers [NUT]).* A key feature of an open economy is that international trade in assets allows a country's GNE to exceed its *gross national disposable income (GNDI)* (net borrowing) or vice versa (net lending).

The various international transactions that account for the difference between GNE and GNDI sum to the *current account* balance. How does a country that spends more than its income finance that expenditure? The answer is that this additional expenditure is financed via the sale of assets to foreign residents. The difference between GNDI and GNE is equal to the sum of the *financial account* and the *capital account.* The flows in the domestic circle of payments (*national income and product accounts*) require that the current account is equal to the sum of the financial account and the capital account (*balance of payments accounts*).

KEY TERMS

Use the space below to record your notes on the following key terms.

Gross national expenditure (GNE) ____________________

____

____

Value added ____________________

____

____

Gross domestic product (GDP) ______________________________

Gross national income (GNI) ______________________________

Imports (IM) ______________________________

Exports (EX) ______________________________

Trade balance (TB) ______________________________

Factor service imports (IM_{FS}) ______________________________

Factor service exports (EX_{FS}) ______________________________

Net factor income from abroad (NFIA) ______________________________

Net unilateral transfers (NUT) ______________________________

Gross national disposable income (GNDI) ______________________________

Current account (CA) ______________________________

Asset exports (EX_A) ______________________________

Asset imports (IM_A) ______

Financial account (FA) ______

Capital account (KA) ______

National income and product accounts ______

Balance of payments accounts ______

REVIEW QUESTIONS

Problem 1: True or false. Please explain your answers.

1a. A country whose GNE exceeds its GDP must be a net exporter of assets. ______

1b. A country's GNE must equal its GDP if it does not engage in trade with the rest of the world. ______

1c. A country's GDP is equal to the total value of the sales of all its firms.

1d. The current account balance is equal to the difference between GNDI and GNE.

TIPS

Figure 16-2 in the textbook is an excellent resource for understanding the structure of the national income and products account and the balance of payments accounts. If you understand and memorize this figure, you are well on your way to doing well in this chapter.

In the "good old days," the financial and capital accounts were collectively called the capital account. Many instructors will have "grown up" using the older nomenclature, and it may slip into their lectures.

2 National Accounts: Product, Expenditure, and Income

ESSENTIAL CONCEPTS

This section carefully describes how the various aggregate measures of economic activity called the national accounts are constructed and provides a flavor of how these measures are used. In a closed economy, aggregate economic activity can be measured by three equivalent measures. The *expenditure approach* counts total spending on final goods and services in the economy (GNE), the *product approach* measures the total value of final goods produced by domestic firms (GDP), and the *income approach* measures the total income of payments to productive factors in the economy (GNDI). In an open economy GNE, GDP, and GNDI differ from each other because of flows between the domestic economy and the rest of the world. These measures are defined in the textbook as a series of identifies. For instance, the *GDP identity* is GDP = GNE + TB, where TB is the trade balance; and the *gross national disposable income identity* (also known as the *national income identity*) is GNDI = $Y = C + I + G + CA$ = GNE + CA, where CA is the current account balance. The national income identity is the most meaningful of the various measures of national well-being because it most closely corresponds to the resources available to a nation's households.

These identities demonstrate that governments must carefully measure a country's transactions with foreigners (the trade balance, net factor income accounts, and unilateral transfers) to measure changes in national welfare. A key example given in the textbook of how the distinction between GDP and GNDI matters is the experience of Ireland. Because of the large portion of Irish manufacturing that is undertaken by foreign multinationals, Irish GDP is much larger, and traditionally faster growing, than Irish GNDI.

Another important identity that can be derived from the national income identity is the *current account identity,*

$$S = I + CA$$

which states that a country's *national savings* ($S = Y - C - G$) must be equal to the sum of investment (I) and the current account balance. A country that wishes to reduce its current account deficit must either increase its savings or reduce its investment. Savings can be broken down further into *private savings* ($Y - C - T$) and *government savings* ($G - T$). In the case of the United States, the rapid increase in the size of its current account deficit is driven by a decline in both private savings and government savings, whereas investment has remained roughly unchanged.

KEY TERMS

Use the space below to record your notes on the following key terms.

Expenditure approach ____

____

____

Product approach ____

____

____

Income approach ______________________________

GDP identity ______________________________

GNI identity ______________________________

GNDI identity ______________________________

National income identity ______________________________

National savings ______________________________

Current account identity ______________________________

Private savings ______________________________

Government savings ______________________________

REVIEW QUESTIONS

Problem 2: Would you expect GNDI to be greater than or less than GDP in a country in which many of the country's citizens work abroad? Explain. ______________________________

Problem 3: Holding fixed other components of aggregate demand, what impact does an increase in investment have for the current account balance? ______________________________

Problem 4: Is it possible that a country's GDP exceeds both its GNE and its GNI?

Problem 5: Consider the following aggregates for a fictional country for the year 2006: $I = 10$, $C = 80$, $G = 10$, and its GNDI is 95.

5a. What is the country's GNE?

5b. What is the country's national savings?

5c. What is the country's current account balance?

5d. Was the country a net exporter or importer of assets?

Problem 6: How might a country's birth rate affect its current account?

Problem 7: Imagine a world in which all countries are identical except that one country has an unusually good investment climate. Would you expect this country to run a current account surplus or deficit?

Problem 8: True, False, or Uncertain. Please explain your answers.

8a. Holding everything else in the economy constant, a decrease in government spending lowers the current account deficit (or raises the surplus).

8b. After everything in the economy is allowed to adjust, a decrease in government spending lowers the current account deficit (or raises the surplus).

Problem 9: (Multiple choice) Home's GDP rises by more than its GNDI. Which of the following are possible explanations?

a. Home has received government aid from a foreign country.
b. A foreign multinational affiliate has just begun production in Home.
c. Many of Home's workers work overseas.
d. all of the above
e. none of the above

3 Balance of Payments Accounts: International Transactions

ESSENTIAL CONCEPTS

The national income accounts include all international transactions involving goods, services, factor services, and non-market transactions. The full set of all international transactions, including trade in financial assets and capital transfers, is documented in a country's balance of payments (BOP) accounts. Because the current account was already covered in detail in the last section, the focus of this section is primarily international trade in assets. There are two types of asset exports. First, domestic residents can sell claims on their home country to foreigners (thereby increasing the country's *external liabilities*). Second, domestic residents can sell claims on foreigners to foreigners (thereby decreasing the country's *external assets*). Similarly, domestic residents can import assets by buying back claims on themselves or by buying claims on foreigners. The actual "movement" that occurs in the asset trade is movement from one country's ownership of an asset to another country. The capital account works similarly but involves capital transfers rather than market transactions.

Now consider the links between the flows of goods, services, income, and assets. By the construction of the national accounts, GNE is equal to the sum of GNDI, the financial account balance *(FA),* and the capital account balance *(KA):*

$$GNE = GNDI + FA + KA$$

which states that expenditure is financed out of earnings or asset sales. GNDI is in turn equal to GNE plus the current account:

$$GNDI = GNE + CA$$

Combining the two expressions yields the *BOP identity,*

$$CA + FA + KA = 0$$

which states that all international transactions either expand or contract the resources available for expenditure in the home country so that a deficit (surplus) in one type of transactions must be balanced by a surplus (deficit) in a different type of transaction. If every international transaction were accurately recorded, the balance of payments would sum to zero by construction because each market transaction involves the exchange of two items of equal value. Every time a domestic resident conducts a transaction with a foreign resident, there must be a *BOP credit* that is exactly offset by a *BOP debit* recorded by balance of payments statisticians. For instance, suppose a Home firm imports a tractor from a Foreign firm and pays by running down its account at a foreign bank. The import is recorded as a debit in the current account balance, and the reduction in the claims on a foreign bank is treated as an asset export in the financial account.

In the aggregate, a country that runs a current account surplus is either running up its stock of claims of foreigners or it is disposing of its liabilities held by foreigners. By convention such a country is called a *(net) lender* because it is in essence providing purchasing power to foreigners. Because the country is buying more assets abroad than foreigners are buying in that country, this is also referred to as a *financial outflow.* A country that runs a current account deficit is called a *(net) borrower* because its GNE is greater than its GNDI. The gap between expenditure and income is filled by a *financial inflow* from abroad.

KEY TERMS

Use the space below to record your notes on the following key terms.

External asset ______________________________

____

____

External liability ____

____

____

BOP identity ____

____

____

BOP credit ____

____

____

BOP debit ____

____

____

(Net) lender ____

____

____

(Net) borrower ____

____

____

Financial outflow ____

____

____

Financial inflow ____

____

____

Official settlements balance ____

____

____

Nonreserve financial account ____

____

____

REVIEW QUESTIONS

Problem 10: (Multiple Choice) Home has a current account deficit of $8 billion, and the capital account balance is zero. Which of the following must be true?

a. Home must have a financial account surplus.

b. Home must be exporting assets to the rest of the world.

c. GNDI must be less than GNE.

d. all of the above

e. none of the above

Problem 11: True, False, or Uncertain. Please explain your answers. A country that runs a current account surplus must be running up its stock of claims on foreigners. ____________

____

____

Problem 12: How are the balance of payments accounts of a country with a fixed exchange rate system likely to differ from the accounts of a country with a floating exchange rate system?

____

____

____

Problem 13: Classify the following transactions on the U.S. balance of payments. Make sure to record both the debit and credit and the appropriate categories (export of good, import of asset on financial account, etc.). Do not concern yourself with the magnitudes involved.

13a. A U.S. manufacturer sells a tractor to a Russian company and the Russian company pays by drawing a check on a Russian bank. ____________

____

13b. A U.S. bank makes a loan to an Argentine firm and creates a deposit in the name of the Argentine firm. ____________

____

13c. The U.S. government gives food to Zimbabwe. ____________

____

13d. A U.S. consultant is paid by a British firm. The British firm draws the funds from its account at an American bank. ____________

____

13e. A middle-aged British rock star plays a free concert for an American audience.

____

13f. A Chinese student enrolls in an American university and pays by drawing on an account at an American bank. ____________

____

13g. An Argentine bank makes an interest payment on its debt to an American bank. It pays by drawing on its deposit at the American bank. ____________

____

13h. An interest payment comes due on an Argentine bank's debt to an American bank. The Argentine bank fails to make the payment. ____________

____

TIPS

Balance of payments accounting questions are tedious, but it is important to understand the structure of these accounts.

Problem 13h can be confusing because it doesn't seem to involve two items of equal value. There are always two items; you must persevere to identify both parts.

4 External Wealth

ESSENTIAL CONCEPTS

A country's *external wealth* is the difference between the value of its total claims on foreigners and the value of foreigners' total claims on it. If this number is positive, we say that the country is a *net creditor.* If this number is negative, as is the case for the United States, we say that this country is a *net debtor.* There are three ways that a country's net wealth can change. First, the financial account of a country records net changes in assets. As is the case for an individual, a country whose income exceeds its expenditure will accumulate external wealth. Second, as wealth is stored in financial assets and the prices of assets vary from day to day, a country's external wealth changes due to valuation effects. For instance, a country that invests in low-risk but low-return assets will tend to see few surprise changes in its external wealth, experiencing little in the way of capital gains or losses. A country that invests in higher-risk but higher-yielding foreign assets could see large swings in its external wealth, but on average it will see a positive valuation effect. Finally, a country's external wealth can change if it receives gifts of assets or if it gives assets to others. A prime example of this sort is debt forgiveness of developing country debt by developed countries.

In practice the size of the valuation effects can be very large relative to the size of financial flows. As pointed out in the textbook, the United States has done well in terms of valuation effects: In 2006 the United States experienced a net financial inflow of $804 billion but saw its external wealth fall by only $302 billion as it enjoyed a half trillion dollar capital gain! These gains were driven in part by the fact that much of the financial claims on the United States are denominated in dollars, whereas most of the financial claims of the United States on foreigners are denominated in other currencies. As the dollar has fallen, the value of its assets has risen relative to the value of its liabilities.

KEY TERMS

Use the space below to record your notes on the following key terms.

External wealth ______________________________

____

____

Net creditor ______________________________

____

____

Net debtor ______________________________

____

____

REVIEW QUESTIONS

Problem 14: Home's current account balance and external wealth (in $ billions) for the years 1990–2000 are shown in the table below. Home's external wealth at the end of 1989 was zero. All external wealth figures are measured at the end of the year (so they include the effects of any borrowing during the year). Assume that KA = 0.

Year	Current Account Balance ($ Billions)	External Wealth at Year End ($ Billions)
1990	10	6
1991	3	10
1992	1	12
1993	−4	8
1994	−7	4
1995	−2	5
1996	3	6
1997	8	15
1998	12	22
1999	10	29
2000	16	43

14a. If there had been no valuation effects over the period, what would Home's external wealth be? ______________________________

____

____

14b. What was the total size of valuation effects over the period? ______________________________

____

____

14c. Which years (if any) were valuation effects positive? ______________________________

____

____

Problem 15: At the end of 2001, Home residents owned €10 million worth of Foreign bonds and $10 million worth of foreign deposits. In turn, foreigners owned $25 million worth of Home bonds. The exchange rate of the dollar in terms of euros was 1. Over the course of 2002, the dollar depreciated against the euro to the rate of 1.5, and Home ran a current account deficit of $5 million. What was Home's external wealth at the end of 2002?

____

____

Problem 16: The external assets of the United States are greatly exceeded by its external liabilities. The NFIA for the United States is positive. Why do economists have difficulty reconciling these two facts? ______________________________

____

____

17

The Balance of Payments I: The Gains from Financial Globalization

Overview

This chapter presents a theory of international trade in financial assets. Countries gain from access to international financial markets in many ways. First, countries can lessen the hardship associated with abrupt, negative shocks to output by borrowing on international markets in order to smooth the necessary reduction in consumption over time. Alternatively, countries can buy foreign assets as precautionary savings should their economy experience a slump. Second, countries can borrow from abroad to finance large investment projects that would require substantial reductions in consumption otherwise. Hence, international financial markets increase the efficiency of international investment. Finally, a country can purchase capital located in other countries in order to diversify its world portfolio and therefore insure itself against shocks. Access to the international financial market does not eliminate the impact of shocks entirely, however, in the sense that any debts incurred must be repaid with interest: A country's behavior must be consistent with its long-run budget constraint (LRBC). Moreover, international financial markets cannot be used to eliminate the risks associated with negative shocks that hit all countries equally.

As intuitive as the theory is, economists have long been surprised by the limited extent to which countries engage in international asset trade. For instance, rich countries invest little in poor countries, where one might expect the return on capital to be higher. Further, investors typically hold their wealth in domestic assets even when they could improve the performance of their portfolios substantially if they held more foreign assets.

1 Intertemporal Macroeconomics

ESSENTIAL CONCEPTS

A country that has access to international financial markets need not spend the same amount as it produces in any given year. For instance, in the absence of international borrowing and lending, a bad harvest would lower the amount of grain available for consumption in an agrarian economy by the amount of the reduction in output. Were the country able to borrow from abroad, it could use the loan to buy foreign grain. Although international markets can break the link between expenditure and income in any given year, it is still true that a country is constrained in its spending ability by the need to finance interest payments on its debt.

This section introduces the concept of the LRBC. To keep things simple, we consider a *small open economy* that takes the *world interest rate* r as given. Ignoring the possibility of transfers and capital gains or losses on a country's external wealth, W, the change in a country's wealth from year $N-1$ to year N is

$$\Delta W_N = W_N - W_{N-1} = rW_{N-1} + TB_N$$

This equation states that the change in external wealth is equal to the investment income on its wealth last year plus any additional borrowing or lending made necessary by the trade deficit or surplus. Reorganizing this equation, we find that

$$W_N = (1 + r)W_{N-1} + TB_N$$

To get a sense of the constraints facing a country over time, consider the two-period example discussed in the textbook. The country begins its life with wealth W_{-1} and exists for two periods, 0 and 1. At the end of the second period, the world ends, so there is no point in having any external wealth. If the country's trade balance in period 0 is TB_0 and its trade balance in period 1 is TB_1, then we have the following equation budget constraint facing our country:

$$-(1 + r)W_{-1} = TB_0 + TB_1 \,/\, (1 + r)$$

This equation states that the *present value* of all present and future trade balances (the right-hand side) must be equal to the present value of a country's initial external wealth. Extending this logic to the long-run case in which there are an infinite number of periods, we can derive the *LRBC* facing the country:

$$-(1 + r)W_{-1} = TB_0 + \frac{TB_1}{(1 + r)} + \frac{TB_2}{(1 + r)^2} + \frac{TB_3}{(1 + r)^3} + \cdots$$

In the case in which the trade balance after time zero is always constant at the level $\overline{TB}$, then the *perpetual loan* formula can be used to simplify this expression to

$$-(1 + r)W_{-1} = TB_0 + \frac{\overline{TB}}{r}$$

which will be a useful simplification for the later sections of the chapter.

What does all this mean? Because the trade balance is equal to the difference between gross domestic product (GDP) and gross national expenditure (GNE) under the model's assumptions, the budget constraint implies that the present value of the country's expenditure must be equal to the value of its starting external wealth plus the present value of its production. In this concrete sense, a country must "live within its means" even if it sometimes spends more than it produces.

Although the LRBC is a useful and important tool, many real-world examples suggest that the assumptions need some modification. For instance, the United States is less constrained than other countries because it can borrow at a lower interest rate than it lends. Developing countries find the opposite to be true, as world financial markets charge a risk premium. Further, many developing countries experience *sudden stops,* which occur when financial markets become unwilling to lend to a country.

KEY TERMS

Use the space below to record your notes on the following key terms.

Long-run budget constraint (LRBC) ______

Small open economy ______

World real interest rate ______

Present value ______

Perpetual loan ______

Sudden stops ______

REVIEW QUESTIONS

Problem 1: Consider a small open country that has an initial external wealth of 100 units. The world real interest rate is 10% in each of an infinite number of years.

1a. Suppose the country runs a trade deficit of 10 units in period 0. What is the level of external wealth at the end of year 0? ______

1b. Could the country run a trade deficit of 10 units in perpetuity? Explain. ______

1c. Suppose the country runs a trade deficit of 12 units in period 0. What is the level of external wealth at the end of year 0? ______

1d. Could the country run a trade deficit of 12 units in perpetuity? Explain. ______

TIPS Occasionally the news will report that a country's pattern of current account deficits is "unsustainable." This means that the deficits could not be repeated indefinitely because they would violate the country's LRBC.

Problem 2: Home is a country that exists for only two periods. It starts with external wealth of zero. In each period (0 and 1) it is able to produce 100 units of output, and it can borrow or lend with the rest of the world at a real interest rate of 10%.

2a. What is the present value of Home's production? ______

2b. What is the largest number of units that Home could consume in the first period and still satisfy its budget constraint? ______

2c. If Home has a trade deficit in the first period, can it also have a trade deficit in the second period? ______

2d. What is the largest trade surplus that Home could run in a single period? ______

2e. What is the largest trade deficit that Home could run in a single period? ______

Problem 3: A country has an initial external wealth of –50, and it will produce 10 units of output in each of an infinite number of future years. The interest rate in each year is 10%.

3a. What is the present value of the country's resources? ______

3b. If the country were to consume a fixed amount every year (including the current year), how much could it consume? ______

3c. What is the maximum that the country could consume in the current year if it were willing to never consume again? ______

TIPS

Problems 2e and 3c are technically correct according to the assumptions of the model but highlight an unrealistic feature of the model. If all of the country's resources were used to pay interest on external debt, leaving no output for consumption, surely the country would renege (default) on its international commitments.

Problem 4: Why would you expect a (net) debtor country to have a deficit on its net factor income from abroad? ______

Problem 5: Explain how the U.S. does not seem to be as constrained as other countries due to the phenomenon of "exorbitant privilege." ______

Problem 6: Which of the assumptions of the simple intertemporal model appear to fail in the case of developing countries? ______

2 Gains from Consumption Smoothing

ESSENTIAL CONCEPTS

When a country experiences a temporary shock to its ability to produce, such as a hurricane, war, or recession, consumption must fall, but the extent to which consumption has to adjust depends on whether the country is able to borrow or lend on international financial markets. A country that shuts itself off to borrowing and lending with the rest of the world can only consume the output that it produces so that consumption must immediately fall by the full amount of the shock. A country that can borrow abroad can reduce the magnitude of disruptive adjustments to consumption by borrowing now and repaying the debt later. The loss of consumption due to a negative shock is smoothed over time rather than incurred all at once. If r^* is the world interest rate, ΔQ is the temporary loss of output due to the negative shock, and ΔC is the change in consumption in every year forever made necessary by the shock (consumption is smoothed), then $\Delta Q - \Delta C$ is the amount borrowed at the time of the shock, $r^*(\Delta Q - \Delta C)$ is the interest payment that must be made every year, and ΔC is the amount that the trade balance must rise to fund the interest payments. Because $r^*(\Delta Q - \Delta C) = \Delta C$, the amount that consumption must fall in every period is

$$\Delta C = (r^* / (1 + r^*))\Delta Q < \Delta Q.$$

If consumption smoothing were not possible, the country would have to reduce its consumption all at once by ΔQ. Consumption smoothing is a fundamental advantage to allowing international trade in financial assets. Note that financial markets cannot ease the pain of all negative shocks: Permanent shocks that reduce output forever require a country to adjust immediately.

Even countries that may have difficulty borrowing abroad because of high levels of existing debts or poor reputations for repayment of loans can still insure themselves against temporary shocks by building up *precautionary savings.* Many countries keep large holdings of foreign securities at their central bank, known as *foreign reserves,* for exactly this purpose. Other countries choose to open *sovereign wealth funds* to invest their stock of foreign assets at a higher return.

KEY TERMS

Use the space below to record your notes on the following key terms.

Precautionary savings ______________________________

____

____

Foreign reserves ______________________________

____

____

Sovereign wealth funds ______________________________

____

____

REVIEW QUESTIONS

Problem 7: True or False. Please explain your answer. Access to international credit markets allows countries to avoid the impact of negative shocks.

____

____

Problem 8: Home is a small open economy that takes the world interest rate of 10% as given. Home can produce 100 units of output each year, and its consumers wish to have smooth consumption over time (same level year in and year out). Finally, Home has no external wealth initially. At time T, Home is hit by a temporary (one-year) reduction in output of 10 units.

8a. If Home is not free to borrow on world markets, how much does consumption fall in year T? ______________________________

____

____

8b. If Home is free to borrow on world markets, how much does consumption fall in year T? ______________________________

____

____

8c. If Home borrows to smooth consumption, how much interest does Home pay each year (assuming the principal is never paid off)? ______________________________

____

____

8d. How would your answer to 8b change if the shock had been permanent rather than temporary? ______________________________

____

____

Now suppose instead that at time T, Home is hit by a temporary (one-year) *increase* in output of 10 units.

8e. If Home is not free to lend on world markets, how much does consumption rise in year T? ______________________________

____

____

8f. If Home is free to lend on world markets, how much does consumption rise in year T?

____

____

8g. How would your answer to 8f change if the shock had been permanent rather than temporary? ______________________________

____

____

TIPS

Much of problem 8 can be answered using a single equation from the textbook. Make sure you understand the economics behind this equation.

Problem 9: Explain the rationale behind Chile's "economic and social stabilization fund."

____

____

____

3 Gains from Efficient Investment

ESSENTIAL CONCEPTS

By definition investment consumes resources now and provides additional resources in the future. An investment that raises national output by ΔQ requires resources of ΔK. In a closed economy the resources to fund this additional investment by ΔK come out of consumption, and the disruptive impact of a large reduction in consumption might be too costly to make the investment feasible. In an open economy, the investment need not reduce consumption at all in any period. If the world real interest rate is r, then the investment will take place as long as the present value of the investment, $\Delta Q / r$, is greater than its immediate cost, ΔK.

International borrowing and lending breaks the link between a country's savings and its investment. Countries with a greater propensity to save or those that lack good investments can provide the immediate funding for countries with lower propensity to save or those that have many good investments. As in the case of international trade in goods, international borrowing and lending allows the world's resources to be used more efficiently, thereby improving the well-being of both borrowers and lenders.

An important question in international finance is why richer, developed countries are not lending more to poorer, developing countries. Everything else equal, economists expect that the marginal product of capital should be higher in developing countries, where capital is scarce, than in the developed world, where it is relatively abundant. Inflows of capital would be expected to raise incomes in developing countries, bringing about *convergence* in levels of development, yet very little capital flows from developed to developing countries.

There are many possible explanations for why capital does not flow from developed to developing countries. One explanation that has received attention is that developing countries suffer from technical and social inefficiencies that lower the *productivity* of capital. To understand this argument, consider the production function $q = Ak^{\theta}$, where q is output per worker, k is the stock of capital per worker, is capital's share in production, and A is a measure of productivity. If the productivity levels A were the same in both countries, then capital would move from countries where it is abundant (k high) to countries where it is scarce (k low). When the capital-scarce country has a much lower level of productivity (low A) than the capital-abundant country, this need not be the case because the marginal product of capital ($\theta A k^{\theta-1}$) might yet be lower in capital-scarce country than in the capital-abundant country. An alternative explanation is that investment in poor countries is deterred by the high-risk premiums there. Understanding the cause of the dearth of capital flows is important because *foreign aid* and lending by bodies such as the *World Bank* will not raise incomes in developing countries much if productivity in these countries is low due to poor institutions.

KEY TERMS

Use the space below to record your notes on the following key terms.

Production function

Productivity

Convergence

Divergence

Foreign aid

World Bank ______________________________

Marginal product of capital (MPK) ______________________________

REVIEW QUESTIONS

Problem 10: Suppose that an investment requires 10 units of current output and delivers a perpetual annual return of one unit of output per year. If the real interest rate is 5% per year, is this investment worth undertaking? ______________________________

Problem 11: Consider a world with Home and Foreign. Suppose that the marginal product of capital is higher in Home than in Foreign.

11a. Are the world's resources being used efficiently? ______________________________

11b. Are world capital markets working properly? ______________________________

11c. What explanation could you provide for why Home's marginal product of capital exceeds Foreign's? ______________________________

Problem 12: Consider the production function described in the textbook, $q = Ak^{\theta}$. Suppose that there are two countries, Home and Foreign. Each country has one worker. Home has a capital stock (k) of 100 units, and Foreign has a capital stock (k) of 49 units. Home's A is 7 and Foreign's A is 10. Capital's contribution to production θ is one half.

12a. Which country has the higher level of output per capita? ______________________________

12b. Which country has a higher marginal product of capital? ______________________________

12c. Which way should capital flow? ______________________________

Problem 13: True, False, or Uncertain. Please explain your answer. Developing countries are poor because they do not receive enough foreign aid from the developed world.

____

____

TIPS If a country banned international borrowing and lending, then its real interest rate is determined by the domestic supply of savings and demand for investment. Consumption is made to fall during an investment boom in order to allow savings to increase (increase in the real interest rate). In a small open economy, there need be no link between domestic savings and investment because the real interest rate is determined abroad.

4 Gains from Diversification of Risk

ESSENTIAL CONCEPTS

Investors who diversify their portfolio of assets can reduce the volatility of their income. This is true of an investor who can buy stocks in different companies within a nation, and it is also true of an investor who can buy stocks of companies in different nations. The basic idea of the gains to international diversification is captured in a two-country model in which Country A and Country B get inversely related output shocks: When times are good in Country A (output is high), they are bad in Country B (output is low), and vice versa. If investors can buy stocks of companies in different locations, they can lower the risk or volatility in their income by putting a large fraction of their wealth in foreign assets. When countries' portfolios are diversified, a country's trade balance and its net factor income balance will move in opposite directions over time. When Country A is in a "good" state, it will run a trade surplus and a deficit on its net factor income balance because Country A assets pay off a lot, whereas Country B assets pay off a little. The opposite occurs when Country A is in a "bad" state. *Diversification* in ownership of capital reduces volatility, but there is a limit: Much of national income accrues to labor, and stocks in "labor" income cannot be bought or sold. Further, many negative shocks (such as a global recession) are common across all countries, and international diversification would not help avoid these shocks.

Given the theoretical gains from international diversification, one would expect enormous volumes of international equity investment. The fact that this is not so is a puzzle that economists have labeled *home bias.* Economists have shown that over the last 20 years the typical investor could have lowered the risk in their portfolio while actually increasing their return.

KEY TERMS

Use the space below to record your notes on the following key terms.

Diversification ____

____

____

Home bias ______________________________

____

____

REVIEW QUESTIONS

Problem 14: Home and Foreign are subjected to random shocks. In either country output in a good year is 50, and it is 10 units in a bad year. The chance of the year being good is 50%. When Home has a good year, Foreign has a bad year, and vice versa.

14a. If international financial markets are closed, what is the variation around the mean?

____

____

14b. If all income were capital income and each country owned 50% of the other country's capital stock, what would the variation in income around the mean be? ______________

____

____

14c. Now suppose that 50% of income was labor income and each country owned 50% of the other country's capital stock. What would the variation in income around the mean be?

____

____

____

14d. Now suppose that the two countries were in the same state every year and each country owned 50% of the other country's capital stock. What would the variation in income around the mean be? ______________________________

____

____

Problem 15: How could you gain some of the benefits of international diversification without buying stocks on a foreign stock market? ______________________________

____

____

Problem 16: (Multiple Choice) Home bias in portfolio ownership might be explained by

a. It is costly to acquire foreign assets.

b. Consumption patterns differ across countries.

c. Foreign investors may face regulatory barriers.

d. all of the above

e. none of the above

18

The Balance of Payments II: Output, Exchange Rates, and Macroeconomic Policies in the Short Run

Overview

Temporary "macroeconomic shocks" can destabilize a country's economy. Some of these shocks have a domestic origin, such as a drop in consumer spending, and some of these shocks originate abroad, such as an increase in international interest rates. This chapter introduces a Keynesian-type model of the macroeconomy to analyze the effect of domestic and international shocks on key macroeconomic aggregates and to analyze the ability of the government to offset these shocks through changes in its policy. The model highlights the role of international markets for goods and assets in determining domestic outcomes. Critically, government policies that affect the return on domestic deposits alter the exchange rate, which in turn alters the trade balance through a phenomenon known as expenditure switching.

A country's choice of exchange rate regime is shown to be paramount in determining the effect of shocks on the economy and in the efficacy of monetary policy for stabilizing the economy. In a country with a fixed exchange rate system, the interest rate must be equal to the world interest rate, which has the implication that the government can only use fiscal policy to combat adverse economic shocks. In a country with a flexible exchange rate system, there is no such constraint on the use of monetary policy because both the exchange rate and the interest rate are free to vary. Finally, real world difficulties in the implementation of policies to stabilize the economy are discussed.

1 Demand in the Open Economy

ESSENTIAL CONCEPTS

The Keynesian model introduced in this chapter attributes fluctuations in national output to shocks to demand for national output. As discussed in Chapter 16, demand for national output is equal to gross national expenditure (GNE) plus the trade balance and so is given by

$$D = C + I + G + TB$$

where C stands for *consumption,* I stands for *investment,* G stands for *government consumption,* and TB stands for the trade balance, or the difference between a country's exports and its imports. This section discusses the model's assumptions over the way in which these four components of aggregate demand behave. Much of the behavior of these components of demand can be attributed to the model's assumption that prices are "sticky," or fixed in the short run.

Demand by consumers is described by the consumption function, $C = C(Y - T)$, which posits that the level of consumption is increasing in *disposable income,* which is the difference between national income, Y, and taxes, T. The rate at which the consumption rises in disposable income is known as the *marginal propensity to consume.* Consumption can also shift as consumer sentiment changes. This is an example of a demand shock.

Demand by investors is assumed to be determined by investor sentiments and by the *expected real interest rate.* The higher is the interest rate, the higher the return that any given investment project would have to generate in order to be profitable. An increase in the interest rate thus reduces aggregate investment as fewer investment projects are undertaken. In summary, the investment function is given by $I = I(i)$, where I is decreasing in i (note that inflation expectations are assumed to be zero so that the nominal interest rate is equal to the real interest rate).

Government consumption, G, and the taxes levied by the government, T, are assumed to be determined only by the government via its *fiscal policy.* Note that not all government spending counts as government consumption, as some spending takes the form of *transfers programs,* such as social security, which do not generate demand for goods and services directly.

The final component of aggregate demand is the trade balance, which is equal to the difference between the value of exports and the value of imports. Demand for a country's exports is assumed to depend on the *real effective exchange rate,* on the level of disposable demand in other countries ($Y^* - T^*$), and on consumer preferences abroad. A country's import demand is also assumed to depend on the real effective exchange rate, on the level of disposable income in the home country ($Y - T$), and on domestic consumer preferences. As a country's real exchange rate depreciates, its goods and services become cheaper relative to foreign goods and services, inducing consumers at home and abroad to engage in *expenditure switching:* Exports are increasing and imports are decreasing in the *real effective exchange rate.* This assumption is generally consistent with the data in the long run but may not hold in the short run, a phenomenon known as the *j curve.* In summary, the trade balance can be written as a function of its determinants: $TB(EP^* / P, Y - T, Y^* - T^*)$.

KEY TERMS

Use the space below to record your notes on the following key terms.

Consumption ______________________________

____

____

Disposable income ____

Marginal propensity to consume (MPC) ______________________________

Expected real interest rate ____

Government consumption ____

Taxes ____

Transfer programs ____

Expenditure switching ____

Real effective exchange rate _______________________________________

Pass-through ____

J curve ____

REVIEW QUESTIONS

Problem 1: Consider the following consumption function, $C = 5 + 0.75 \cdot (Y - T)$. Y is national income and T is government taxes.

1a. What is the marginal propensity to consume? ______

1b. If disposable income is 100, what are consumers' savings? ______

1c. What form might a "consumption shock" take given the structure of this consumption function? ______

1d. If each individual consumer had the same consumption function, would a government transfer program, such as social security, affect aggregate consumption? ______

1e. True or False. Please explain your answer. If the government were to cut taxes T by 15 units and Y were to stay the same, aggregate demand would increase by 11.25. (Hint: Take into account demand for foreign goods and services.) ______

TIPS

Savings and consumption are assumed to not rely directly on the interest rate. This assumption may be different than in other textbooks.

Transfer programs can affect aggregate consumption spending if the marginal propensity to consume differs across consumers with different income levels.

Problem 2: There are seven potential investments available in Home. Each investment requires one unit of input. The rate of return on each investment is shown in the following table.

Project	Rate of Return
1	10
2	9
3	6
4	5
5	3
6	2
7	1

2a. If the real interest rate were 4%, how many units of output are demanded for investment?

______

2b. If the interest rate were to rise to 7%, how many units of output would be demanded for investment? ______

2c. Suppose that there was a productivity boom so that the rate of return on each investment doubled. If the interest rate continued to be 7%, how many investments would be undertaken? ______

Problem 3: Home's exchange rate is fixed for many years. At time *t*, the currency appreciates. Use the following graphs to plot the response of Home's exports, imports, and trade balance over time. (Hint: Think about the j-curve.)

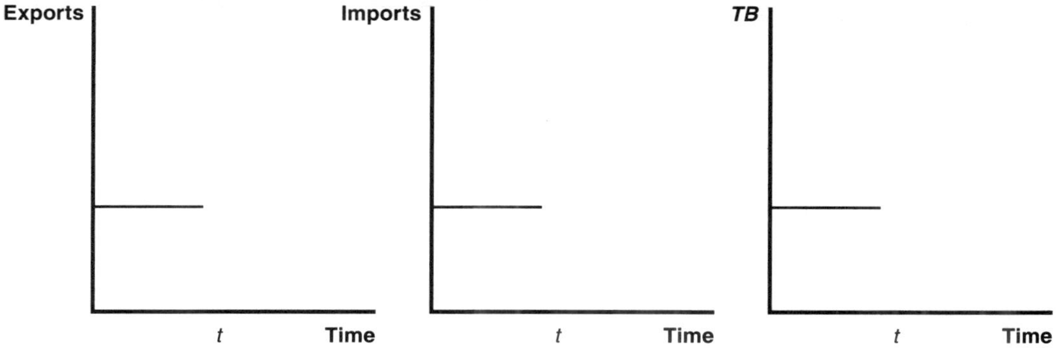

Problem 4: (Multiple Choice) A 10% depreciation is observed to lead to a 4% increase in import prices. Which of the following phenomenon could explain the incomplete pass-through?

a. dollar invoicing

b. distribution costs

c. j-curve effects

d. a & b

e. all of the above

Problem 5: (Multiple Choice) Home's trade balance surplus might increase as a result of

a. a real effective exchange rate depreciation

b. a decrease in Home's disposable income

c. an increase in the rest of the world's disposable income

d. all of the above

e. none of the above

2 Goods Market Equilibrium: The Keynesian Cross

ESSENTIAL CONCEPTS

In a Keynesian model all changes in short-run aggregate supply are induced by a shock (change) in one or more components of aggregate demand *D*. Because aggregate demand is a function of the same variables on which its components depend, it can be written

$$D(Y - T, I, G, EP^* / P, Y^* - T^*) = C(Y - T) + I(i) + G + TB(EP^* / P, Y - T, Y^* - T^*)$$

Holding fixed national income *Y*, an increase in *G*, *i*, *E*, or Y^*, or a reduction in *T* or T^* will raise some component of aggregate demand, so aggregate demand will increase as well (note that Home and Foreign prices *P* and P^* are fixed in the short run). The short-run equilibrium in the goods market requires that aggregate supply *Y* equals aggregate demand *D* or

$$D(Y - T, I, G, EP^* / P, Y^* - T^*) = Y$$

The level of output that satisfies this *goods market equilibrium condition* is generally analyzed using the Keynesian cross diagram shown in Figure 18-1.

FIGURE 18-1

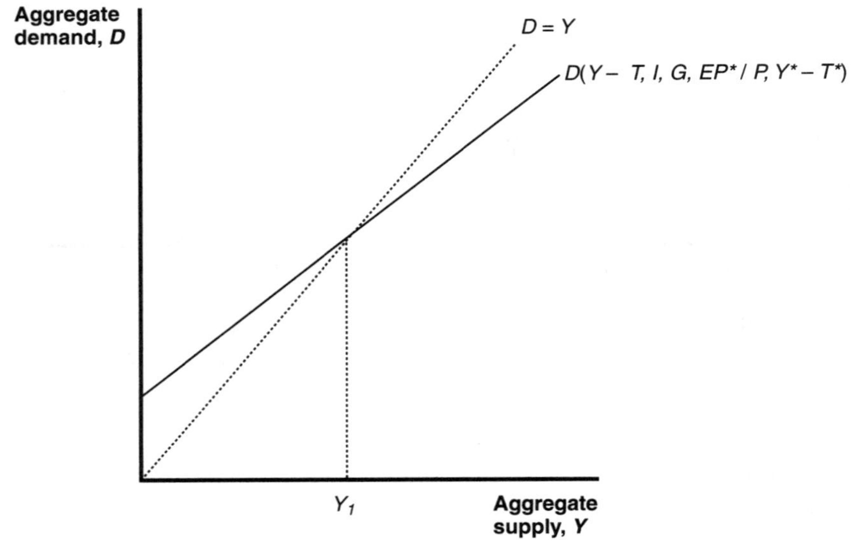

The Keynesian Cross

The solid upward sloping line D is the aggregate demand curve. Aggregate demand is increasing in national output because consumption expenditure rises in national income. The slope of D is less than one because the marginal propensity to consume is less than one and because some of consumption falls on foreign rather than domestic goods. The equilibrium level of output Y_1 induces a level of aggregate demand that is exactly equal to that level of output. From Figure 18-1 it is clear that any shock that increases aggregate demand for any level of national output causes the aggregate demand curve to shift up, causing the short-run equilibrium level of output to rise.

KEY TERMS

Use the space below to record your notes on the following key term.

Goods market equilibrium condition ______________________________

____

____

REVIEW QUESTIONS

Problem 6: What is the effect of the following shocks on the short-run level of national output?

6a. A fall in interest rates? ______________________________

____

6b. An appreciation of the Home currency? ______________________________

____

6c. A tax cut? ______________________________

6d. A tax cut in Foreign? ______________________________

____

6e. A drop in consumer confidence (consumers want to spend less)? ______________

____

6f. News that imported products make you sick? ______________________________

____

TIPS

With prices sticky in the short run, we assume that any change in demand is immediately translated into a change in supply. Put another way, firms and workers have committed themselves to supply whatever is demanded no matter how big or small.

"Shocks" to aggregate demand shift the D curve up and down. Clearly, any shock to demand can be directly offset by a change in G and indirectly through a change in T, i, or E. This observation will motivate an activist government policy later in the chapter.

3 Goods and Forex Market Equilibria: Deriving the IS Curve

ESSENTIAL CONCEPTS

The *IS curve* shows the combinations of the nominal interest rate and national output (i, Y) that are consistent with goods market equilibrium when all other determinants of aggregate demand are held fixed. There are two channels that connect interest rates to national output. First, a change in interest rates directly lower investment spending $I(i)$. Higher interest rates make investment less attractive. Second, changes in interest rates also spark changes in exchange rates. In the short run, prices are sticky so that all changes in nominal exchange rates are also changes in real exchange rates. A reduction in interest rates leads to a real depreciation, which induces expenditure switching and a higher trade balance. Because these two effects reinforce each other, an increased interest rate lowers aggregate demand and so lowers national output: The IS curve is downward sloping.

A change in ***any*** other variable that affects aggregate demand D other than the interest rate will induce a ***shift*** in the IS curve. For instance, an increase in government spending directly increases aggregate demand and so increases the volume of output in the short run for any initial level of interest rates. As a result, the new relationship between interest rates and national output features a higher level of national output for each level of interest rates.

KEY TERMS

Use the space below to record your notes on the following key term.

IS curve ______________________________

____

____

REVIEW QUESTIONS

Problem 7: How do the following shocks shift the IS curve? Explain.

7a. A fall in interest rates? ______

7b. An increase in the expected future exchange rate? ______

7c. A tax cut? ______

7d. A tax cut in Foreign? ______

7e. A drop in consumer confidence (consumers want to spend less)? ______

7f. News that imported products make you sick? ______

TIPS

Any change in a component of aggregate demand that changes the level of output for a given level of the interest rate (see Problem 6) will *shift* the IS curve. Changes in components of aggregate demand that are due to a change in the interest rate are associated with a movement *along* the existing IS curve.

4 Money Market Equilibrium: Deriving the LM Curve

ESSENTIAL CONCEPTS

The *LM curve* is used to summarize the combinations of the nominal interest rate and national output that are consistent with equilibrium in the money market while holding fixed the real money supply and any other determinants of money demand. The key equation is

$$M / P = L(i)Y$$

An increase in the interest rate i lowers money demand, whereas an increase in real output Y increases money demand. Hence, an increase in real output is associated with an increase in interest rates. This means that the LM curve is upward sloping.

There are only two shocks that can shift the LM curve. First, a change in the nominal money supply M or a change in the price level P both alter the real money supply. An increase in the real money supply is associated with a downward shift in the LM curve. Second, the function L can shift. For example, if people become fearful of the financial system and want to hold more cash, the function L would shift up (a rush to liquidity). An increase in money demand holding fixed i must shift the LM curve up.

KEY TERMS

Use the space below to record your notes on the following key term.

LM curve ____

____

____

REVIEW QUESTIONS

Problem 8: (Multiple Choice) Which of the following could result in a shift of the LM curve?

a. a depreciation of the exchange rate

b. a rise in consumer spending

c. an increase in investment

d. a fall in the price level

e. all of the above

Problem 9: True or False. Please explain your answer. The LM curve is upward sloping because prices are assumed to be sticky. ____

____

____

5 The Short-Run IS-LM-FX Model of an Open Economy

ESSENTIAL CONCEPTS

In a short-run equilibrium, the nominal interest rate and level of real output make aggregate demand equal to aggregate supply in the goods market and ensure that the demand for real balances is equal to the real money supply. In other words, the interest rate and level of real output are determined by the intersection of the IS curve and the LM curve. In the background (and on a separate diagram typically drawn to the right of the IS-LM diagram), the interest rate and exchange rate lead to equilibrium in the foreign exchange market.

In this section, we use the complete model to analyze the effect of temporary shocks to the economy on the endogenous variables, such as national output, exchange rates, and trade balances. It is important to understand that a temporary shock is one that has no impact in the long run and so has no impact on people's expectations concerning future variables. For instance, a temporary investment boom results in an increase in one component of aggregate demand and so shifts the IS curve at the moment, but everyone in the economy understands that investment will soon fall and the IS curve will shift back to its initial location. The textbook's focus is on shocks that are created by changes in a government's *fiscal policy* (government consumption and taxation) and in its *monetary policy* (the money supply).

The effects of changes in fiscal and monetary policy on the economy depend on the country's exchange rate regime. The government of a country that has a flexible exchange rate system is in principle free to shift its IS curve (through fiscal policy) or its LM curve (through monetary policy). Mixtures of monetary and fiscal policy can be used to target particular interest rates and levels of national output. As noted in Chapter 15, a country that chooses to have a fixed exchange rate system and allows capital movements between countries loses control of its interest rate. To maintain the fixed exchange rate system, the government must adjust the country's money supply (and hence its LM curve) to keep the interest rate fixed. A change in fiscal policy that would tend to change the interest rate can only be achieved if the central bank alters the money supply to shift the LM curve in the same direction so as to prevent interest rates from changing.

KEY TERMS

Use the space below to record your notes on the following key terms.

Monetary policy ______________________________

____

____

Fiscal policy ______________________________

____

____

REVIEW QUESTIONS

Problem 10: Suppose that you are a government official in charge of your country's fiscal policy. The country maintains a flexible exchange rate system. You are asked by your country's "Grand Poobah for Life" to use fiscal policy alone to expand the country's output and to reduce its trade deficit simultaneously.

10a. Is it possible for you to obtain these two goals using only fiscal policy? Use the following diagram in your explanation.

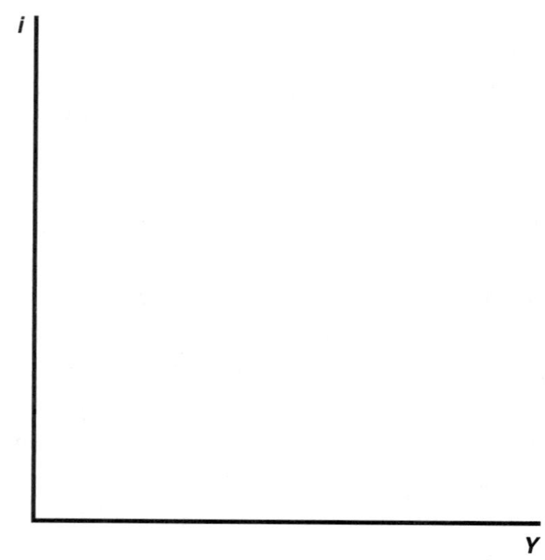

____

____

10b. Now suppose instead that you were in charge of the country's money supply. Is it possible for you to obtain these two goals using only monetary policy? Use the following diagram in your explanation.

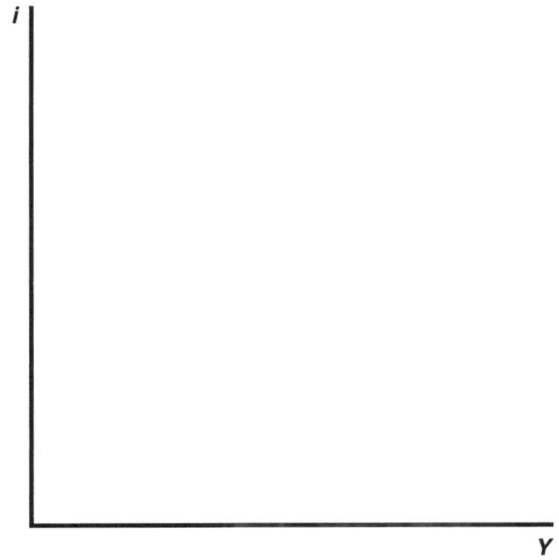

10c. Now suppose that the country has a fixed exchange rate system. Is it possible to use either monetary or fiscal policy to lower the trade deficit and expand national output simultaneously? Use the following diagram in your explanation.

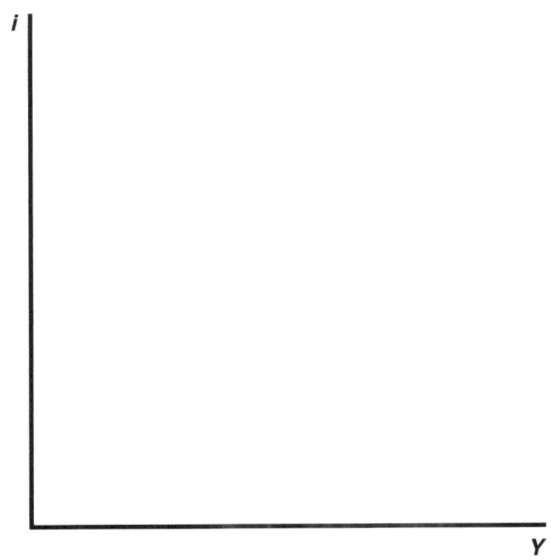

Problem 11: True or False. Please explain your answer. A policy of fixing the nominal interest rate at a set level has the same consequences as a policy of fixing the exchange rate.

6 Stabilization Policy

ESSENTIAL CONCEPTS

Economic shocks are those that shift either the IS curve or the LM curve so that output is not at its natural, long-run level. When used correctly, fiscal and monetary policy can be used to "shock" the economy back to its long-run level by offsetting the effects of other shocks in the economy. When the government acts in this manner, it is following a *stabilization policy.* The ease with which one can shift curves around on paper makes stabilization policy appear to be easy. In practice, however, there are two major problems facing policymakers. First, policymakers generally have incomplete information about the state of the economy. Measuring economic aggregates is an immense undertaking and subject to error. The difficulty of formulating policy due to the slow collection of data is called the inside lag. Second, even after government policies are formulated and implemented, it takes time for their effects to take hold. The effects of fiscal or monetary policy may not be felt until after the adverse temporary shock to the economy has already receded. The slow response of the economy to government policies is called the outside lag.

One area in which the effects of economic policy are likely to take time is in the effect of changes in the exchange rate on the trade balance. Firms may not pass-through exchange rate changes to local currency prices in order to avoid alienating their hard-won local clientele, especially if they know that the movement in the exchange rate is only temporary. Further, to the extent that international contracts for exports and imports are set in advance, changes in the real exchange rate may fail to have a stimulating effect through the trade balance until long after the adverse shock has faded.

KEY TERMS

Use the space below to record your notes on the following key term.

Stabilization policy ____

____

____

REVIEW QUESTIONS

Problem 12: Suppose that all investors simultaneously have midlife crises. They are so distracted by the loss of their youth that they invest less at every given interest rate.

12a. What is the impact on the economy if the country has a flexible exchange rate system? Use the following diagram in your explanation.

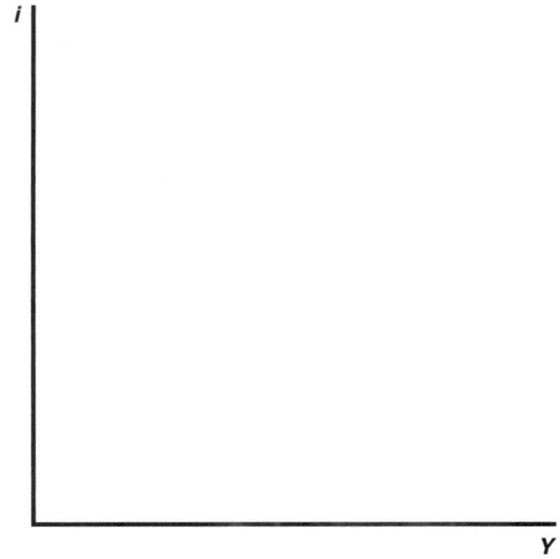

12b. How might the government combat the effects of the investment shock under a flexible exchange rate system?

12c. What is the impact on the economy if the country has a fixed exchange rate system? Use the following diagram in your explanation.

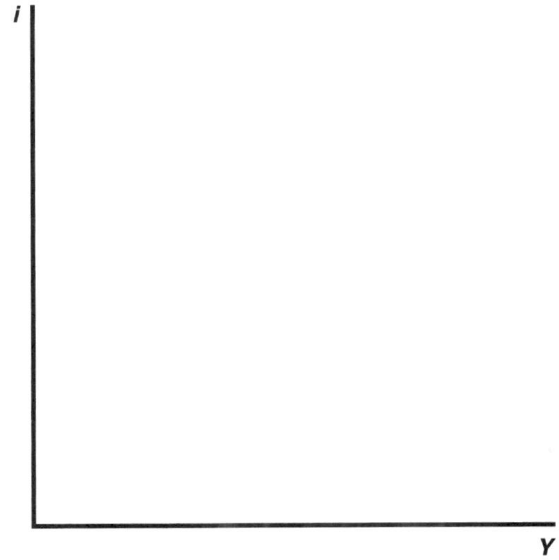

12d. How might the government combat the effects of the investment shock under a fixed exchange rate system?

____

____

TIPS Problem 12 makes the point that any shock to a component of aggregate demand has a similar effect to a change in a government's fiscal policy. A reduction in investment demand has the same impact as a sudden cut in government expenditure in the short run.

Problem 13: Compare and contrast the effect of an increase in Foreign interest rates on Home's economy under fixed and floating exchange rate regimes. Use the following two diagrams in your answer. The top panel corresponds to a flexible system, and the bottom corresponds to a fixed system. Explain your answers below.

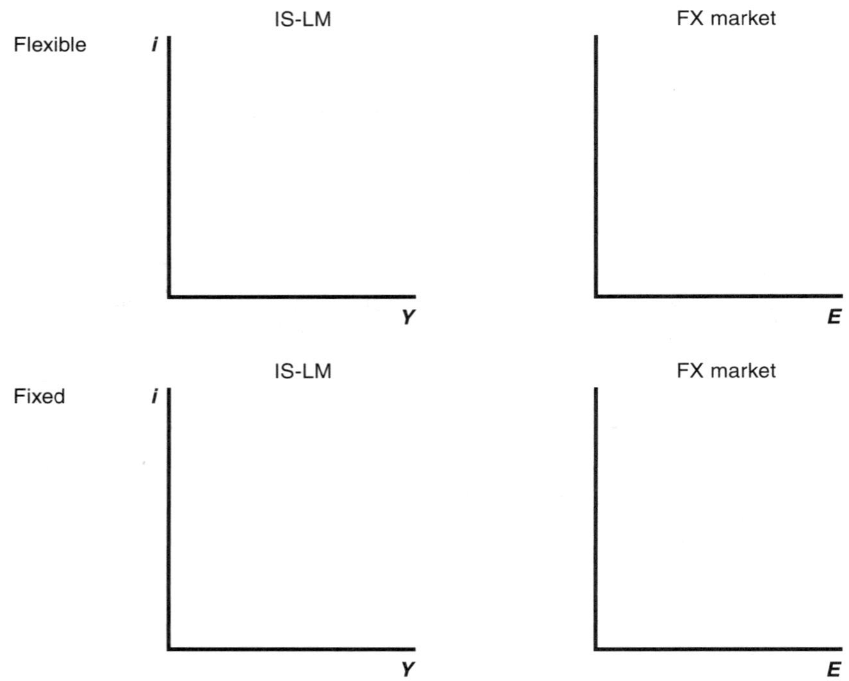

____

____

____

Problem 14: (Multiple Choice) Which of the following complicates the use of stabilization policy?

a. lag in information collection
b. slow response of investors to changes in interest rates
c. j-curve effects
d. all of the above
e. none of the above

19

Fixed versus Floating: International Monetary Experience

Overview

This chapter discusses the benefits and costs of a fixed exchange rate system relative to a flexible exchange rate system. The primary benefit of the fixed exchange rate system is that it can lower the cost of international transactions by reducing exchange rate volatility. Hence, the benefits for Country A of fixing its exchange rate to the currency of Country B are likely to be large when Country A and Country B engage in a high volume of transactions. The primary cost of a fixed exchange rate system is that a country that pegs the value of its currency to the currency of another has to adopt the same monetary policy of that country. Thus, the costs facing Country A to fix its exchange rate to the currency of Country B are likely to be relatively low when the two countries are exposed to similar economic shocks, so the monetary policy appropriate for Country B is also appropriate for Country A. For a number of developing countries, there may be additional benefits to a fixed exchange rate system. First, a country whose external wealth is very sensitive to currency movements may shield itself from wealth shocks by fixing its exchange rate. Second, a country that lacks a credible monetary anchor (a poor reputation for inflation) may see the loss of monetary policy autonomy as a partial blessing.

In practice, many exchange rate systems can be quite large and complex. The Bretton Woods system, for instance, included most of the world's developed countries. This system had formal arrangements that were designed to discourage competitive devaluations and other beggar-thy-neighbor policies that had plagued earlier monetary systems. Finally, the difficulties maintaining these cooperative arrangements in specific and the reasons for the demise of other exchange rate systems are illustrated in a discussion of the modern history of the exchange rate systems.

1 Exchange Rate Regime Choice: Key Issues

ESSENTIAL CONCEPTS

Some countries fix the value of their currency in terms of another, whereas others allow their currency to float freely. A country that has chosen a fixed or floating exchange one year might change its mind the next. Differences across time and across countries in countries' choices of exchange rate regimes reflect differences in the magnitude of the costs and benefits of fixing an exchange rate. The benefits of fixing the value of one country's in terms of another country's currency is that the peg reduces the degree of uncertainty in cross-border transactions by eliminating exchange rate volatility. Empirical studies have shown that a reduction in exchange rate volatility allows the volume of trade in goods, services, and assets between the countries to expand. The cost of a fixed exchange rate system is that the country fixing finds that it cannot follow a monetary policy that is independent of the base country. Because a fixed exchange rate eliminates a country's ability to pursue an independent monetary policy, countries that fix their exchange rate tend to be less stable than those with floating exchange rate systems.

Two countries should be part of a fixed exchange rate system if they are sufficiently similar in terms of the economic shocks (common stabilization priorities) and if their markets are sufficiently integrated. This idea is captured in Figure 19-1. Above the fix line at a point like *B*, the two countries are either sufficiently integrated or experience sufficiently similar shocks to make a fixed exchange rate system viable. Below the fix line at a point like *A*, the two countries would be better not to be part of the same fixed exchange rate system.

FIGURE 19-1

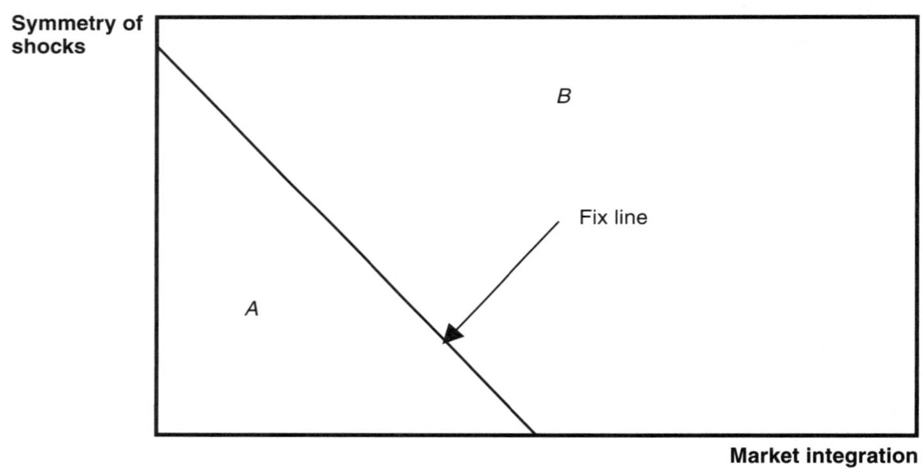

Symmetry-Integration Diagram

Over time, two countries could become more appropriate partners for a fixed exchange rate system moving from *A* toward *B*, or they could grow less appropriate, moving from *B* to *A*. It is therefore not surprising that fixed exchange rate systems come and go.

KEY TERMS

Use the space below to record your notes on the following key terms.

Gold standard ______________________________

Base currency

Center currency

Asymmetric shocks

Symmetry-integration diagram

REVIEW QUESTIONS

Problem 1: Suppose that Home fixes its exchange rate relative to Foreign (the center country). Suppose that Home is hit by a negative shock to investment that lowers Home's output but has no effect on Foreign's output. Assume that the Foreign does not adjust its policies. Must Home remove its fixed exchange rate in order to stabilize its economy?

TIPS

Problem 1 reminds us that adopting a fixed exchange rate does not prevent a country from using fiscal policy to stabilize the economy.

Problem 2: Why might a country that had previously pegged its exchange rate to one currency begin to peg its currency to another?

Problem 3: Suppose that Texas and Massachusetts were countries with their own currencies (the steer and the bean, respectively). Is it obvious that Texas would benefit from fixing the steer to the bean?

Problem 4: Why might a country with a fixed exchange rate contemplate capital controls?

2 Other Benefits of Fixing

ESSENTIAL CONCEPTS

A fixed exchange rate system may benefit developing countries through additional mechanisms. First, for a country with a poor history of managing inflation, a fixed exchange rate system may be the only credible nominal anchor. Second, a fixed exchange rate may benefit countries whose external liabilities are denominated in major foreign currencies like the dollar, whereas their assets tend to be primarily in domestic currency. Countries exhibiting liability dollarization find that their total wealth is highly sensitive to exchange rate movements: A depreciation of the country's currency can swell the value of its liabilities relative to its assets. Developing countries are more likely to exhibit such as a currency mismatch because foreigners are reluctant to expose themselves to the exchange risk associated with buying local currency assets. Countries with poor institutional histories are said to suffer from original sin: A country cannot borrow abroad in its own currency because of its reputation.

When a country's foreign exchange liabilities outweigh its foreign exchange assets, a depreciation of its currency makes its citizens poorer by raising the value of its liabilities relative to its assets. If this loss of wealth suppresses consumption and investment, then depreciation can actually depress rather than stimulate output. This possibility is supported by empirical evidence: Countries experiencing losses of wealth due to dramatic depreciations experience large reductions in output. Given the problems associated with exchange rate movements that occur under a flexible exchange rate system, many developed countries are said to have a *fear of floating*.

These additional benefits of a fixed exchange rate lower the threshold tradeoff between symmetry of shocks and degree of economic integration necessary to induce a country to adopt a fixed exchange rate system. It is therefore not surprising that fixed exchange rate systems are relatively common among small, developing countries.

KEY TERMS

Use the space below to record your notes on the following key term.

Fear of floating ______________________________

____

____

REVIEW QUESTIONS

Problem 5: The Republic of Inflationstan announces that it will fix its currency to the U.S. dollar in order to control inflation, a perennial problem in the country. Why might you be skeptical about the likelihood that the country will tame inflation? ______________________________

____

____

Problem 6: Home's currency, the blott, is fixed in terms of the U.S. dollar. Home has external assets of \$100 million and external liabilities of €100 million. Suppose the dollar depreciation against the euro from $E_{\$/€} = 1$ to $E_{\$/€} = 1.5$.

6a. What is the impact of the currency movements on Home's net external wealth?

6b. What is the impact of the currency movement on Home's national output if the behavior of consumers and investors is sensitive to total wealth?

Problem 7: Most of Home's trade is with the European Union, but most of Home's net foreign liabilities are denominated in U.S. dollars. Discuss the challenge facing Home in determining its foreign exchange regime.

TIPS

Problem 7 sheds some light on why countries sometimes fix their currency relative to a basket of other currencies.

Problem 8: Why might a country have a difficult time borrowing in its own currency?

3 Fixed Exchange Rate Systems

ESSENTIAL CONCEPTS

Fixed exchange rate systems can involve many countries. Examples of complex fixed exchange rate systems include the Bretton Woods System, developed after World War II, and the European Exchange Rate Mechanism (ERM). These systems are based on a *reserve currency* system in which the member countries fix the value of their currency relative to a single reserve currency, such as the U.S. dollar, or in terms of a commodity, such as under the gold standard. A key feature of these systems, with the exception of the gold standard, is that only the country of the reserve currency is able to pursue an independent monetary policy. However, each country within the exchange rate system might be hit by an economic shock that is special to that country. The key question addressed in this section, therefore, is what kind of *cooperative arrangements* can be established in order to facilitate burden-sharing across countries.

Suppose that one country within a reserve currency system is hit by an adverse shock so that its output falls below its full employment level. Because the country's interest rates must be fixed to maintain the fixed exchange rate, the country cannot unilaterally ease its monetary policy to combat this shock. There are two mechanisms that could be used to maintain the fixed exchange rate system while simultaneously maintaining the fix. First, all countries within the system could agree to lower their interest rates a little, but not as much as the country receiving the adverse shock would like. In this way the adverse shock is partially stabilized in the directly affected country, whereas the other countries find their economies slightly overstimulated. Alternatively, the adversely affected country could *devalue* its currency by changing the rate at which its currency trades for the reserve currency. In this case, the phenomenon of expenditure switching steers some aggregate demand away from other countries in the reserve system to the devaluing country. In this case, the devaluing country stabilizes its economy at the expense of other reserve currency system countries. Non-cooperative devaluations are a *beggar-thy-neighbor* policy that raises frictions among system members.

KEY TERMS

Use the space below to record your notes on the following key terms.

Fixed exchange rate systems ____________________

____

____

Reserve currency system ____________________

____

____

Cooperative arrangements ____________________

____

____

Devaluation ____________________

____

____

Revaluation ____________________

____

____

Beggar-thy-neighbor policy ____________________

____

____

REVIEW QUESTIONS

Problem 9: Suppose that Home and Foreign are two countries that are (non-center) members of a reserve currency system. Both countries are initially in full employment.

9a. Suppose that Foreign cuts its taxes. If Home's government takes no action, what happens to Home's output?

____

____

9b. Now suppose that Foreign revalues its currency. If Home's government takes no action, what happens to Home's output?

____

____

Problem 10: Why might it be desirable to fix the value of your currency to gold than to fix it to the currency of another country?

____

____

Problem 11: Suppose that Home fixes the value of its currency relative to Foreign. Foreign complains that Home's currency is now "undervalued."

11a. If Foreign takes no action, what is the impact of Home's action on Foreign's national output?

____

____

11b. Can Foreign use monetary policy to offset the effect of Home's action on Foreign's national output? If so, what is the impact on Foreign's trade balance?

____

____

TIPS

Problem 9 points out that there are all kinds of interconnections between countries, even in the presence of a fixed exchange rate system.

Problem 11 captures some of the flavor of the recent economic history of relations between China and the United States.

4 International Monetary Experience

ESSENTIAL CONCEPTS

This section uses the conceptual framework developed in this chapter to interpret the modern history of the exchange rate systems. A key tenet of this framework is that one of the most important benefits of fixing the exchange rate is to facilitate international trade and other transactions. The rapid growth of such transactions during the period 1870 to 1914 explains in part why the number of countries pegging their currency to gold increased from 15% to 70%. Moreover, as more countries pegged their currency to gold, the integration benefit increased to other countries doing the same. This is an example of a network externality.

The collapse of the gold standard can also be understood through the framework. The collapse of world trade during World War I and the subsequent increase in protectionism after the war reduced the benefit of a fixed exchange rate system. Further, the rising political activism in countries previously controlled by a handful of elites made the instability costs of a fixed exchange rate system more relevant. Finally, during the inter-war period, countries were buffeted by asymmetric economic shocks, and the practice of beggar-thy-neighbor–type devaluations increased the cost of pegging to gold.

World War II ushered out the gold standard from the international stage permanently. The Bretton Woods System designed by the United States and the United Kingdom in the waning years of the war was a reserve currency system in which all participating countries pegged their currencies to the dollar while the United States in turn pegged its currency to gold. Initially most countries participating in the system imposed capital controls in order to allow themselves some monetary policy autonomy. Over time, however, these capital controls became hard to enforce. The subsequent decline in monetary policy autonomy combined with growing concerns that the United States would remove the peg on gold led to the demise of this fixed exchange rate system in 1971. Since then, countries have chosen their exchange rate regime based on narrow individual needs with substantial variation across countries in the choice of regime and with substantial variation over time for many countries in their choice of exchange rate regime.

REVIEW QUESTIONS

Problem 12: Under the Bretton Woods System, the United States was accused of exporting its inflation. If the center country in an exchange rate system increases its money supply, what is the impact on the price levels in the other countries in the system? ________________

____

____

Problem 13: Why does it become more attractive to fix your currency to the same currency to which other countries are fixing their currency? ________________________

____

____

Problem 14: Why do capital controls make a fixed exchange rate system easier to manage?

____

____

____

20

Exchange Rate Crises: How Pegs Work and How They Break

Overview

Throughout modern history, many countries have found themselves in a cycle in which they fix their exchange rate one year and then are forced to let it float a few years later. When the fixed exchange rate breaks, countries often plunge into an exchange rate crisis, experiencing rapid exchange rate depreciation, deep recession, and other forms of financial turmoil, such as widespread bank failures.

This chapter develops a theoretical framework that can be used to understand the factors that give rise to exchange rate crises. The starting point of this framework is the observation that the central bank of a country with a fixed exchange rate must hold foreign currency assets (reserves) so that it can intervene in support of the fixed exchange rate. Any shock or policy action that reduces the holding of foreign assets by the central bank increases the risk that a country will experience such an exchange rate crisis. These shocks can take two forms: (1) a reduction in money demand that induces a contraction of the liabilities and assets of the central bank and (2) central bank lending that induces a change in the composition of its assets.

First- and second-generation models of exchange rate crises are discussed in turn. First-generation models focus on the role of fiscal policies that are inconsistent with maintaining a fixed exchange rate. First-generation models fit the history of exchange rate crises in Latin America in the 1980s. Second-generation models focus on how the inability of governments to commit to maintain a given fixed exchange rate can interact with investor expectations to precipitate an exchange rate crisis. If investors suddenly fear that an exchange rate crisis is imminent, interest rates may rise and force the government to abandon an exchange rate peg. Such self-fulfilling exchange rate crises have become prevalent in recent years.

1 Facts about Exchange Rate Crises

ESSENTIAL CONCEPTS

An *exchange rate crisis* occurs when there is a sudden and large depreciation of the exchange rate. They can occur in countries at every level of development, but they are more likely to have costly social effects in developing countries than in developed countries. For instance, although both developed and developing countries are likely to be in a recession at the onset of an exchange rate crisis, developed countries recover quickly after the onset of the crisis, whereas developing countries are likely to fall deeper into recession.

One reason exchange rate crises are associated with great economic and social costs is that they are typically accompanied by large-scale bank failures, a *banking crisis,* and by government's failure to repay its debts, a *default crisis.* When an exchange rate crisis occurs in tandem with a banking or default crisis, the situation is called *twin crises.* When an exchange rate crisis occurs simultaneously with both banking and default crises, the situation is known as *triple crises.* Given the social and economic dislocation that occurs during an exchange rate crisis, it is not surprising that these crises are associated with political upheavals.

KEY TERMS

Use the space below to record your notes on the following key terms.

Exchange rate crisis ______________________________

____

____

Banking crisis ______________________________

____

____

Default crisis ______________________________

____

____

Twin crises ______________________________

____

____

Triple crises ______________________________

____

____

REVIEW QUESTIONS

Problem 1: How big a depreciation is large enough to be called an "exchange rate crisis"?

____

____

____

Problem 2: What conditions in the financial sector are likely to increase the severity of a large depreciation of the exchange rate? ______________________________

____

____

Problem 3: How could a banking crisis induce an exchange rate crisis? ______________

____

____

TIPS

As you work through the problems in the remainder of this chapter, think about the observation that banking and exchange rate crises tend to occur simultaneously.

2 How Pegs Work: The Mechanics of a Fixed Exchange Rate

ESSENTIAL CONCEPTS

The central bank maintains a fixed exchange rate system by being willing and able to buy or sell foreign exchange at the fixed exchange rate. To do so, the central bank must own a stock of foreign exchange assets, known as *reserves.* Central bank assets that are not denominated in foreign currency are collectively called *domestic credit.* Both types of assets are purchased by the central bank by issuing money so the money supply M (assumed to be equal to the monetary base) is equal to the sum of reserves R and domestic credit B, or $M = B + R$. Much of the analysis of this chapter is of the *central bank balance sheet* because changes in the bank's *liabilities* induce changes in its assets, $B + R$. The composition of the bank's assets also matters because a central bank that has run out of reserves cannot maintain the fixed exchange rate. That is, an exchange rate crisis occurs when reserves are gone, $R = 0$.

The analysis of exchange rate crises thus begins with the money demand equation, $M = P \times L(i)Y$, where P is the price level that is assumed to be fixed in the short run. Assuming that the monetary base is the central bank's only liability, we have $R + B = M$. Combining these two equations yields the key equation

$$R = P \times L(i)Y - B$$

Given money demand and the existing level of domestic credit B, the central bank's reserves must adjust so that money supply is equal to money demand. Suppose that equilibrium is disturbed by an increase in money demand so that money supply now exceeds money demand. If domestic credit is held fixed, capital must flow into the country and thereby expand R. Otherwise local interest rates would have to rise above world levels, which, given the fixed exchange rate, they cannot do in equilibrium. A reduction in domestic credit would have the same effect. The bottom line is that reserve levels adjust automatically to changes in money demand or changes in domestic credit.

This situation is illustrated in Figure 20-1. Money demand determines the level of the money supply, which is shown on the horizontal axis and in the example is 1,000. Given our simple assumptions, the money supply equals the domestic credit (B) plus reserves (R). Reserves are equal to money demand less domestic credit, in this case 500.

FIGURE 20-1

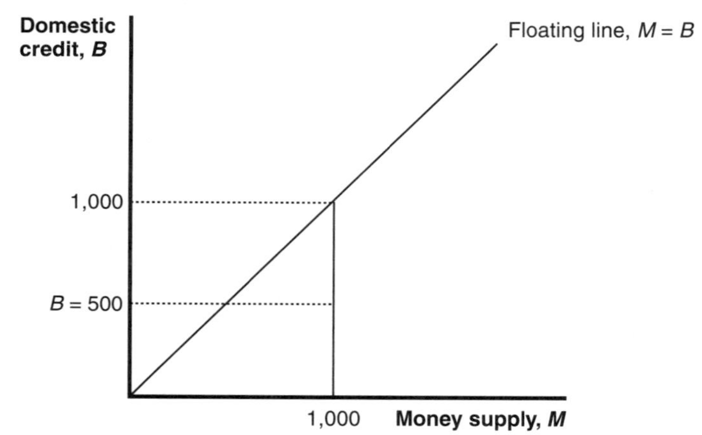

Central Bank Balance Sheet

Should domestic credit rise from 500 to 1,000, then reserves will be squeezed to zero, and the country will be forced to float the exchange rate. This explains the float line shown in the diagram. Any monetary shock that works through $L(i)Y$ or through B will have an impact on the reserves. A big enough reduction in money demand, caused by an increase in i, a decrease in Y, or a big enough increase in B, will result in a fall in R and a potential exchange rate crisis. The larger the share of reserves in central bank assets (the *backing ratio*) and hence the more of the money supply backed by foreign exchange, the smaller the risk of an exchange rate crisis. A currency board is thought to be a particularly "safe" type of fixed exchange rate system because the backing ratio is 100%.

Several shocks are important in generating exchange rate crises. First are those shocks that reduce money demand, $L(i)$. One source of fluctuations in money demand is variation in a country's risk premium: the extra return a country's assets must offer to compensate investors for the risk that the country's currency will depreciate *(exchange rate premium)* or that the borrowers will fail to repay *(default premium)*. An increase in the *interest rate spread* between countries indicates movement in risk premiums. Another type of shock occurs when the banking system becomes *insolvent* and the central bank is forced to bail out the banking system by extending domestic credit.

Finally, the section considers a more realistic central bank balance sheet by allowing for the possibility that the central bank will issue sterilization bonds. These bonds are not money but do allow the country to change the level of its assets. Many developing countries have issued such bonds in order to increase their backing ratio, but such a policy comes at a cost because the bonds pay a higher interest rate than the reserves.

KEY TERMS

Use the space below to record your notes on the following key terms.

Domestic credit ____

____

____

Reserves

Central bank balance sheet

Assets

Liabilities

Floating line

Fixed line

Backing ratio

Currency board

Risk premium

Interest rate spread

Currency premium

Country premium

Sterilization bonds ______________________________

Credibility ______________________________

Contagion ______________________________

Sterilization ______________________________

Insolvent ______________________________

Bailout ______________________________

Illiquid ______________________________

Bank run ______________________________

Lender of last resort ______________________________

REVIEW QUESTIONS

Problem 4: Why is a currency board the safest configuration of the central bank balance sheet? ______________________________

Problem 5: How could a central bank increase its reserves without changing the money supply or its stock of domestic credit? Why is this method of increasing reserves costly to the central bank? ______________________________

Problem 6: A country called Home has money demand of 100 pesos and domestic credit of 50 pesos. The central bank has no outstanding sterilization bonds.

6a. What must the level of reserves be? ______________________________

____

6b. Suppose the central bank is forced to extend domestic credit by 45 pesos in order to bail out failing financial firms. Is the direct effect enough to induce an exchange rate crisis?

____

6c. What additional factors could push the country into an exchange rate crisis given the shock described in the previous section? ______________________________

____

____

Problem 7: Suppose interest rates in a country with a fixed exchange rate suddenly jump from 5% to 30%, but no policy change has been announced.

7a. Is the country credibly pegged? ______________________________

____

7b. If the government does not carry out open market operations, what happens to the backing ratio? Use the following diagram in your answer. ______________________________

____

____

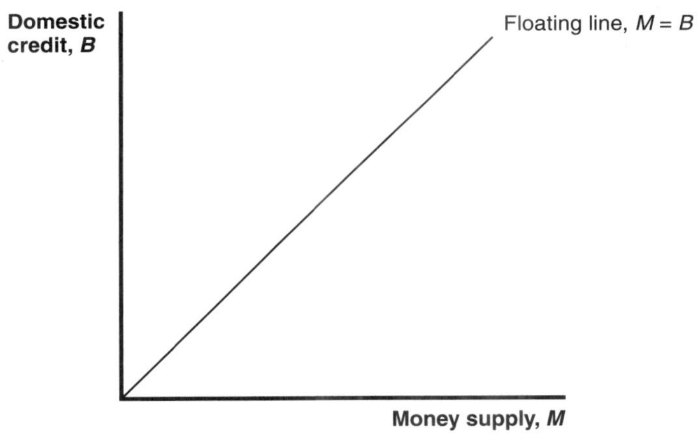

Problem 8: How could an international institution such as the International Monetary Fund (IMF) help a country that is on the brink of an exchange rate crisis? ______________________________

____

____

Problem 9: Why is a bank bailout risky for a central bank, but providing liquidity to a solvent bank is not so? ______________________________

____

____

Problem 10: (Multiple Choice) Suppose that many citizens in Home hold local deposits in dollar accounts, whereas others hold peso accounts. The interest rate differential between dollar accounts and U.S. interest rates is 5%, and the interest rate differential between peso accounts and U.S. interest rates is 10%.

a. The country premium is 15%.
b. The currency premium is 10%.
c. The currency premium is 5%.
d. The country premium is 10%.
e. none of the above

TIPS Understanding the structure of the central bank's balance sheet and its implications for the level of reserves and the level of the money supply is absolutely critical to understanding the content of this chapter.

3 How Pegs Break I: Inconsistent Fiscal Policies

ESSENTIAL CONCEPTS

In the late 1970s and 1980s a common cause of exchange rate crises was fiscal policies that were inconsistent with maintaining a fixed exchange rate system. These policies arise when the government can impel the central bank to buy its bonds, a situation known as *fiscal dominance.* When a government relies on the central bank to expand domestic credit in order to finance a large and persistent fiscal deficit, the central bank will lose reserves. Once these reserves are gone, the exchange rate crisis ensues.

The *first-generation crisis model* formalizes the implications of deficit driven monetary growth for exchange rate crises. The model builds on the monetary approach to the exchange rate that was introduced in Chapter 14. The key assumptions are over investor's expectations concerning the timing of the exchange rate crisis. In the *myopic case,* investors do not anticipate the crisis and only react once the exchange rate has become unsustainable. With continued growth in domestic credit, reserves gradually go to zero and the fixed exchange rate system breaks. On this date, investors realize that the nominal anchor of the exchange rate has been eliminated and so expect that inflation will now proceed at the rate of monetary growth. By the Fisher effect, the interest rate rises and so money demand falls. The reduction in money demand immediately leads to higher prices, and absolute purchasing power parity (APPP) requires the exchange rate to depreciate dramatically. As a result, any investor holding local currency assets will suffer a capital loss.

Given the potentially large capital loss that investors can experience when the exchange rate regime collapses, it makes sense that investors would like to anticipate the break in the exchange rate system. If investors are forward-looking instead of myopic, they may mount a *speculative attack* and suddenly buy up all of the central bank's reserves, thereby precipitating an exchange rate crisis. The speculative attack will occur as soon as the drop in the money supply that would be caused by the loss of the central bank reserves is equal to the fall in money demand implied by the Fisher effect. This criteria is captured in the following equation:

$$R / M = -\Delta M / M = \phi \times \mu$$

where the left-hand side is the backing ratio, and the right-hand side is the "responsiveness of money demand to interest rate changes" multiplied by the future growth rate of domestic credit. Unlike the myopic case, this scenario implies a smooth transition from a fixed exchange rate to a continuously depreciating exchange rate.

KEY TERMS

Use the space below to record your notes on the following key terms.

First-generation crisis model ____

Fiscal dominance ____

Speculative attack ____

International Monetary Fund ____

REVIEW QUESTIONS

Problem 11: Home's currency, the peso, is pegged to the dollar at a rate of 1 peso per dollar, Foreign's currency. Foreign's price level is $P^* = 1$, its inflation rate is zero, and its interest rate is 5%. Home's fiscal deficit is being financed by a 30% rate of domestic credit growth. Assume that investors are myopic. The following questions progressively add information about Home's situation.

11a. Suppose Home holds a positive level of reserves. What is the inflation rate in Home?

11b. Now suppose that Home's reserves go to zero at time *t*. What is the interest rate in Home at time *t*? ____________________

11c. Suppose that real money demand $L(i)Y$ is 200 before time *t* and 100 at time *t*. What has happened to the price level in Home at time *t*? ____________________

11d. Explain why real money demand may fall at time *t*? ____________________

11e. What happens to the exchange rate in Home at time *t*? Provide exact numbers.

11f. Suppose that as an investor, you own 10 pesos and 10 dollars. What happens to the dollar value of your assets at time *t*?

TIPS

A sudden large depreciation of a country's currency leads to large capital losses to the wealth of domestic savers because most of their assets tend to be in the home currency.

The sharp drop in the exchange rate that occurs in the myopic model is consistent with the "freely falling" exchange rate system noted in Chapter 13.

Problem 12: Home has a fixed exchange rate system. Suppose that domestic credit in Home is expanding at a rate of 20%. The responsiveness of money demand to interest rate changes is equal to 2.

12a. Suppose that the backing ratio is equal to 50%. Is an exchange rate crisis imminent?

12b. Suppose that a new government is elected at time *t* that promises to increase government spending. People expect that money growth will therefore expand to 40%. What happens to the exchange rate?

Problem 13: Suppose you are an official at the IMF. A country with dwindling reserves approaches you and asks for an emergency loan to replenish its reserves. Under what circumstances would you be reluctant to make loan to this country?

TIPS

Problem 12 highlights the importance of expectations in the timing of exchange rate crises.

In the myopic model, the loss of reserves is smooth, and the exchange rate makes an abrupt jump when the exchange rate crisis begins. In the forward-looking model, reserves abruptly jump to zero, whereas the exchange rate depreciates smoothly.

Problem 13 highlights a problem that the IMF has faced over the years. If a country is following policies that are inconsistent with maintaining its exchange rate, a loan will only delay an inevitable exchange rate crisis. For this reason the IMF often requires countries to reduce budget deficits and to restrict the growth of domestic credit.

4 How Pegs Break II: Contingent Monetary Policies

ESSENTIAL CONCEPTS

The *second-generation crisis model* explains how countries that are following rational and consistent fiscal policies may yet experience an exchange rate crisis for no apparent reason. The key observation to the model is that governments will let the exchange rate float if the cost to fixing the exchange rate gets sufficiently high. The government has a *contingent commitment* to the exchange rate peg, maintaining it as long as it suits the government.

Suppose that investors wake up one day fearing that a country will drop its exchange rate peg and let its currency float. This sudden change in investor sentiment, whether it be based on solid reasoning or not, raises the risk premium for the country in question and forces interest rates up in that country. High interest rates may harm the economy and so raise the cost of maintaining the fixed exchange rate, inducing the government to abandon the exchange rate peg. In the model a change in expectations induces an exchange rate crisis that would otherwise not have occurred. That is, expectations were self-fulfilling. This model has *multiple equilibria:* Either no one expects a crisis (the peg is credible) and none occurs, or everyone expects a crisis (the peg is not credible) and it occurs.

KEY TERMS

Use the space below to record your notes on the following key terms.

Second-generation crisis model ______________________________

____

____

Contingent commitment ______________________________

____

____

Multiple equilibria ______________________________

____

____

Self-fulfilling equilibrium ______________________________

____

____

Corners hypothesis ______________________________

____

____

REVIEW QUESTIONS

Problem 14: What kind of information can be used to glean whether a country's peg is credible or noncredible? ______________________________

____

____

Problem 15: Why are fixed exchange rate systems more likely to break down during recessions?

Problem 16: Could a currency board help to prevent a self-fulfilling exchange rate crisis?

TIPS

It is important to understand the concept of equilibrium used in this section. Governments and investors are choosing their best action given the action of others, yet both can be made worse off.
Governments have to be very careful in their actions to avoid creating the perception that an exchange rate crisis is possible. A careless remark by a finance minister could induce a change in investors' expectations.

21

The Euro

Overview

The Eurozone is a group of countries that belong to the European Union and that share the euro as their currency. The euro has existed as a full-fledged currency since it was created in 2000 after years of careful planning and an even longer period of economic and political integration in Europe. The goal of this chapter is to understand as fully as possible the logic of the euro project. The economic logic of the euro can be analyzed using the theory of the optimum currency area. The greater the economic integration of a set of countries and the greater the symmetry of shocks between these countries, the more likely they are to benefit on net from using a common currency. The political logic is that sharing a common currency helps to increase the feeling of unity among a set of countries that have fought numerous wars throughout modern history. The analysis suggests that as an economic project, the euro makes little sense, so the euro's primary justification is political.

Key areas of contention among citizens of the Eurozone are the goals and the structure of the European Central Bank (ECB). The ECB is highly independent, answering to no governmental institution, and its primary goal is to prevent inflation. Critics worry that other goals of central banks, such as fighting recessions and lending to troubled financial institutions, receive insufficient attention at the ECB. On the other hand, the desire of countries to join the ECB must partially be to enjoy the benefits of price stability. The criteria for entry into the Eurozone require countries to demonstrate that they are willing to undergo monetary and fiscal discipline associated with low-inflation environments.

1 The Economics of the Euro

ESSENTIAL CONCEPTS

Should two or more countries share a currency, or should they each have their own currency? The theory of *optimum currency areas (OCA)* addresses exactly this question. The costs and benefits of sharing a currency share much in common with the costs and benefits of a fixed exchange rate system. As discussed in Chapter 19, a fixed exchange rate eliminates exchange rate fluctuations and so makes international commerce easier to conduct (efficiency benefits of market integration), but it makes it impossible for individual countries to pursue a monetary policy that reacts to country-specific economic shocks (stability costs). Everything else equal, countries that are economically highly integrated and that are subjected to common (rather than asymmetric) shocks are more likely to gain from using a common currency. This situation is illustrated in Figure 21-1. Points in this box that are above the solid diagonal line, such as points *B* and *C*, correspond to economic benefits that outweigh the economic costs of a fixed exchange rate, whereas points that are below the solid line, such as point *A*, correspond to a situation where the costs of fixing outweigh the benefits.

FIGURE 21-1

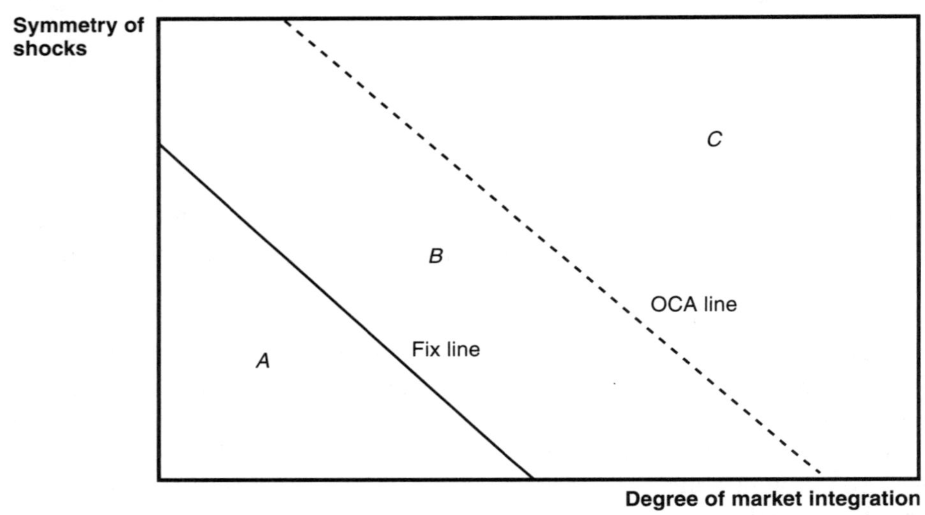

Fixed Exchange Rate Compared to OCA Criteria

A key difference between a fixed exchange rate system and a currency area is that countries following a fixed exchange rate system may revert to a floating system with its own monetary policy, whereas countries in a currency area would have to incur enormous costs associated with introducing a new currency. Given the more limited options facing a country in a currency area relative to a country in a fixed exchange rate system, the criteria for an OCA are stronger. So, for instance, in Figure 21-1 Country C would benefit from an OCA, whereas Country B would benefit from a fixed exchange rate system but not an OCA.

There are three other criteria that are relevant to an OCA but not to a fixed exchange rate system. First, the greater the ability for workers to move between countries, the less important are asymmetric economic shocks across countries because workers can move to the country with the better outcome. Second, the existence of a government apparatus for redistributing government spending from countries receiving good shocks to countries receiving bad shocks also reduces the cost of integration. Third, countries with a history of poor monetary policy (perhaps showing *inflation bias*) may gain by ceding monetary control to an outside body. Finally, there may be political objectives that offset economic costs.

The section concludes by comparing the United States and Europe in terms of their optimum currency area criteria. On market integration and symmetry of shocks criteria, the United States and Europe are relatively similar, but on the other criteria, Europe falls far behind the United States. The OCA itself might help increase the degree of integration, however.

KEY TERMS

Use the space below to record your notes on the following key terms.

Currency union __________

Eurozone __________

Euro __________

Optimum currency area (OCA) __________

Inflation bias __________

REVIEW QUESTIONS

Problem 1: Ecuador, a small developing country with little in common with the United States, dumped its currency and opted to use the dollar. What might explain Ecuador's decision to adopt the dollar rather than to peg its currency? __________

Problem 2: What economic argument can be made for joining the European Monetary Union even if the typical OCA criteria are not currently satisfied? __________

Problem 3: Is it possible that countries might satisfy the criteria for adopting a common currency only to find that years after doing so, they do not? __________

2 The History and Politics of the Euro

ESSENTIAL CONCEPTS

The development of the euro project follows a gradual and organic progression of integration that began with the systematic rebuilding that occurred in Europe after World War II. Institutions designed for European cooperation go back to the European High Authority, which was created to allocate and administrate the funds for rebuilding Europe provided for by the *Marshall Plan*. Another important milestone in this integration process was the *Treaty of Rome* in 1957, which created plans to create the European Economic Community. The collapse of the Bretton Woods System of fixed exchange rates in the early 1970s led to an impetus for a currency system that would foster economic union in Europe. The European Monetary System (EMS) in 1979 gave rise to the *Exchange Rate Mechanism (ERM),* which was essentially a mini-system of fixed exchange rates (allowing fluctuation within a band) in Europe in which the German mark was the de facto reserve currency.

The fall of the Berlin Wall in 1989 raised new questions about European identity and the appropriate scope of economic integration. The 1991 *Maastricht Treaty* created the *European Union (EU)* along with a notion of EU citizenship and a process for the entry of new countries into the union. The treaty proposed the creation of the single currency, the euro, to replace the constellation of fixed European currencies. Almost immediately in 1992, Europe experienced the *ERM crisis,* and the pegs of several countries broke. Among the countries most affected, Britain to this day has yet to adopt the euro. Since 1992, the euro has passed through its planning phases, becoming a unit of account in 1999 and replacing the currencies of 11 European countries in 2000. Since then the number of countries in the Eurozone has expanded to 13, and others wait in the wings.

KEY TERMS

Use the space below to record your notes on the following key terms.

Marshall Plan ____________________

Treaty of Rome ____________________

Exchange Rate Mechanism (ERM) ____________________

Maastricht Treaty ____________________

European Union (EU) ____________________

Economic and Monetary Union (EMU) ______________________________

____

____

ERM crisis ______________________________

____

____

European Central Bank (ECB) ______________________________

____

____

REVIEW QUESTIONS

Problem 4: How did the 1995 Schengen Treaty help set the stage for the euro?

____

____

____

Problem 5: How does the ERM crisis cast doubt on the proposition that Europe is an optimal currency area? ______________________________

____

____

3 The ECB and the Eurozone in Theory and Practice

ESSENTIAL CONCEPTS

When the euro was introduced as the official currency of the Eurozone, the ECB took over the role of monetary policy from the national central banks. The ECB is structured after the German model, which puts a premium on price stability or low inflation. The primary goal of the ECB is to "maintain price stability." It is forbidden from financing fiscal deficits, it cannot extend credit to financial institutions in a crisis, and it is not subject to any external governmental oversight. The ECB's decisions are made by its governing council, which consists of the central bank governors of the Eurozone central banks and six members of its Executive Board, and are made primarily by consensus. Supporters of the ECB's independence and its focus on price stability believe that it lends credibility to the young institution. Critics point out that the independence is antidemocratic and the obsession with price stability rules comes at the expense of output stability.

To join the Eurozone, a country must first satisfy the five *convergence criteria* laid out in the Maastricht Treaty. Three of these criteria require countries to demonstrate that they are willing to experience the rigor of a low-inflation environment. They must peg their currency to the euro, allow inflation rates to fall, and reduce the difference between their interest rates and those of the Eurozone. Countries must also demonstrate that they are capable of maintaining fiscal discipline by keeping the budget deficit below 3% of gross domestic product (GDP) and by keeping the government debt level to less than 60% of GDP. The logic again is that countries that demonstrate this discipline are unlikely to favor high inflation in order to erode the real value of government debt. Once countries are part of the Eurozone, they are supposed to meet the fiscal criteria of the *Stability and Growth Pact (SGP),* but these limits on budget deficits have been widely ignored.

KEY TERMS

Use the space below to record your notes on the following key terms.

Convergence criteria ______________________________

____

____

Stability and Growth Pact (SGP) ______________________________

____

____

REVIEW QUESTIONS

Problem 6: Why is the SGP occasionally referred to as the stupidity pact? ______________

____

____

Problem 7: What purpose do the nominal convergence criteria of the Maastricht Treaty serve?

____

____

____

Problem 8: A key controversy associated with the ECB surrounds its complete independence from elected bodies.

8a. Given the ECB's independence, what check is there on its behavior? ______________

____

8b. What is the primary argument in favor of this independence? ______________

____

____

8c. What is the primary argument against this independence? ______________

____

____

8d. Why is this arrangement sometimes called the "German model"? ______________

____

____

Problem 9: What economic justification is there for the growth and stability pact's limit on fiscal deficits to 3% of GDP instead of the more cautious 2% of GDP? ________________

____

____

Problem 10: How does EU enlargement complicate ECB governance? ________________

____

____

Problem 11: Suppose a country wished to adopt the euro as its currency. Could this country do so without the consent of the EU? ________________________________

____

____

TIPS

Central bank independence is widely understood to be important for overcoming inflation bias. Everywhere central banks are independent, however, there are some who criticize this independence.

22

Topics in International Macroeconomics

Overview

Each of the four sections in the chapter presents a separate issue of long-standing interest in international macroeconomics. The first section analyzes systematic movements in real exchange rates over time and across countries that can arise because of trade costs that limit the amount of arbitrage possible internationally. Movements in the real exchange rate can be broken down into long-run trends and short-run deviations from the trends. Long-run trends can be forecast using the Balassa-Samuelson Model, which attributes real exchange rate appreciation to rapid productivity growth. Short-run deviations from long-run trends are shown to decay slowly over time so that real exchange rates tend to converge toward their long-run equilibrium levels.

The second section analyzes systematic failures in the uncovered interest parity (UIP) that allow speculators to "beat the market." These "excess returns" are not arbitraged away, however, because the necessary investments are highly risky. The excess returns are necessary to compensate investors for the additional risk. The third section analyzes growing global imbalances that manifest themselves as large United States current account deficits. The section explains why these imbalances have happened, whether they can long continue, and what consequences would occur if the imbalances were to disappear.

The final section addresses the phenomenon of sovereign default: the failure of governments to repay their debts to international creditors. Because countries are free to default on their debt whenever they please, the model used to analyze the phenomenon weighs the costs and benefits of default. A key result is that the greater output variability in developing countries explains why they are allowed to borrow very little, why the interest rates they are charged are high, and why these countries are most likely to default on their debts.

1 Exchange Rates in the Long Run: Deviations from Purchasing Power Parity

ESSENTIAL CONCEPTS

Price levels vary across countries in systematic ways. For instance, prices are lower in developing countries than they are in developed countries. Such failures of purchasing power parity (PPP) can be attributed to costs of moving goods and information internationally. These *trade costs* create limits to arbitrage across countries, allowing the real exchange rate the freedom to vary within a *no-arbitrage band*. The larger the trade costs, the wider the band. Empirical studies of trade costs, defined so as to include local distribution costs, suggest that they may be as large at 74% of the price of the typical good. This is a large cost indeed.

The concept of trade costs can be used not only to explain why PPP often fails in the data but also why it fails in the ways that it does. The Balassa-Samuelson Model shows how trade cost can explain why price levels are higher in developed countries. The typical price basket used to measure the price level in a country includes both traded manufacturing goods and non-traded services. Suppose that labor is more productive in making traded manufacturing products in developed countries than it is in developing countries, but there are no productivity differences across countries in non-traded services. If both countries produce manufacturing goods and there are no trade costs in manufacturing, then the wage in the developed world will be higher than it is in the developing world. A higher wage drives up the price of services in the developed world; this is known as the *Balassa-Samuelson effect.*

Movements in a country's real exchange rate can include long-run trends (such as how quickly a country's productivity grows) and short-run deviations from the long-run trends. When the real exchange rate is above its long-run trend (undervalued), there is a tendency for it to appreciate gradually over time. When the real exchange rate is below its long-run trend (overvalued), there is a tendency for it to depreciate gradually over time. This process of convergence is slow, taking approximately 5 years for half the difference between actual and long-run equilibrium level to disappear. In summary, forecasts of future movements in the real exchange rate need to account for trend and reversion to the trend.

KEY TERMS

Use the space below to record your notes on the following key terms.

Trade cost ______________________________

____

____

No-arbitrage band ______________________________

____

____

Balassa-Samuelson effect ______________________________

____

____

Equilibrium real exchange rate

REVIEW QUESTIONS

Problem 1: Suppose that trade costs are 15%. How overvalued may the real exchange rate become?

Problem 2: Trade costs have been thought to have fallen over the last 30 years. Everything else equal, would this phenomenon have affected the degree of volatility in the nominal exchange rate?

Problem 3: Suppose the country Home has a real exchange rate of 0.6. Does this necessarily imply that the real exchange rate is over- or undervalued?

Problem 4: The Balassa-Samuelson effect is built on several assumptions.

4a. Would the Balassa-Samuelson effect occur if all goods and services were freely traded?

4b. Would the Balassa-Samuelson effect occur if productivity across countries in traded goods were mirrored in non-traded goods?

Problem 5: In what sense can rapid productivity growth be associated with inflation?

Problem 6: Suppose that a country has a fixed exchange rate and the real exchange rate is undervalued.

6a. What mechanism allows the real exchange rate to converge to its equilibrium level?

6b. Is convergence likely to be slow or fast relative to a country with a floating exchange rate?

2 Exchange Rates in the Short Run: Deviations from Uncovered Interest Parity

ESSENTIAL CONCEPTS

Throughout the book, we have assumed that the foreign exchange market is an *efficient market* in which the expected return was driven to be the same on all assets as long as capital was free to move internationally. Empirical research has shown, however, that the UIP condition is subject to systematic *forecast error.* Individuals engaged in the carry trade (i.e., those borrowing in a low interest rate currency and then using the proceeds to buy deposits in a high interest rate currency) may make *excess returns* (above-average profits).

To explain the fact that the foreign exchange market is inefficient, economists use a variant of the limits to arbitrage argument. Exchange rates are exceptionally volatile, so those engaged in the carry trade are exposed to risk. Relative to other types of investments, such as buying shares in domestic companies, the carry trade has a low *Sharpe ratio,* or the ratio of expected excess return to the standard deviation of excess return. In a sense, the small excess return has to be possible in order to compensate investors for the risks that they take in foreign exchange speculation. Put another way, investors are unwilling to arbitrage away small differences in expected profits given the high level of risk that it entails. In the case of developing countries that are perceived as particularly risky, local interest rates can be very high, a situation known as the *peso problem:* The fear of exchange rate volatility may result in large profits but at the expense of large risks.

KEY TERMS

Use the space below to record your notes on the following key terms.

Carry trade ____________________

Peso problem ____________________

Efficient markets hypothesis ____________________

Forecast error ____________________

Rational expectations hypothesis ____________________

Limits to arbitrage ____________________

Inefficient market ______________________________

Excess return ______________________________

Sharpe ratio

REVIEW QUESTIONS

Problem 7: Suppose that you have ¥100,000 to invest. Annual interest rates in Japan are zero, and they are 10% in Australia. The current spot rates for the U.S. dollar and Australian dollar are $E_{US\$/¥} = 100$ and $E_{Aus\$/¥} = 0.75$, respectively.

7a. You invest your ¥100,000 in Australian dollar deposits. If the exchange rate does not change over the year, how many yen will you have at the end of the year? ______________

7b. Given your answer to 7a, what is the "forecast error" associated with UIP?

7c. What is the "excess return" associated with your answer to 7a? ______________

7d. Does the fact that you made money in your trade disprove the efficient markets hypothesis?

7e. Now suppose that you borrowed an additional ¥900,000 to invest in Australian bonds on top of the ¥100,000. At the end of the year, how many yen would you earn if the exchange rate were to stay the same? ______________

7f. Now repeat the exercise in 7e under the assumption that the **yen** appreciates by 14% (be careful to get your exchange rates right). ______________

Problem 8: What would the Sharpe ratio on exchange rate arbitrage if UIP held always?

Problem 9: What do the solutions to the failure of PPP and UIP share in common?

____

____

TIPS

Problems 7e and 7f highlight the impact of "leverage" on investment returns. The more of the funds that are borrowed, the higher the potential return (or loss) on your investment.

3 Global Imbalances

ESSENTIAL CONCEPTS

In recent years, the current account deficit of the United States has reached enormous proportions. To fund the $800 billion current account deficit of the United States takes almost the combined current account surpluses of the remaining countries on the earth. This section addresses three issues. First, what is the economic cause of these large imbalances? Second, could these imbalances persist far into the future, or must they soon come to an end? Third, how large and disruptive would exchange rates changes have to be to remove these imbalances?

To understand the cause of these imbalances, a very simple model is introduced that is built upon the current account identity

$$CA(r^w) = S - I(r^w),$$

where CA is Home's current account balance, S is Home's savings, I is Home's investment spending and r^w is the world real interest rate. Because an increase in r^w is assumed to reduce investment, Home's current account balance is increasing in r^w. Because Home's current account surplus or deficit must be balanced by the Foreign's deficit or surplus, we have

$$CA(r^w) + CA^*(r^w) = 0,$$

where $CA^*(r^w)$ is Foreign's current account balance. Any increase in the supply of world savings $(S + S^*)$ will result in a reduction in the price of world savings r^w. Any increase in the demand for world investment given $r^w(I(r^w) + I^*(r^w))$ will result in an increase in r^w. The simple model can be used to understand the causes of global imbalances. If there is a positive shock to Home investment demand or to Foreign savings, or if there has been a negative shock to Home savings and Foreign investment demand, Home's current account will sink into deficit. Statistical data suggests that the big shock has been a decline in Foreign's investment demand, which has led to a *savings glut,* a lower world real interest rate, and a current account deficit in the United States.

The growth in global imbalances has led many economists to be concerned that the present situation is not sustainable in the long run and that a painful adjustment might be necessary. As covered in Chapter 17, a current account deficit of a given size is not sustainable if it implies explosive growth in a country's debt, or put another way, if it violates the country's long-run budget constraint. If the present imbalances are not sustainable, then spending power will need to shift away from the United States toward the rest of the world. How large a change in the real exchange rate would be necessary to eliminate the imbalance? This question is called the *transfer problem.* If relative demand for Home and Foreign goods is identical across countries, then a shift of spending power (or wealth) from Home to Foreign has no impact on the relative demand and so does not affect the real exchange rate (the price of Home goods in terms of Foreign). If, however, there is home bias so that demand for Home products drops and demand for Foreign products increases when income is transferred from Home to Foreign, then Home's real exchange rate depreciates substantially.

KEY TERMS

Use the space below to record your notes on the following key terms.

Savings glut ______________________________

____

____

Transfer problem ______________________________

____

____

REVIEW QUESTIONS

Problem 10: Use the savings–investment model with Home and Foreign to analyze the effects of the following shocks on Home's current account balance and on the world real interest rate.

10a. A reduction in Home savings. ______________________________

____

____

10b. An investment "boom" in Home. ______________________________

____

____

10c. If real interest rates have fallen, could either a fall in domestic savings or a rise in Home investment demand be primarily responsible for a current account deficit?

____

____

Problem 11: Home is running a current account deficit when it puts a tax on borrowing from abroad. What is the effect of the tax on Home's current account deficit?

____

____

Problem 12: True, False, or Uncertain. Please explain your answer.

12a. Home is a net debtor (its net wealth is negative). Home cannot run a trade deficit perpetually. ______________________________

____

____

12b. Home is a net creditor (its net wealth is positive). Home cannot run a trade deficit perpetually. ______________________________

____

____

Problem 13: Home's citizens become more sophisticated and increase their demand for high quality foreign products. What is the effect on Home's real exchange rate?

____

____

Problem 14: When does a reduction in the current account deficit require a real exchange rate depreciation? ______________________________

____

____

TIPS

A trade balance is "sustainable" if it can be repeated perpetually. Any trade deficit is "not sustainable" if a country is already a net debtor.

Problems 13 and 14 focus on alternative reasons for change in demand for a country's products.

4 Debt and Default

ESSENTIAL CONCEPTS

Sovereign default occurs when a government fails to make payments on its debt. Because creditors have little recourse when a sovereign debtor does not make a payment, it is a matter of choice whether a government repays its debts or does not. Sovereign debt is thus called a *contingent claim:* The government will repay if the costs of not paying outweigh the benefits of default. The benefits of default are obvious: There is more money left to spend. The costs are harder to pinpoint, but most involve various financial market penalties (e.g., temporary loss of access to international financial markets) and broader macroeconomic costs (e.g., higher risk premiums and local banking failures).

A model is developed to understand the forces at work in the decision of whether to default. A country is expected to repay the principle L of its debt plus interest of $r_L L$ for a total payment of $(1 + r_L)L$. The country's output level is random and equal to $\overline{Y} - V$, where V (the negative output shock) varies between zero and V. If the country defaults, it saves $(1 + r_L)L$, but it faces financial disruption costs that are proportional to output of $c(\overline{Y} - V)$. The benefit of repayment outweighs the cost of default if the negative shock is not too big, or $V < V^*$, where

$$V^* = \overline{Y} - (1 + r_L)L / c$$

is called the repayment threshold. The lower the threshold, the smaller the negative output shock needed to induce the country to default. The model thus predicts that a country is more likely to default if its debt burden, $(1 + r_L)L$, is larger, the cost of default is lower, or more subtly, the volatility of output (range of V) gets larger. Assuming a competitive banking system, a bank must be offered a higher interest rate to lend to a borrower that is more likely to default on its debt. Finally, by assuming the supply curve for loans is upward-sloping, the probability of default, the lending rate, and the volume of loans can be determined. Under certain circumstances, the model predicts that emerging markets (where output is more volatile than in developing countries) should experience (1) higher interest rates on their debts, (2) smaller debts, and (3) more frequent defaults. These predictions are consistent with international experience.

KEY TERMS

Use the space below to record your notes on the following key terms.

Sovereign default ______

Contingent claim ______

Repayment threshold ______

REVIEW QUESTIONS

Problem 15: A bank is accused of charging exorbitant interest rates to a sovereign borrower. What must be true about the output volatility in that country? ______

Problem 16: True, False, or Uncertain. Please explain your answer. A country could lower its cost of repaying its debt if it could raise its cost of defaulting on its debt.

Problem 17: How could a default trigger a local financial crisis? ______

TIPS

Problem 16 makes the point that a country that faces no cost of default would be worse off than one that does face a cost. Because a country with nothing to lose will always default, no one would ever lend to such a country.

Answers to Study Guide Problems

1

Trade in the Global Economy

1. In the example given in the book, the United States has a large trade deficit with China. But this does not mean that the goods are built entirely in China. In fact, China imports a lot of inputs from other countries, which in turn are part of the value of the good. In a sense, then, these imports contain value added from many countries.
2. Small countries that have many nearby trading partners have higher ratios of trade to GDP. Because the internal market is so large in a country like the United States, its international trade is a relatively small portion of its total output.
3. Hong Kong and Malaysia import a lot of goods, add a little value to these goods, and then re-export them to the rest of the world. The trade volumes are "gross" in the sense that they include value added from abroad, but GDP is "net" in the sense that it includes only local value added.
4. There have been two "golden eras" of globalization interrupted by a very long period when countries were more inward looking. The extent of outward orientation of an economy (the degree of globalization) depends in large part on government policies. A big increase in trade barriers can stop globalization.
5. False. There are substantial volumes of migration between countries at similar levels of development. It is important to remember that restrictions on immigration have a strong impact on who can move where.
6. A country may produce the same good in many different countries if the cost of shipping the good is high or if there are high tariffs. Either trade barrier makes local production desirable.
7. Vertical FDI is more likely to lead to an expansion of trade. Production of a good is moved overseas with the intention of lowering the cost of production. For instance, a U.S. multinational may produce washing machines in Mexico for the U.S. market. Horizontal FDI is more likely to lead to a contraction of trade because firms are substituting local production for exports from the country in which the multinational originates.

2

Trade and Technology: The Ricardian Model

1a. There is more than one way to arrive at this answer. The first is to reproduce the method used in the textbook: Calculate how many shirts can be produced if all 100 workers make shirts (100 workers · 2 shirts per worker), plot that on the Y axis, make the same calculation for the X axis (100 workers · 5 apples per worker), and then draw a line between them. The slope is then the rise (200) over the run (−500).

A more complicated (but illuminating) alternative is to formulate an equation for the PPF. Suppose that L_A is the number of workers making apples and L_S is the number of workers making shirts. If all workers are employed (which we assume!), then $100 = L_A + L_S$. The technology means that the amount of apples produced is $Q_A = 5 \cdot L_A$ and the amount of shirts produced is $Q_S = 2 \cdot L_S$. Combining this information we have

$$100 = \frac{Q_S}{2} + \frac{Q_A}{5} \Rightarrow Q_S = 200 - \frac{2}{5}Q_A.$$

This is the equation that is graphed in Figure 2-2.

FIGURE 2-2

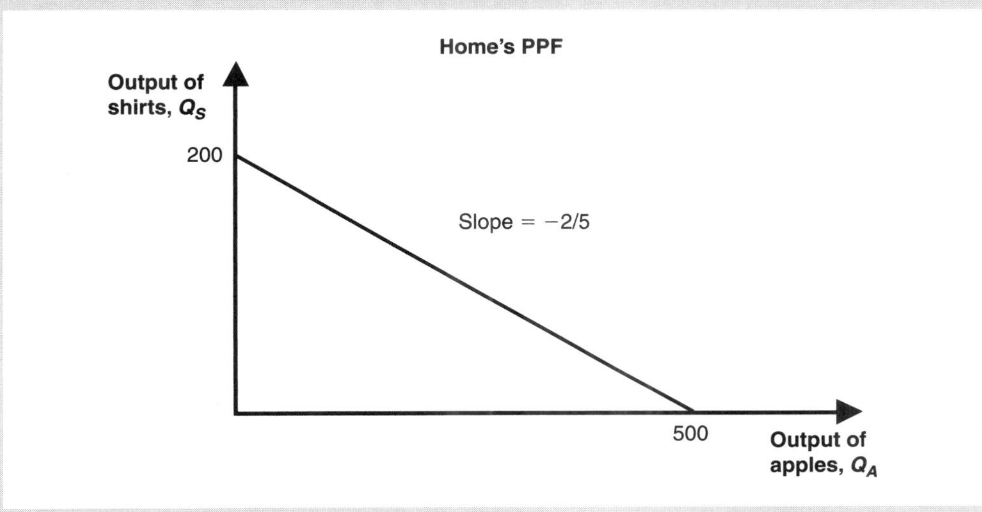

1b. We have assumed that the technology features no *diminishing returns.* No matter how many apples or shirts are being made, one worker can produces two shirts, or five apples. Thus, if one more worker is taken out of making shirts, the output of shirts always falls by 2 and the amount of apples always goes up by 5.

1c. The opportunity cost of apples is 2/5 shirts. This is the absolute value of the slope of the PPF drawn in problem 1a but only because apples are on the X axis and shirts are on the Y axis. To produce one more apple, 1/5 of a worker is required because $MPL_A = 5$. The 1/5 of a worker could produce 2/5 of a shirt (1/5 workers · 2 shirts per worker).

1d. The opportunity cost of shirts is 5/2 apples. This is *not* the slope of the PPF drawn in problem 1 because apples are on the X axis and shirts are on the Y axis. To produce one more shirt, 1/2 of a worker is required because $MPL_S = 2$. The 1/2 of a worker could produce 5/2 of a shirt (1/2 workers · 5 apples per worker).

1e. This is illustrated in Figure 2-3.

FIGURE 2-3

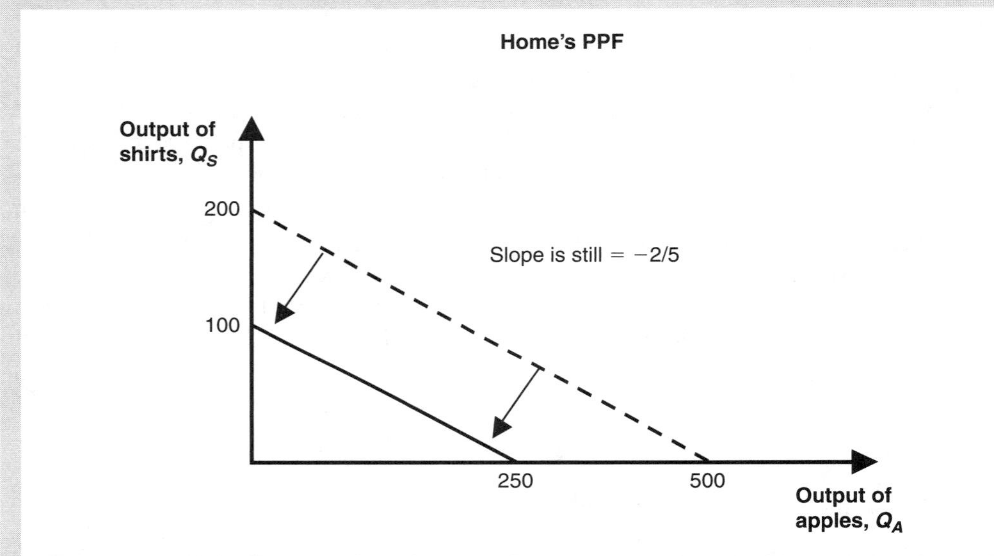

1f. Changing a country's size just changes the X and Y intercepts, but it does not change the slope of the PPF and so does not affect the opportunity of cost of one good in terms of the other.

1g. In exactly the same way as it did in problem 1e, the PPF shifts inward so that the intercepts are half of what they had been before. See Figure 2-3.

1h. See Figure 2-4.

FIGURE 2-4

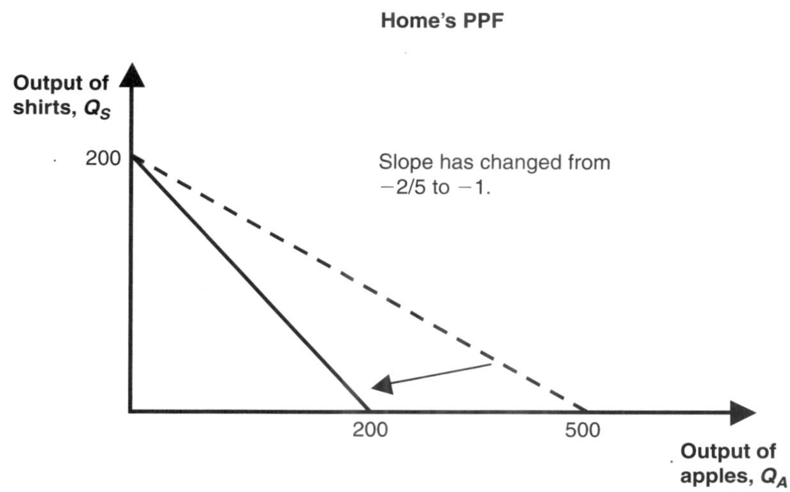

1i. This change alters the opportunity cost of apples in terms of shirts because it has changed Home's "technology" in only one of the two goods. Now to make one apple, 1/2 of a worker is needed. Moving a worker out of the shirt industry reduces shirt production by 1/2 worker · 2 shirts per worker = 1 shirt.

2a. Firms are willing to supply any mixture of goods on the PPF (see Figure 2-2). A firm that makes shirts is willing to hire a worker if the cost of doing so is no greater than the value of sales generated by hiring that worker. A shirt-making firm will then hire a worker if the wage is no more than

$$MPL_S \cdot P_S = 2\,\frac{\text{shirts}}{\text{worker}} \cdot \frac{\$5}{\text{shirt}} = \frac{\$10}{\text{worker}}.$$

An apple-making firm will hire a worker if the wage is no more than

$$MPL_A \cdot P_A = 5\,\frac{\text{apples}}{\text{worker}} \cdot \frac{\$2}{\text{apple}} = \frac{\$10}{\text{worker}}.$$

A worker creates \$10 worth of output making either good. Perfect competition and the fact that workers are free to move between industries mean that the wage must equal \$10. Because firms make zero profits whatever level of output they produce (at the prices given), they are willing to make as much as consumers want of either good as long as the PPF allows it.

2b. The country will produce 500 apples. Plugging the information into the equations in the previous answer, it should be clear that one worker will create \$20 of sales making apples and only \$10 of sales making shirts. The wage of workers will then be bid up to \$20 and so make it impossible for a shirt-making firm to break even. All workers then make apples, and the maximum number of apples they can make is 500.

3a. The budget constraint is

$$D_S = \frac{\$100}{\$1/2} - \frac{\$1/5}{\$1/2} \cdot D_A = 200 - 2/5 \cdot D_A.$$

This equation is graphed in Figure 2-5. If you did problem 1, this graph should look familiar. If the prices charged by firms reflect the opportunity costs in production, then the consumer's budget constraint is the same as the PPF in the Ricardian model.

FIGURE 2-5

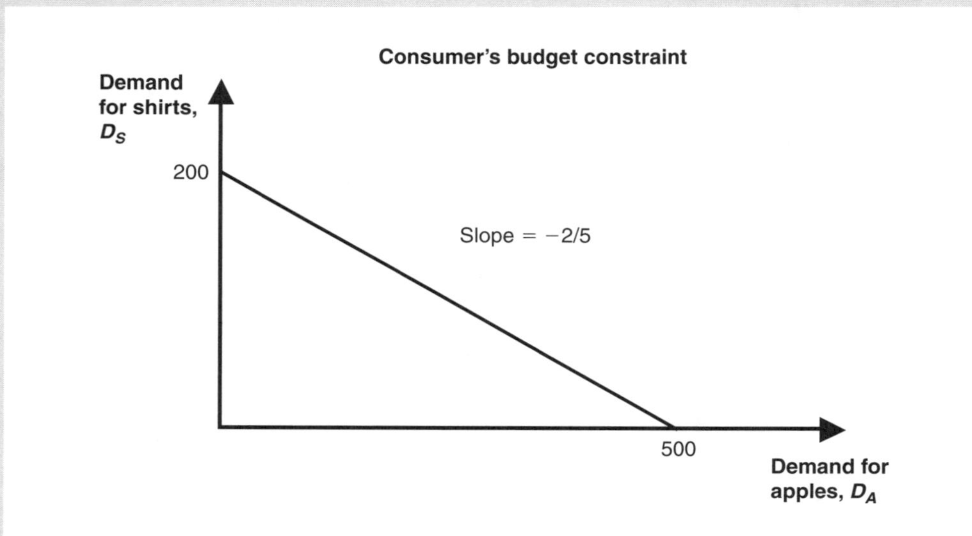

3b. There would be no change in the graph. Plugging the information into the budget constraint equation gives you exactly the same equation as for the last question. Equivalently, if the consumer were to spend all her income on shirts, she could buy \$200/(\$1 per shirt) = 200 shirts. If the consumer were to spend all her income on apples she could buy \$200/(\$0.40 per apple) = 500 apples. A straight line drawn between these two points on the graph will have a slope of −2/5 (see Figure 2-5).

3c. See Figure 2-6. The opportunity cost of an apple for the consumer has gone up even though the dollar price of an apple stays the same! Now, it costs the consumer 4/5 of a shirt to purchase one additional apple.

FIGURE 2-6

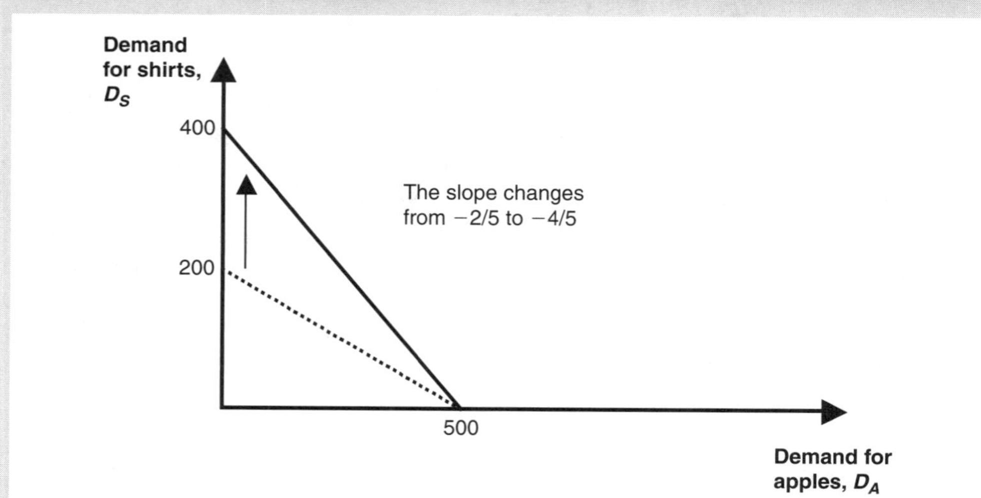

3d. See Figure 2-7. The opportunity cost of an apple has fallen by half. To obtain one more apple one needs only give up 1/5 of a shirt rather than 2/5 of a shirt.

FIGURE 2-7

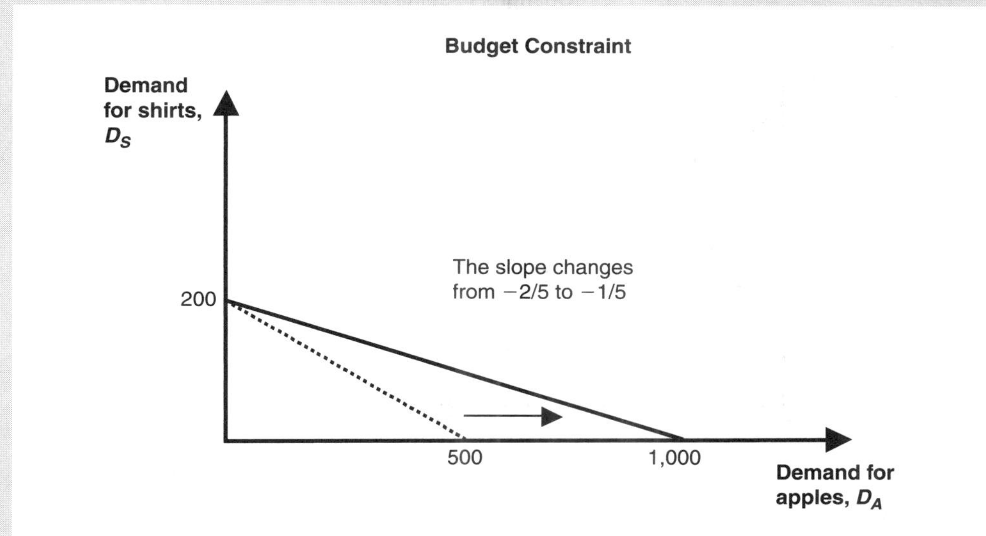

4a. Because consumers like more of both goods, when given a choice between A, B, and C, the consumer would always choose C.

4b. If given a choice between A and B, there is no way of knowing which will be chosen because the consumer gets the same amount of satisfaction out of both A and B.

4c. See Figure 2-8.

FIGURE 2-8

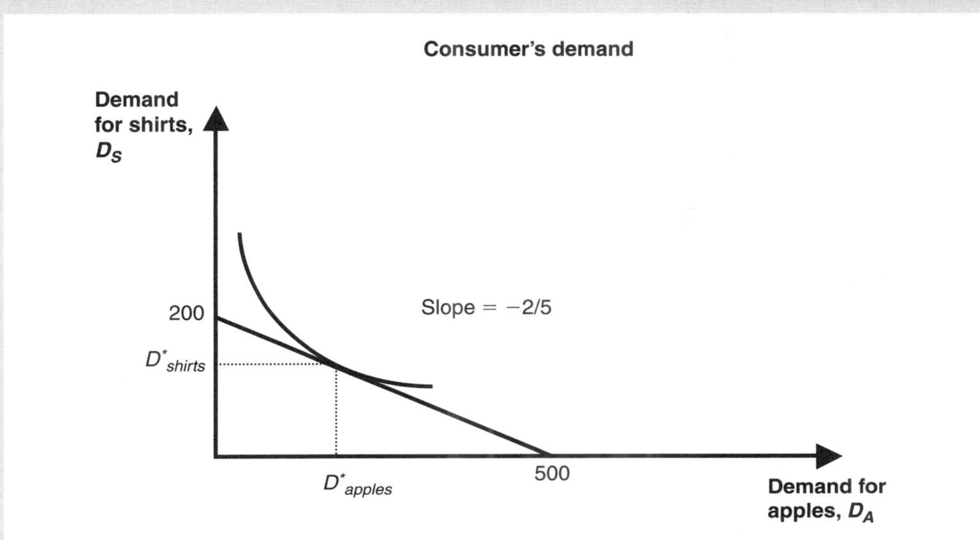

4d. See Figure 2-9.

FIGURE 2-9

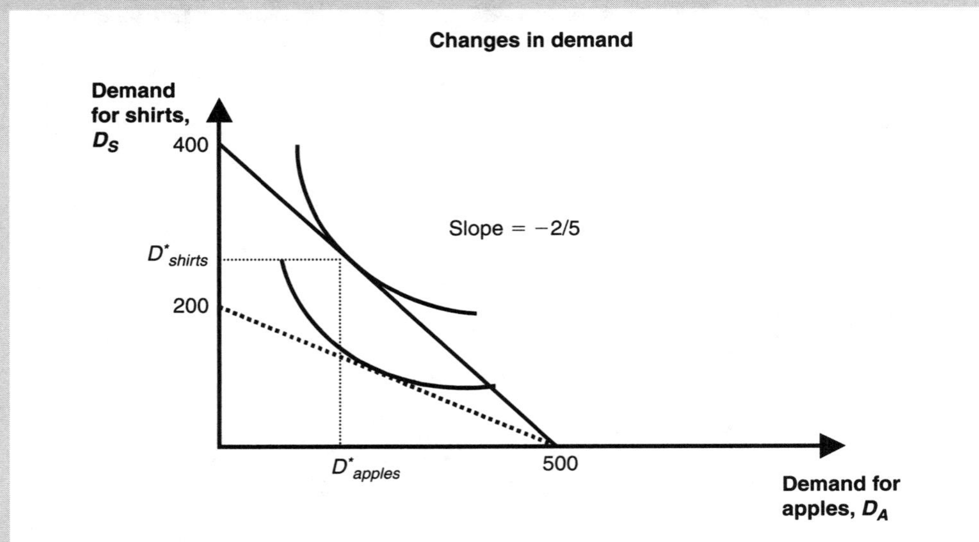

5a. As long as the relative price of apples is 2/5, firms are willing to produce anywhere along the PPF. Whatever firms produce, workers' wages will equal the value of the sales of those firms because of perfect competition (and the fact that they are the only factor). Given this income and relative prices, workers' budget constraint is the same as the PPF. Whatever bundle they choose (where the indifference curve is tangent to the budget constraint), firms will supply. An example of an equilibrium is shown in Figure 2-10.

FIGURE 2-10

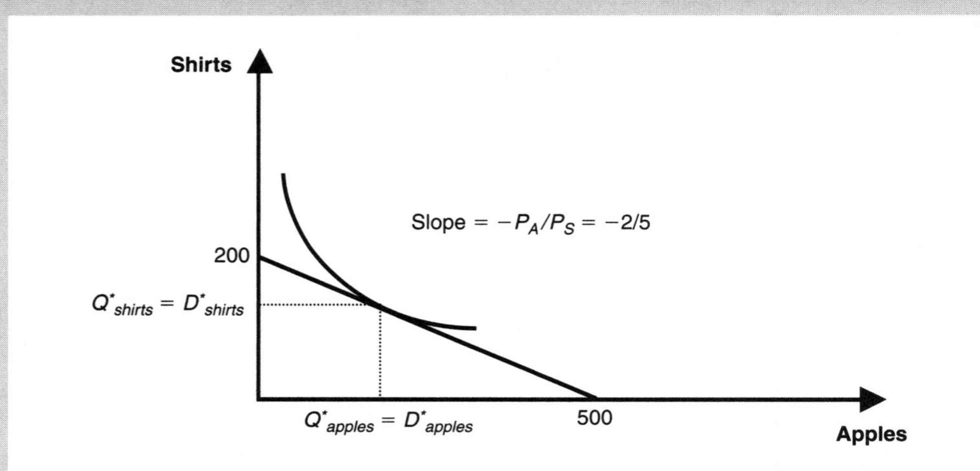

5b. In Figure 2-11, the quantity of apples demanded and supplied rises and the quantity of shirts demanded and supplied falls as the technology for producing apples improves. Note, however, that given the outward shift in the budget constraint, the consumer is free to consume more of both goods. The consumer purchases fewer shirts because apples have become relatively cheaper. Notice that the indifference curves will *not* cross.

FIGURE 2-11

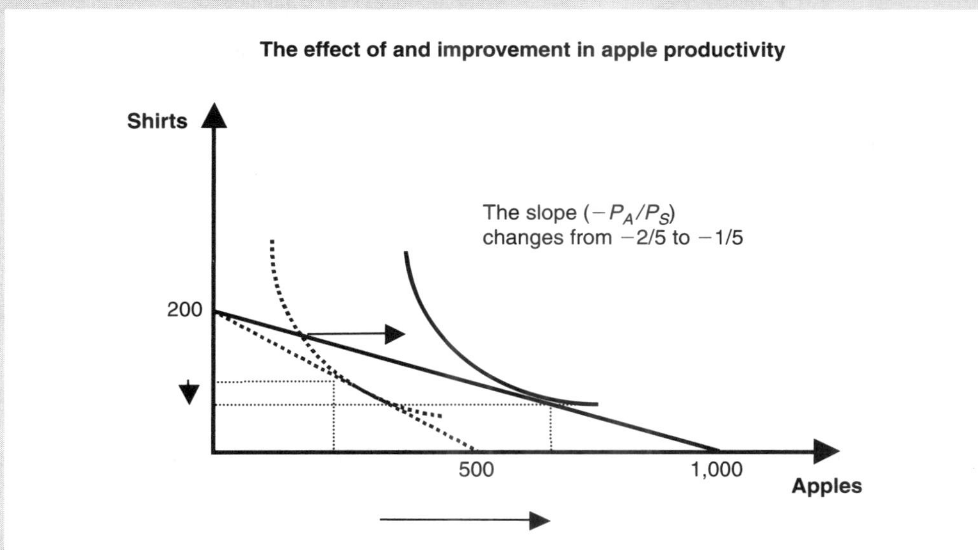

5c. The higher relative price of apples on world markets induces apple firms to expand, driving up the wage and driving shirt producers out of business. Hence, the economy produces only apples. The income of workers is then 500 apples, which are worth P_A, so that their budget constraint is

$$P_A 500 = P_A D_A + P_S D_S.$$

After some algebra, the country's budget constraint (or consumption possibilities frontier) becomes

$$D_S = \frac{P_A}{P_S} 500 - \frac{P_A}{P_S} D_A = 500 - D_A,$$

which is graphed in the Figure 2-12.

FIGURE 2-12

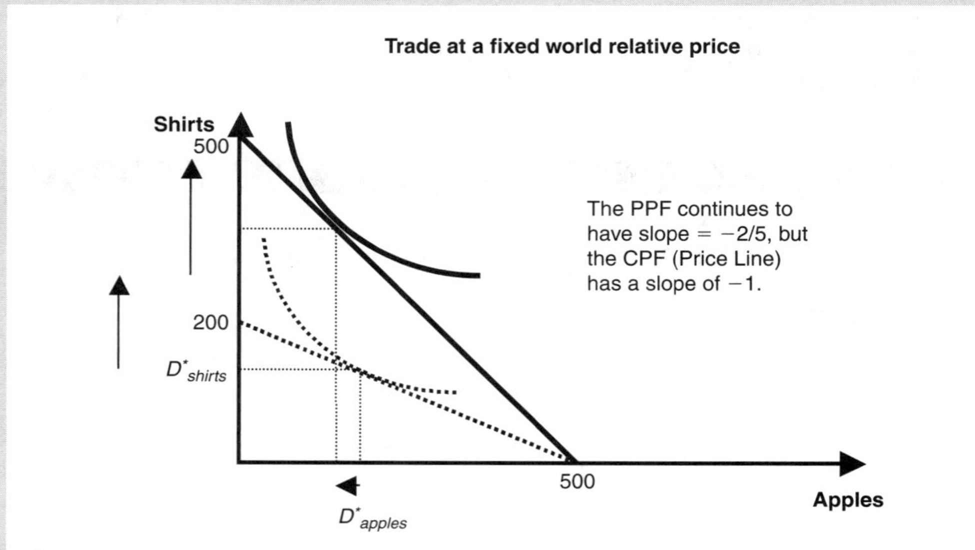

6a. For Foreign to have a comparative advantage in apples, the opportunity cost in production for apples in Foreign must be less than one. Hence, a marginal product of labor in shirts in Foreign can be any number less than 6. If it were less than 4, then Home would also have an absolute advantage in shirts.

6b. There are no gains from trade if the opportunity cost of producing each good is the same in both countries. Because the opportunity cost of apples is one shirt in Home, any numbers for which the marginal product of labor was the same in both goods would create a situation in which there was no comparative advantage and so no gains from trade. For the wage to be twice as high in Foreign, Foreign labor must be twice as productive (in both goods in this case), so MPL for apples and shirts in Foreign must be 8.

7. The good in which a country has a comparative advantage will have a lower relative price than in the other country, and the opposite will be true of the good in which it has a comparative disadvantage. Firms in the industry of comparative advantage tend to expand into the foreign market, where the relative price is higher. A trade equilibrium then involves new relative prices in at least one country, and at least one country will specialize.

8a. The price of apples in terms of shirts P_A / P_S must lie between the autarky (no-trade equilibrium) relative prices in Foreign and Home, respectively. For if $P_A / P_S > 1$, then both countries would produce exclusively apples, and if $P_A / P_S < 3/4$, both countries would produce exclusively shirts. Hence, for both goods to be produced it must be the case that $3/4 \leq \frac{P_A}{P_S} \leq 1$.

8b. Foreign has a comparative advantage in apples because the opportunity cost of producing apples is lower than in Home. Hence, Foreign will export apples and import shirts. Because the question assumes that the world relative price is halfway between the no-trade equilibrium prices in each country, it must be true that $P_A / P_S = 7/8$ (halfway between 8/8 and 6/8). Because the price of apples in a trading equilibrium is higher than in the no-trade equilibrium, producers in Foreign specialize in apples. Given world prices, if the consumers in Foreign traded all their apples for shirts, they could afford 700 of them (7/8 · 800). The tangency of the indifference curve with the consumption possibilities frontier gives the actual amount demanded. The country exports 800 − D^*_{apples} units of apples and imports D^*_{shirts}. Foreign is illustrated in panel (a) of Figure 2-13, and Home is shown in panel (b).

FIGURE 2-13

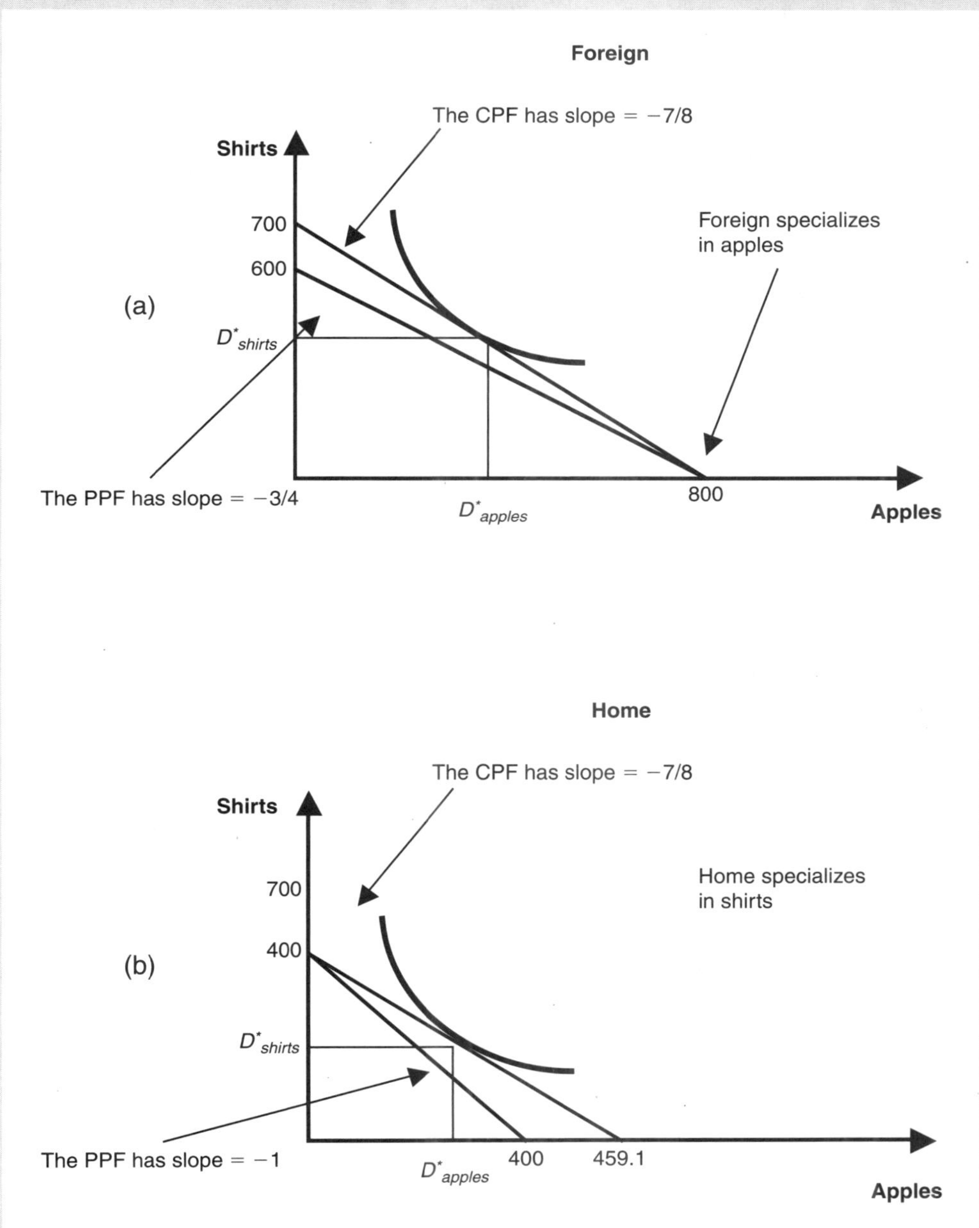

9a. The first step is to identify which good Home exports. Because the opportunity cost of shirts is lower in Home than in Foreign, Home will export shirts. Producers in Home are willing to make up to 400 units of shirts as long as the relative price of shirts is 1 and at this relative price consumers buy 225 shirts (400 − 175 = 225). This means that if Home is fully specialized in shirts and consumers buy 225 of them, there are 175 shirts available to export. This explains the flat portion of the export supply function shown in Figure 2-14. To get any more shirts available for export, Home consumers have to cut back their demand, which they will do if the relative price of shirts rises. The supply curve is getting steeper because consumers become less willing to substitute shirts for apples. Note also that Home can never export more than 400 shirts because this is the maximum amount of shirts that Home is capable of making!

FIGURE 2-14

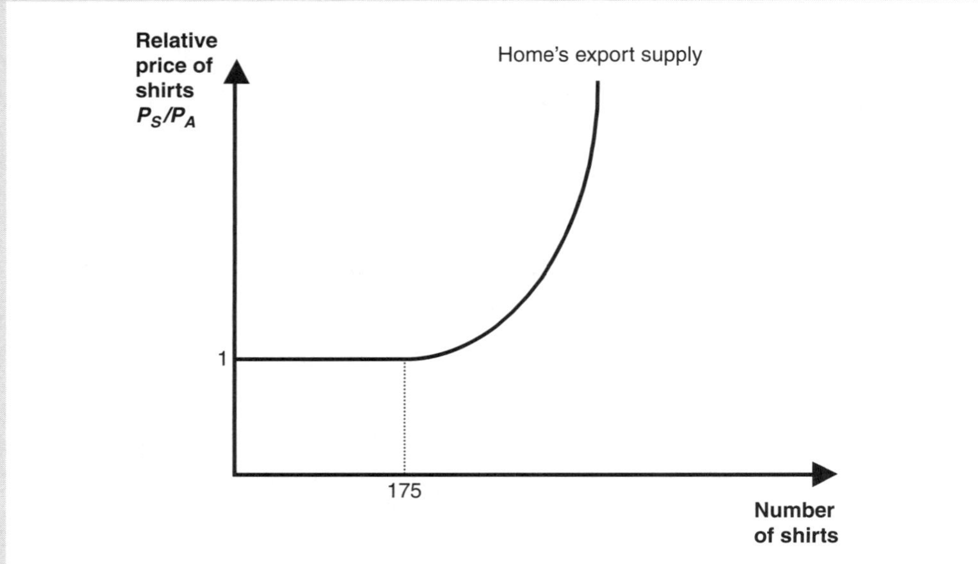

9b. Home export supply and foreign import demand is shown in Figure 2-15. If the world relative price of shirts in Foreign is 4/3, the foreign producers are willing to produce both goods. In this situation, Foreign shirt firms will produce some of the domestic consumption of 300 and import the rest on the flat portion of Foreign's import demand. If the world relative price of shirts falls below 4/3, then there is no production of shirts in Foreign and Foreign consumers start to buy more of the now cheaper good. Hence Foreign's imports begin to rise. This explains the downward-sloping part of Foreign's import demand.

FIGURE 2-15

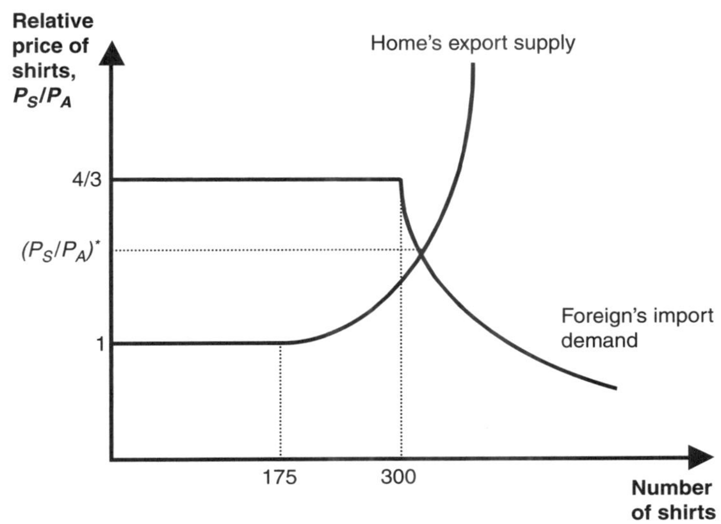

9c. Doubling the size of Home's economy doubles both its ability to produce and its desire to consume. Hence, as shown in Figure 2-16, when Home is completely specialized in producing shirts but the relative price of shirts is still 1, its consumers will produce 800 shirts, of which it will consume 450 shirts, leaving 350 for export. The shift in the export supply curve will reduce Home's *terms of trade,* that is, the value of what it exports in terms of the price of what it imports. The case shown here has Home not fully specialized in its export good; that is, it continues to produce some, but not all, of its import good. The reduction in Home's terms of trade could have been less extreme.

FIGURE 2-16

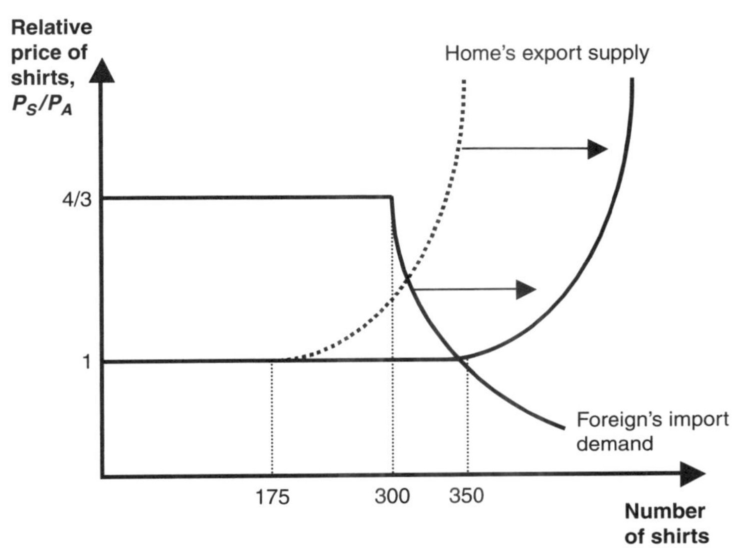

3

Who Gains and Who Loses from Trade?

1a. If the use of both inputs is doubled, then the volume of output is doubled as well. This is an example of a "constant returns to scale" technology.

1b. If the use of only one input is increased, then output will rise but at a decreasing rate. If labor is increased by a factor of 2, then output will increase by a factor of $\sqrt{2}$. Note that it is the same constant returns to scale technology, but there are diminishing returns if only one factor is increased.

1c. Suppose that there are 100 units of capital, so that $Q_M = 10\sqrt{L_M}$. A reduction of employment by 1 lowers output by $\Delta Q_M = 10\left(\sqrt{L_M} - \sqrt{L_M - 1}\right)$. Plugging in the numbers and using a calculator to solve it, reducing employment by one unit lowers output more when $L_M = 10$ than when $L_M = 100$. This highlights the implications of diminishing marginal product of labor.

2a. The opportunity cost of M in terms of A is given by the absolute value of the slope of the PPF. This is higher at point 2 than point 1. Figure 3-1 shows an example of an "increasing opportunity cost PPF."

2b. When all labor is put into Agriculture, the marginal product of labor in Agriculture (MPL_A) is very low (little land per laborer) and the marginal product of labor in Manufacturing (MPL_M) is high (lots of unused machines). Hence, as labor is moved out of Agriculture into Manufacturing, initially there is only a very small drop in Agricultural production and a very large increase in Manufacturing output: The opportunity cost of M in terms of A is low. As more labor is moved, the MPL_A is getting larger and MPL_M is getting smaller. Hence, output of agriculture starts falling at a faster rate and output of manufacturing expands at a slower rate: The opportunity cost of M in terms of A is high.

2c. A profit-maximizing firm will choose a labor force that makes the value of the marginal product of labor equal to the wage. In this example, the value of the marginal product is \$20 per worker, so in equilibrium it had better be the case that the wage is \$20.

2d. Because $P_M MPL_M = W = P_A MPL_A$ in equilibrium, $MPL_A > MPL_M$ because $P_M > P_A$.

2e. The value of the marginal product of labor is \$40, and workers are being paid only \$25. This means that revenues could be expanded by more than costs if another worker is hired. Hence, you are employing too few workers.

2f. If P_M / P_A falls (e.g., suppose that P_M drops while P_A is fixed), then workers will be induced to move out of manufacturing into agriculture. As more workers enter agriculture, the land/labor ratio falls. Hence, the marginal product of labor in agriculture falls. This can be seen directly in Figure 3-3. The fall in the price of a unit of manufacturing goods reduces the value of the marginal product of labor in manufacturing from the dotted curve to the solid curve. This reduction in labor demand lowers the nominal wage and so induces the agricultural industry to expand (a movement along the demand curve for labor in agriculture). Because the amount of land is fixed, the land/labor ratio falls and the marginal product of labor in agriculture falls as well.

FIGURE 3-3

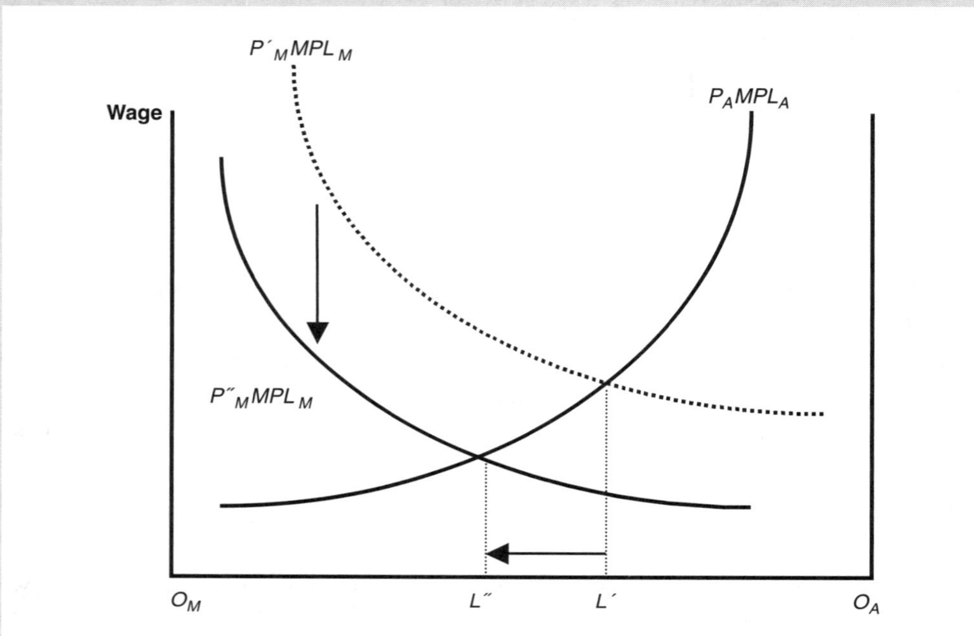

The Effect of a Change in the Price of a Good on the Allocation of the Mobile Factor

3a. See Figure 3-4 on the next page.

FIGURE 3-4

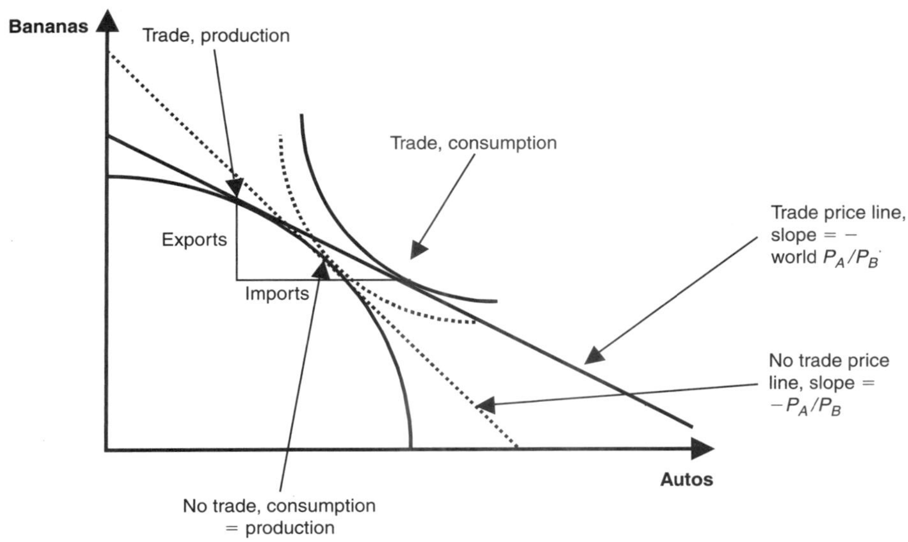

National Welfare: Autarky versus Trade

3b. The country is better off because the opportunity cost of producing a good in autarky is different than the opportunity cost of the good on international markets. By reorganizing production in the country and changing consumption patterns, the country can then expand the production of the good in which its opportunity cost in production is less than the opportunity cost on international markets, thereby obtaining more of both goods.

3c. Recall that the price of autos in terms of bananas is higher in Foreign than in Home in a no-trade equilibrium. In a trading equilibrium, the relative price of a good must lie between the autarky relative prices of the two countries because if it were not the two countries would like to export the same good. Hence, Foreign adjusts to international trade by cutting back production of autos, expanding production of bananas, and exporting bananas to Home in return for autos. Notice that the law of comparative advantage must hold: A country exports the good in which its autarky relative price is lower and imports the other good.

3d. In a free-trade equilibrium, the two countries face exactly the same relative prices. Producers adjust their production until the ratio of the value of the marginal product of labor is the same in both industries. Hence, the ratio of the marginal product of labor in autos to the marginal product of labor in bananas is the same in both countries. This in turn is equal to the slope of the PPF at the point where production occurs: The opportunity cost of producing autos in terms of bananas must be the same in the two countries.

4a. See Figure 3-5. Note that the diagram already expressed all variables in terms of the price of bananas. So a reduction in the relative price of autos (P_A / P_B) involves the shift in the value of the marginal product of autos when expressed in terms of bananas. This shift induces labor to move from auto production to banana production.

The amount of labor that moves across industries is captured by the distance L_1L_2. The wage expressed in terms of bananas (W / P_B) falls.

FIGURE 3-5

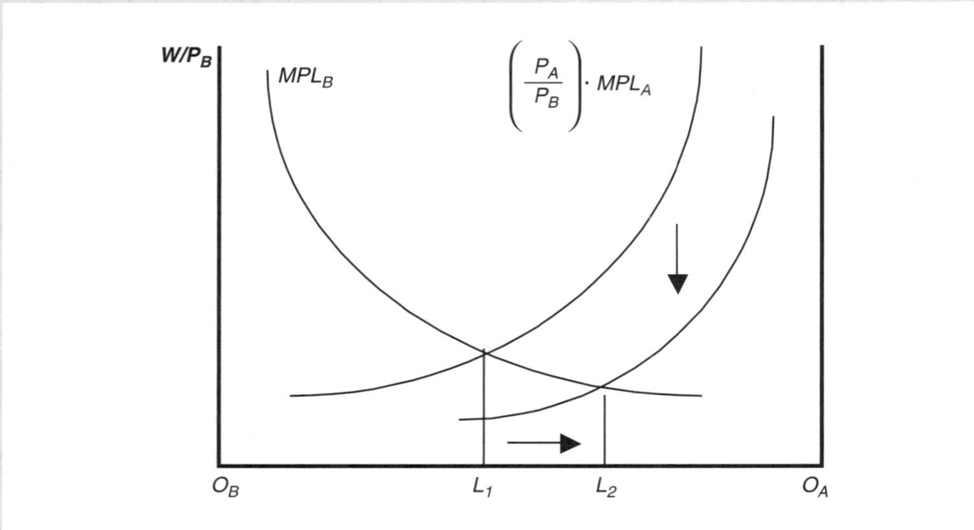

The Effect of a Reduction in the Relative Price of Autos

4b. Because $P_AMPL_A = W$, it follows that $MPL_A = W / P_A$. MPL_A rises because the amount of labor employed making A declines. Because MPL_A rises, it follows that W / P_A rises. Workers can afford more autos.

4c. Because $P_BMPL_B = W$, it follows that $MPL_B = W / P_B$. Because MPL_B falls (see Figure 3-5), it follows that W / P_B falls. Workers cannot afford as many bananas.

4d. The effect of trade on the well-being of workers is ambiguous if the workers spend their income on both goods.

5a. If labor were truly mobile between industries, then it would move into the higher paid industry until the wages were equalized.

5b. Workers may have skills that they have learned in their industry that cannot be transferred to other industries. Their wages fall when they are displaced because they lack the skills that are valuable to another industry. In some sense, these skills can be thought of as being specific to an industry. This idea helps explain why TAA includes providing retraining to workers displaced by trade.

6a. Because labor is unable to move, the marginal product of labor in computers must stay the same. Hence, the wage must rise by the same amount as the price of computers. This means that the real wage of computer workers in terms of computers is the same. Because the price of tulips has not changed, the real wage of computer workers in terms of tulips has risen.

6b. Because labor is unable to move, the marginal product of labor in tulips must remain the same, so the real wage of tulips in terms of tulips has stayed the same. Because computer prices have risen, however, the real wage of tulip workers in terms of computers has fallen.

7a. See Figure 3-6. (Autarky information is displayed in dotted lines, and trade information is displayed in solid lines.) Home has the higher autarky relative price of autos and so is the exporter of bananas. Home's supply of bananas increases and its supply of autos decreases, whereas the opposite is true in Foreign. Home's consumption of bananas is less than its supply of bananas, and its consumption of autos is greater than its supply of autos. The opposite is true in Foreign.

FIGURE 3-6

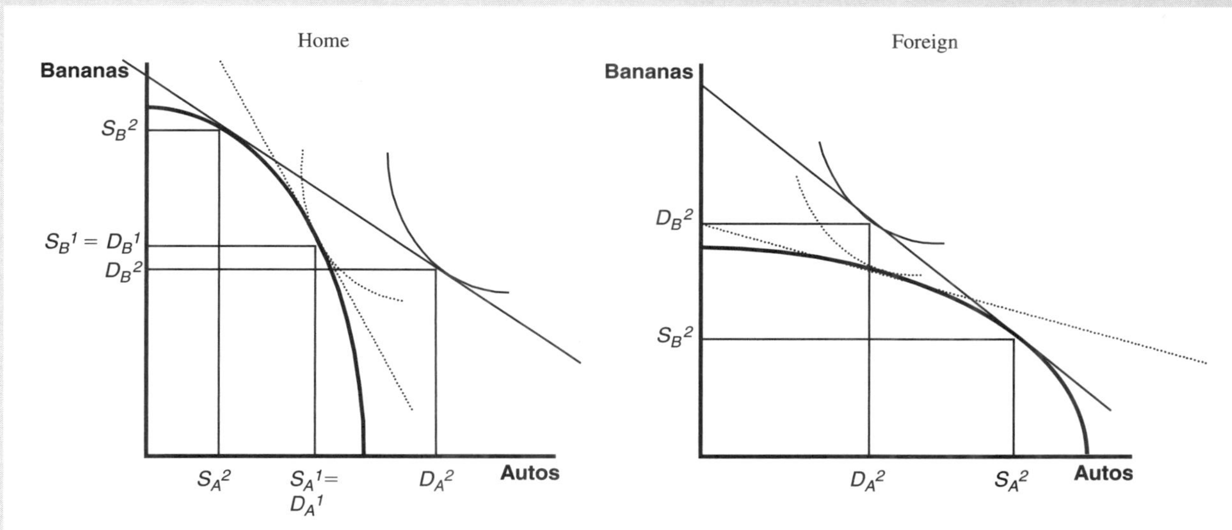

Trade versus Autarky in Home and Foreign

7b. The real rental of capital falls in Home. As labor is pulled out of auto production, the marginal product of capital (MP_K) falls. Because

$$MP_K = \frac{R_K}{P_A},$$

the income of a unit of capital has fallen relative to the price of autos. Now notice that

$$\frac{R_K}{P_B} = \frac{P_A}{P_B} \cdot \frac{R_K}{P_A}.$$

Because P_A / P_B goes down when the country trades, and because R_K / P_A falls as well, the nominal earnings of a unit of capital will buy less of both goods!

7c. Note that the relative price of autos goes up for Foreign, and so the argument for 7b applies here but in reverse. The real rental of capital rises in Foreign.

7d. The demand for land in Home rises as the country increases its production of bananas. The marginal product of capital rises as labor is moved from auto production into banana production. The value of the marginal product of land is the demand curve for land.

7e. Because global resources are used more efficiently, both countries can consume more than they did when they were not trading. Because the country gains-from-trade means that winners win more than losers lose, the winners could compensate the losers and everyone could be made better off.

4

Trade and Resources: The Heckscher-Ohlin Model

1a. The answer is displayed in Figure 4-5. Shoes have a higher labor/capital ratio than computers when the wage/rental ratio is high and have a relatively low labor/capital ratio when the wage/rental ratio is low. Hence, one cannot call either good labor or capital intensive. The Heckscher-Ohlin model explicitly rules out this possibility!

FIGURE 4-5

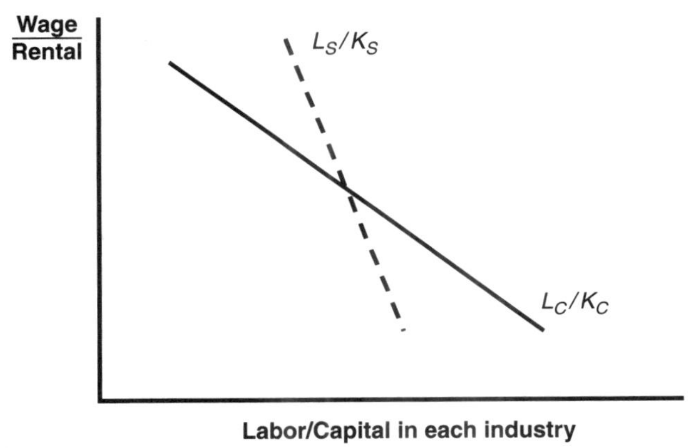

An Example of a *Factor Intensity Reversal*

1b. Factor abundance is measured as the ratio of the endowments of the factors. The capital/labor ratio in Home is 2, and it is 2.5 in Foreign. Foreign is capital-abundant relative to Home even though it has less capital than Home.

2a. Because consumers' tastes are the same in every country, the differences in relative prices in the two countries must stem from differences in the shape of the production possibility frontiers. A situation in which Home has a higher relative price of computers in a no-trade equilibrium is shown in the Figure 4-6. The curves relevant to Home are represented by solid lines, and curves relevant to Foreign are in dotted lines. Home's PPF is bowed out toward shoes, and Foreign's PPF is bowed out toward computers. Because tastes are the same in both countries, it is the difference in the shape of the PPFs that give rise to the difference in the no-trade equilibrium prices.

Why is Home's PPF bowed out toward shoes and Foreign's PPF bowed out toward computers? As capital is added to an economy, the PPF tends to bow out toward the capital-intensive good (computers in this example). As labor is added to an economy, the PPF bows out in favor of the labor-intensive good (shoes in this example). Thus, Foreign must have a higher capital/labor ratio than Home, so it is relatively capital-abundant.

FIGURE 4-6

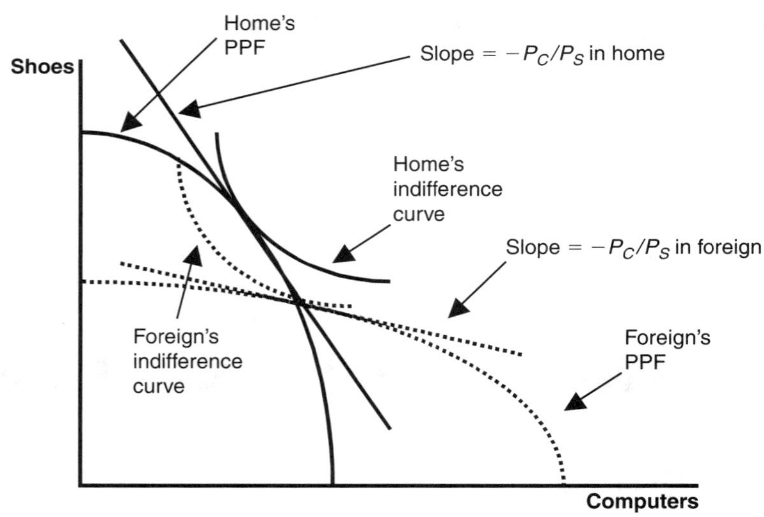

Autarky

2b. Foreign is producing a higher ratio of computers to shoes in a no-trade equilibrium than Home. The tastes are the same in the two countries, and the relative price of computers is lower in Foreign than in Home. This means that Foreign consumers must be consuming relatively more computers than shoes compared with Home consumers. Because the country must supply its own goods (there is no trade), Foreign must be producing a higher ratio of computers to shoes than Home.

3a. Because Home is labor abundant relative to Foreign and shirts are labor intensive relative to airplanes, the *Heckscher-Ohlin theorem* establishes that Home will export shirts.

3b. Assumption six of the Heckscher-Ohlin model is that countries have the same tastes. Because the countries are engaged in free trade, the price of the goods is the same in both countries. Hence, consumers in Foreign consume goods in the same ratio as those in Home.

3c. An increase in the endowment of capital will tend to further skew its PPF toward the capital-intensive good, airplanes. This means that for any relative price of airplanes, Foreign will supply more airplanes and fewer shirts, as shown in the left-hand side of the Figure 4-7. As a result, Foreign's export supply curve for airplanes shifts to the right, causing the relative price of airplanes to fall.

FIGURE 4-7

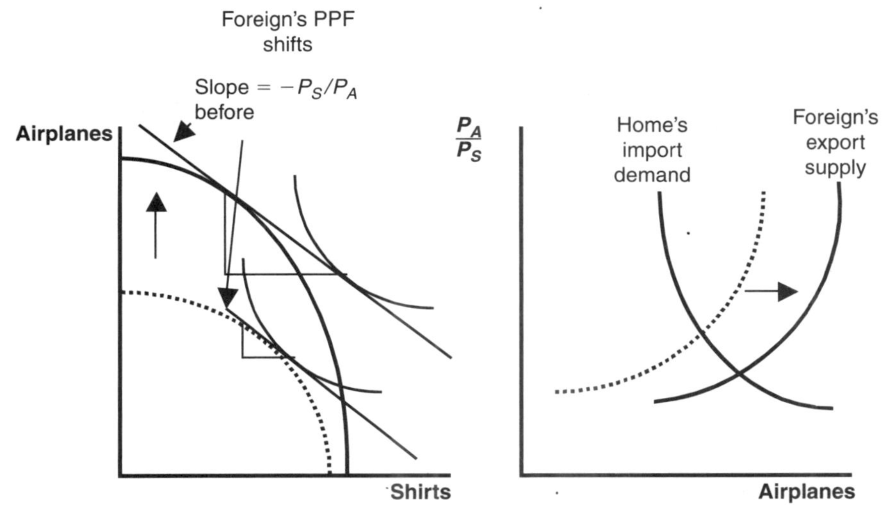

Increase in Capital Endowment

3d. As established in the last problem, an increase in Foreign's endowment of capital reduces the relative price of airplanes and so increases the relative price of shirts. This is a terms-of-trade improvement for Home, the exporter of shirts. Therefore, Home can get to a higher indifference curve. (See Figure 4-8.) Note that shirt output increases and airplane output falls as a result.

FIGURE 4-8

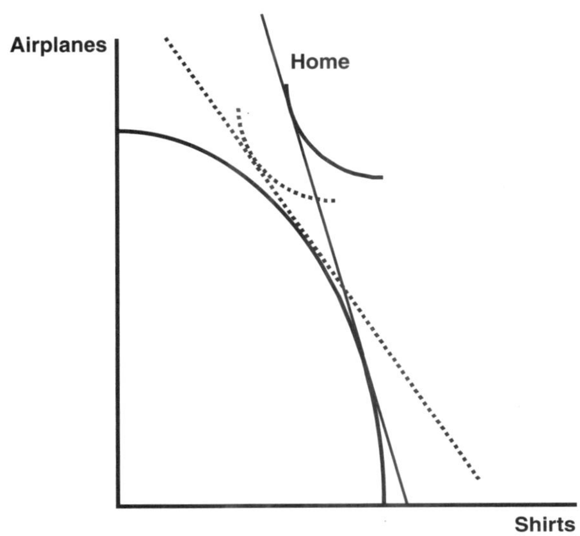

Terms of Trade Improvement for Home

4. Suppose that the capital-abundant country (Foreign) has consumers who have strong preferences for airplanes, whereas the labor-abundant country (Home) has consumers with strong preferences for shirts. Then it is possible that the trade pattern is exactly the opposite of that predicted by the Heckscher-Ohlin theorem, as can be seen in Figure 4-9.

FIGURE 4-9

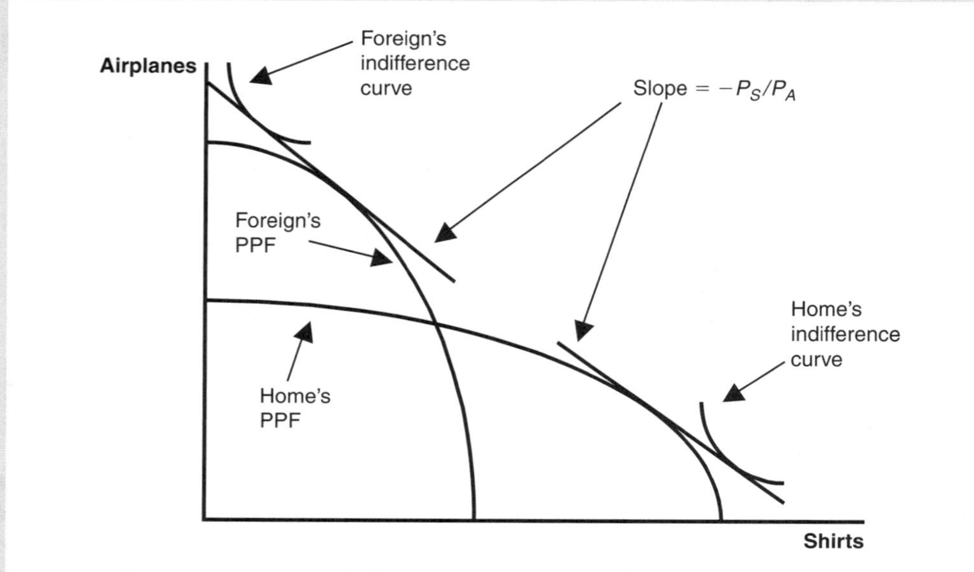

The Importance of the Tastes Assumption in Heckscher-Ohlin

5. There could be (1) factor intensity reversals, (2) technologies that differ across countries, and (3) tastes that differ across countries.

6a. The highest relative wage that could occur in this country is 10. The relative demand for the whole economy cannot exceed the relative demand for the shoe industry because it is a weighted average of the relative demands in the two industries.

6b. As resources are moved out of computers and into shoes, the relative demand curve for the economy shifts up. The weights in the weighted average now favor shoes over computers.

6c. An upward shift in the relative demand curve causes the relative wage to rise. Because the industry relative demand curves do not shift, this means that L / K must fall in each industry.

7a. The capital/labor ratio used by Ubetchan producers in both industries would rise. Engaging in free trade would lower the relative price of autos and thereby induce the auto industry to contract and the hat industry to expand. As factors are moved out of autos and into hats, the relative demand for capital would decrease, because autos are relatively more capital intensive than hats. This is shown as the leftward shift in the relative demand curve in Figure 4-10. The reduction in the relative demand for capital lowers the rental/wage ratio, which induces firms in the both the auto and shoe industry to substitute capital for labor. Note that the relative supply of factors in the economy, given by K^* / L^* in Figure 4-10, does not change.

FIGURE 4-10

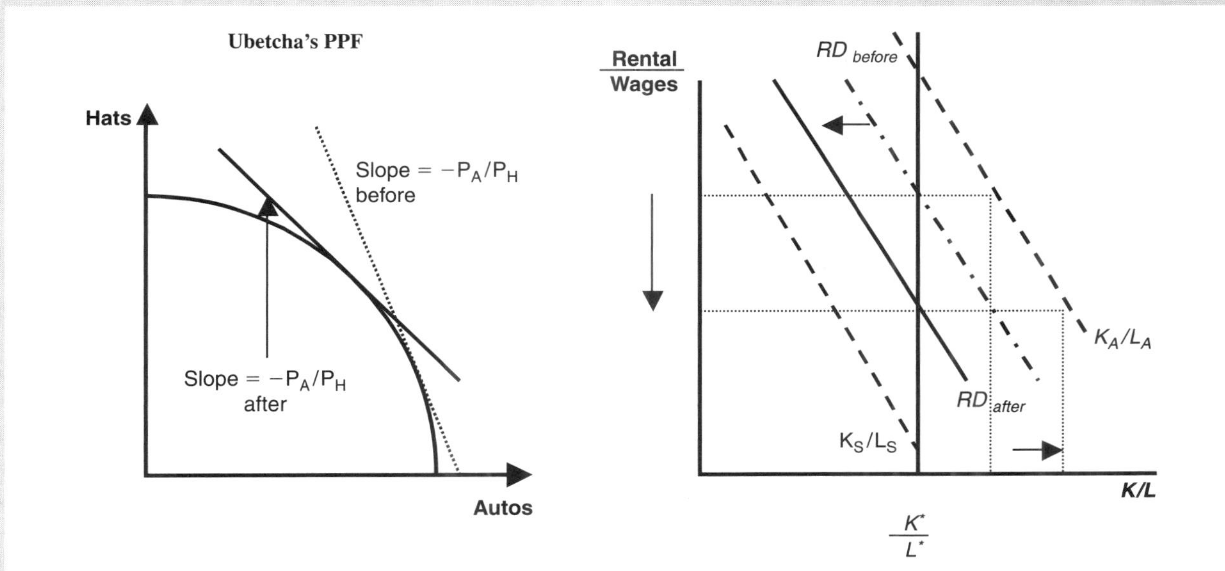

The Effect of Trade on Factor Prices

7b. Because the capital/labor ratio used by producers rises, the marginal product of capital should fall, as each machine has fewer workers using it.

7c. A political group that represented the economic interests of capital owners would lobby against free trade. By the Stolper-Samuelson theorem, the decrease in the relative price of the capital-intensive good induced by free trade would lower the real rental and raise the real wage.

8a. By the Heckscher-Ohlin theorem, the United States has a comparative advantage in skill-intensive goods, so free trade raises the price of skill-intensive goods. By the Stolper-Samuelson theorem, trade raises the real income of skilled workers while lowering the real income of unskilled workers. Hence, the Heckscher-Ohlin model is consistent with the survey results.

8b. One would expect exactly the opposite response in a skill-scarce country compared with the response in the skill-abundant country. Trade causes the relative price of goods to move in the opposite direction for this type of country.

9a. Because the two countries are absolutely identical, they should have exactly the same relative price of goods and factors in a no trade equilibrium. Hence, there is no motive for migration.

9b. Moving capital from Foreign to Home will skew Foreign's PPF (it shrinks but in a skewed way) toward doughnuts and Home's PPF outward toward sofas. The relative price of sofas will fall in Home and rise in Foreign. Applying the Stolper-Samuelson theorem, the real earnings of labor will rise in Home and fall in Foreign. Because they were starting at the same level (before the capital moved), Home must now have a higher real wage than Foreign.

9c. Labor would want to move from Foreign to Home.

9d. The migration of labor from Foreign to Home would tend to skew Home's PPF toward doughnuts and Foreign's PPF toward sofas. This has the opposite impact on the relative price of doughnuts and so has the opposite impact on real wages. Real wages tend to converge between the two countries through the response of goods prices.

9e. Yes, migration causes the relative price of doughnuts to fall (and sofas to rise). By the Stolper-Samuelson theorem, this implies an increase in the real rental to capital.

10. According to the Heckscher-Ohlin model, international trade increases the real income (through the Stolper-Samuelson theorem) of the abundant factor and reduces the real income of the scarce factor. In developing countries, labor is the abundant factor and so should gain from trade. If Bob were educated and fast thinking, he could say, "Oh yeah, what about the Leontief paradox?" Then you'd be pretty much sunk.

11. If Leontief had found that a bundle of U.S. exports contained a higher ratio of capital to labor than imports, then he would have concluded that the U.S. trade pattern was consistent with Heckscher-Ohlin. There would be no paradox.

12a. Because the country has a larger share of world GDP than it has of labor, it should be a net importer of labor services.

12b. If workers in Home are paid better than in the rest of the world, then they may be more productive than workers elsewhere. In this case, it could be that if effective labor were measured, Home in fact has a share of world effective labor that is greater than its share of GDP.

12c. Yes. A country's relative abundance or scarcity is its share of the world's stock of a type of factor relative to its share of world income. Differences in technologies would show up as differences in shares of the world's income that are not accounted for by differences in factor ownership. A really productive country will appear to be scarce in a larger set of factors and a less productive country will appear to be abundant in a larger set of factors.

5

Movement of Labor and Capital between Countries

1a. The expansion of land increases the marginal product of labor in agriculture for every level of possible employment. Because the prices of goods are fixed on world markets, this change raises the value of the marginal product of labor in agriculture from $P_A MPL_A$ to $P_A MPL'_A$ as illustrated in Figure 5-2. At the old level of employment (measured by the distance $L^* O_A$ in the figure) $P_A MPL'_A > W$, so agricultural firms hire additional labor until the labor employed in A is given by $L' O_A$. This drives up the wage and leads to a movement along the curve $P_M MPL_M$ until $P_M MPL_M = P_A MPL'_A = W'$.

FIGURE 5-2

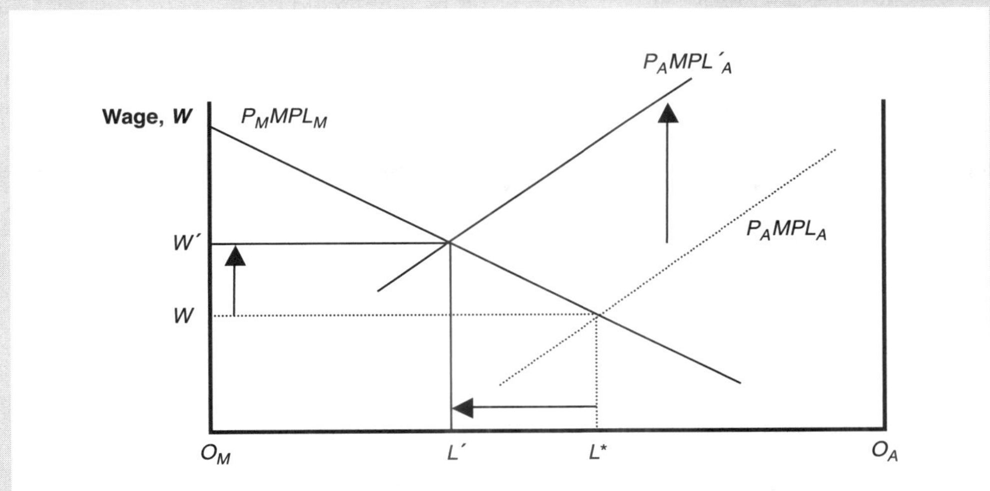

An Increase in Land Endowment Raises the Wage in Home

1b. Immigration leads to an increase in Home's labor endowment and so increases the size of the base of the diagram as illustrated in Figure 5-3. Note that the apparent shift in the $P_A MPL_A$ is not the result of any actual change in the value of the marginal product of labor in agriculture for a given level of employment. It is due to a shift in the origin O_A to the right, reflecting the increase in the labor endowment. The increase in the labor endowment is measured by the distance from O_A to O'_A. The wage will drop as a result of the increase in the endowment of labor. If there are no *moving costs,* then labor will move into Home until its wage level is equal to the world wage level.

FIGURE 5-3

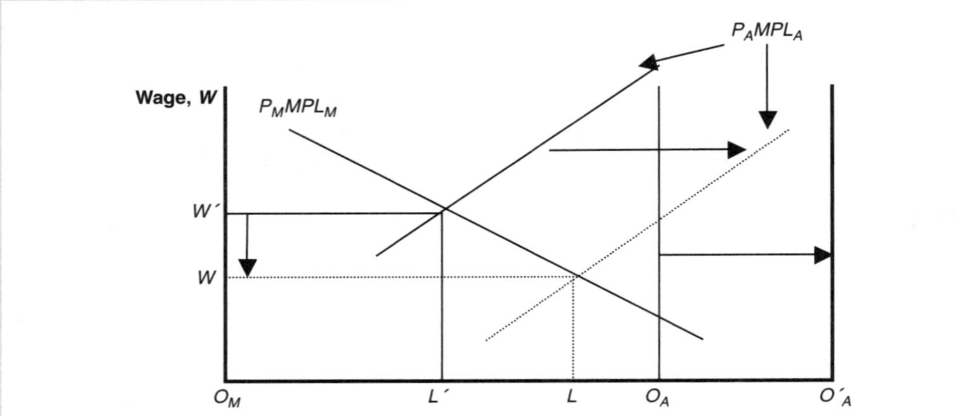

An Increase in the Labor Endowment Due to Immigration

1c. As shown in the answer to 1b, the increase in the endowment of labor reduces the wage. This induces both agriculture and manufacturing to add workers. Hence, the marginal product of capital and the marginal product of land both increase (the capital/labor ratio and the land/labor ratio rise). Because the prices of goods are fixed, this means that the real income of a unit of capital (R_K) and (R_T) both increase. Capitalists and landowners are made better off by immigration.

1d. The PPF shifts outward when more of the mobile factor is available, as shown in Figure 5-4. Because there are more workers employed in both industries after the inflow of workers, the level of output of each good must rise.

FIGURE 5-4

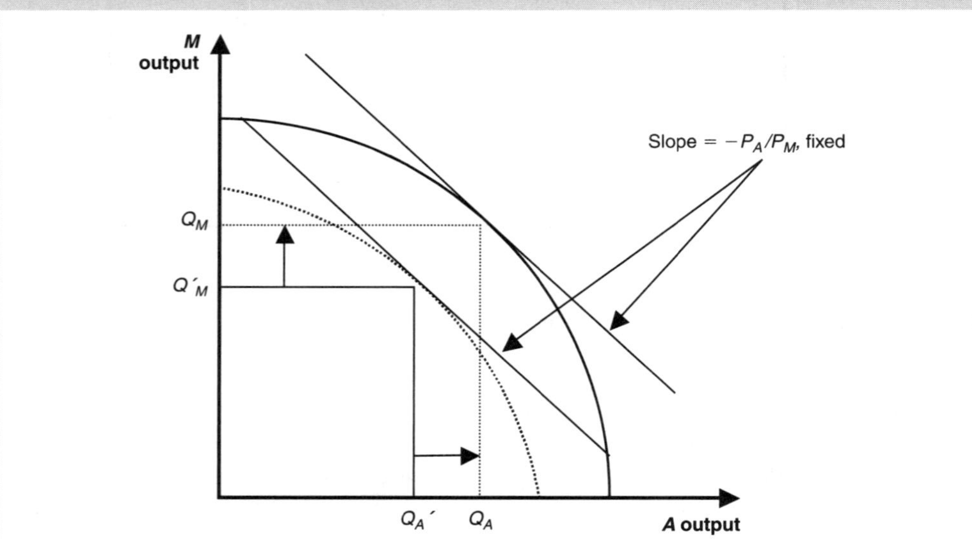

Effect of Expanding the Endowment of the Mobile Factor

2a. Airplanes are capital intensive relative to shirts because the capital/labor ratio is 5/3, which is greater than the capital/labor ratio in shirts, which is 1.

2b. To answer this question, we use the box diagram shown in Figure 5-5. The height of the diagram is the size of the country's endowment of capital, and the length of the base is the original size of the labor endowment. In the diagram, the slope of the line from O_S through point *a* is equal to 1, which is the capital/labor ratio in shirts, and the slope of the line from *a* to O_A is equal to 5/3, which is the capital/labor ratio in airplanes. Initially, the amount of capital employed in airplane manufacturing is given by the length of the line from *K* to O_A and the amount of labor used in making airplanes is given by the length of the line *L* to O_A. When laborers leave, the box becomes narrower and so we relabel the airplane origin O_A' to reflect this fact. The slope of the line from *b* to O_A continues to be 5/3. The new intersection at *b* shows clearly that even though there is less labor available in the country, the amount of labor and capital employed in airplane manufacture has increased!

FIGURE 5-5

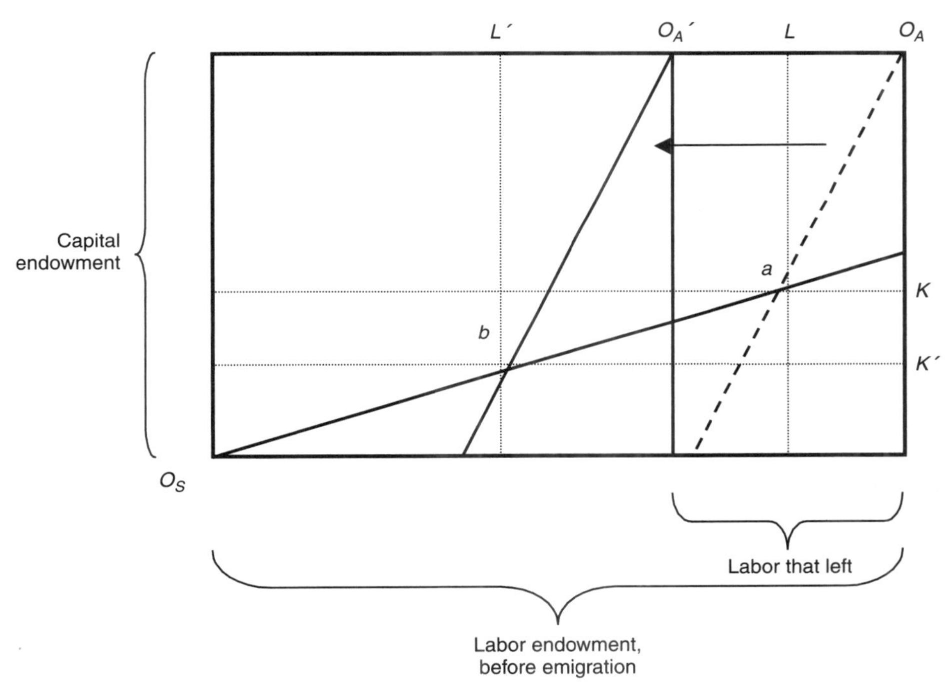

The Box Diagram and a Shrinking Labor Force

2c. Let Q_A be the output of airplanes and Q_S be the output of shirts. Let $\overline{K}$ be the country's endowment of capital, and let $\overline{L}$ be the country's endowment of labor. Using the production information in the question we have

$$\overline{K} = 5 \cdot Q_A + 2 \cdot Q_S$$

and

$$\overline{L} = 3 \cdot Q_A + 2 \cdot Q_S.$$

Doing a little algebra, we find that

$$Q_A = \frac{\overline{K} - \overline{L}}{2} \text{ and } Q_S = \frac{5\overline{L} - 3\overline{K}}{4}.$$

2d. The answer is shown in Figure 5-6. The shift in the PPF is consistent with the Rybczynski theorem in reverse: At fixed relative prices, a decrease in the endowment of labor leads to a reduction in the production of the labor-intensive good and an expansion in the production of the capital-intensive good.

FIGURE 5-6

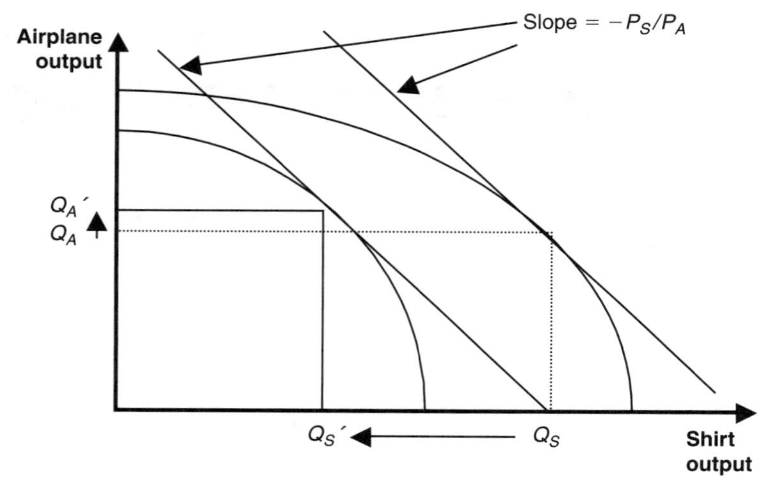

The Effect of a Reduction in Labor Endowment in the Long-Run

3a. The entry of computer workers into the country raises the marginal product of capital in the computer industry for any level of capital used in that industry, as shown in Figure 5-7. This induces capital to move into the computer sector, as shown by the shift from K to K'. Because the rental must rise, it must be that the marginal product of capital increases in both industries. This means that marginal product of both computer workers and shirt workers must fall (falling ratio of specific factor to mobile factor in each industry). Hence, both types of workers are hurt.

The fall in real income across computer and shirt workers will not be of the same magnitude, however.

FIGURE 5-7

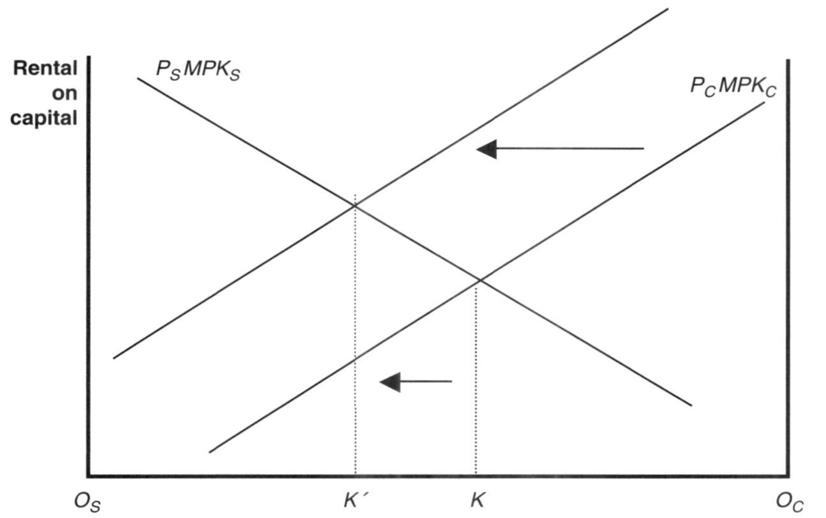

The Effect of an Increase in the Endowment of Skilled Labor

3b. In the long run the factor price insensitivity result must hold: There is no effect on the real wage of either computer or shirt workers. This is because workers can retrain and switch industries in the long run.

3c. In the short run the real rental must rise. Figure 5-7 demonstrates that the rental must rise, and because goods prices are fixed, an increase in the nominal rental is also an increase in the real. In the long run, the factor price insensitivity result must hold so there is no long-run impact on the real rental rate. Output of the labor-intensive good will expand and the capital-to-labor ratios in each industry will return to their normal level.

4a. True. It is estimated that there are 12 million illegal immigrants into the United States, but the number of legal immigrants is much higher. As a portion of the U.S. population, immigrants are most represented among the least and the most educated.

4b. False. Many immigrants into the United States are unskilled. However, a very substantial portion of the most highly skilled workers in the United States are immigrants. There is a U-shaped relationship between immigrants' share of the population and level of educational attainment.

4c. True. Low-skill apparel industry output expanded and high-skill industries contracted relative to other American cities.

5a. The problem involves the specific-factors model. Because Home has more labor than Foreign and everything else is the same, the marginal product of labor in Home must be lower than the marginal product of labor in Foreign in both industries. Hence, wages will be lower in Home. If the marginal product of labor is lower in Home than in Foreign in both industries, it must be true that the marginal product of capital is higher in Home than in Foreign. Hence, the rental rate in Home must be higher as well. This creates the motive for capital to leave Foreign, where the rental on capital is low, and enter Home, where the rental on capital is high.

5b. The increase in capital expands Home's PPF in favor of M as in Figure 5-8. Because labor is drawn out of agriculture into manufacturing, the output of agriculture must fall.

FIGURE 5-8

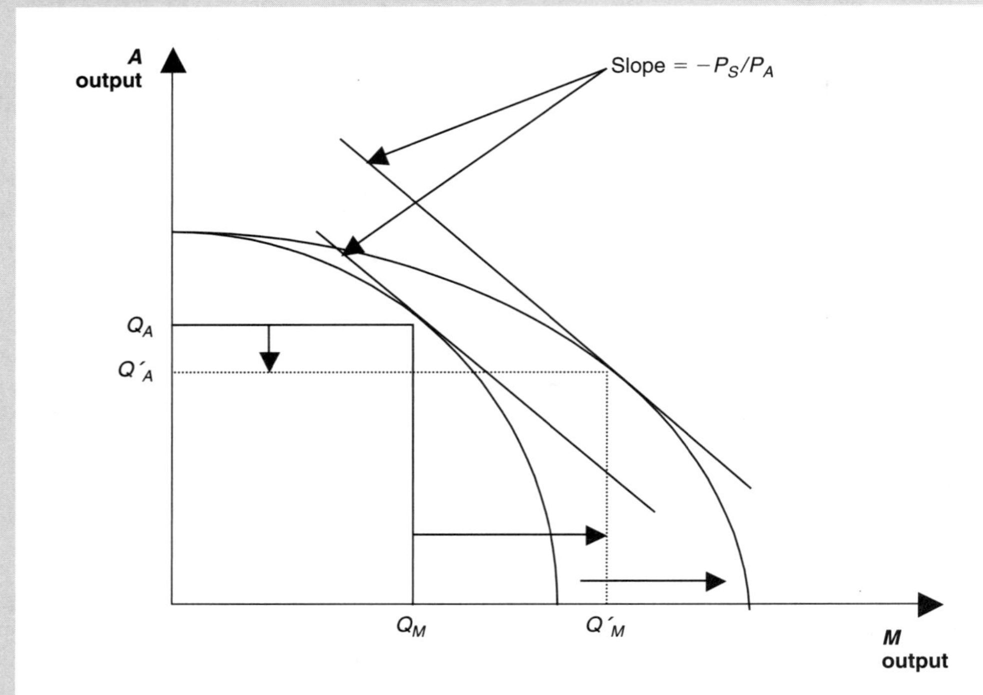

The Effect of an Increase in Home's Capital Stock in the Short-run

5c. The effect of FDI into Home is to raise the real wage. As shown in Figure 5-9, an increase in the capital endowment due to the inflow of capital shifts up the marginal product of labor in manufacturing for every level of manufacturing employment. The new capital increases the demand for labor in manufacturing and so drives up the wage. Because the prices of goods are fixed, this nominal increase in the wage is also a real increase. Because labor is drawn out of agriculture, the land/labor ratio rises so that the marginal product of land falls. Hence the earnings of the owner of a unit of land fall. Note that the capital/labor ratio must rise. To see this, note that the marginal product of labor in manufacturing has risen. For the marginal product of labor to rise in manufacturing, the capital-to-labor ratio must have increased. Hence the marginal product of capital falls, making the earnings of a unit of capital decline in real terms.

FIGURE 5-9

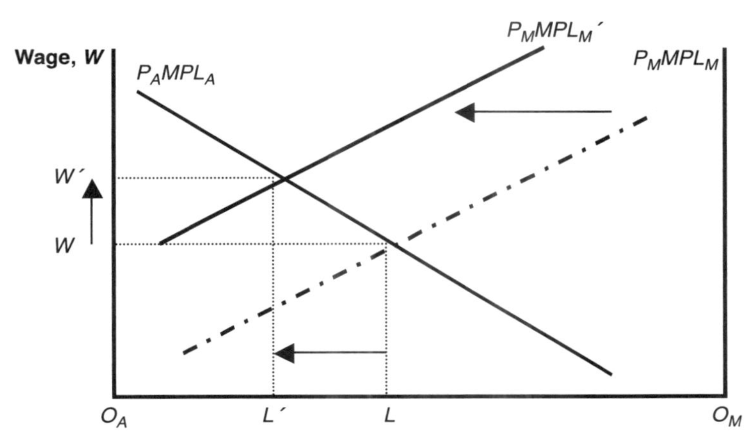

An Inflow of Greenfield Investment

5d. The effect of the outward flow of capital in Foreign is to lower labor demand by shifting down the marginal product of labor in manufacturing. Hence, the nominal and real wage falls in Foreign.

6a. The output of shirts rises! Why is this? Because capital is completely mobile between industries, we can simply apply the Rybczynski theorem. A reduction in the country's stock of capital reduces the output of the good that is intensive in that factor (airplanes) and increases the production of the other good (shirts).

6b. In the long run, the fall in the capital stock has no impact on the real wage because the reallocation of capital and labor between industries leaves the original capital/labor ratios in each industry unchanged. Because marginal products do not change in the long run, the real returns to factors stay the same. This is the factor price insensitivity result.

7a. The value of output is the area under the value of marginal product of labor curve. Given the straight line, this can be calculated as $25 \cdot 50 + (1/2) \cdot (30 \cdot 25) \cdot (150 - 100) = 1375$.

7b. The increase in output was 1375, but of this $25 \cdot 50 = 1250$ is paid to foreigners who have entered the country. Hence, the total gain to the country is 125.

7c. Home-specific factors gain from access to lower cost labor. They receive the 125 calculated in the previous problem plus the direct effect of paying the same workers less to the tune of $5 \cdot 100 = 500$, so the total gain to specific factors is 625.

8. There are big upfront moving costs to immigration. It may take years for immigrants to earn enough additional income to pay off these moving costs. Older workers expect to work for fewer years than younger workers and so may not be able to pay off these moving costs.

6

Increasing Returns to Scale and Imperfect Competition

1a. See the following table.

Quantity Sold	Price	Revenue	Marginal Revenue
1	7	7	7
2	6	12	5
3	5	15	3
4	4	16	1
5	3	15	−1
6	2	12	−3
7	1	7	−5

1b. The firm should make 3 units. The marginal revenue associated with selling the third unit is \$3, which is greater than the marginal cost of \$2.5, so selling the third unit increases revenue by more than it increases costs. For the fourth unit, the marginal revenue is \$1, so the increase in sales revenue is less than the increase in cost.

1c. The firm's profit is (price − marginal cost) · quantity sold. If the firm makes 3 units, profit is (\$5 − \$2.5) · 3 = \$7.5. Notice that the firm's profits fall to \$6 if it sells one more unit.

2. The optimal price and quantity and the associated profits are shown in Figure 6-1.

FIGURE 6-1

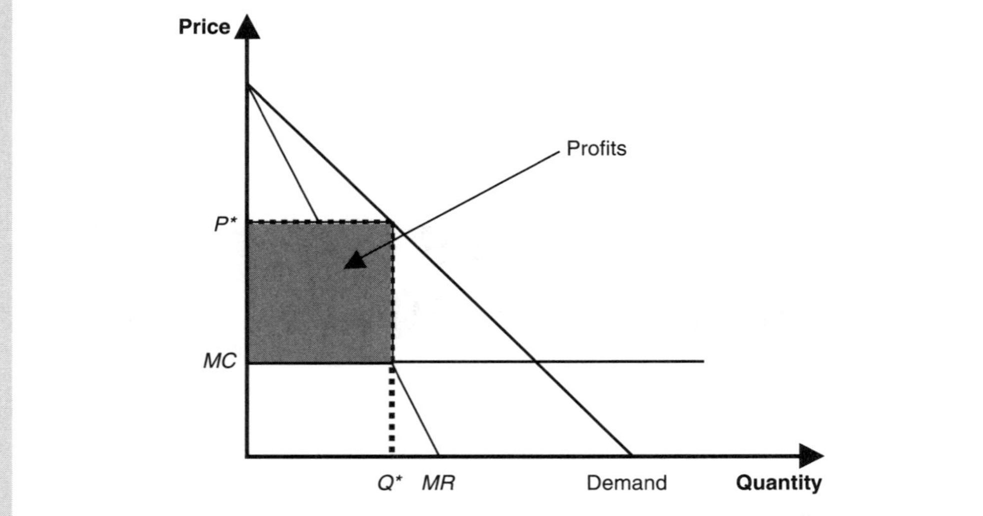

Monopoly Profits

3. The demand curve, $D / 2$, shows how industry demand is split across two firms that charge identical prices for their own differentiated product. The demand curve d shows how much demand there will be for a firm's product if it should deviate from the typical industry behavior and charge a different price. If it lowers its price, it steals some customers from its competitor's variety, but if both firms lowered their price, then no firm steals customers from its competitors.

4. The firm's average total cost is $(\$2 \cdot Q + \$100)/Q$. When $Q = 10$, $AC = \$12$. A firm selling 10 units must be getting a price of \$12 to break even.

5a. The effect of increasing the number of products in the market is shown in Figure 6-2. The solid curve in D / N is demand per firm when each firm charges the same price before the increase in the number of products, and the dotted line labeled D / N' is the curve after the increase in products. The solid line labeled d is demand before the increase, and the broken curve labeled d' is demand after the increase.

FIGURE 6-2

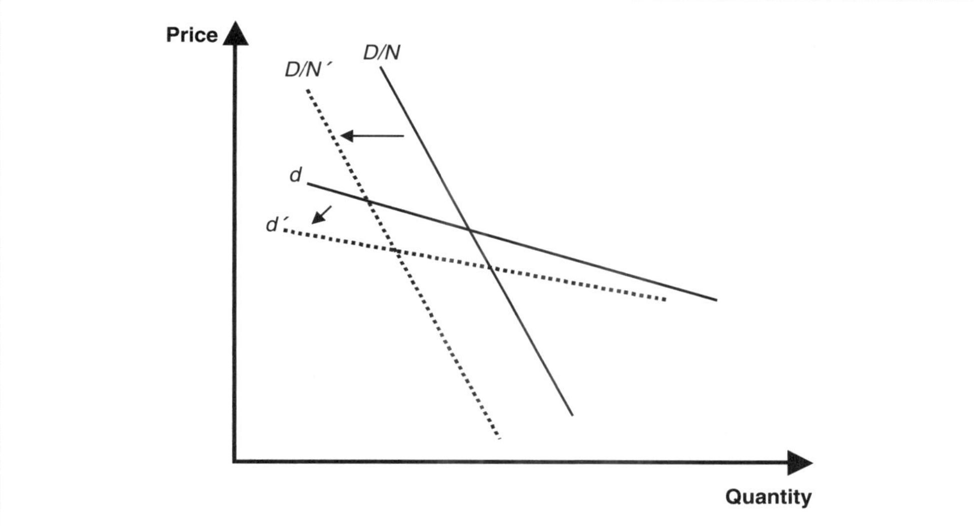

The Effect of Entry on Demand Curves when Products Are Differentiated

5b. The shift in the D / N curve is simple: The same amount of demand is split over a larger number of firms. The shift in the *d* curve is more complicated. The curve shifts down because the more products in the market, the less demand there is for any given product. It also becomes flatter because with increased product choice consumers become more sensitive to price differences across products.

6a. See the left-hand panel of Figure 6-3.

FIGURE 6-3

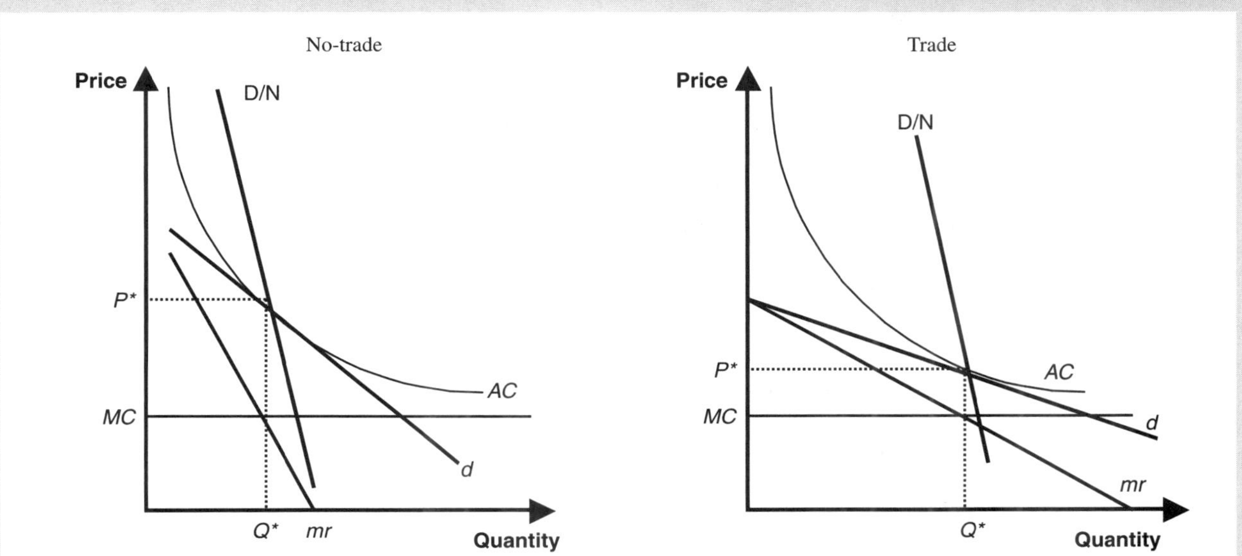

Equilibrium

6b. See the right-hand panel of Figure 6-3.

6c. The D / N curve has shifted to the right. The demand curve d has had its P intercept fall but has also become flatter. The associated marginal revenue curve has moved in a similar fashion. Finally, the price charged by the typical firm has fallen and the quantity sold has increased. In both cases, zero profits are being made.

6d. When international trade is allowed between the two identical countries, the size of the total market doubles, but the number of operating firms in this market, although larger than in each individual country in autarky, is less than twice the number of firms in each market in autarky. Hence, the D / N curve shifts to the right. Because more firms are operating in the integrated world market than in each country in autarky, the demand curve d has shifted down while also becoming flatter. Firms that stay in the market compensate for the lower price they can charge by selling a larger quantity of output so that price continues to be equal to average cost.

6e. The gains from trade include the availability of increased product variety, and these goods have become cheaper. Trade expands the product range available to consumers. This can be seen in the change in the demand curve d. (It is flatter or more elastic because there are more competing varieties.) Demand per firm has increased, however, as can be seen by the shift in the demand curve D / N to the right. Higher demand per firm allows firms to move down their average cost curve and therefore charge lower prices.

6f. The adjustment costs are associated with the closing of some firms and the subsequent dislocation of the employees at those plants. The fact that the D / N curve has shifted to the right indicates that some of the firms in each country must close and so lay off workers.

7a. The larger a market is, the more variety that market will support. The more variety in a market, the flatter the demand curve d and the lower the price charged for each variety. Hence, the real wage should be higher in the large country in a no-trade equilibrium.

7b. The small country gains more from trade because it gets access to the larger number of varieties that are produced in the larger market.

8. No, the monopolistic competition model would not be appropriate for this industry because with so few firms in the industry, the firms are likely to behave strategically. The monopolistic competition model dispenses with strategic behavior among firms by assuming that there are many of them.

9. Yes. Wine is differentiated to some extent merely by where it is produced. In principle, this is enough to generate intra-industry trade: People may consume both wine from California and from France merely for variety.

10. If workers move across industries, then trade between countries is probably motivated by comparative advantage rather than product differentiation, increasing returns, and imperfect information. Trade causes firms to reallocate resources across industries in comparative advantage models and across firms within industries in the monopolistic competition model.

11. Because the Heckscher-Ohlin model does not give rise to a gravity equation, a gravity equation is more likely to fit the data between countries that have similar endowments.

12. Because product differentiation gives rise to intra-industry trade, the index of intra-industry trade is likely to be closer to 100 when goods in that industry are highly differentiated and closer to 0 when goods are homogeneous.

13. As shown in the textbook, the gravity equation can be made to distinguish between trade between regions within a country and between regions in different countries.

The difference in the constant across borders from the constant within borders can be used to gauge the size of the "border effect."

14. As shown in the textbook, the number of goods being exported from Mexico can be used as the smallest reasonable estimate of the expansion of variety available in the United States. Doing the same for Canada would give a crude measure of the expansion in variety due to NAFTA.

15a. At home, $MR = 10 - 2Q$. In Foreign, $MR = 6 - 2Q$.

15b. Setting marginal revenue equal to marginal cost in each market, we find that the amount sold in Home is 4 units and the amount sold in Foreign is 2 units. This translates into a price in Home of 6 and a price in Foreign of 4.

15c. See Figure 6-4. The key feature of the diagram is that the demand curve in the exporter's home market has been drawn steeper than the importing country. The higher price charged by the firm in the exporter's home market is evidence of dumping.

FIGURE 6-4

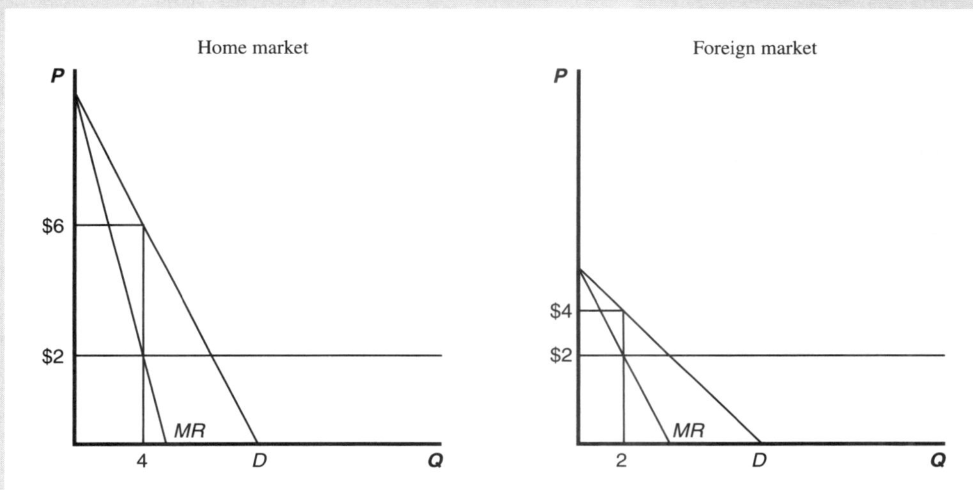

International Price Discrimination

16. Yes. The firm could be accused of dumping if the average cost is greater than $10 (as might happen during a recession) or if the price being charged in the foreign market is not increased above the home price by the amount of any shipping cost incurred.

17a. See Figure 6-5. (Note that the actual level of demand in Foreign has been assumed to be large relative to the amount sold by the firm.)

FIGURE 6-5

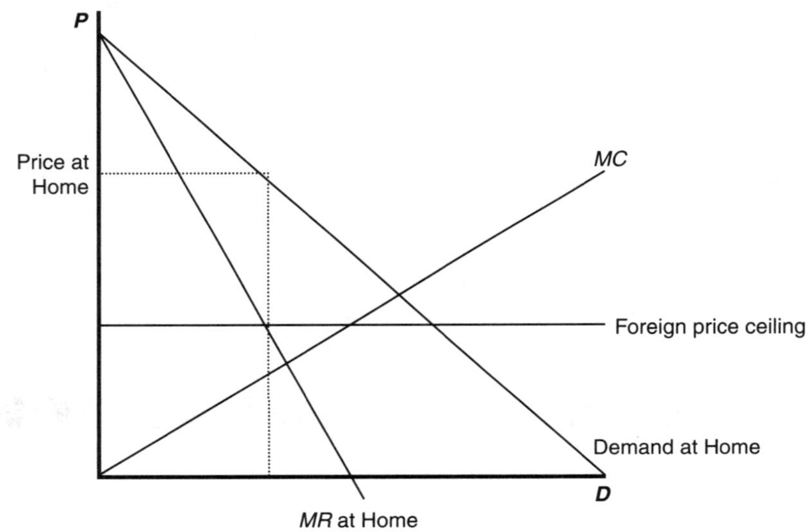

The Market for Beddybuy

17b. If the drug company finds that consumers at Home are buying their product abroad, they may cease to sell their product in Foreign if the profits from being able to charge them the monopoly price at Home are large relative to the profits of supplying both markets when consumers are paying the regulated price.

18. International trade turns a monopoly into an oligopoly. Because international trade allows more firms to compete in the country's market, prices should be lower. This is good for consumers and is a form of gains from trade.

19a. $MR = 95 - 2Q$.

19b. Setting marginal revenue equal to marginal cost, we have $10 = 95 - 2Q$. So $Q = 42.5$. Plugging this back into the demand equation, we have $P = 95 - 42.5 = 52.5$.

19c. Economic profit is $(\$52.5 - \$10) \cdot 42.5 = \$1{,}806.25$.

19d. The marginal revenue facing a firm in each market is $MR = P - q$, where q is the amount sold by that firm.

19e. Setting marginal cost equal to marginal revenue in a firm's home market, we have $\$10 = P - q_H$. Setting marginal cost equal to marginal revenue in the foreign market, we have $\$15 = P - q_F$. From the demand curve we have $P = 95 - q_H - q_F$ (because sales in each country are due to local and foreign firms). Putting all these equations together, we have $P = 95 - (P - 10) - (P - 15)$. Solving this equation, we find $P = \$40$. Hence, the firm sells $40 - 10 = 30$ in its home market and $40 - 15 = 25$ in the foreign market.

19f. Although the firm is charging the same price in each market, the export sales have higher costs, and so \$5 should be subtracted from the foreign price to make it comparable to the home price.

19g. The profit in a firm's home market is $(\$40 - \$10) \cdot 30 = \$900$. The profit in foreign market is $(\$40 - \$15) \cdot 25 = \$625$. The total profit is then $\$900 + \$625 = \$1{,}525$, which is lower than the firm's profits when trade was not allowed.

7

Foreign Outsourcing of Goods and Services

1a. First, we calculate the cost of each activity in each country. These calculations are shown in the following table:

	a	b	c
Home	$4 · 1 + $2 · 4 = $12	$4 · 2 + $2 · 3 = $14	$4 · 3 + $2 · 2 = $16
Foreign	$5 · 1 + $1 · 4 = $9	$5 · 2 + $1 · 3 = $13	$5 · 3 + $1 · 2 = $17

In the absence of transport costs, Foreign is the cheaper producer for activities a and b, whereas Home is the cheaper producer in activity c. With transport costs of $2, the gap in costs would have to be at least this large to induce Home firms to outsource the activity to Foreign. Hence only a is produced in Foreign and b and c are produced in Home.

1b. From the table in the answer to 1a, we see that if there are no transport costs, then a and b would be outsourced to Foreign and only c would remain in Home.

1c. Before the transport costs fall, the amount of Home's skilled labor used in the production of a good is 2 + 3 = 5 and the amount of Home's unskilled labor is 3 + 2 = 5, so the ratio is 1. After the reduction in transport cost, the ratio is 3:2 because only c is done in Home. Hence, the ratio increases from 1 to 1.5. In Foreign the ratio is initially 1:4 but rises to (1 + 2):(4 + 3) or 3:7. Hence, relative demand rises in both countries.

1d. No, only the interpretation of the trading pattern would be different.

2. Banning foreign investment may keep the stock of capital in the country low and the rental high. The high rental to capital would raise the cost of performing each production activity and so limit the amount of outsourcing.

3. If only trade in final goods were allowed, then comparing the factor intensities of goods makes sense. However, once activities can be split into pieces, it is only the factor intensities of the activities that matter for the location of production, not the factor intensities of goods.

4a. The actual assembly-line kinds of jobs done by blue collar workers increasingly may have been outsourced to lower-wage countries, leaving primarily white collar jobs in the United States.

4b. The relative wage of white collar workers has risen over this same time. In the Heckscher-Ohlin model this would mean that firms would substitute blue collar workers for white collar workers. But exactly the opposite appears to be happening.

4c. There could have been skill-biased technical change that resulted in the automation of blue collar jobs.

5a. See Figure 7-2. The diagram shows an improvement in the terms of trade for a country with a comparative advantage in R&D. Because R&D activity will buy more components, firm output increases from Y_0 to Y_1.

FIGURE 7-2

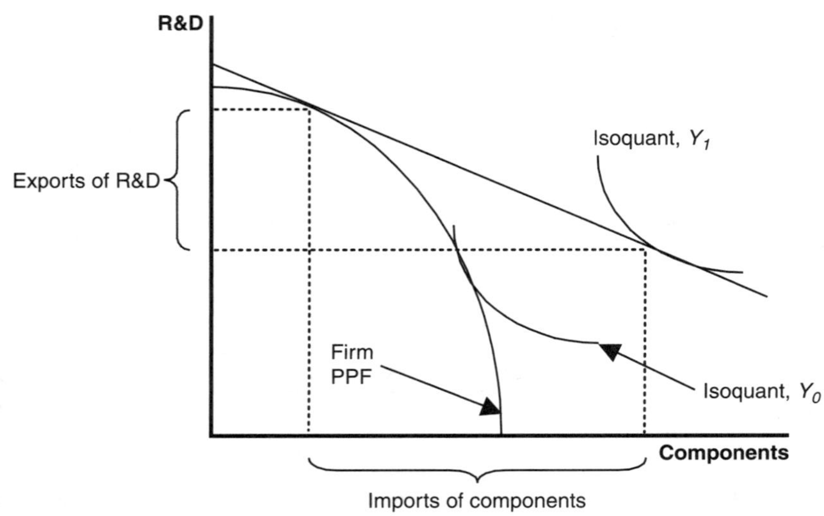

From Autarky to Free Trade in the Outsourcing Model

5b. Home firms export R&D to Foreign firms in return for imports of components that Home firms use (along with R&D that they keep) to produce final goods.

5c. Home firms are able to produce more final output with the same quantity of inputs. Hence, their apparent productivity has increased.

5d. As in the Heckscher-Ohlin model, the increase in the output of the skill-intensive activity (rather than good) increases the relative demand for skilled workers.

5e. See Figure 7-3. An improvement in the terms of trade allows the firm to purchase more components with the same amount of R&D. This change induces the firm to shift resources output of components production into R&D production, expand its trade, and ultimately increase its output from Y_1 to Y_2.

FIGURE 7-3

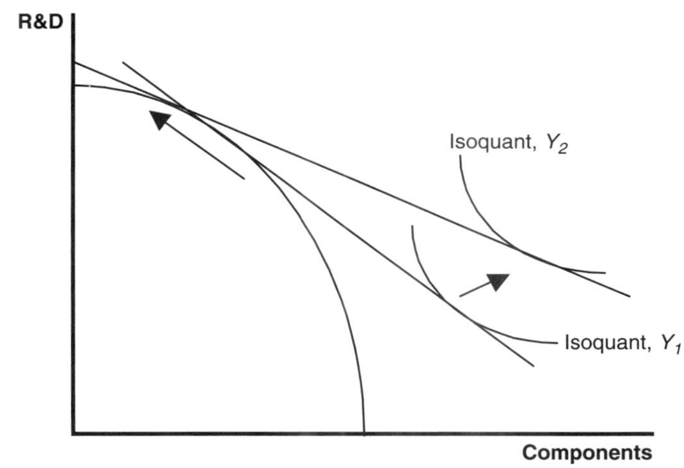

An Improvement in the Terms of Trade for Components Importer

5f. The terms-of-trade improvement increases the amount of final output that the firm can produce with the same quantity of inputs. Hence, the firm appears to be more productive.

6a. Improving Foreign's ability to produce components would help Home if it results in an improvement in Home's terms of trade: A decline in the relative price of components makes Home better off.

6b. Improving Foreign's ability to conduct R&D would hurt Home if it results in a deterioration in Home's terms of trade.

7. According to the study, 14% to 19% of productivity growth can be attributed to outsourcing, whereas less than 7% can be attributed to high-technology capital.

8a. See Figure 7-4. The diagram shows that if transport costs are high for the least skill-intensive activities and low for the most skill-intensive activities, then the slicing of the value chain could be very different.

FIGURE 7-4

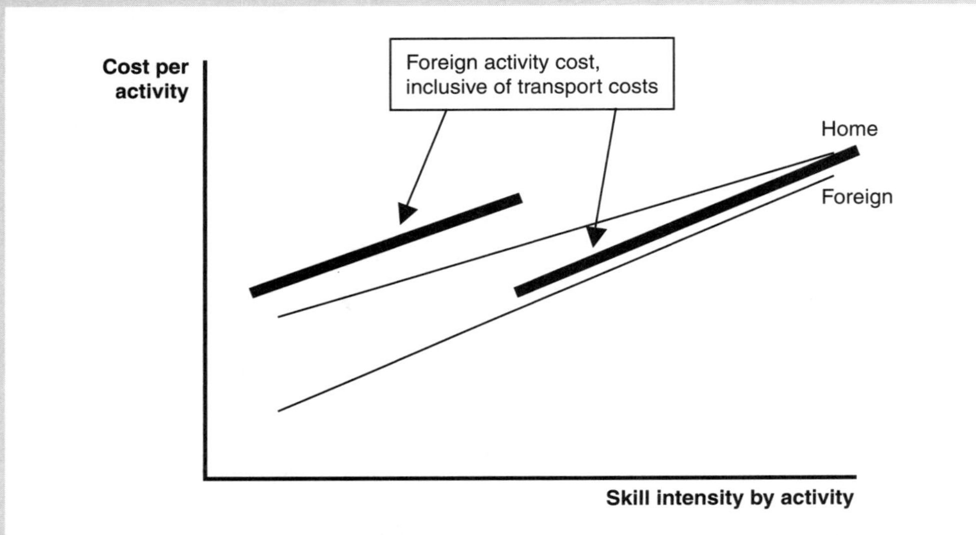

Outsourcing of Skill-Intensive Activities

8b. Yes, once we have nonuniform transport costs across activities, any number of permutations could actually arise. An example is illustrated in Figure 7-5. Transport costs are low for very low skill-intensive activities and for very high skill-intensive activities while being high for activities of moderate skill intensity. As a result, the least and most skill-intensive activities are outsourced in this example while those "in the middle" stay put.

FIGURE 7-5

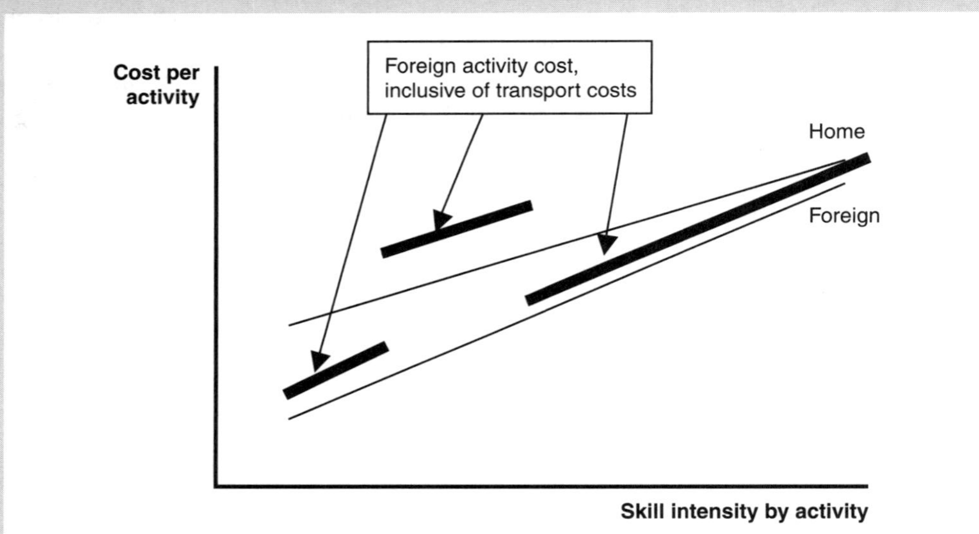

Non-uniform Transport Costs across Activities

9. India's growing output of business services could hurt the United States if it causes a deterioration in the terms of trade for the United States.

10. As services become more tradable, the United States could begin to export a larger volume of them. As output of services expands, factors could be pulled out of manufacturing and into services. This is essentially what is happening in the gains-from-outsourcing example given in the textbook and considered again in problem 5.

8

Import Tariffs and Quotas under Perfect Competition

1a. The firm would be selling its product in your market at less than the normal price. Normal price would mean the price in the exporting country's market, the price in a third country, or the average cost of production.

1b. This is an example of a free-trade agreement, which is allowed under Article XXIV of the GATT.

1c. "Normal trade relations" perhaps better conveys the actual meaning of "most favored nation status," which is the principle of nondiscrimination.

2. Anne's consumer surplus is \$1, the difference between the \$3 that she was willing to pay for the first tomato and the price of the tomato, \$2.

3. Producer surplus is the payment to the fixed factor of production. Hence, the producer surplus in this case is revenue minus the wage bill, or \$40.

4a. The autarky price is the price at which the country would not want to import any of the product, or \$10.

4b. The triangle in Figure 8-2, with area $\frac{1}{2} \cdot (\$10/\text{unit} - \$6/\text{unit}) \cdot 15 \text{ units} = \$30$, is the gains from trade. This is equal to the difference between the gain in consumer surplus and the loss of producer surplus, which is also a triangle, with a height of $\$10/\text{unit} - \$6/\text{unit}$ and a base of 15 units. See triangle D in Figure 8-2 in the textbook.

4c. See Figure 8-5.

FIGURE 8-5

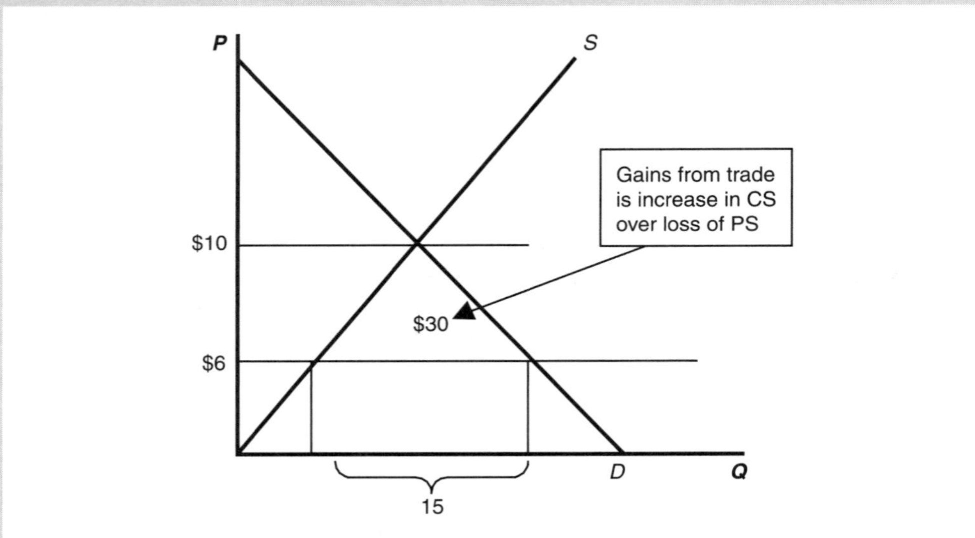

The Gains from Trade

5a. The price at Home rises to \$8 (which is $P_W + t$).

5b. The tariff is \$2 per unit and 7.5 units are imported, so the total tariff revenue is \$15.

5c. The deadweight loss of the tariff is equal to the reduction in imports (15 units − 7.5 units) multiplied by half the \$2 increase in price: 1/2(\$2/unit)(7.5 units) = \$7.5.

5d. The change in producer surplus is equal to the difference between the change in revenue minus the change in payments to variable factors of production, or \$5.

5e. Consider Figure 8-6. The figure shows the effect of the tariff on the home country. The labeled geometric figures correspond to components of the welfare change that were calculated earlier in the problem. The total loss of consumer surplus is equal to the area $f + g + h + i$. From 5d, the area f is \$5. From 5c, the area $g + i$ is the deadweight loss of \$7.5. From 5b, the area h is the size of the tariff revenue, \$15 as calculated. Hence, the total loss of consumer surplus is \$27.50.

FIGURE 8-6

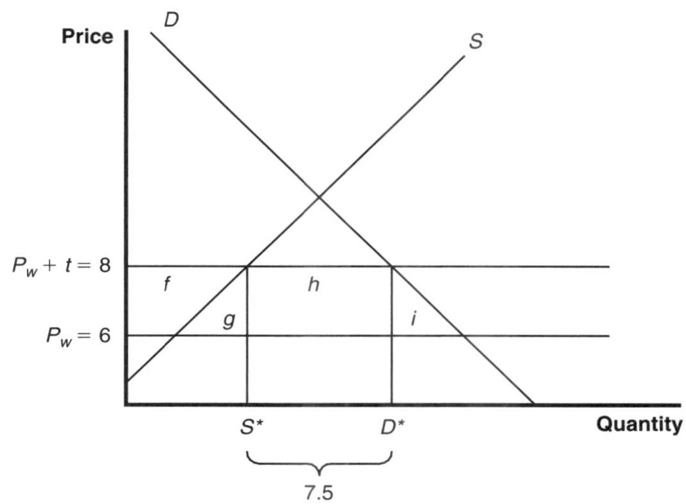

The Welfare Effects of a Small Country Tariff

5f. See Figure 8-6 and the numbers for *f, g, h,* and *i* provided in the answer to 5e.

6a. Producer surplus decreases by \$175. This is equal to the reduction in revenue (holding fixed output) of \$200 and subtracting the production loss of the tariff 1/2(\$2)25 = \$25.

6b. Consumer surplus increases by \$625. Holding fixed the quantity sold, the \$2 fall in price raises consumer surplus by \$600. Add to this the consumption loss under the tariff 1/2(\$2)25 = \$25.

6c. Tariff revenue falls by \$400 = \$2(300 − 100)

6d. The deadweight loss of the tariff is equal to \$50, and the removal of the tariff gets rid of this deadweight loss, making the country better off.

6e. The information is displayed in Figure 8-7.

FIGURE 8-7

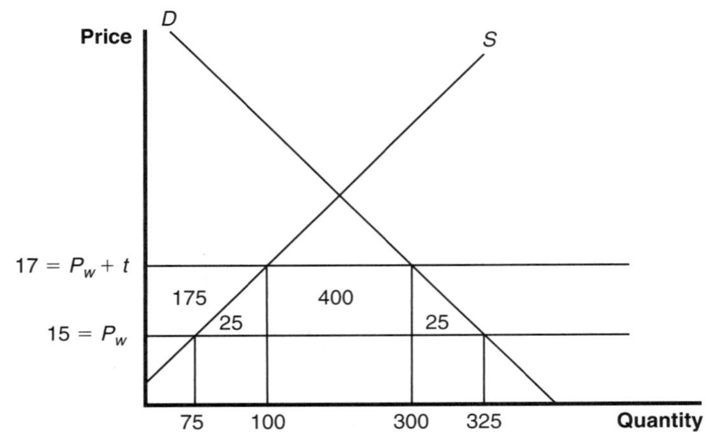

The Welfare Effect of Trade Liberalization: Small Country

7a. Because the home price is \$11 and the tariff is \$2, the world price with the tariff must be \$9.

7b. The revenue raised by the tariff is \$2/unit multiplied by 50 units or \$100.

7c. Using the deadweight loss formula we have (1/2)(\$11/unit − \$10/unit)(100 units − 50 units) = \$25.

7d. The total effect on national welfare is the terms-of-trade gain minus the deadweight loss. The terms-of-trade gain is (\$10/unit − \$9/unit)50 units = \$50. This is greater than the deadweight loss by \$25. Hence, Home gains from this tariff.

7e. The welfare effect on foreign is its terms-of-trade loss (Home's gain) plus its deadweight loss. The deadweight loss is (1/2)(\$10/unit − \$9/unit)(100 units − 50 units) = \$25. Hence, the total welfare loss to Foreign is \$75.

7f. The effect on world welfare is the sum of the deadweight losses in both Home and Foreign, or \$50.

7g. See Figure 8-8.

FIGURE 8-8

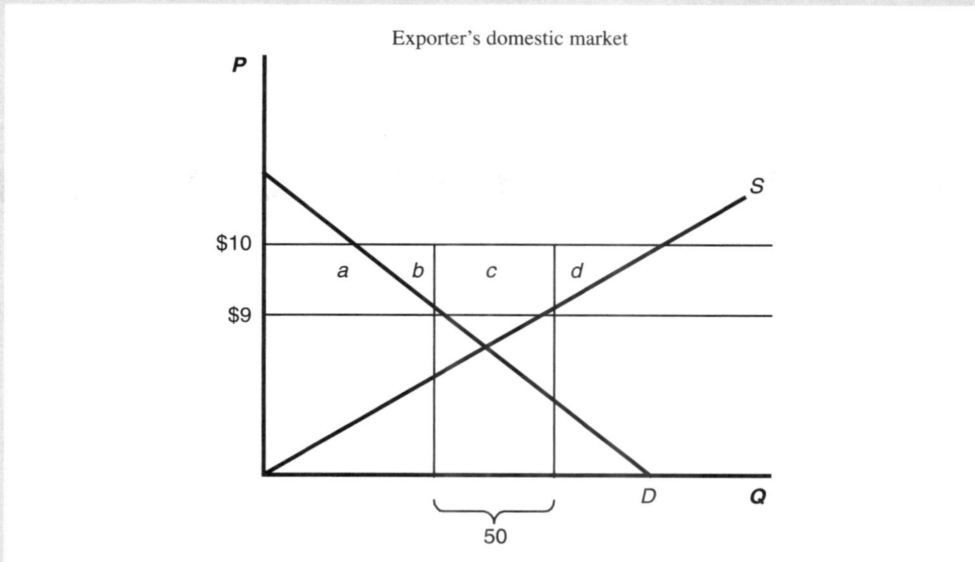

The Welfare Effect of a Tariff on an Exporter

The diagram shows consumer surplus gain a, producer surplus loss of $a + b + c + d$, and net loss of exporting country welfare of $b + c + d$, which is equal in value to the sum of deadweight loss of $b + d = \$25$ and terms-of-trade loss of $c = \$50$.

8. The elasticity of the supply curve is related to its steepness. The steeper the supply curve, the lower the elasticity. When the supply curve is very steep, the more the incidence of the tariff falls on the exporting country. The more of the tariff borne by the foreigners, the larger the optimal tariff.

9a. In the case of perfect competition and quota licenses that are distributed via a perfectly competitive auction, the welfare effect of tariffs and quotas are equivalent. Both raise the domestic price of the good above the world price (and so alter producer and consumer surplus in the same way), and both raise exactly the same amount of revenue for the government.

9b. A producer would rather be protected by a quota than a tariff in this case. In the case of the quota, the domestic price is determined solely by domestic demand, domestic supply, and the size of the quota. Changes in the world price then have no effect on producer surplus. In the case of the tariff, the price at home is equal to the price on world markets plus the tariff. A reduction in the world price would then reduce the home price as well, thereby lowering producer surplus.

10a. The value of the quota rent is the difference between the domestic and world price of the good (\$5/units) multiplied by the size of the quota (50 units). Hence, the value of the quota rent is \$250.

10b. The deadweight loss to the exporting country is equal to (1/2)(\$10/unit − \$8/unit)(100 units − 50 units) = \$50. In addition, the exporting country suffers the terms-of-trade loss of (\$10/unit − \$8/unit)(50 units) = \$100. Hence, the total welfare loss to the exporting country is \$150.

10c. The importing country enjoys the terms of trade gain of \$100 and a deadweight loss equal to (1/2)(\$13/unit − \$10/unit)(100 units − 50 units) = \$75. Hence, Home enjoys an increase in national welfare of \$25.

10d. See Figure 8-9. The box of size \$100 is the terms-of-trade loss (gain) for the exporter (importer), the triangle with size \$50 is the deadweight loss in the exporting country, and the triangle with size \$75 is the deadweight loss in the importing country.

FIGURE 8-9

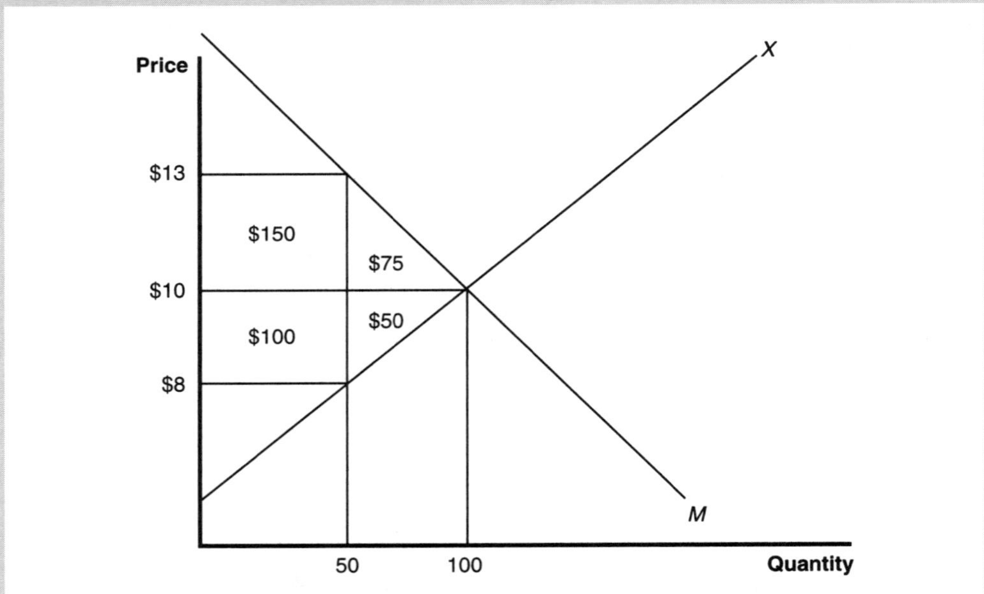

Welfare Effects of a Quota: Large Country Case

10e. If the importing country were to give the quota rents to the exporting country, then the exporter would see the quota raise its welfare by \$100 = \$150 − \$50, whereas the importing country would see its welfare fall by \$225 = \$150 + \$75.

11. By giving the quota rents to the exporting country, the importing country reduces the incentive for the exporting country to retaliate or seek redress from the WTO. As we found in the last question, the exporting country can actually be made better off. In fact, the case study on Japanese automobiles is consistent with this hypothesis.

9

Import Tariffs and Quotas under Imperfect Competition

1a. See Figure 9-2. When international trade is not allowed, the firm is a monopoly and therefore chooses its quantity so that marginal cost is equal to marginal revenue (Q_1). This level of output implies a monopoly price of P^M.

FIGURE 9-2

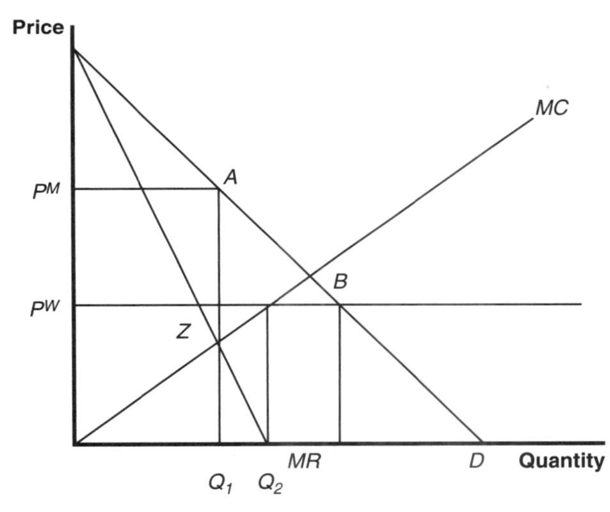

Free Trade versus Autarky with a Home Monopoly

1b. International trade forces the firm to lower its price to P^W.

1c. When the firm is exposed to international trade, the best it can do is choose the quantity that sets the world price (its new marginal revenue curve) equal to its marginal cost (Q_2). Given the way that the diagram is drawn, this actually implies an increase in output.

1d. The international market constrains the monopoly power of the firm and so lowers its producer surplus.

1e. The price charged by the monopolist in autarky (P^M) exceeds the world price, so free trade improves consumer surplus.

1f. Consumers gain the trapezoid, P^MABP^W. This gain in consumer surplus contains within it the lost monopoly profits (the rectangle P^MAZP^W). Hence the country is better off with trade.

1g. If the world price were below the intersection between the marginal revenue and marginal cost curve, then the monopolists' output would fall rather than rise.

2. Yes. Consider Figure 9-2. Suppose that P^W were above the intersection between the demand curve and the marginal cost curve but below P^M. In this case the monopolist would be willing to satisfy all domestic demand at that price. The fact that the country could import at that price is all that is needed to force the domestic price down.

3a. See Figure 9-3. Note that the marginal revenue curve has been omitted to avoid cluttering up the diagram. The result is very similar to the perfect competition small-country case. The tariff increases the price, expanding the producer surplus by the area a, and decreasing consumer surplus by $(a + b + c + d)$. The tariff collects revenue c, so the total impact on national welfare is $-(b + d)$.

FIGURE 9-3

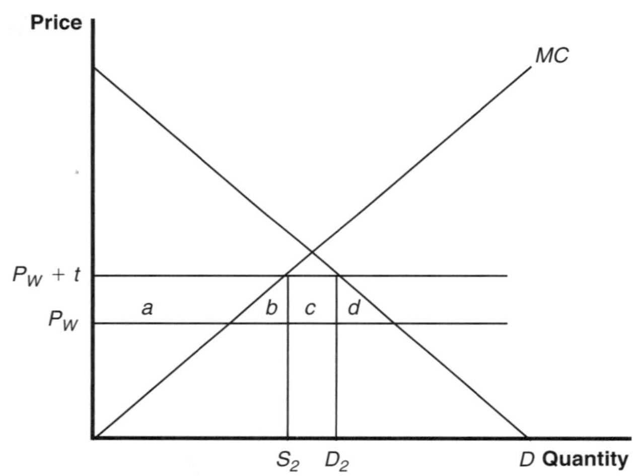

Tariffs and a Home Monopolist

3b. Because the quota does not allow imports to expand above the size of the quota when the price on the domestic market rises, the Home firm has monopoly power. As shown in Figure 9-4, the quota that under perfect competition would lower imports by the same amount as a tariff of size t has the effect of shifting the demand curve and marginal revenue curve facing the monopolist to the left. The firm charges a markup over its marginal cost that exceeds the size of the tariff t. As a result the domestic price with a quota P^Q exceeds the domestic price with a tariff $P^W + t$, so consumer surplus is lower under a quota than it is under a tariff.

FIGURE 9-4

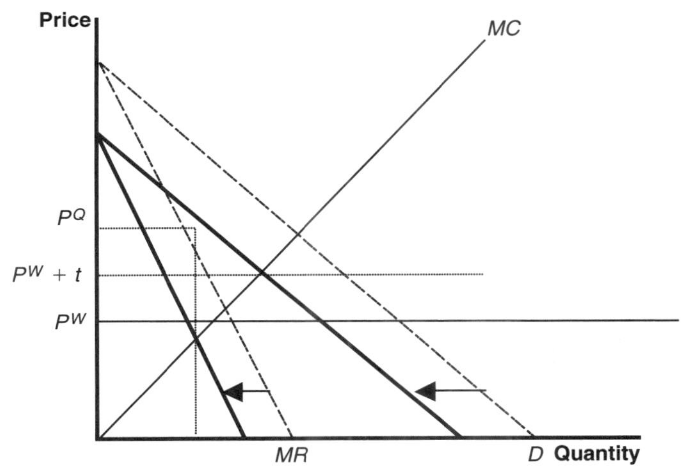

Quotas Hit Consumers More than Tariffs when There Is a Single Home Firm

3c. Suppose a tariff t resulted in M units imported. The tariff revenue would be $t \cdot M$. A quota of size M would imply quota rents of $(P^Q - P^W) \cdot M$ because each quota license allows the owner to buy at the low world price of P^W and to sell at the high domestic price of P^Q. Because $P^Q - P^W > t$, it follows that the quota rent associated with imports of M exceeds the tariff revenue associated with import with imports of M.

4a. By raising the price of cucumbers above the world price, the tariff would lower consumer surplus in every year that the domestic price is above the world price.

4b. In order for infant industry protection to be appropriate, P must be below the average cost of production for the home cucumber firm now but must be no less than the average cost of product for the home cucumber firm in 5 years.

4c. If capital markets were perfect in Home, then one argument for infant industry protection would not be valid. A firm that will eventually be competitive should be able to borrow against future earnings if these earnings are to materialize. An argument might still be made if there were positive externalities in the cucumber industry.

4d. The existence of positive externalities, such as knowledge spillovers, could justify infant industry protection, but in the cucumber industry that might be a hard sell.

5a. If the reason for infant industry protection were purely that capital markets were imperfect, then it would make no sense to offer the protection. This is because the producer surplus accrues to the foreign multinational rather than to a domestic firm.

5b. If the argument were that this is an industry with knowledge spillovers, then domestic entrepreneurs might benefit from having the foreign multinational. These spillovers would lower the cost of domestic firms and so might justify the tariff. The application to China's auto industry suggests that multinationals may have played a role in getting the auto industry started in China.

6. From the application in the textbook, it appears that Harley-Davidson could not get a loan from the banking system in the absence of the temporary protection. There is no suggestion that it had to do with any positive externalities.

7a. See Figure 9-5. If there is no tariff, then the marginal cost of serving the market is \$10. Setting marginal cost equal to marginal revenue ($10 = 100 - 2Q$) and solving, we find that the optimal quantity to sell is 45 units. Plugging this number into the demand function ($P = 100 - 45$) gives us a price of \$55.

7b. See Figure 9-5. The tariff raises the marginal cost of serving the market to \$20. Setting marginal cost equal to marginal revenue ($20 = 100 - 2Q$), we find that the optimal quantity to sell is now 40 units. Plugging this number into the demand function ($P = 100 - 40$) gives us a price of \$60. Here is an example of a tariff that is not fully passed on to consumers. A \$10 tariff increased the price by only \$5.

FIGURE 9-5

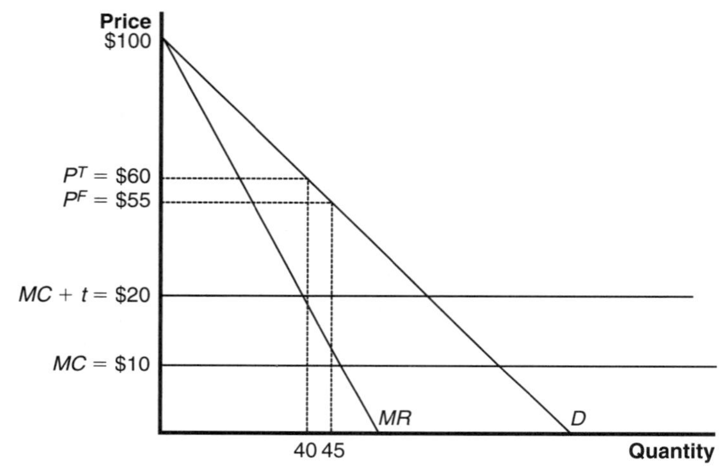

The Effect of a Tariff on a Foreign Monopolist

7c. Using the formula for the area of a triangle, consumer surplus is equal to \$1,012.50 with free trade ($1/2 \cdot [100 - 55] \cdot 45$) and \$800 with the tariff ($1/2 \cdot [100 - 60] \cdot 40$). Tariff revenue collected by the government is equal to 0 without the tariff and \$400 with the tariff ($10 \cdot 40$). National welfare is the sum of consumer surplus plus tariff revenue, so the tariff made the country better off.

8a. See Figure 9-6. The key point is that the marginal revenue curve is not as steep as the demand curve and so the domestic price rises by more than the tariff. Before the tariff is applied, the foreign monopolist sells quantity Q_1 where the marginal cost (MC) of serving the market is equal to the marginal revenue (MR). This quantity implies a home market price of P_1. The tariff increases the marginal cost by t per unit ($MC + t$) and so induces the monopolist to cut back supply to Q_2, which implies a price of P_2. Because the demand curve is steeper than the marginal revenue curve, the price increase $P_2 - P_1$ is larger than the size of the tariff t.

FIGURE 9-6

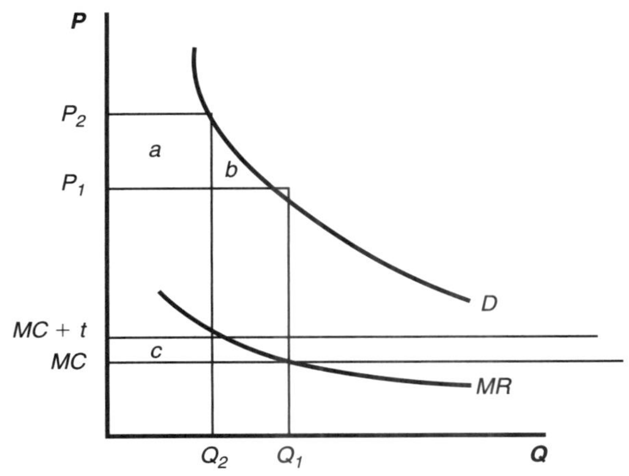

Demand Curve Steeper than the Marginal Revenue Curve

8b. No, in this case the loss in consumer surplus (area $a + b$ in Figure 9-6) must exceed the increase in government revenue, which is equal to $t \cdot Q_2$ (area c in Figure 9-6). This must be so because $P_2 - P_1 > t$.

9. As pointed out in the text, the mere threat of antidumping tariffs can induce foreign firms to raise their price in the importing country. Hence, the government official's statement is potentially misleading because foreign producers may have been induced to change their behavior even if no antidumping cases are filed.

10. It is relatively easy to file a dumping case, and there is a good chance that the government will find in favor of a dumping claim. Even when a dumping case is not fully prosecuted, the threat of dumping duties is often enough to induce foreign firms to increase their price.

11. For antidumping tariffs to be applied, there must be evidence of "material injury" to domestic producers. If there are no domestic producers, then there can be no evidence of material injury.

10

Export Subsidies in Agriculture and High-Technology Industries

1. By increasing the supply of food, the aid drives down the price of food on world markets, a phenomenon that hurts developing-country exporters of food. A more helpful policy is to provide aid in cash.

2. A tax credit on fertilizer would lower the cost of agricultural producers and so may be construed as a production subsidy.

3. An export subsidy increases the price of the good in Home to a level above the world price. This would allow arbitragers to buy a good at the low world price, import the good, and then request the export subsidy. Hence, the government must put an import tariff in place to prevent this possibility.

4a. The country exports 120 units and the government pays $1 for each unit, so the total cost to the government is $120.

4b. Because this is a small country, the effect of the subsidy on national welfare is the deadweight loss. This is equal to one half of the increase in exports multiplied by the increase in the Home price of the good, or $10.

4c. See Figure 10-4. The deadweight loss is equal to $10, and the total cost of the subsidy is $120.

FIGURE 10-5

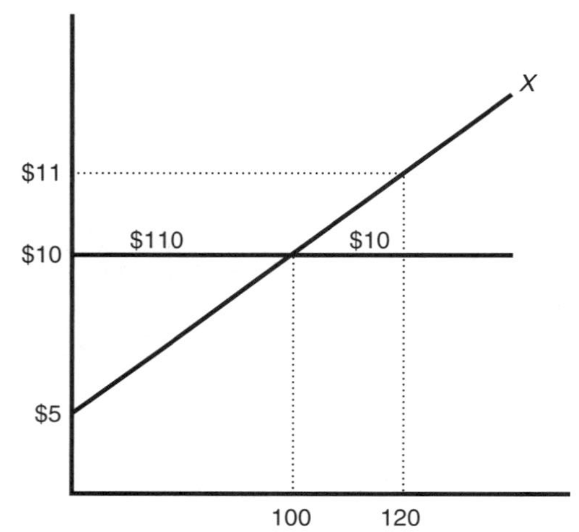

The Effect of an Export Subsidy on a Small Country

5a. The cost of the subsidy to the government is the area $(b + c + d)$.

5b. Producer surplus increases by $(a + b + c)$.

5c. The size of the consumption loss is equal to $s \cdot (D0 - D1) / 2$. This is the formula for the area of a triangle.

6. For a high enough price in the Home market, producers will be willing to supply even more than consumers demand. A large enough export subsidy (combined with a tariff) can raise the price above the autarky price in Home and induce the country to export.

7a. The cost of the subsidy is the volume of exports multiplied by the subsidy per unit exported: (\$10/unit) · (150 units) = \$1,500.

7b. Home suffers a terms-of-trade loss = (\$100/unit − \$95/unit) · (150 units) = \$750 and a deadweight loss equal to (1/2) · (\$105/unit − \$100/unit) · (50 units) = \$125. Hence the total loss of welfare to Home is \$750 + \$125 = \$875.

7c. The subsidy raises Foreign's national welfare because consumer surplus increases more than producer surplus falls. However, Foreign's gain is not as large as Home's terms-of-trade loss. In Foreign, there is deadweight loss = (1/2) · (\$100/unit − \$95/unit) · (150 units – 100 units) = \$125. The deadweight loss accrues because Foreign's producers make too few units and consume too many relative to free trade. Foreign's gain is then Home's terms-of-trade loss less Foreign's deadweight loss, or \$625.

7d. See Figure 10-5. Consumers gain $a + b$, while producers lose a.

FIGURE 10-5

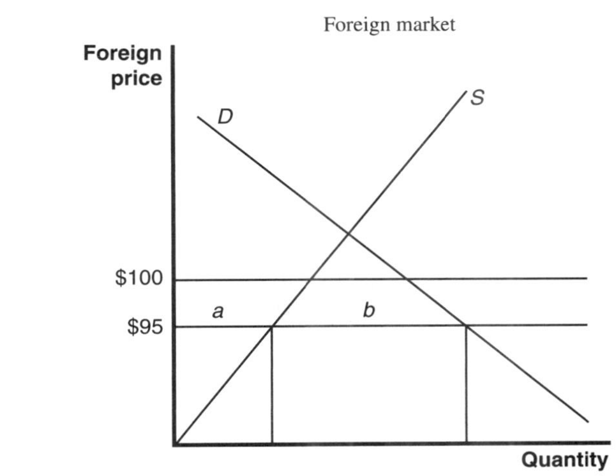

Effect of an Export Subsidy on Importing Country Welfare

7e. See Figure 10-6. Home losses include its deadweight loss d and its terms of trade loss $a + b + c$. Foreign enjoys terms-of-trade gain $a + b + c$ but suffers deadweight loss of c.

FIGURE 10-6

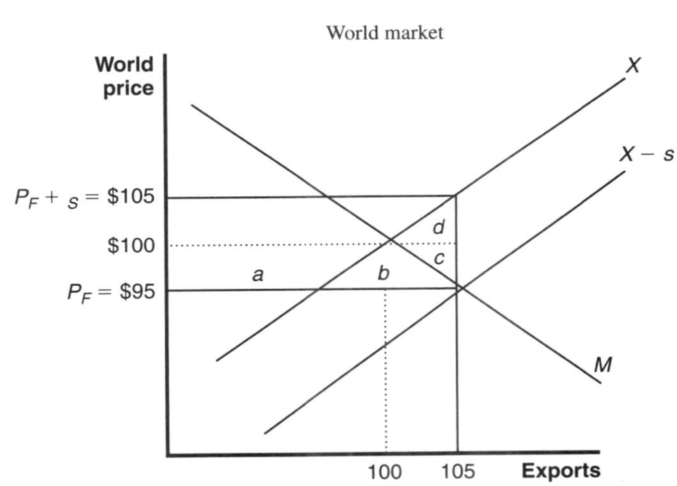

Deadweight Losses and Terms of Trade Effect in the World Market Diagram

7f. Yes. The price being charged by firms in their own market is $P_F = \$95$, and the price being charged by the same firms in Home's market $P_F + s = \$105$, where s is the subsidy of $10. Because the price charged by these firms is lower in their domestic market than in Home, the criteria for dumping are satisfied.

7g. The importing country could impose countervailing duties to offset the effect of the subsidy.

8a. See Figure 10-7. The export tax lowers supply on the world market from Q_1 to Q_2 and therefore drives up the world price from P_1 to P_2. The price in the home market is the world price less the export tax (because the tax does not need to be paid on domestic sales). Exports drop.

FIGURE 10-7

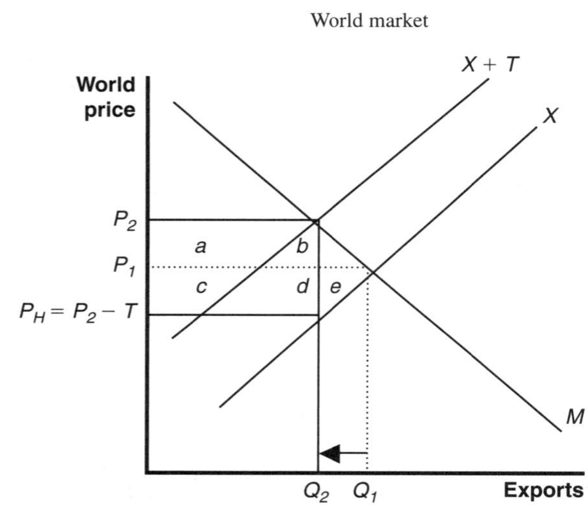

The Effect of an Export Tax on the World Market

8b. Because Home's price falls from P_1 to P_H, its producers are made worse off while its consumers are made better off. The loss of producer surplus exceeds the gain in consumer surplus by the area $c + d + e$ in Figure 10-7. The government collects tariff revenue on exports equal to $T \cdot Q_2$, which is equivalent to the area $a + b + c + d$ in the figure. Some of the tax revenue is paid by foreign consumers ($a + b$) because the export tax improves the exporter's terms of trade.

8c. The export subsidy unambiguously reduced the exporter's welfare. In addition to the deadweight loss, a loss is associated with a deterioration of the terms of trade. The export tax also creates deadweight loss, but it causes a terms-of-trade gain. If the terms-of-trade gain is large relative to the deadweight loss, the country is better off with the tax. If an export subsidy is favored over an export tax, it must be that governments seek to increase producer surplus because the export subsidy increases producer surplus whereas the export tax reduces producer surplus.

9a. The production subsidy costs the government $5 per unit produced multiplied by the 200 units that are produced, or $1,000 (area $a + b + c + d$ in Figure 10-8). The export subsidy costs the government $5 per unit exported multiplied by the volume of exports of 150 units (200 − 50), or $750 (area $b + c + d$ in Figure 10-8). Hence, the production subsidy costs the government an additional $250.

9b. In both cases the production distortion is given by the area *d* in Figure 10-8, which can be calculated as (1/2) · ($15/unit − $10/unit) · (200 units − 150 units) = $125.

FIGURE 10-8

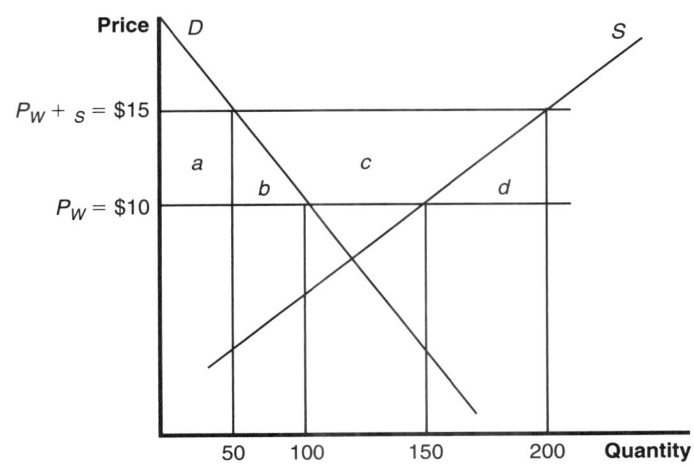

Production versus Export Subsidy

9c. The consumption distortion in the production subsidy case is zero because the price facing consumers has not changed. In the case of the export subsidy, the consumption distortion is given by the area *b* in Figure 10-8, which can be calculated as (1/2) · ($15/unit − $10/unit) · (200 units – 150 units) = $125.

9d. In Figure 10-8, the effect of the export subsidy on national welfare is –(*b* + *d*) and the effect of the production subsidy on national welfare is –*d*. Hence, the export subsidy reduces national welfare by $125 more than the production subsidy because of the consumption distortion –*b*.

9e. If Home is large, the export subsidy has a bigger impact on the country's exports because it reduces consumption and increases production, whereas the production subsidy only increases production. Because exports are less affected, the export supply curve shifts by less and the impact on the terms of trade is smaller.

9f. If Home were a large country, its production subsidy would reduce the world price. The reduction in the world price increases Home's consumer surplus.

10. Yes. If the subsidy is sufficiently large, producers can be induced to produce more than consumers demand and the country will then become an exporter of a good that it would otherwise import.

11a. Assuming that there is no retaliation or asymmetry of production so that only one country is producing the good, there is no deadweight loss. The subsidy simply results in the transfer of a fixed amount of profit from one country to another.

11b. If the United States were to retaliate against the European Union, then plausibly both countries would end up producing and so there would be no profits. In this case, both countries would be worse off than if neither were offering subsidies.

11c. The two countries might have found themselves in an international prisoner's dilemma. Their efforts to increase their own well-being could have made the two countries collectively worse off. The 1992 agreement might have been an attempt to get out of this situation.

11

International Agreements: Trade, Labor, and the Environment

1. The multilateral agreement will only work if there are mutual gains to the parties involved. If only one country is large, then that country may have no incentive to agree to tariff reduction.
2. If many small countries join a customs union, they may collectively become large on international markets. Because large countries are better off with restrictions on imports and small countries are better off with free trade, these countries may raise the tariff on outsiders.
3. This odd possibility is possible. Suppose that marginal costs of production are constant in Home and outside the free-trade area. It could be that Home's external tariff is low enough that countries outside the free-trade area have a lower marginal cost than Home and so supply the Home market. Now suppose that another country (Foreign) in the free-trade area has very high tariffs. Because there are rules of origin, Home producers get better access to Foreign's market than countries outside the area and so are the lowest-cost producer for the Foreign market while being a high-cost producer for their own market.
4. See Figure 11-2. Let the marginal cost of production for a country within the free-trade agreement be *C*. The free-trade agreement lowers the cost for this country to supply the domestic market and so trade rises. This is nothing different than we saw in Chapter 8.

FIGURE 11-2

Home market

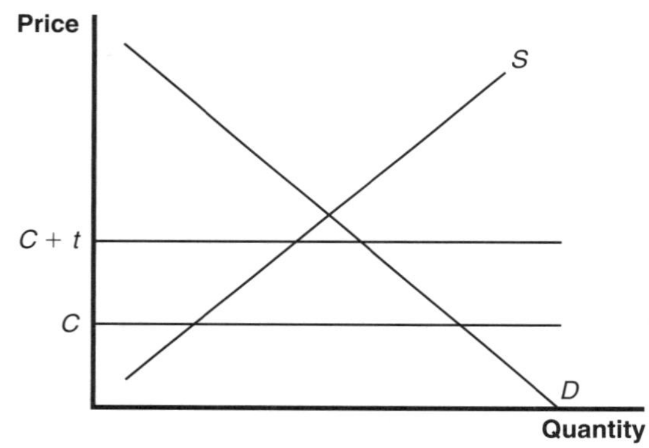

Trade Creation

5a. There can be no trade diversion in this example because country A has the lowest marginal cost of the three countries. It would be the supplier before and after the agreement.

5b. An RTA with country B could lead to trade creation if the initial tariff was high enough that home did not import the good from either country A or B.

5c. See Figure 11-3. Before the regional trade agreement, a tariff t is applied to imports of both A and B so that the marginal cost of A serving Home is $C_A + t$ and the marginal cost of B serving Home is $C_B + t$. Because $C_A + t < C_B + t$, the low-cost country A is the sole supplier when the tariff is equally applied to each country. Now suppose that country B joins a regional trade agreement with Home and the tariff is sufficiently large that country B is now the lowest cost supplier. Because $C_B < C_A + t$, trade is diverted from the low-cost producer A to the high-cost producer B.

FIGURE 11-3

Home market

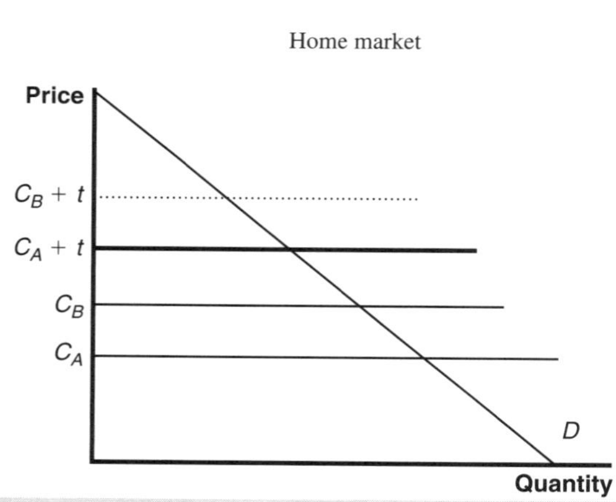

Trade Diversion

5d. Yes. Before the RTA, the price in Home was $C_A + t$. After the RTA, the price fell to C_B. It is true that tariff revenue has been lost, but it is also true that consumer surplus has risen because the price does fall.

6. Fair Trade Coffee, which is discussed in Chapter 3, is an example of an NGO that has had some success raising living standards. Consumers pay extra for coffee made under appropriate circumstances.

7. They worry that this is a form of disguised protectionism intended to raise the cost of production in low-wage countries.

8a. This question describes a specific-factors–type framework. If the wage rises in the formal sector, then the value of the marginal product of labor must rise as well. This means that employment in the formal sector must fall.

8b. Labor pushed out of the formal sector finds employment in the unregulated informal sector. As labor employed in that sector rises, the value of the marginal product of labor falls and so too does the wage paid in the informal sector.

9a. As in the tuna-dolphin case, there is a strong chance that the WTO will rule against Home because it is imposing a production process method on Foreign.

9b. No. As long as the reporting is nondiscriminatory, this would be fine with the WTO.

10. Rich countries will have tighter regulations on pollution than poorer countries. If these regulations raise the cost of highly polluting industries more than less-polluting industries, then tariff reduction could cause highly polluting industries to move to poorer countries. Pollution could increase as a result.

11a. If the pollution is primarily local, then an international prisoner's dilemma is less likely to arise because one country's pollution does not affect another.

11b. If the marginal costs of all producers rise, then the global supply curve for these goods shifts inward, resulting in a higher price for sneeds. The exact amount of the price increase depends on the shape of the demand and supply curves.

11c. Your country's sneed industry benefits from the higher price for sneeds on world markets while its marginal cost curve stays the same. Therefore your country's producer surplus rises.

11d. There is a free rider problem. If all other countries sign on to the agreement, your country gets the benefit of less global pollution from its actions and it benefits in terms of producer surplus because the price of sneeds has risen.

12

The Global Macroeconomy

1. The price of all foreign goods, services, and financial assets relative to domestic goods, services, and financial assets changes with the exchange rate.
2. An appreciation of the exporter's currency puts them at a disadvantage relative to foreigners, whereas a depreciation puts them at an advantage.
3. Brazil's country risk is 10% − 4% = 6%.

4a. It should decline as the country is forced to borrow more.

4b. Capital gains might improve the country's external wealth by enough to offset borrowing.

5. Anything that eases the cost of international transactions, including policy changes and technological improvements, such as improved communication and transport technology.

13

Introduction to Exchange Rates and the Foreign Exchange Market

1a. $E_{\$/€} = 1.2$ (American terms), $E_{€/\$} = 1 / 1.2 = 0.833$ (European terms).

1b. The dollar depreciated by 20% against the euro: $(1.2 - 1) / 1$.

1c. The euro appreciated by 16.7% against the dollar: $(0.833 - 1) / 1$.

1d. $E_{\$/¥} = 1 / 120 = 0.0833$ (American terms), $E_{¥/\$} = 120 / 1 = 120$ (Japanese terms).

1e. The dollar appreciated by 16.667% against the yen: $(1 / 120 - 1 / 100) / (1 / 100)$.

1f. The percent change in the effective exchange rate is equal to the trade-weighted average of bilateral exchange rates.

$$\frac{\Delta E_{eff}}{E_{eff}} = \left(\frac{1.2 - 1}{1}\right)\left(\frac{\$200bil.}{\$200bil. + \$400bil.}\right) + \left(\frac{0.0833 - 0.1}{0.1}\right)\left(\frac{\$400bil.}{\$200bil. + \$400bil.}\right)$$

The first term on the right side of the equals sign is the percentage depreciation of the dollar against the euro multiplied by Europe's trade weight. The second term is the percentage appreciation of the dollar against the yen multiplied by Japan's trade weight. Doing the calculation, we find that

$$\frac{\Delta E_{eff}}{E_{eff}} = -0.044 = -4.4\%.$$

So the dollar appreciated against this basket of currencies.

2a. The dollar price of the ale in Munich is $3€ \cdot E_{\$/€}$ which is equal to \$2 when $E_{\$/€} = 2/3$.

2b. If $E_{\$/€} = 1$, then the ale is cheaper in Boston. Party on, Volker!

3a. No, Home cannot fix its exchange rate vis-à-vis multiple currencies if those currencies float. To see this, suppose that there are two countries, A and B, and Home fixes its exchange rate vis-à-vis at one. For simplicity assume that one unit of currency A buys one unit of currency B initially. Now suppose that A's currency appreciates vis-à-vis B so that one unit of A's currency buys 2 units of B's currency. One unit of Home's currency buys one unit of A's currency, which buys 2 units of B's currency, but one unit of B's currency buys one unit of Home's currency because of the fixed exchange rate! The exchange rates are not consistent!

3b. Home could fix its currency vis-à-vis its largest trading partner. Alternatively, Home could dollarize by using the currency of its largest trading partner or agreeing to a currency union with its largest trading partner.

4. Spreads are higher for individuals (small players) because there are more middlemen between the final transaction and the underlying foreign exchange market than there are for the large interbank traders who directly transact on the interbank market.

5a. If you buy euros forward at this rate, then the dollar cost in 30 days will be (1.25\$/€·€10 million) or \$12.5 million. Since you have contracted to sell the wine for \$13 million, you will make \$500,000.

5b. If the spot rate for the euro rises above 1.3\$/€, then your dollar cost will exceed your dollar income, and you will lose money.

5c. If you were to own this call option, then in 30 days you are guaranteed a positive dollar return on the wine. If the spot rate exceeds 1.27, then you will exercise the option, buy the wine, and come away with \$300,000. On the other hand, if the spot rate were less than 1.27, you would not use the option and buy euros on the spot market. The benefit of owning the option relative to the forward contract is that if the spot rate is less than 1.25, you will get a better price for the euros and make more money. If the spot rate is more than 1.25, you would have been better off using the forward market.

5d. Your \$1 million will buy \$1 million / 1.25 \$/€ = €800,000 at the forward rate. If the spot rate is 1.3, then this amount of euros converts into (1.3 \$/€)·(€800,000) = \$1.04 million. Hence, you would make \$40,000 in the transaction.

5e. In this scenario, the €800,000 that you bought forward would only be worth \$960,000, so you would have lost \$40,000.

6. The answer is c. $E_{\$/€} \div E_{\$/£} = E_{£/€} = 3/2 \div 2 = 3/4$.

7. The answer is d, all of the above. Answer a is true: $E_{¥/\$} = 100$, $E_{\$/€} = 2$, so $E_{€/\$} = 0.5$ and $E_{€/¥} = E_{€/\$} \div E_{¥/\$}$. Answer b is true: $E_{\$/¥} = 1 / E_{¥/\$}$. And answer c is true: $E_{¥/€} = E_{¥/\$} \times E_{\$/€}$.

8. The cross rates are not consistent, so there is a triangular arbitrage opportunity. First, trade your \$1 million for £500,000. Second, trade your £500,000 for Yen 110 million. Third, trade your Yen 110 million for \$1.1 million. Realize profits of \$100,000.

9. Yes, arbitrage prevents the price of the same thing from being different in different locations. For arbitrage to occur, it must be possible to transact across these locations. Capital controls by their very nature prevent arbitrage.

10. The answer is d, depreciate by 2%. According to UIP, the interest rate differential is equal to the expected change in the exchange rate.

11a. The amount of euros that \$1 million buys is (\$1 million) / (1.25\$/€) = €800,000.

11b. At the end of the year you would have (€800,000)(1+0.03) = €824,000. This is the principal plus the interest.

11c. At the end of the year you would have (\$1 million)(1.05) = \$1,050,000.

11d. To make the amounts identical, the forward exchange rate would have to satisfy the equation \$1,050,000 = $F_{\$/€}$(€824,000), where the left side is the amount of dollars you would get from the U.S. deposit, whereas the right side is the amount of dollars you would get from the German deposit if the forward rate were $F_{\$/€}$. Solving for this we find that $F_{\$/€}=1.274272$.

11e. If investors were risk neutral (i.e., they do not care about risk), then uncovered interest parity ought to hold as well. This means that the expected future spot rate would have to be equal to the forward exchange rate.

11f. The expected rate of depreciation of the dollar is equal to (1.274272 – 1.25) / 1.25 = 1.94%. Note that this is approximately equal to the difference in the interest rates between the United States and Germany.

11g. If U.S. deposits were more liquid and less risky than German deposits, then the rate of return on U.S. deposits might be somewhat less than that on German deposits. (Put another way, investors would have to be compensated to hold German deposits.) This means the expected rate of depreciation of the dollar might be somewhat larger to boost German returns.

12a. To answer these questions, we use the uncovered interest parity equation. Holding fixed U.S. interest rates *and the expected future spot rate,* it is clear that the spot rate must increase. That is, the dollar must depreciate.

12b. If U.S. interest rates rise, it must be that the expected dollar return on British deposits rises as well. Otherwise, the no-arbitrage condition would not hold. There is more than one way for this return to rise: either the expected rate of depreciation of the dollar must rise, or the interest rate on British deposits must rise.

12c. Assuming that capital controls have not been imposed so that the no-arbitrage condition holds, it must be that the expected future spot rate has risen (i.e., depreciated).

14

Exchange Rates I: The Monetary Approach in the Long Run

1. Using the law of one price equation, we find that the price in Germany must be €0.80.

2a. No. For the law of one price to hold for guns, the exchange rate would have to be 2/3. For the law of one price to hold for doctor's visits, the exchange rate would have to be 3.

2b. The cost of an American basket is $175 (the average of the $200 and $150).

2c. The cost of a French basket is €175 (the average of €300 and €50).

2d. Yes, at that exchange rate the cost of the French basket is $175.

2e. This would be a real depreciation of the dollar because it would imply that it takes more U.S. baskets of goods to buy a French basket.

2f. For any $E_{\$/€} < 1$, the dollar is overvalued because it takes less than one U.S. basket to buy a French basket.

2g. No, with the different weights placed on guns, the prices of these baskets would be different. The U.S. basket would cost $180, whereas the French basket would cost €150. The dollar would appear to be undervalued if these two differently calculated baskets were compared.

3. The real exchange rate must be depreciating at a rate of –1% (or appreciating at a rate of 1%) because $\Delta q_{F/H} \,/\, q_{F/H} = \Delta E_{\$/blot} \,/\, E_{\$/blot} + \pi_F - \pi_H = 5\% + 2\% - 8\%$.

4. The answer is b, a straightforward application of the RPPP formula.

5. True. The percent change in the nominal exchange rate is equal to the percent change in the real exchange rate plus the differences in the inflation rates of the two countries. RPPP holds when changes in the real exchange rate are zero, and it fits better when changes in the real exchange rate are small relative to differences in inflation rates.

6. The answer is d, the law of one price implies both PPP concepts, but the reverse is not true.

7. All three choices are correct, so the answer is d.

8. The rate of inflation should be equal to the rate of money growth, so inflation in Home should be 3% and inflation in Foreign should be 5%. Now apply RPPP to find that Home's currency ought to appreciate at a rate of 2%. Hence the answer is a.

9a. We plug the information into the money market equilibrium equation for the United States $25 = (1/2)(100 units)$P$, so $P = 0.5$$/unit.

9b. Using the APPP equation, we have $(0.1\$/¥)P_{Japan} = 0.5\$/\text{unit}$, so $P_{Japan} = 5¥/\text{unit}$.

9c. Using the money market equilibrium equation for Japan, we have $M_{Japan} = (5Y/\text{unit})(80 \text{ units})(3/4) = 300$ yen.

10a. The inflation rate in the United States is the difference between the rate of growth of money and the rate of growth of the economy, or 2%.

10b. The inflation rate in Canada is 9%.

10c. The Canadian dollar is increasing (depreciating) at a rate of 7%.

11. During hyperinflations nominal money balances held are rapidly losing value, imposing a severe cost on the holders of that money. People become anxious to exchange their money for things that will hold their value, like goods.

12. A decrease in money demand would tend to increase the price level in Home. To maintain PPP, Home's exchange rate would have to depreciate.

13a. From the Fisher effect we know that Country A has the higher inflation rate.

13b. Assuming arbitrage in financial and goods markets, the real interest rate is the same. Real interest parity arises.

13c. According to the monetary theory, the rate of inflation should be the difference between the rate of money growth minus the rate of growth in real output. Hence, the inflation rate in Country B is 4%.

13d. The real interest rate must be 3% because the interest rate in Country B is 7% and the inflation rate is 4%. Because the real interest rate is the same in Country A, the inflation rate there must be $10 - 3 = 7\%$. Because the inflation rate in A is equal to the money growth rate in A minus the growth in real output, the money growth rate in A must be 9%.

13e. A decrease in the growth of money from 6% to 2% eliminates inflation in Country B in the long run. Hence, the interest rate falls to 3%, which is equal to the real interest rate.

13f. By assumption the liquidity ratio must rise.

13g. The increase in the liquidity ratio increases money demand at time *T*. Because the money supply is fixed at time *T*, the sudden increase in the money demand must lead to an immediate decrease in the price level.

13h. The sudden decrease in Country B's price level leads to a sudden decrease (appreciation) in Country B's exchange rate. The appreciation is necessary for APPP to hold.

13i. After time *T*, RPPP requires that Country B's exchange rate appreciate at a rate equal to Country A's inflation rate of 7%.

14. All of the choices are associated with an appreciation so the answer must be e.

15. Money demand must be increasing in Home, which drives down Home's price level, which has two implications. First, Home's currency must be appreciating because prices are falling. The Fisher effect implies that interest rates in Home are less than in Foreign. Hence, c is the only true response.

16a. With a constant money growth rate of 10% in Home, the inflation rate in Home would be 10%. With a constant money growth rate of 5% in Foreign, the inflation rate in Foreign would be 5%. (*Y* is constant, and the nominal interest rate is constant at the real interest rate plus the rate of expected inflation). By RPPP the dollar must lose value at a rate equal to the difference in inflation rates, or 5%.

16b. By the Fisher effect, the interest rate differential between Home and Foreign is equal to the inflation rate differential between Home and Foreign. Hence, Home's interest rate is higher than Foreign's interest rate by 5%.

16c. With a lower expected rate of money growth, there is now a lower expected rate of inflation (5% instead of 10%). By the Fisher effect, the interest rate should fall by 5% at time *t*.

16d. The fall in the interest rate leads to an increase in money demand: $L(i, Y)$ jumps. Because $P = M^S / L(i, Y)$ and M^S is fixed at the moment of *t,* the price level should fall. By APPP, the dollar should strengthen, that is, E should drop to keep foreign prices equal to domestic prices.

16e. Because the rate of money growth is now the same in the two countries, there should be no difference in inflation rates, and hence by RPPP the exchange rate should be constant over time.

17a. Home's exchange rate would have to appreciate at a rate of 3%.

17b. Home's money supply would need to grow at a rate of 5%.

17c. By the Fisher effect and the difference between Foreign's nominal interest rate and inflation, the world real interest rate must be 3%. Because Home wishes to the inflation rate to be 2%, Home must target a nominal interest rate of 5% (2 + 3).

17d. A fall in the growth rate of real output would alter the relationship between inflation and the rate of growth of the money supply. Hence, it would alter the government's money supply anchor. Neither the interest rate target nor the exchange rate target would have to change.

15

Exchange Rates II: The Asset Approach in the Short Run

1. The answer is d. Applying UIP, the dollar must be expected to depreciate by 2% in order for the expected returns to be the same in both currencies.

2a. UIP requires the dollar to depreciate by 2% in order to make the expected dollar return on foreign assets equal to the dollar return on domestic assets.

2b. The expected change in the exchange rate is 2%, and the current spot is 1, so the future expected spot rate must be 1.02 because (1.02 – 1) / 1 = 0.02.

2c. It has increased. There is now a greater gap between interest rates on deposits in the United States and Europe that must be accounted for by a faster rate of expected dollar depreciation.

2d. It must appreciate so as to allow for a greater depreciation in the future.

2e. See Figure 15-1. The increase in domestic interest rates results in a need for a faster rate of dollar depreciation. Because the expected level of the exchange rate has not changed, the downward sloping curve does not move.

FIGURE 15-1

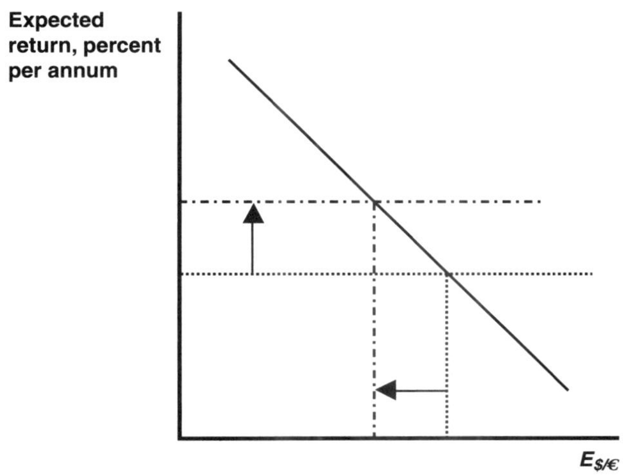

Temporary Home Monetary Shock and the Exchange Rate

2f. Because the interest rate gap has become smaller, the expected rate of dollar depreciation has become smaller.

2g. The dollar would have to appreciate.

2h. See Figure 15-2. An increase in the foreign interest rate means that the expected rate of home currency depreciation does not have to be as large to equalize expected returns.

FIGURE 15-2

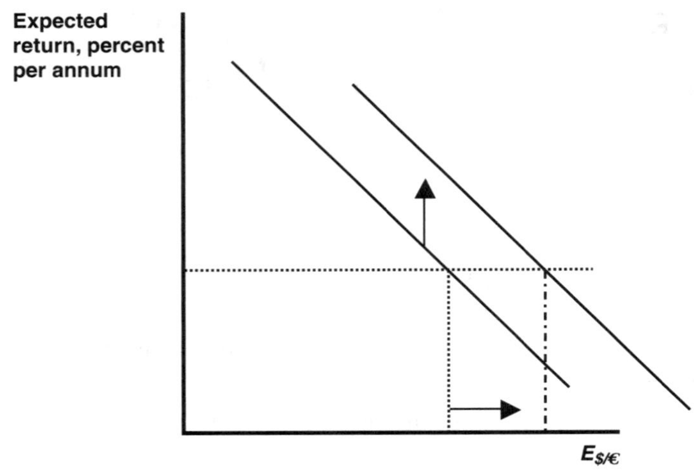

Temporary Foreign Interest Rate Shock and the Exchange Rate

3a. There is no effect on prices at time *T* because prices are assumed to be sticky.

3b. To get people to hold the increased real balances, the interest rate must drop. This is shown in Figure 15-3 as a rightward shift in the real money supply leading to a movement along real money demand.

FIGURE 15-3

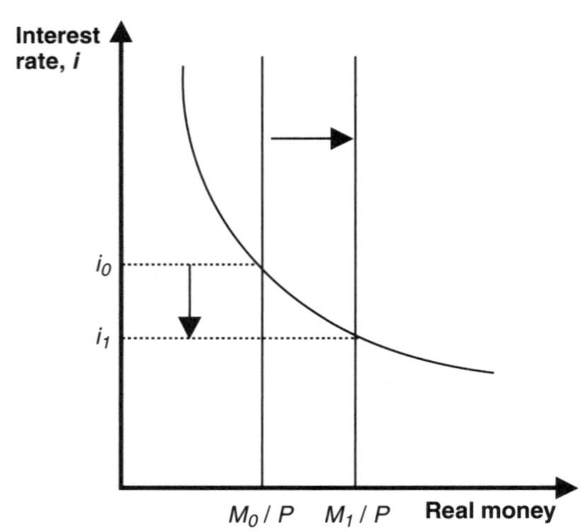

An Increase in the Real Money Supply

3c. In the long run, the price level must also rise by 10%.

3d. There is no long-run effect of the increase in M on the interest rate because inflation in the long run will be driven back to zero after prices have jumped 10%. When prices rise from P to P_1, it must be that $M_1 / P_1 = M_0 / P$.

4a. There is no effect on prices at time T because prices are assumed to be sticky.

4b. The interest rate must rise at time T because the increase in real output raises the demand for real balances shown in Figure 15-4 as the upward shift in the $L(i, Y)$ curve. To get people to be willing to keep their demand constant, the cost of real balances must rise.

FIGURE 15-4

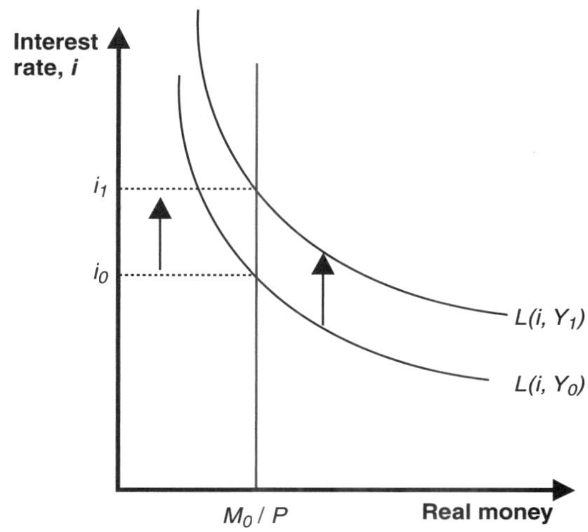

An Increase in the Real Money Demand

4c. In the long run the price level must fall to increase the quantity of real balances.

4d. There is no long-run effect on the interest rate because prices are flexible in the long run. That is, the price level falls so that the real money supply expands until the interest rate returns to i_0.

5. See Figure 15-5. A temporary increase in Home's money supply lowers its interest rate (left-hand panel) and so leads to a depreciation in the Home currency (right-hand panel).

FIGURE 15-5

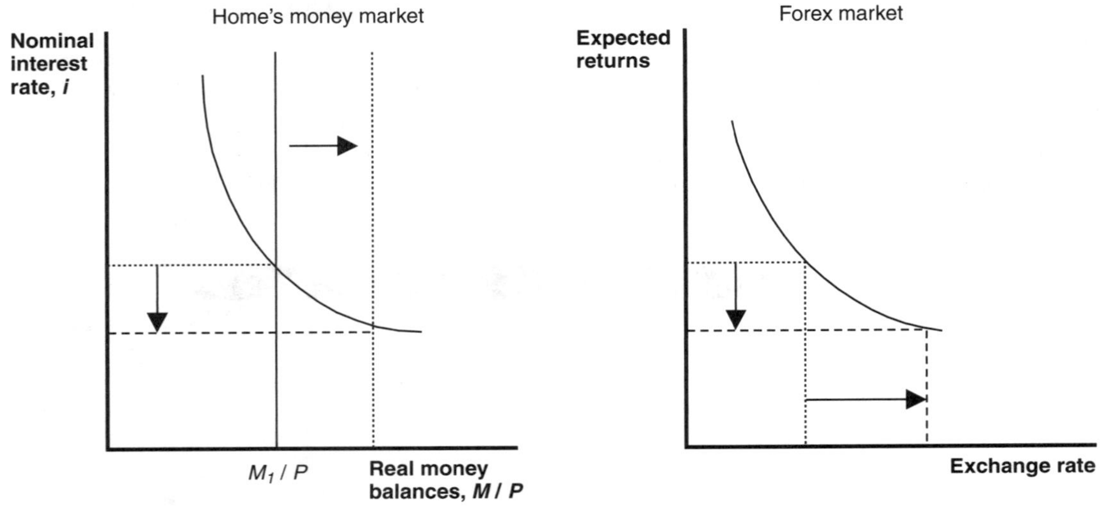

The Effect of a Temporary Increase in Home's Money Supply

6. See Figure 15-6. A temporary increase in Home's real output increases its demand for money (left-hand panel), thereby increasing Home's interest rate. The increase in the interest rate has the effect of causing an appreciation in the exchange rate in order to give Home's currency more room to depreciate in the future (right-hand panel).

FIGURE 15-6

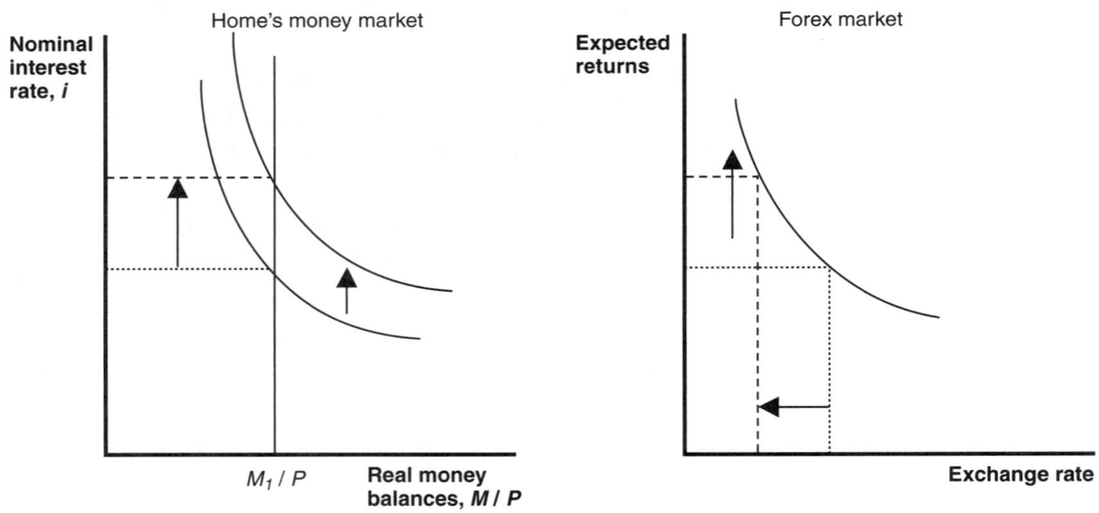

The Effect of a Temporary Increase in Home's Real Output

7. See Figure 15-7. An increase in Foreign's real output increases its money demand and so drives up Foreign's interest rate. This results in an increase in the return on foreign assets, which is represented in the right-hand panel of Figure 15-7 as a rightward shift in the curve. Home's currency depreciates relative to Foreign's currency.

FIGURE 15-7

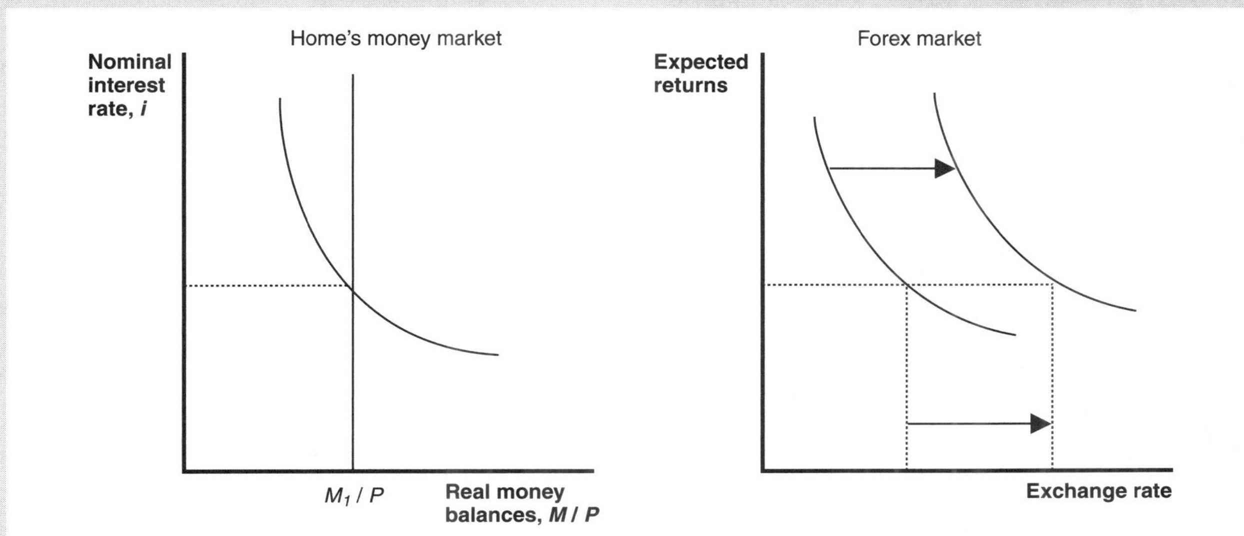

The Effects of a Temporary Increase in Foreign's Real Output

8a. True. If prices were perfectly flexible, then there would be no short-run effect on interest rates that cause overshooting.

8b. Uncertain. Although a sharp drop in the dollar could be consistent with a permanent increase in the money supply and a jump in inflation, it could also be consistent with other possibilities. For instance, there could be a large but temporary increase in the money supply in the United States. Alternatively, a foreign country could have tightened its monetary policy.

8c. Uncertain. Interest rates could increase because of a reduction in the money supply combined with sticky prices, or they could increase because inflation expectations have risen combined with the Fisher effect. The connection between interest rates and exchange rate movements depends on the context.

9a. Because we are in a long-run equilibrium, we can use the monetary approach developed in Chapter 14. Because $L(i)$ is the same in both countries, the exchange rate is equal to the ratio of money supplies ($1,000/€500) multiplied by the ratio of real outputs (5,000/10,000) or 1$/€.

9b. Using the same approach as 9a, we find that the expected future spot rate is 1.5$/€.

9c. They are 5%. Recall that the expected rate of depreciation prior to time T was zero, so by UIP the interest rates must have been the same in the two countries. There is no monetary shock in Europe, so interest rates must have stayed the same after time T.

9d. By UIP, the dollar must be expected to appreciate by 3% at time T because interest rates in the United States are below those of Europe by 3%.

9e. At time T the expected rate of depreciation in the dollar is equal to –0.03 (the dollar is expected to appreciate), which is the gap between interest rates in the United States and Europe. The expected future spot rate is 1.5$/€, so if x is the current spot rate, then $(1.5\$/€ - x) / x = -0.03$. Hence, $x = 1.546\$/€$.

10a. See Figure 15-8. The increase in output from Y_0 to Y_1 shifts up money demand and raises the interest rate. People expect prices to fall in the future when they cease to be sticky. By absolute purchasing power parity (APPP) this implies an appreciated future spot rate. Hence, the expected return curve shifts down in the foreign exchange market. The two effects reinforce one another and the exchange rate falls.

FIGURE 15-8

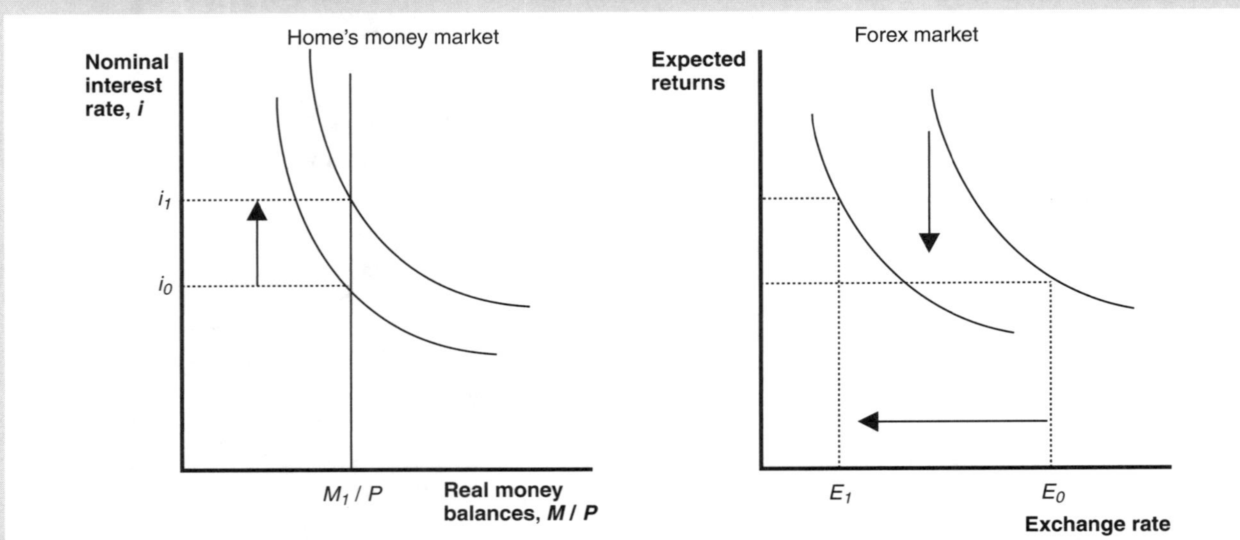

The Short-run Effect of a Permanent Increase in GDP

10b. See Figure 15-9. In the long-run prices fall from P_0 to P_1, and this expands the supply of real money. This lowers the interest rate and leads to a depreciation of the currency to E_2. Notice that the currency has appreciated relative to its initial value, E_0.

FIGURE 15-9

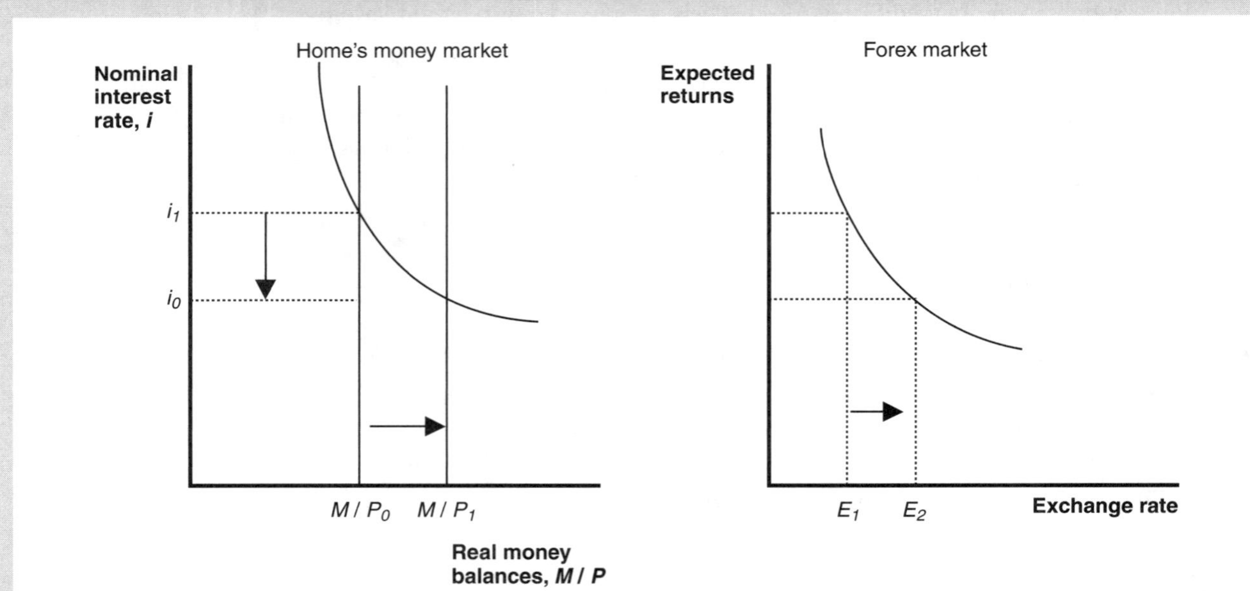

The Long-run Effect of a Permanent Increase in GDP

11. No, as long as PPP holds in the long run, monetary policy ultimately affects the price level, which in turn affects the exchange rate in the long run.

12a. Because Home has pegged its currency to Foreign, it must have the same interest rate as Foreign, so Home's interest rate rises.

12b. Home's real money demand rises, and this would tend to raise interest rates. Because interest rates cannot rise, Home's money supply must rise.

16

National and International Accounts: Income, Wealth, and the Balance of Payments

1a. False. The country may be a net exporter of factor services, or it may be receiving unilateral transfers from abroad.

1b. True. If no goods or services are being contributed to the economy from abroad, then supply equals demand dictates that expenditure equals product.

1c. False. A country's GDP includes only sales to final customers. It does not double count intermediate input production.

1d. True. Consult Figure 16-2 on the next page. Along the circular flow, all the current account items can be found between GNE and GNDI.

2. Domestic citizens working abroad are a source of NFIA or NUT. As a result, GNI exceeds GDP in countries like Jordan.

3. The current account identity tells us that the current balance is equal to the difference between national savings and investment. Holding fixed the savings rate, an increase in investment ought to lower the current account balance.

4. Yes. If a country has a trade surplus, its GDP will exceed its GNE. If, in addition, it has a deficit on its factor income account, its GNI will be less than its GDP.

5a. $GNE = C + I + G = 100$.

5b. $S = Y - C - G = 95 - 90 = 5$.

5c. $CA = S - I = 5 - 10 = -5$.

5d. A net exporter. A country that runs a current account deficit must export assets to obtain income to fund expenditure.

6. Recall that a country's current account balance is equal to the difference between saving and investment. A country with a high birth rate will tend to have a relatively large number of young citizens relative to other countries. If young people have different savings behaviors than older people, then the country may have very different current account behavior.

FIGURE 16-2

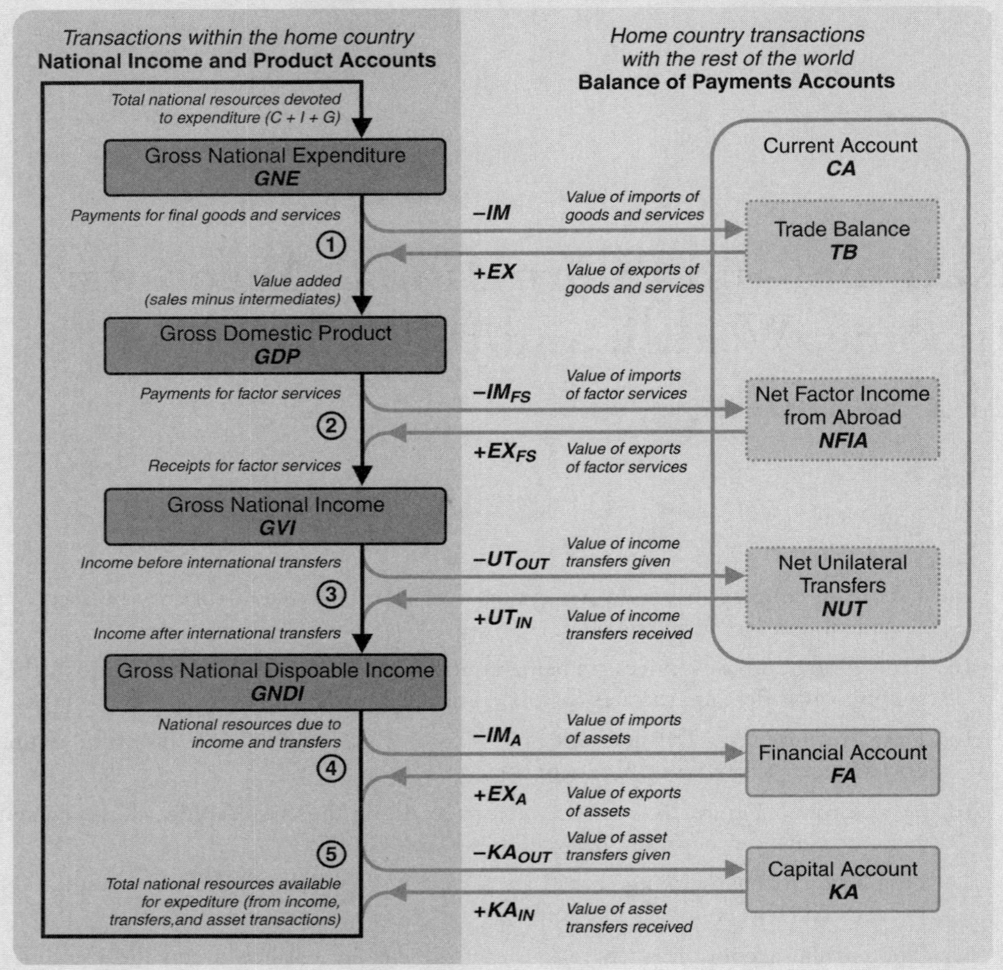

The Open Economy

7. A country with a very good investment climate will tend to have a higher investment rate. If the country has the same savings rate, then we would expect the country to be running a current account deficit.

8a. True. Government savings increases, and because all other components of savings are held fixed, the current account deficit must shrink.

8b. Uncertain. The chief question is how consumption spending responds. The phenomenon of Ricardian equivalence suggests that consumers will increase their spending in response to lower projected future taxes. If so, this might erode the savings gain.

9. The answer is b. The output of the affiliate is part of GDP, but its earnings will not be counted toward domestic income. Foreign aid does not increase GDP directly, and workers abroad do not affect domestic GDP.

10. The answer is d.

11. Uncertain. A country could use its current account surplus to pay down its existing liabilities to foreigners.

12. A country with a fixed exchange rate system is likely to intervene frequently in the foreign exchange market. As a result, it should have a much larger official settlements balance.

13a. The tractor sale is an $+EX$, and the payment is $-IM^F_A$.

13b. The loan is an import of a foreign asset $-IM^F_A$, and the deposit is an export of a home asset $+EX^H_A$.

13c. The food is exported to Zimbabwe $+EX$, which is balanced by a unilateral transfer $-UT_-$.

13d. The consultant's pay is an export of a factor service $+EX_{FS}$, and the payment is accomplished via a reduction on foreign claims on the American bank, so $-IM^H_A$.

13e. The concert is a service import $-IM$, but it is a gift $+UT_+$.

13f. The Chinese resident is receiving a service $+EX$, and the payment is $-IM^H_A$.

13g. The interest payment is factor service payment $+EX_{FS}$, and the payment method is $-IM^H_A$.

13h. The interest payment is factor service payment $+EX_{FS}$, and the payment method is an import of a foreign asset $-IM^F_A$ because the American bank now has a larger claim on a foreign entity.

14a. Summing over all the current account balances, we find that the external wealth would have been 50.

14b. The difference between the sum of current account balances and the actual external wealth is –7.

14c. The years that external wealth was greater than what was predicted by financial flows are 1991, 1992, 1994, 1995, and 1997.

15. If the current account deficit had been zero, the valuation effect would have increased the country's assets to $25 million, so external wealth would have been zero. The current account deficit increased the country's net wealth by –$5 million.

16. If the rate of return on assets and liabilities were the same and equal to r, then we would expect net income of $r(A - L)$, where A is assets and L is liabilities. Because $A < L$, we would expect these payments to be negative, yet they are positive.

17

The Balance of Payments I: The Gains from Financial Globalization

1a. Using the equation $W_N = TB_N + (1 + r)W_{N-1}$, we have $-10 + (1.1)100 = 100$.

1b. Yes. Using the equation $-(1 + r)W_{-1} = TB_0 + TB_1 / r$, we have $-110 = -10 + (-10 / 0.1) = -110$. The LRBC is satisfied.

1c. Using the equation $W_N = TB_N + (1 + r)W_{N-1}$, we have $-12 + (1.1)100 = 98$.

1d. No. The present value of trade deficits exceeds the initial wealth, so the LRBC is not satisfied with a perpetual trade deficit of 12.

2a. The present value of home production is 100 + 100 / 1.1 = 190.91.

2b. The present value of expenditures must be no greater than 190.91. According to the simple model, this could be spent all at once in the first period.

2c. No. Home would have to borrow in the first period to fund its trade deficit, and it would have to run a trade surplus in the second period in order to repay its debt.

2d. The trade surplus is equal to production minus consumption, so the largest trade surplus the country could run is 100.

2e. The largest trade deficit the country could run is 110 in the second period. Suppose the country ran a trade surplus of 100 in the first period. In the second period, the country would have external wealth of 110, which could then be spent on foreign goods.

3a. The present value of the country's resources is $(1.1)\cdot(-50) + 10 + 10 / 0.1 = 55$.

3b. Let X be the amount consumed in every period. Then the long-run budget constraint requires $X + X / .1 = 55 = X(1 + 10)$. So, $X = 5$.

3c. 55.

4. If the interest rate on assets and liabilities were the same, then a net debtor will have larger payments on its debts than on its assets.

5. The United States pays a lower interest rate on its debts than it receives on its assets. This means that although it is an external net debtor, its factor service payments are not actually negative.

6. A couple of assumptions fail in the case of developing countries. First, developing countries often pay higher interest on their debts than they receive on their assets. Second, international financial markets often set debt limits for these countries so that they are not so free to run trade deficits in any given period.

7. False. The present value of consumption must fall, but it is spread out over many years rather than incurred all at once.

8a. If Home is not free to borrow, its consumption must fall by 10 units.

8b. Using the formula for the size of adjustment necessary, we have $(0.1 / 1.1)\cdot(-10) = -0.9091$, so consumption falls 0.9091 units.

8c. Home borrows approximately 9.1 units (99.1 – 90) and each year pays an interest rate of 10% on this debt. Hence, the interest paid each year is approximately 0.91 units.

8d. If the shock had been permanent, then the country would have been forced to reduce its consumption by 10 units in every period because one cannot use international borrowing and lending to offset permanent shocks.

8e. If Home had not been free to lend on international markets, its consumption would increase by 10 units.

8f. If Home had been free to lend, its consumption would rise by $(0.1 / 1.1)\cdot(10) = 0.9091$ units.

8g. If the shock were permanent, then Home would increase its consumption by 10 units in each period.

9. This is an effort to build up precautionary savings as a shield against bad shocks in the future.

10. The present value of the perpetual return is $1 / 0.05 = 20$, which exceeds the current investment cost. Hence, the investment is worth undertaking.

11a. If the world's resources were being used efficiently, the marginal product of capital would be the same in the two countries.

11b. No. If they were, then resources would be directed to their highest return.

11c. Assuming that capital is free to move internationally, there are two possibilities. First, it could be that Home has a smaller amount of capital per worker than Foreign. Second, it could be that Home has higher technical or social efficiency than Foreign so that it gets more out of its capital than Foreign.

12a. Using the production function, we find that in each country output per worker is equal to 70.

12b. The marginal product of capital in this case is proportional to output divided by the capital stock, so Foreign has a higher marginal product of capital.

12c. Investors should invest exclusively in Foreign until the marginal product of capital is the same in the two countries.

13. Uncertain. If capital does not flow to developing countries because of high risk premium and not because of low A productivity, then foreign aid can be helpful. If, however, A is low because of poor institutional quality (including corruption) then foreign aid does little to aid the development process.

14a. The mean is (50 units + 10 units) / 2 = 30 units. Half the time output is 20 units above the mean, and half the time output is 20 units below the mean. Because expenditure equals output, expenditure varies in the same way.

14b. International diversification ensures that the country *always* gets 30 units of expenditure.

14c. International diversification of capital income ensures that the country always gets capital income of $(1 / 2)\cdot(25 + 5) = 15$. Labor income is undiversified, however, so it varies between 25 units in good years to 5 units in bad years. Hence, in good years income is $25 + 15 = 40$, and in bad years income is $15 + 5 = 20$. Therefore, income varies 10 units around the mean.

14d. If the two countries experienced the same shock each year, then there would be nothing gained from international diversification. The variation around the mean would be 20 units as in problem 14a.

15. You could buy stocks in American multinationals. Because multinationals produce and sell some of their output in foreign markets, they are somewhat diversified.

16. The answer is d.

18

The Balance of Payments II: Output, Exchange Rates, and Macroeconomic Policies in the Short Run

1a. The marginal propensity to consume is 0.75.

1b. Recall that $S = (Y - T) - C$. Plugging in the equation for C, we obtain $S = 0.25(Y - T) - 5$. Because disposable income $Y - T$ is equal to 100, we have $S = 20$.

1c. A consumption shock could take the form of a change in the intercept or the marginal propensity to consume. A consumption boom could take the form of an increase in either.

1d. A transfer of disposable income from one consumer to another will have no impact on aggregate consumption if both consumers have the same marginal propensity to consume.

1e. False. Although consumption spending will rise by this amount, some of the spending will fall on imports, and these are not part of domestic aggregate demand.

2a. All projects with a rate of return greater than the interest rate will be undertaken. Hence, investment will be 4 units.

2b. All projects with a rate of return greater than the interest rate will be undertaken. Hence, investment will be 2 units.

2c. All projects with a rate of return greater than the interest rate will be undertaken. Hence, investment will be 4 units. This answer is arrived at by doubling the numbers in the table.

3. The answer is illustrated in Figure 18-2. Note that the immediate impact of an appreciation of Home's currency is to reduce the cost of its imports and thereby improve the trade balance. Over time, the real appreciation of the currency induces expenditure switching by Home and Foreign consumers so that exports fall and imports increase. Eventually the trade balance deteriorates.

FIGURE 18-2

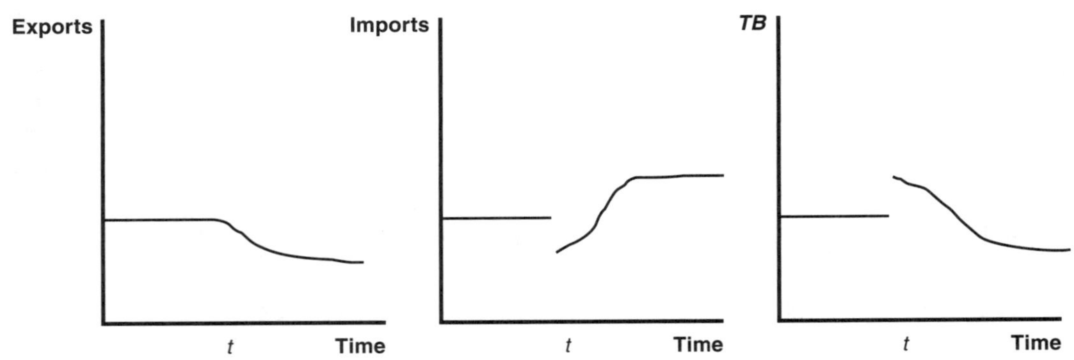

The J curve in Reverse, the Case of an Appreciation

4. The answer is d because both dollar invoicing and distribution costs reduce the share of the final price that is affected by exchange rate movements. They reduce the link between movements in the nominal exchange rate to movements in the real exchange rate. J-curve effects involve imperfect transmission of changes in the real exchange rate to the trade balance, which is a conceptually different issue.

5. The answer is d, all of the above.

6a. A fall in the interest rate increases investment spending, *I,* and leads to a depreciation of the exchange rate, which in turn increases the trade balance. Hence, aggregate demand increases and the national output rises.

6b. An appreciation of Home's currency tends to reduce the trade balance, which lowers aggregate demand and national output.

6c. A tax cut raises disposable income and so increases consumer spending. Although some of this spending goes to imports and so does not raise expenditure on domestic goods and services, consumption rises by more than imports. As a result, aggregate demand expands and so does domestic output.

6d. A Foreign tax cut raises consumer expenditure in Foreign, and some of this increased spending falls on Home's goods and services. Hence, aggregate demand in Home expands and so does national output.

6e. A drop in consumer confidence shifts the function $C(Y - T)$ down and so reduces aggregate demand for every level of national output. The downward shift in aggregate demand lowers national output.

6f. This is a sudden drop in the demand for imports. Consumers switch their expenditure away from imports toward domestic goods even with an unchanged nominal exchange rate. As a result, domestic demand increases and national output rises.

7a. A fall in interest rates is associated with a movement along the same IS curve rather than a shift in the IS curve.

7b. An increase in the expected future exchange rate is associated with a rightward shift in the IS curve.

7c. A tax cut is associated with a rightward shift in the IS curve.

7d. A foreign tax cut is associated with a rightward shift in the IS curve.

7e. A drop in consumer confidence is associated with a leftward shift in the IS curve.

7f. A shift in expenditure toward domestic goods and services is associated with a rightward shift in aggregate demand.

8. The answer is d because a fall in the price level increases the real money supply. None of the other options has any direct effect on the LM curve.

9. True. The LM curve is upward sloping because when prices are sticky, real money demand has to be equal to a constant. An increase in national output raises real money demand, and this increase in money demand has to be offset by an increase in the nominal interest rate. If prices were flexible, then an increase in national output would result in a decrease in the price level and an increase in the real money supply.

10a. No. See Figure 18-3. An increase in the government spending or a reduction in taxes will shift the IS curve to the right, thereby increasing national output. The higher interest rate leads to an appreciation of the currency, however, reducing the trade balance. Moreover, the expansion of disposable income raises demand for imports further reducing the trade balance.

FIGURE 18-3

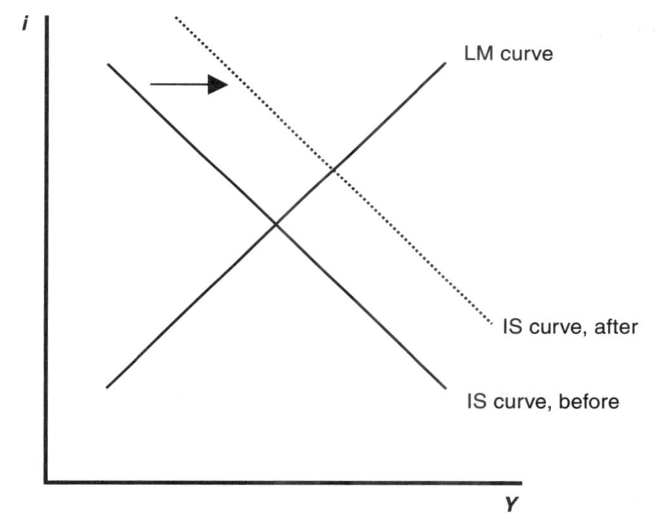

Fiscal Policy Alone Causes *i* and *Y* to Move in the Same Direction

10b. Yes. See Figure 18-4. An increase in the money supply shifts the LM curve to the right, thereby increasing national output and lowering interest rates. The lower interest rate causes the exchange rate to depreciate and tends to improve the trade balance. Although the increase in national output raises demand for imports, which tends to lower the trade balance, the exchange rate depreciation increases the trade balance. Therefore, it is possible that monetary policy alone could achieve both aims.

FIGURE 18-4

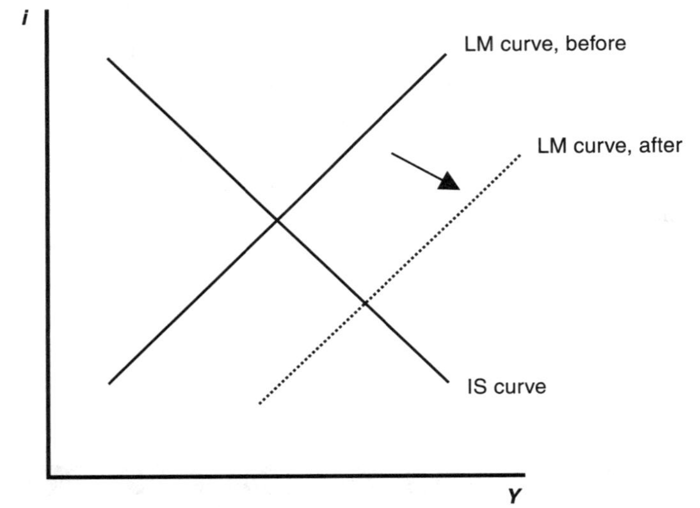

Monetary Policy Alone Causes *i* and *Y* to Move in Opposite Directions

10c. No. See Figure 18-5. An increase in the government spending or a reduction in taxes will shift the IS curve to the right, thereby increasing national output and putting upward pressure on interest rates. Because the higher interest rate would tend to appreciate the currency, the government must increase the money supply in order to maintain the fixed exchange rate. While the real exchange rate is unchanged, the increase in disposable income will tend to increase imports and worsen the trade balance.

FIGURE 18-5

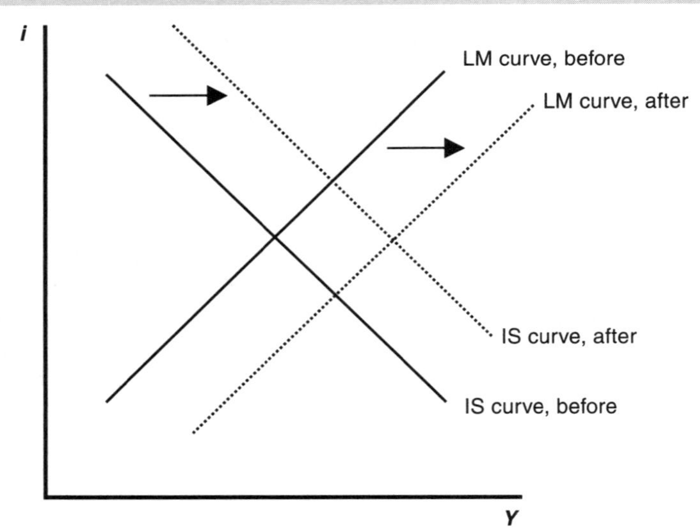

With Fixed Exchange Rate System, Changes in Fiscal Policy Cause Shifts in Both IS and LM Curves

11. False. There is some similarity in the sense that the domestic interest rate is fixed and the LM curve must be adjusted to accommodate movements in the IS curve. However, there is no sense in which the interest rates of Home and Foreign must be the same so that changes in the Foreign interest rate can change the exchange rate.

12a. See Figure 18-6. An exogenous drop in investment shifts the IS curve to the left, lowering output and the interest rate. The exchange rate depreciates and the trade balance improves, which offsets some of the recessionary impact of the shift.

FIGURE 18-6

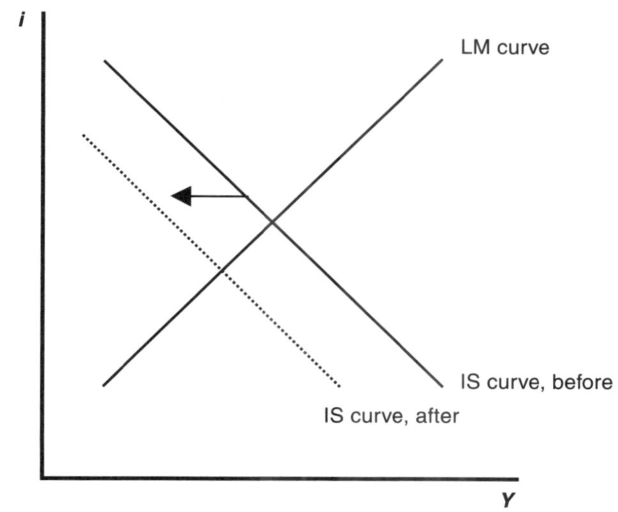

Effect of Investment Bust with a Flexible Exchange Rate System

12b. The most natural thing to do would be to cut taxes or raise government spending in order to shift the IS curve back to its initial level. Alternatively, the government could increase the money supply to shift the LM curve to the right.

12c. See Figure 18-7. Because the fixed exchange rate system requires the interest rate to be fixed, the leftward shift in the IS curve caused by the decline in investment spending induces the LM curve to shift to the left as well as the central bank lowers the money supply. The effects of the shock are therefore magnified under a fixed exchange rate system.

FIGURE 18-7

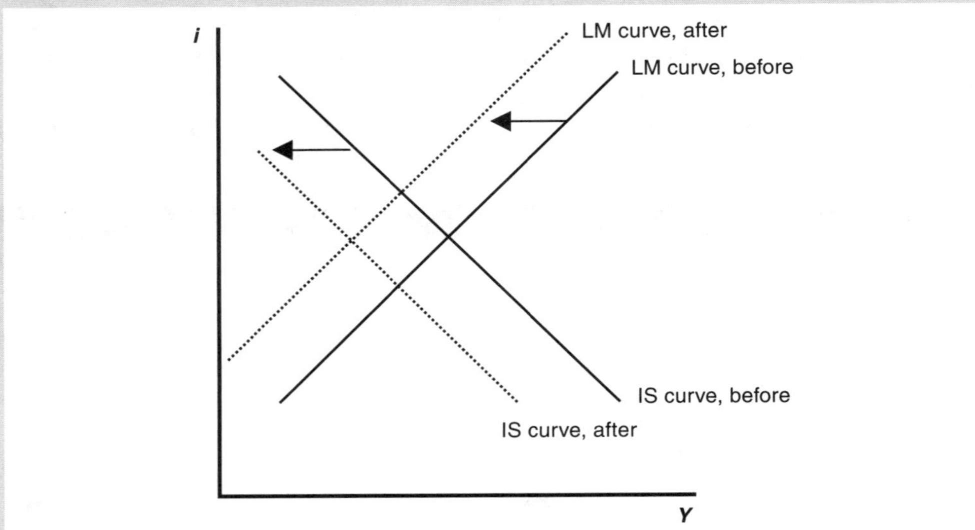

Effect of Investment Bust with a Fixed Exchange Rate System

12d. Fiscal policy could be used to offset the effect of the investment bust, but monetary policy is not an option.

13. See Figure 18-8. In both cases, the return on Foreign assets rises from FR_0 to FR_1 and the IS curve shifts from IS_0 to IS_1. In the case of a flexible exchange rate system, Home's exchange rate will depreciate, and this will tend to expand exports and contract imports, shifting the IS curve to the right. Output rises, and this drives up the local interest rate but by less than the rise in interest rates in Foreign (note that part of the expected return in Foreign is due to a faster rate of depreciation). In the case of the fixed exchange rate system, Home's exchange rate cannot change, so the interest must go up in Home by exactly as much as in Foreign. Hence, the LM curve must shift to the left. This reduces investment in Home and may result in reduced output.

FIGURE 18-8

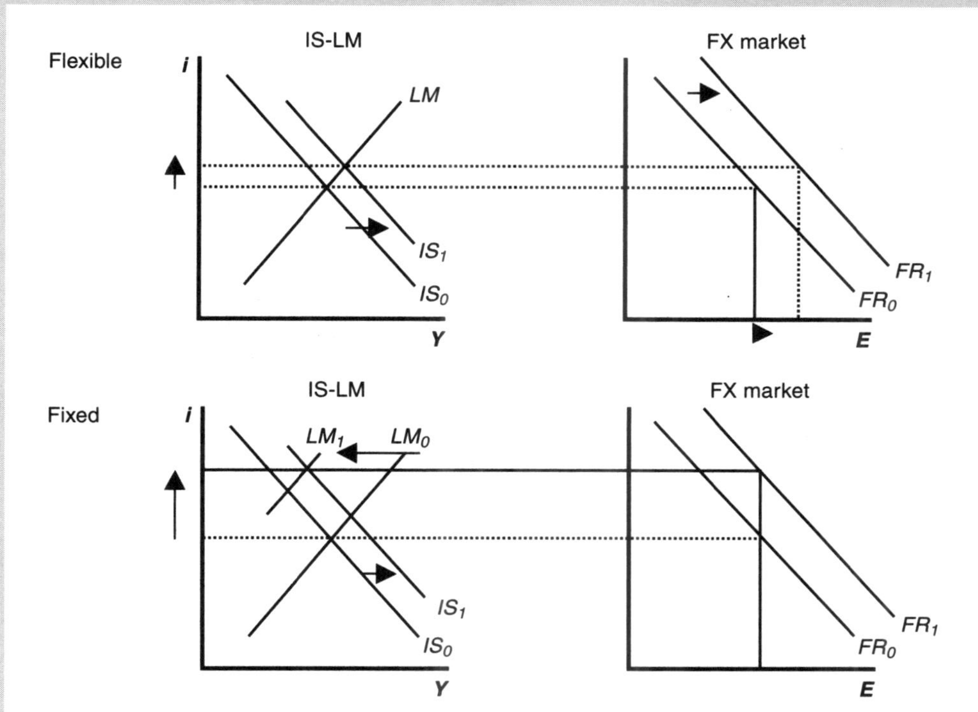

The Impact of a Rise in Foreign Interest Rates Under a Flexible and Fixed Exchange Rate System

14. The answer is d, all of the above.

19

Fixed versus Floating: International Monetary Experience

1. No, a country retains control over its fiscal policy even when it fixes its exchange rate. The decline in investment could be offset by either a tax cut or an increase in government spending.

2. It could be that trading patterns have changed so that the volume of trade with the country to which the currency is pegged has been eclipsed by trade with the other country.

3. Perhaps not. To the extent that the two states do not trade much with each other and may be exposed to asymmetric shocks (a fall in oil prices is good for Massachusetts but bad for Texas), it may be that the states would be better with different currencies.

4. By imposing capital controls the country regains its ability to conduct an independent monetary policy.

5. Countries have many nominal anchors at their disposal. If a country cannot commit to maintain a nominal anchor of a different sort, then it is unclear why it will be any more successful fixing its nominal exchange rate.

6a. The depreciation of the dollar swells Home's liabilities relative to its assets, reducing its total wealth.

6b. If consumption and investment is sufficiently sensitive to changes in total wealth, then it is possible that the depreciation of the dollar will result in a contraction of both investment and consumption and a fall in output. As shown in the textbook, there is evidence that very large depreciations can have this effect on the economy.

7. Ideally, Home's trade in goods and its trade in assets would be with the same trade partner so that the economic integration and the currency mismatch arguments for fixing the exchange rate with a single country would be possible. In this case, however, fixing the currency in terms of the dollar means not fixing it with respect to the euro and vice versa. Thus, Home must choose between fixing its currency with the European Union to gain from market integration or fixing its currency with the U.S. to avoid the currency mismatch of its assets and liabilities.

8. The problem of original sin. If a country has a reputation of high inflation and an unstable currency, foreign firms may be reluctant to hold assets denominated in the local currency.

9a. If Foreign cuts its taxes, its expenditure rises, and some of the additional expenditure is directed to Home's goods and services. The increase in aggregate demand raises output in Home. Because Home was initially in full employment, its economy begins to overheat.

9b. If Foreign revalues its currency, then its real exchange rate will rise, and some of the expenditure will be shifted toward Home's products. If Home takes no action, its trade balance will rise, and the economy will again begin to overheat.

10. If a country fixes its currency to gold, it does not expose itself to arbitrary policy changes from the base country. Further, if there are enough adherents to the gold standard, it will also benefit from the network externality.

11a. A real devaluation of Home's currency causes expenditure switching away from Foreign toward Home. The reduction in aggregate demand can result in output falling below its full employment level in Foreign.

11b. Foreign could stimulate its economy by lowering the interest rate, thereby expanding investment. The reduction in interest rates in Foreign would have to be matched in Home to prevent Home's currency from appreciating.

12. If the center country increases its money supply, the non-center countries will also have to increase their money supplies in order to prevent their currencies from appreciating. The increase in the money supply in the non-center country could result in inflation if it is permanent.

13. The more countries that are fixed to a given country, the larger the volume of potential transactions that are not subject to exchange rate volatility.

14. Capital controls allow the countries within the system to have some modicum of monetary policy. The extent of policy autonomy is partially disciplined by the strength of the controls.

20

Exchange Rate Crises: How Pegs Work and How They Break

1. According to the text, an exchange rate crisis in a developed country typically involves a 10%–15% depreciation and a 20%–25% depreciation in a developing country.

2. When a banking system or the government has assets in local currency and liabilities in foreign currency, then a depreciation of the exchange rate causes the value of liabilities to swell, causing banking crises and government defaults.

3. When a bank fails, the central bank may be tempted to prop up the bank by extending credit to it. This expansion of domestic credit may expand the money supply and destabilize the fixed exchange rate system.

4. Currency boards have a backing ratio of 100%, so as long as there is positive money demand, there will be positive reserves. As long as the currency board continues to operate, the fixed exchange rate will be maintained.

5. A central bank could sell sterilization bonds that are a liability of the central bank but which are not counted as money. The policy is costly because the sterilization bonds are likely to require a higher interest rate than the reserves earn, so the policy can induce losses at the central bank.

6a. The central bank should have reserves worth 50 pesos.

6b. Without any additional effect, the increase in domestic credit should lower reserves to only 5 pesos, but this is not zero, so there should be no exchange rate crisis.

6c. The loss of reserves and the financial crisis could induce a rise in the risk premium. Higher domestic interest rates would then lower money demand, pushing the country into an exchange rate crisis as reserves go to zero.

7a. The rise in interest rates suggests that either the exchange risk premium or the default risk premium have risen. To the extent that the exchange risk premium is responsible for the rise in the interest rate, the information suggests that the currency is not credibly pegged.

7b. See Figure 20-2. Money demand will fall from M_0 to M_1 as interest rates rise from i_0 to i_1 (decrease in money demand), so the value of central bank assets must fall. Because the level of domestic credit stays fixed, reserves must fall. By definition the backing ratio has decreased.

FIGURE 20-2

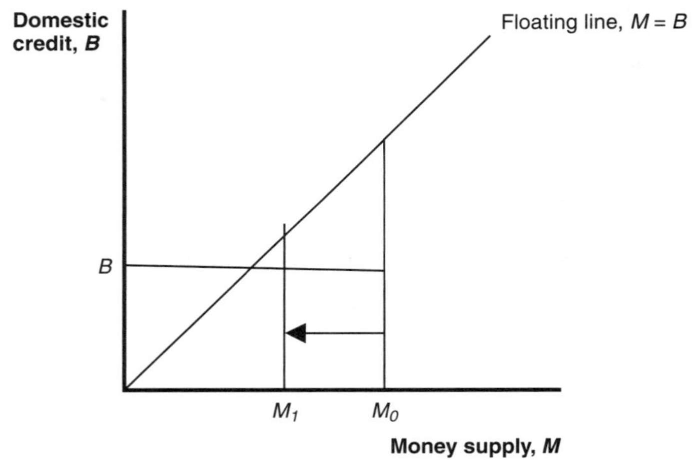

8. It could make a loan of foreign exchange to the country's central bank. The higher reserves could tide the country over until money demand rises.

9. A bailout implies a generalized rise in domestic credit but does not raise the money supply so that it must squeeze out reserves. Providing liquidity to a solvent bank raises both the assets and liabilities of the central bank, so it does not squeeze out reserves because money demand has risen.

10. The answer is c. The interest rate differential for peso accounts includes both currency and country premiums. The dollar deposit interest rate differential does not contain the currency premium. Hence, the currency premium is equal to the total differential minus the default premium or 5%.

11a. As long as the currency remains pegged, the money supply remains constant, and prices are constant. Inflation is zero.

11b. Now the money supply grows at a rate of 30%, so inflation is 30%. By the Fisher effect, the nominal interest rate must rise from 5% to 35%.

11c. Because at time t the money supply is fixed, the decline in the money demand must be offset by an increase in the price level. Hence, prices double at time t.

11d. Real money demand falls at time t because interest rates have risen.

11e. The exchange rate jumps from 1 to 2, reflecting APPP and the doubling of the local price level.

11f. Before time t, the value of the portfolio is \$20. After time t, the 10 pesos are worth only \$5, so the value of the portfolio is \$15.

12a. No, the threshold for the crisis is equal to $2 \times 20\% = 40\%$, which is less than the existing backing ratio.

12b. Now the threshold backing ratio rises to $2 \times 40\% = 80\%$, which exceeds the existing backing ratio. Hence, the currency depreciates.

13. As long as the country continues to finance a budget deficit through central bank domestic credit, the country will experience reserve losses. The loan will only have a temporary effect as long as fiscal policy is inconsistent with maintaining the fixed exchange rate.

14. A sudden increase in the interest rate spread indicates a loss of faith in a country's commitment to the exchange rate.

15. During recessions the cost of maintaining the fixed exchange rate system is higher than during normal times. Any change in expectations that raises the interest rate deepens the already high cost of maintaining the peg, thereby reducing the credibility of the peg.

16. A currency board might make it appear less likely that a country will abandon a peg. As Argentina's experience suggests, however, the government can always get rid of the currency board if the cost of maintaining the fixed exchange rate is too high.

21

The Euro

1. Ecuador had a reputation for not being able to control its money supply. A fixed exchange rate system might not have been credible because the peg is a contingent obligation. Adopting the dollar raises the cost of going back to the old days.
2. By removing exchange rate volatility, the currency union may foster rapid growth in trade between countries and thereby lead to greater integration.
3. The fear is that by fostering additional trade, countries may be induced to specialize in different products. Specialization may result in the countries being exposed to more asymmetric shocks.
4. Optimum currency area theory emphasizes the importance of labor mobility. Currency unions are more likely to raise welfare if workers can leave areas receiving bad shocks and enter countries experiencing good shocks. The 1995 Schengen Treaty eases restrictions on labor mobility across countries.
5. Faced with asymmetric shocks, many countries in Europe found it too painful to keep their exchange rates fixed during the ERM crisis. This is a hint that the countries are not sufficiently similar to make a common currency worthwhile.
6. The fiscal restrictions limit the ability of governments to adjust their fiscal policy to fluctuations in aggregate demand, leaving governments with no recourse to fight recessions. Further, there is no theory that suggests that low government deficits have anything to do with optimum currency areas. Finally, the criteria are widely ignored by even Germany, the country with the greatest interest in price stability.
7. Because they can be painful, the criteria allow countries to demonstrate their commitment to low inflation policies.

8a. Decisions are made by consensus by representatives from all member countries.

8b. Central bank independence appears to be necessary to avoid the time inconsistency of monetary policy that leads to inflation bias. Governments that can control the central bank are too tempted to expand the money supply.

8c. The central bank's preferences might be inconsistent with the desires of the majority of citizens.

8d. Among European countries, the German central bank was structured so as to keep inflation low. The Maastricht Treaty tries to screen out countries that might want to have a more interventionist central bank.

9. There is no such justification in theory. The number is largely arbitrary.
10. As the number of members expands, the diversity of economic shocks to which countries in the Eurozone are exposed also rises. Because the ECB makes its deci-

sions by consensus, it becomes ever more difficult to agree on the appropriate policy when each member has a different opinion about what is appropriate.

11. There is nothing stopping a country from adopting the euro as its currency, but joining the Eurozone requires admission. The difference is that countries not in the Eurozone have no input into the ECB's decisions.

22

Topics in International Macroeconomics

1. The no-arbitrage band is 100 / 115 = 0.87 and 115 / 100 = 1.15, so the most that the real exchange rate can appreciate before arbitrage becomes profitable is 0.87.

2. One cause of movements in nominal exchange rates is movements in real exchange rates. If a reduction in trade costs leads to a narrowing of the no-arbitrage band, the real exchange rate should become less volatile.

3. No. This could be the equilibrium real exchange rate.

4a. No. If all goods and services were freely traded, then the price of the same good (or service) must be the same in every country, so there can be no variation in price indexes across countries.

4b. No. If developed countries had an equal productivity advantage in services, then the cost of production would be the same in both countries despite the fact that wages are higher in the developed world.

5. Suppose that a country's productivity in manufacturing is growing rapidly. Then its real exchange rate must be appreciating. If the nominal exchange rate is fixed, then the real appreciation must occur through inflation.

6a. Either price levels or nominal exchange rates must move in the right level. Therefore, if the exchange rate is fixed, adjustment can occur only through movements in price levels.

6b. It is more likely to occur rapidly in a country with a floating exchange rate because price levels are indeed sticky. Adjustment that requires price levels to change will be slow.

7a. Because the exchange rate didn't move, the investment has a return of 10% in yen so that the investment earned ¥10,000. Hence, you end the year with ¥110,000.

7b. UIP would have predicted a 10% yen appreciation, but there was none. Hence, the forecast error was 10%.

7c. The excess return was also 10%.

7d. No. On average the excess return on an investment should be zero, but any particular outcome is random.

7e. At the end of the year you would have ¥1,100,000, of which you would have to repay your loan of ¥900,000. Hence, you would have ¥200,000, which implies a return of 100%.

7f. Consider the realized yen return on Australian dollar assets: $i_{Aus\$} + \Delta E_{¥/Aus\$} / E_{¥/Aus\$}$. If the yen were to appreciate by 14%, then the yen return would be $0.1 - 0.14 = -0.04$. Hence, your return on each yen invested would be roughly –4%, so you are left with ¥1,000,000 × (1 – 0.04) = ¥960,000. Because you have to return ¥900,000 to repay the loan, this leaves you with a loss of ¥40,000 or a 40% loss.

8. Expected excess return would be zero, so the Sharpe ratio would be zero.

9. Both solutions are due to "limits to arbitrage." In the case of PPP this involves trade costs. In the case of UIP the limit is due to the desire to avoid risk.

10a. A reduction in savings drives up the world interest rate and increases Home's current account deficit.

10b. An investment boom raises the world interest rate and increases Home's current account deficit.

10c. No. There must have been a shock abroad that lowered the real interest rate and induced investment to expand in Home.

11. A tax t on borrowing from abroad raises the interest rate at Home to $r^w + t$. An increase in the cost of borrowing lowers investment and so lowers Home's current account deficit.

12a. True. Because net wealth is negative, there are interest payments that must be made abroad, making it necessary for Home to run a trade surplus to pay.

12b. False. Home will earn a steady stream of interest payments from abroad that make it possible to fund consumption greater than output.

13. This is a decrease in the relative demand for Home goods and services, so the price of these goods and services must drop. Home's real exchange rate must depreciate.

14. A transfer of spending power from Home to abroad will require a real exchange rate adjustment when it results in a change in aggregate spending on Home and Foreign goods. In the case of Home bias, shifting income from Home to Foreign results in a drop in demand for Home goods and services.

15. According to the model, an increase in output volatility has the effect of increasing the country's cost of borrowing because the probability of default increases. Hence, if the model is correct, this particular country must have volatile output.

16. True. By raising the cost of defaulting on its debt, the less likely it will be that the country will default on the debt. Knowing this, banks are willing to lend at a lower interest rate than they would otherwise.

17. An increase in the risk premium due to a default raises domestic interest rates, which puts pressure on the domestic financial system and increases the likelihood of an exchange rate crisis if the country has a fixed exchange rate system.